I0120624

THE TOURIST STATE

THE TOURIST STATE

Performing Leisure, Liberalism, and Race in New Zealand

MARGARET WERRY

A Quadrant Book

UNIVERSITY OF MINNESOTA PRESS

MINNEAPOLIS • LONDON

Quadrant, a joint initiative of the University of Minnesota Press and the Institute for Advanced Study at the University of Minnesota, provides support for interdisciplinary scholarship within a new, more collaborative model of research and publication.

QUADRANT

Sponsored by Quadrant's Environment, Culture, and Sustainability Group (advisory board: Bruce Braun and Dan Philippon) and by the Institute on the Environment at the University of Minnesota.

Quadrant is generously funded by the Andrew W. Mellon Foundation.

Publication of this book has been supported by an annual award from the University of Minnesota Provost's Office, Imagine Fund for the Arts, Design, and Humanities.

An earlier version of chapter 1 was previously published as "Tourism, Race, and the State of Nature: On the Bio-Poetics of Government," *Cultural Studies* 22, no. 3/4 (2008): 391–411. An earlier version of chapter 3 was previously published as "Translate, Translocate, Perform," in "On the Road," special issue, *Performance Research* 12, no. 2 (2007): 125–37. An earlier version of chapter 3 was previously published as "The Greatest Show on Earth: Spectacular Politics, Political Spectacle, and the American Pacific," *Theatre Journal* 58, no. 3 (2005): 4–35. An earlier version of chapter 5 was previously published as "National Cinema, Global Markets, and the Politics of Post-Ethnicity: Notes from Middle Earth" (Occasional Papers on Globalization, vol. 1, no. 5, Globalization Research Center, University of South Florida, Tampa, 2004).

Copyright 2011 by the Regents of the University of Minnesota

All rights reserved. No part of this publication may be reproduced, stored in a retrieval system, or transmitted, in any form or by any means, electronic, mechanical, photocopying, recording, or otherwise, without the prior written permission of the publisher.

Published by the University of Minnesota Press
111 Third Avenue South, Suite 290
Minneapolis, MN 55401-2520
http://www.upress.umn.edu

Library of Congress Cataloging-in-Publication Data

Werry, Margaret.
  The tourist state : performing leisure, liberalism, and race in New Zealand / Margaret Werry.
    p. cm. — (A Quadrant book)
  Includes bibliographical references and index.
  ISBN 978-0-8166-6605-8 (hc : alk. paper) — ISBN 978-0-8166-6606-5 (pb : alk. paper)
  1. Tourism—Social aspects—New Zealand. 2. Tourism—Political aspects—New Zealand.
  3. Leisure—New Zealand. 4. National characteristics, New Zealand. 5. Maori (New Zealand people)—Social conditions. 6. Liberalism—New Zealand. 7. New Zealand—Race relations. I. Title.
  G155.N5W47 2011
  306.4'8190993—dc23

                    2011017086

Printed in the United States of America on acid-free paper

The University of Minnesota is an equal-opportunity educator and employer.

17 16 15 14 13 12 11   10 9 8 7 6 5 4 3 2 1

CONTENTS

NOTE ON ORTHOGRAPHY

Following the convention in Aotearoa New Zealand, Māori words are not italicized and are (contextually) translated the first time they are used in each chapter. I have also followed current orthographic conventions in the use of the macron accent, except when quoting sources written before these conventions were normalized. I have likewise not normalized Māori usage in earlier sources.

INTRODUCTION: TOWARD A
PERFORMANCE THEORY OF THE STATE

PROLOGUE

For much of the new millennium, New Zealand has been the hot global ticket. Twice named Lonely Planet's top destination, it is touted for its bicultural dynamism, can-do creativity, fair-go egalitarianism, and laid-back leisure-loving lifestyle. And then, of course, there is the scenery. No longer the dreary sheep farm at the end of the world, the *new* New Zealand—Aotearoa New Zealand—is at the world's fresh cutting edge: clean, green, technologically capable, aesthetically innovative "Islands of Imagination" whipped by the Pacific's brisk winds of change.[1] Yet in 2001, when Aotearoa New Zealand strode onto the world stage, it did so not as a cosmopolitan, competitive Asia-Pacific knowledge-industry hub. Instead, it made its entrance as sublime scenic backdrop to a premodern fantasy Europe that never was: "Home of Middle-earth," where the race of Man battled savage hordes in an epic struggle for supremacy.

The two faces of the nation were, in fact, intimately related, yoked by a governmentwide national rebranding strategy that piggybacked on *Lord of the Rings* mania to cement tourism's status as number one foreign-exchange earner. The campaign's tagline ran "100% Pure New Zealand," its brand values engineered to encompass a spirit of enterprise and associations with leisured adventure and untrammeled nature.[2] But for Māori appointees working within newly bicultural state agencies overseeing tourism promotion and policy, these *terra nullius* proclamations were understandably troubling, for their sidelining of Māori tourism initiatives (on which development hopes were pinned) as much as for their colonial overtones. Māori committees and culture workers rang changes on the campaign, proposing versions in which the land might be storied by epic tales of indigenous, not neocolonial, origin. Māori culture, they suggested, might offer the nation what advertising guru Kevin Roberts called a Lovemark, lending the brand distinction, authenticity, and affective charge, inspiring—as the nation of yore had aimed to—"loyalty beyond reason."[3]

The elements of this destination image—at once a site of contest and collaboration, a call to belonging and a call to passage—are woven through every dimension of public life, from the highest echelons of diplomacy to the most mundane features of everyday life. When Prime Minister John Key visited Shanghai in July 2010, for example, he also wore the hat of Minister of Tourism, custodian of the national brand. Between signing off on scientific research collaboration initiatives and a film coproduction agreement, he presided over a ceremony at the Shanghai Expo to present a carved waharoa (a ceremonial Māori gateway) as "a visible and lasting symbol of the strengthening ties between New Zealand and China" and of "the cultural experiences that Chinese visitors can expect when they come to New Zealand" as tourists.[4] Back in New Zealand, the bus stops and drain covers of its "creative capital," Wellington, received a swish design overhaul in what architects have called the new Pacific aesthetic (in which the curvilinear motifs of Māori carving meet materials and design elements drawn from the natural landscape). Collision is mutated into proudly pluralist consensus and difference into capital, identity capital—the sign by which the state is known to its citizenry, to itself, and to the world at large.

As a nation, Aotearoa New Zealand is a community not so much imagined as *imagineered.* It is a state production and a participatory drama, the work of culture agents across business, civil society, policy, and entertainment. Index and agent of a broader synergy, tourism is implicated in virtually every industry sector, regional economy, event cluster, and domain of governmental responsibility or cultural practice. Viticulture, film production, marine conservation, sports events, arts exchanges, higher education, wool marketing, and revitalization projects in ailing ex-industrial towns or tribal districts are all linked by tourism in a dense network of multiplier effects and collateral benefits, leveraging potentials and opportunities for adding value (to borrow the policy jargon). Meanwhile, tourists themselves—witnesses, pleasure seekers, story bearers—move to the rhythms of this new national story. Aotearoa New Zealand, one might say, is a tourist state.

Pull back the curtains of this national scene, however, and you will find the set of a larger drama called the New Zealand Experiment: the ruthless reforms of the 1980s that shook off the nation's post-Fordist malaise, demolished its century-old welfare state, and saw its ascendance as neoliberalism's poster child. It is a drama with a comic conclusion—a long-awaited return to prosperity at the hands of a *post*neoliberal administration that softened the harsh corners of neoliberal fundamentalism with social-democratic compromise—and a remarkable subplot: biculturalization. This new commitment to biculturalism is the consummation of a generation of Māori resistance and revitalization that has seen the settling of reparations claims, a new legislative status for tribal collectives, and the integration of Māori custom, conduct, and language into many dimensions of governmental and public life, from social service delivery to parliamentary ceremony to public broadcasting.

But behind the New Zealand Experiment stands still another, earlier experiment: the so-called Liberal era (1890–1914), in which the young settler colony touted itself as the social laboratory of the world. It was, according to the political commentators and leisure travelers who flocked there as witnesses, an exemplar of benevolent, managerial statehood, dedicated to the welfare of its population and to engineering the perfect conditions for economic prosperity. Raw, humming, new settler townships, aglow with the righteousness of progress, celebrated their pastless, classless modernity against the background of a transcendent landscape by turns bucolic, primeval, and triumphantly sublime. The project of image management was taken on by the state and taken up by the business syndicates and provincial development lobbies, between the state and which there existed but a thin and frequently transgressed line.

Like Aotearoa New Zealand, this earlier imagineered nation had a name, Maoriland, that pinpointed the racial calculus at its core.[5] At the same time as politicians and pundits tolled the death knell for their picturesque indigenes (and pursued policies that many hoped would ensure it), they paired progressive liberalism with Māori culture at the forefront of diplomatic pageantry, nationalist historiography, and artistic production as the coin of national distinction. The decorative kowhaiwhai patterns on the borders of every illustrated weekly, the Māori-language brand names that trademarked products for export, the encounter plots and Māori motifs in nationalist drama, music, and literature (often crafted with an eye toward tourism-related marketing potential)—these were Maoriland's truck and trade. Awash in imperialist nostalgia and parochial pride, Maoriland was the brand under which the state in the making sold itself both to its citizens and to prospective migrants as a natural, prosperous, Anglo-Saxon paradise that had solved the race problem plaguing other colonies through a combination of good fortune (being blessed with a "better class of native") and good government.[6]

In the Liberal era, also, tourism was the hub of the machine of state. Overseen by its own government department, it was the organizing principle behind most civic occasions, its interests invoked to argue for everything from new railways to treaties with foreign powers. Almost without exception, Maoriland's spokesmen—the historians, playwrights, editors, advertisers, ethnologists, curators, and other culture workers of the young nation—spent time both in the employ of the state and in the service of its pet industry, tourism. If you had paid a visit in 1906–7 to the government-planned New Zealand International Exhibition in Christchurch, for example, you would have found these spokesmen there: Alfred Hill, composer of the "Exhibition Ode," whose other works, also performed at the exhibition, banked on tested touristic commodities; James Cowan, official recorder of the exhibition, author of government tourism and settlement guides, and one of the nation's most prolific historians; and Augustus Hamilton, curator of the Colonial Museum and influential tourist art-market patron, to name just a few. Throngs of visitors from New Zealand, Australia, and around the world witnessed this triumphal proclamation of progressive statehood and the findings of its social laboratory, which these men helped to orchestrate: displays of the colony's bounteous natural resources, demonstrations of its progress in industry and manufacturing, galleries of images attesting to its scenic splendors, and courts documenting the good works of its many government departments.

Also at the exhibition, however, were prominent rangatira (leaders) and members of several Māori tribes: Mahutu Te Toko of the Waikato confederation that had prosecuted a war of resistance against the colonizers a mere three decades earlier; Tuta Nihoniho of Ngāti Porou and Te Heuheu Tukino of Ngāti Tuwharetoa, both powerful politicians and vociferous critics of the state's rapacious policies regarding taxation and acquisition of Māori land; and Apirana Ngata and Te Rangi Hīroa, Māori members of Parliament, present and future. They were resident at Te Araiteuru, a model pā (fortified village) constructed by government experts on the exhibition grounds to entertain and edify the visitors in the imperial tradition of the World's Fair native village—a heritage attraction essentially, documenting the ancient and barbarous past that had given way to national modernity.[7] They had been invited (in some cases employed) by the state to ornament a romantic spectacle of their own political obsolescence. Yet they came. And they performed, daily staging magnificent haka dances or intricate poi demonstrations. These were Maoriland's spokespeople also. For these peoples, tourism represented an opportunity, a foothold in the Liberal-era order. At the pā, a revalorized Māori culture took up residence at the symbolic heart of the state project with which, like it or not, they were now enmeshed. The treasures of their ancestors were "gazed on by the world"; tourism was a stage on which to present their communities as claimants to, or members of, supranational and national publics (all the while forging new, politically actionable bonds between themselves and their distant kin). It was a chance also to travel, to enjoy for themselves tourism's pleasures and prerogatives of self-cultivation and knowledge: "many are the lessons to be learnt there."[8] Ultimately, this touristic opportunity—strategically engaged, in the language of cultural performance—could put Māori in the (Pākehā, or non-Māori) public eye as a vigorous, well-organized, corporate force in New Zealand modernity, a vital variable in the national experiment.

THE TOURIST STATE: A GUIDE

What is remarkable here is not that a state should twice undertake to brand itself in the manner of a corporation (a commonplace in a global economy, then as now, especially for the small or geopolitically marginal) but that the process should reach so deep into the fabric of everyday life, implicating Māori and Pākehā in a radical reordering of self-recognition and mutual recognition, economic possibility and political agency.[9] Why is tourism so pivotal to this process? And what can this small, remote, and in some respects quite unusual country tell us about the part the global culture industries have played, and continue to play, in the racial constitution of liberal states and their citizens?

The relationship between nationalism and tourism is a well-established one. From Colonial Williamsburg to Skansen, from ninja villages in Japan to Taman Mini Indonesia Indah, scholars have documented tourism's production (and sometimes contestation) of hegemonic representations of nationhood as a form of public pedagogy. They have demonstrated the ways, also, in which iconic tourist landscapes—the White Mountains of New England, or the British Lake District—participate in the invention of tradition, becoming the coin of international recognition or loci for experiences of national belonging. Where national hegemony is forged across deep (racial or ethnic) disparities in power or entitlement, however, its touristic representation manifests as a form of symbolic violence. In the island Pacific, environmental desecration, the expropriation of land, and exploitation of resources by colonial, corporate, or military forces have proceeded in lockstep with the growth of tourism's myth machine. In what postcolonial scholars have dubbed soft primitivism, cultural prostitution, or militourism, tourism stages the spectacle of happy, hula-dancing natives welcoming with open arms the kin of those who robbed them: a neocolonial farce of choreographed, counterfeit consensus.[10] Tourism, for these scholars, is an epiphenomenon of political–economic domination, a spectacular screen that conceals the reality of dispossessed lives, mesmerizing the dominators as with the reflected aura of their own beneficence. It is colonialism by other means, a new kind of sugar for former plantation economies.[11] For historians of settler states such as Aotearoa New Zealand or Australia, the complicity between tourism and nation takes yet another turn, that of cultural appropriation, in which settlers declare their new-found national identity by presenting those they have displaced as their symbolic surrogates, nostalgically borrowing the authenticity of indigenous belonging, profiting from the traffic in indigenous images and property, and buttressing the racial distinctions between primitivism and modernity that undergird the whole edifice of nation.[12]

In this book, I do not take issue with these arguments, which I believe to be necessary and illuminating ones, especially in the context of Pacific travails. I do question, however, whether an emphasis on tourism's symbolic power risks underestimating its material efficacy and complexity. In positing tourism as a representational projection—a simulacrum *behind which* causal or explanatory entities (such as empire, the state, or capital) remain invisible, untouchable, and all-powerful—the postcolonial analysis can divert us from the very questions it might illuminate: How can tourism enroll the energies and imaginations of so many individuals and communities in shaping environments, institutions, economies, and conditions of opportunity? How does it mold the behaviors, aspirations, and self-understandings of those who witness and those who perform (who are neither pawns nor dupes but participants in this never-innocent process)? How, in short, does it contribute to state making?

The Tourist State shifts focus from tourism's *representation* of nation or culture to anatomize its *performance* (by which I mean both materialization and expression) of the state.[13] My research in Aotearoa New Zealand has led me to consider the possibility that tourism is not simply a cultural symptom of liberal statehood and its racial logic but can operate as one of its most fundamental mechanisms. Tourism, like the state itself, is inseparably material *and* ideational. It brings bodily practices, natural environments, symbolic materials, geopolitical actors, economic forces, and social fantasies together in powerful and mobilizing networks. This process is never only a matter of representation. In tourism, the state is revealed as a performance: "a doing and a thing done," taken up, and played out in flesh.[14] This state making can occur in tourism's work of imag(in)ing or branding, in infrastructure and institution building, or in spatial management or development. It can occur in tourism's shaping of the intimate conduct of citizens (the bodily take-up of racialized forms of taste, habitus, affect, relationality, consumption, discipline, and pleasure). It can occur when tourists produce, consume, and circulate knowledge about a population, or in the deliberate staging of rituals of interracial recognition, from routine attractions to the highest level of diplomatic encounter. It can occur as tourism publicity differentiates populations or as tourism businesses market culture, bringing the commons into the ambit of the national economy. It can occur in tourism's generation both of statements about nation and of transitory experiences emphasizing belonging and loyalty. Because this process rests on its constant and necessary enactment, it is porous and fractal: the state thus conceived is neither monster nor monument but an ongoing and incessantly contested process, the cumulative effect of myriad performances.

The state, in other words, does not preexist tourism's evolutions, only to be reflected, refracted, or reproduced through them. Rather, the doing of tourism helps to give the state its "effect"—its appearance of solidity, efficacy, and representative authority—even as the state shapes the conditions under which and the ends to which tourists and tourism providers act.[15] Following the passage of actors—that is, tracing how people (and things and places and policies) act, and act on one another—can help us grasp what we might call (after Foucault) the practical systems and political rationality of a liberal state, in all their intimacy and intricacy and in all their geographical and historical specificity. Tourism, I argue, is engine and compass of liberalism's contradictions as well as its achievements. It exposes the state as a fundamentally, constitutively racial entity, rather than an entity to which race is an inconvenience, impediment, or unfortunate remainder, as liberal *doxa* contends. Race, in a very basic sense, makes liberal states go.

The Tourist State, then, is an attempt to capture New Zealand state-making and racial formation in motion.[16] It is part interpretive history, part performance ethnography, and part cultural criticism. The chapters that follow do not restrict themselves to any one genre of tourism, to tourist practice itself, or even to the territorial boundaries of the state. Instead, they follow touristic associations where they lead: military diplomacy at the dawn of the American Pacific; the exotic blandishments of Broadway and Coney Island; landscape preservation, health reform, and town planning; blockbuster film and knowledge-economy policy engineering; and tourist attractions themselves. Each chapter seizes critically on an event, place, institution, personage, or practice in which tourism and liberal governmentality coincide in provocative ways. And each theorizes a signature trope of liberal life through the lens of racial performance: territoriality and welfare, the public sphere and cosmopolitan civil society, international relations and global mobility, cultural policy and property, and transnational capital and mass culture. Together, these chapters extend performance methodologies to the study of the state, addressing the bodied, emplaced, artful, and imagined dimensions of statehood. They offer ways to think about race, whiteness, and particularly indigeneity under (neo)liberalism and about the place of human agency in processes of state making.

Throughout, I try to render the complex interpenetration of touristic, governmental, and ethnic projects, the ways in which actual and imagined acts of travel enabled citizens, denizens, and nonnationals to shape, picture, perceive, and feel (or feel a part of) the national welfare. Together these constitute what I call New Zealand's tourist state. A state, semantically speaking, can be understood as both an apparatus of political rule and a condition of being and feeling, a predicament. New Zealand's tourist state, as it appears in these pages, is both these things: a powerful governmental assemblage patterned and produced by racial inequality and a shifty, anxious structure of feeling that is dependent on treating with global forces for survival. Tourism accentuates a paradox that is also the subject of this book, a paradox familiar from theories of nationalism and globalization: those political formations that appear most stable, hermetic, and enduring—nation, ethnic collectives, and the state—are constituted through circulation.[17] The constant passage of people, ideas, images, and capital, both within their own borders and abroad, makes these constructs *imaginable*, but their continual translation and their becoming through motion is an unsettling condition, always threatening to unseat the certainties of permanence and power to which they pretend. To live in a tourist state, then, is to live with this perpetual disturbance, to live on the edge of semantic availability, in a space of both glimmering possibility and painful uncertainty.[18]

UNSETTLED STATES:
THE HISTORY OF A SOCIAL LABORATORY

New Zealand is an apt site to assay these claims about the relationship between tourism and state making. It is not the only state to have linked tourism with ethnic governance or development, nor to have taken a policy interest in tourism management. One could point to the Indonesian government's long-standing investment in Bali tourism (from the 1920s to the present) or to Singapore tourism's more recent efforts to discipline and display its multicultural population. In the early twentieth-century U.S. Southwest and Hawai'i, state and federal administrations explicitly supported private business interests that yoked territorial expansion to the lure of indigenous tourism. Other settler colonies, such as the prefederation Australian states, had government tourism and publicity bureaus, although none of these marketed Aboriginal attractions. But the New Zealand effort was both the earliest (establishing the first state tourism department in 1901) and arguably the most systematic, centralized, long-standing, and well documented.

I have chosen to focus here on two discrete periods: the Liberal era (1890–1914) and the decade following the nation's neoliberal reinvention

(1998–2009). In both eras, the nation styled itself as the social laboratory of the world. The laboratory, Actor Network Theorists have argued, "is a space in which persons and objects can be organized, made to act on one another, *leading to generalizable results*" that can be "mobilized in social programmes."[19] During these two periods, New Zealand was a global exporter of ideas about liberal government, neoliberal reform, and indigenous empowerment; tourism functioned both as a means to publish the laboratory's findings and (I shall argue) as a crucial site of its experimental process. The two periods were both unsettled times, characterized by highly reflexive governmental practice. They were times when the balance of ethnic power was hotly contested and when the nation turned its face increasingly toward global horizons, with high levels of both immigration and emigration. Commentators have described these periods as moments of both innovation and foundation, setting the pattern for longer intervals of (supposed) stability. They were also, not coincidentally, periods in which tourism became the focus of intense governmental interest.

From its inception, New Zealand was a promotional state. It was declared a British colony in 1840 following the signing of the Treaty of Waitangi by representatives of a number of Māori tribes, and it was a self-governing colony by 1856. The Treaty extended to Māori liberal rights to equal treatment as subjects of the Crown and rights to possession of lands and other properties. Despite its provisions being flagrantly violated over the following century and a half, the document lent the gloss of legitimacy to the ensuing campaign of organized commercial settlement. For a small and distant colonial economy built on the acquisition and resale of (Māori) land, immigrant capital, and the investment of British taxpayers (including a costly war to suppress Māori resistance), effective publicity was a manifest necessity. From panorama displays in London, to magic lantern lectures in the British provinces, to a veritable avalanche of travel accounts—all extolling the natural splendors of a "better Britain," its wealth of resources and investment opportunities, and its well-managed, peaceable natives—the discourses of travel, settlement, colonial knowledge-production, and state making were often inseparable.

In 1890, the fiftieth anniversary of its founding, the colony turned a corner. For the first time, native-born citizens outnumbered immigrants, urbanites outnumbered rural residents, federation with the Australian states was debated and declined, and (after decades of land acquisition and conversion from forest to farm) agriculture now anchored the economy. The following twenty years, known as the Liberal era, have been called the "hinge" of New Zealand history.[20] The cultural urgings of nascent colonial nationalism, the administrative unification of the islands and exponential growth of the state apparatus, and participation in foreign wars and the development of territorial (one might argue, imperial) interests in the island Pacific all pointed to an emerging sense of the nation's distinctive modernity.

The state's turn to tourism exemplified the gregarious spirit of capital expansion and social managerialism that characterized the era (in which state bodies oversaw everything from industrial arbitration to pensions, life insurance, and public housing). Boosterist parliamentarians argued that tourism offered an instrument of regional development, a rich source of export earnings, and a vital instrument of publicity that would draw immigrant labor and investment as a by-product. While it had been the focus of programmatic state efforts from the 1870s onward, in 1901 the state established an agency entirely devoted to tourism promotion, development, and management, a sign of the importance it was coming to hold in the arts of government. Tourism soon became as integral to the material work of state making (driving, for example, transportation infrastructure investment, or urban planning and public health efforts) as it was to the poetics of nationhood. "No beggars to haunt you, and a paternal government that treats her visitors as honoured guests," one tourist shilled, concluding, "that's the way to do things, by gad,—it's top hole!"[21]

Who were these tourists? Over half were white settlers from Australia, members of the professional class from the eastern cities who were escaping the summer heat or visiting friends and relatives. The next largest group was British travelers touring the imperial circuit. Finally, Europeans and Americans also came in roughly equal numbers.[22] The long journey time meant that only the relatively moneyed or leisured could afford to make the trip. Many who traveled were precareer (about to establish themselves in New Zealand or another colony), retirees, women visiting friends who had migrated, or professional travelers (the authors, journalists, and commentators whose work is the archive on which the following chapters draw). The line between settler and tourist, national and non-national, was always a fuzzy one. But to the state that courted them, who these tourists were was less important than who they were *imagined to be*.

State tourism policy, I argue throughout these chapters, was performative rather than pragmatic. (Despite strong growth, tourism remained a tiny sector of the economy throughout the Liberal era, and the state's investments in it consistently ran at a loss.) Just as it worked to bring into being the state it proposed, tourism conjured the subject it imagined as a citizen: the white, wealthy, cosmopolitan witness to and consumer of the self-enunciation of a nation.

Nowhere was the performative character of tourism more evident than in its interface with ethnic politics. During the Liberal era, the Māori population climbed steadily from a low of 6 percent of the national total, recorded in the 1896 census. The resurgent population presented an impediment to the Liberal-era mandate of closer settlement and industrially efficient, capital-intensive farming. The Pākehā demand to individualize Māori land title (and thus bring the last remaining holdings into the market and its inhabitants into the labor force) was the defining feature of parliamentary ethnopolitics during this era. It was accompanied by an outright state assault on Māori lifeways, targeting "outdated" and "injurious" customs and particularly any practices that reeked of "communalism."[23] But the Liberal era also saw the revitalization of beleaguered tribal confederations, and the rise of new representative Māori bodies, which mediated between tribal structures and the liberal apparatus, using parliamentary avenues to press for a share in Liberal modernity's promised gains.[24] At the onset of the Liberal era, policy makers largely (wishfully) assumed Māori to be a dying race; by its conclusion, assimilationist frameworks were beginning to give way to accommodationist ones. If Pākehā saw Māori ethnic expression as an intractable obstacle to a homogenous national modernity, in the context of tourism it could be assigned new forms of value and incorporated into schemes of capital expansion.[25] Māori culture was soon recognized as an asset that would distinguish the nation in a competitive international marketplace—in essence, as a brand.

Ethnic tourism proper (as I detail in chapter 1) was at the outset a *Māori* initiative. Certain entrepreneurial hapū (descent groups) in the central North Island owned the land on which some extraordinary geological attractions were located. Their entertainment of sightseers soon became a lure and a tradition in its own right, and it remained so long after the state and Pākehā investors had wrested their territorial assets from their hands. Tourism was not, however, a *pan*-Māori initiative: ethnic tourism per se remained confined to the thermal regions, and many tribes privately took a dim view of Arawa engagement with it. The Arawa hapū involved were kūpapa (loyal to the Crown during the Land Wars of the mid- to late-nineteenth century) and addressed the state as strategic collaborators in this industry, albeit ones with increasingly little bargaining power. Still, touristic practices, aesthetics, techniques, discourses, and analytics had come to define the Liberal-era state, and they would soon help to define the broad terms of Māori recognition, both the intelligibility and value of Māori as subjects of the state and their visibility to those with whom the state treated.

The short twentieth century in New Zealand, from 1914 through 1984, was lived in the Liberal-era legacy. Liberal-era governmental experiments bequeathed the style of communitarian, highly interventionist social democracy (sometimes called state socialism) that fast became a model (or a cautionary tale) for reform advocates in other liberal states.[26] The Liberal era also passed down its ethos of accommodationist ethnic paternalism: at around 12 percent of the population, with an economic base in farming, agricultural labor, and state industries, Māori gained some recognition in the party political system as a working-class vote bloc courted by the Labour Party. But the national faith in the state's egalitarian benevolence, and entrenched racism, allowed Pākehā New Zealand to avoid reckoning with the brutal structural and social legacies of colonial dispossession. The "Maoriland" brand endured, growing more dated by the decade, while inbound tourism was consistently slight during these years. Political stability, economic protectionism, a slowly growing population, low immigration, and an economy dominated by agricultural produce bound for British markets left the nation insulated from global currents, with little need for expansion or publicity. The state's efforts focused instead on conserving the national estate and making this patrimony accessible to Pākehā, who adopted rational recreation (particularly hiking, camping, and boating) as a right and rite of citizenship.

This all changed when the fifth Labour government took office in 1984, amid the global meltdown of Fordist economics. The New Zealand economy was reeling from the oil shock, tightening agricultural markets, high deficits, inflation, and mounting public debt. Pleading that "there was no alternative," Labour embarked upon a textbook example of neo-liberal reform, the New Zealand Experiment, which the World Trade Organization touted as a success story for other neoliberalizing welfare states. Deregulation and decentralization swept away a century of public provision overnight: the government slashed farming subsidies, foreign investment restrictions, and protectionist tariffs, floated the currency, auctioned off state-owned assets on the global market, reduced taxes on the wealthy, privatized public services, abolished welfare provisions, and deregulated immigration and the labor market. This was pure, abstract "economic fundamentalism" pursued (in the then–Prime Minister's retrospective assessment) with a zealotry "more like religious belief than professional practice."[27] The subsequent ten years of miserable economic performance laid bare the social cost of the experiment: wages plummeted, unemployment climbed, and one-sixth of the nation found itself living below the poverty line.

Neoliberal reforms hit already economically vulnerable Māori communities with disproportionately devastating force. But they also precipitated an impending revolution in the relationship between Māori and the state.[28] In the 1950s and 1960s the urban migration of Māori for industrial labor had accentuated the racial and class rather than tribal basis for Māori politics, making starkly visible the legacies of structural discrimination: least income, least wealth, lowest educational achievement, highest incarceration rates, lowest life expectancy, and so on.[29] A second Māori renaissance, at once political and cultural, gathered momentum in the 1970s, inspired by international civil rights and decolonization struggles and airing generations of unaddressed grievances, including the kinds of abuses to cultural property and pride committed in the name of tourism. By the mid-1980s, the pressure of this movement on the state was overwhelming. The incoming Labour government responded by extending the purview of the Waitangi Tribunal (appointed in 1977 to investigate contemporary violations of the Treaty of Waitangi's terms) to claims dating back to the signing in 1840. Tribal collectives, given new political recognition as claimants, were granted reparations of confiscated land (including many tourism-related assets), percentage shares in national assets and public goods (from fishing rights to the broadcasting spectrum), and legislative protections for cultural property. Moreover, the Treaty process introduced a principle of bicultural partnership to the state, requiring all Crown agencies to represent and serve Māori in ways consonant with Māori cultural and spiritual values, social organization, traditional relationships, and protocols.

The fractured postreform state turned to tourism for reasons akin to those of its Liberal-era forebear: to aid devastated regional economies, bolster export earnings, and gain publicity. Its eyes turned outward, searching for the new global markets, investors, and immigrants that would be crucial to its survival. Tourism's ultimate ascendance, however, came with Aotearoa New Zealand's *post*neoliberal turn, which began in 1999 with Prime Minister Helen Clark's fifth Labour government.[30] This typically "third way" administration reversed many of the most damaging cuts in public provision, aiming to rebuild confidence in the mandate of government through an emphasis on partnering, community, and (significantly for tourism) identity, culture, and social cohesion. But the neoliberal bedrock, sedimented by the earlier decade of reform, remained: business interests and managerialism ruled, and the peculiar jargon of economic rationalism (such as "value added," "fiscal responsibility," or "measurable output") was the cultural dominant. Meanwhile, flexibilized, insecure, tertiary-sector employment, high debt levels, scarcity of social services, and widely stratified incomes were the unquestioned reality of most citizens' lives. For this state, tourism would not only be the lynchpin of a new knowledge economy but an expression and engine of biculturalism, incorporating Māori into the flow of capital to provide the "point of difference" that would add value to the national brand and unleash their "store of untapped intellectual capital."[31] Tourism, then, would play a crucial role in establishing the practical systems and the ethnic and political rationality of the (post)-neoliberal state, the conduct and self-identity of its subjects, transforming Aotearoa New Zealand from a hidebound, homogenous, and stagnant place, marked by colonial "cultural cringe," into a dynamic, competitive, creative, plural, proud, gregarious global leader.

GOVERNMENTALITY, TOURISM, AND THE (NEO)LIBERAL STATE

The success of this strategy, I suggest, owes something to the affinity between tourism and the liberal state—an affinity not just historical but also practical and philosophical. Liberalism can be defined as that body of thoughts, feelings, expectations, discourses, modes of governance, and political fictions that takes the autonomy and rights of the individual as the basis for collective life. My use of the term in this volume is distinct from formal liberalism (in the sense defined by political scientists) or ideological liberalism (in the sense used, either pejoratively or approvingly, in common parlance). Liberalism is not a thing but, as Elizabeth Povinelli has argued, a "moving target developed in the European empire and used to secure power in the contemporary world," an ideal whose global dissemination has been pivotal to the extension of both democracy and capitalism, forming the "normative horizon" of global modernity.[32] In this sense, liberalism is so ubiquitous as to be nearly invisible. More often than not, we study *with* liberalism's imperatives, rather than studying those imperatives themselves. The cultivation of the self, the ideal of authenticity, the exercise of freedom (including rights to mobility, action, or expression), the sanctification of property (and the construal of all things of value *as* property), the benefit of boundaries between the state, civil society, and the market, and the drive to limit the powers of the state over the autonomous, authentic individual are all liberal *doxa* that quietly anchor scholarly ideals in the humanities.

The starting point of Foucault's groundbreaking critique of the liberal state—and the inspiration for the following chapters—was to note that the dominant tradition of conceptualizing the state as a determined and determining entity ("the regulator of social life and locus of territorial sovereignty and cultural legitimacy") was itself an artifact of liberal discourse. It pitted the state against the subject's autonomy, thus lending an aura of "unity, individuality, and rigorous functionality" to an entity that is in fact a "composite reality and mythicized abstraction."[33] Foucault, by contrast, approached this set of liberal *doxa* not as political ideals (opposed by a monstrous, cold, and oppressive state) but as themselves elements in the liberal state's apparatus of rule.

The liberal state's mandate, Foucault argued, was not to compel or dominate but to elicit autonomous action while creating the conditions that would direct it to specific ends. His theory of governmentality detailed the ensemble of dispersed practices, technologies, and forms of regulation and incitement that characterize the liberal state. Distinct from regimes both of sovereign rule and of disciplinary society (although often overlapping with them), governmentality takes as its object the population—its measurement, management, welfare, and productivity—and works through producing and organizing knowledge about that population, thus creating the conditions by which governing appears to do itself. Liberalism's arts of government mobilize tactics rather than laws, the foremost of which is to link governance with self-governance, guidance with self-guidance, by recursive work on subjects' conduct. This work can take place in the programmatic activities of both state and nonstate agencies (corporations, charities, unions, or networks of voluntary association, for example), or in broader cultures of self-fashioning in which subjects participate. Governmentality thus harnesses social and individual capacities, self-managed according to the "internal rule of maximum economy," which means, in contemporary terms, market ideals of efficiency, productivity, and competitiveness.[34] Ultimately, politics is less relevant to this process than policy, that connective tissue between the political rationality of institutions and the practical rationality of everyday life, which can take the forms both of authorizing edicts and of managerial interventions that organize the capabilities and conduct of citizenry.

Governmentality, then, is a political technology that works in classically liberal fashion at arm's length, organizing populations, assigning value, and producing values, not through the top-down application of power but through the promulgation of desire, habit, and commitment on the part of its subjects. Tourism's historical complicity with liberalism rests on this fact. The culture industries are pivotal to governmentality's system, as scholars such as Toby Miller and Tony Bennett have argued.[35] The forms of consumption, sociality, spatial practice, behaviors, expectations, tastes, and skills—the performance repertoires, essentially—that the culture industries cultivate lead subjects to bind themselves to the state. Tourism, particularly, is a remarkable apparatus for extracting (and globally distributing) monetary value from those things whose worth lies outside the market (ethnic lifeways, marginal lands, and so on), by channeling the interests, self-interest, and energies of a free population. In New Zealand, tourists and tourism workers came to align their individual conduct with an idea of the general welfare, participating in the production and circulation of knowledge about the Māori population, for instance, assuming particular habits of the body, or cultivating and expressing particular forms of identity. They did so not in response to a directive but for pleasure, for personal gain, or because the organization of things disposed them to conduct themselves in that way.

Governmentality ultimately works through incorporating and directing energies that do not conform to its ends. Its animating question is, How can those for whom the contract with the state is not free be brought to express and experience freedom within its ambit and its limits? It is on tourism's many and varied answers to this question that I focus in this volume. This incorporative impetus lends a blush of benevolence to the foundational and ongoing violence of state making, for which Foucault has often stood accused as an apologist. To be sure, governmentality's incorporation and valorization of intelligible subjects is always matched by its exclusion or exception of unintelligible (dissenting) ones from liberal protections.[36] The annals of New Zealand tourism are peppered with examples of such genocidal biopolitics. When, for instance, Liberal-era campaigns against Tūhoe separatism in the Urewera region faltered, the state appropriated part of the forest to the national estate, promoting it as a virgin space emptied of its picturesque but savage denizens past, for the recreation of citizens and foreign visitors. Tourism's benevolence stepped in where military force failed, extinguishing the rights—indeed the very legitimacy—of outliers to the state. Recent police raids on Māori-activist communities in the same region, prompted by post–9/11 antiterrorism provisions, were a brute reminder of this history. Yet the work of negotiation and incorporation on which I concentrate here, in which the state and free subjects collaborate in the mundane border-work of tourism, is no less a part of this apparatus of rule. The more benign and unremarkable it appears, the more it should demand our critical and ethical attention.

To see the liberal state governmentally is to commit, as I do in this book, to a capillary-level analysis of its analytics, networks, and techniques, in their constantly reflexive process of change and in all their local variance and historical specificity. As Barry Hindess has argued, "there may be very little of value to be said for or against, or even simply about, liberalism in general," and our scholarly goal should not be to develop an ideal or typical model of governmentality, nor to rank actually existing governmentalities against it.[37] Liberal and neoliberal states continually encounter other forms of authority, other political imaginaries, and they evolve in the midst of vastly different cultural, economic, and social milieus: the state thus begs ethnographic attention, a focus on local, emic, vernacular notions of governance as well as on the deliberative and programmatic dimensions of state praxis.[38]

This conjunctural, ethnographic approach is of redoubled importance in the study of *neo*liberal governmentalities, in part because neoliberalism (as it has made its way into common scholarly parlance in the academy) has been so consistently misunderstood as a novel, unanimous doctrine or epochal calamity, rather than (like liberalism) a mode: a heterogeneous, evolving, disjunctive, globally distributed but locally variant ensemble of practices.[39] Insofar as neoliberalism owes its global spread to bodies such as the International Monetary Fund and the World Trade Organization and to the U.S.–driven global economy, it has indeed assumed the appearance of doctrine. But even in Aotearoa New Zealand, where these organizations' dictates were initially applied with almost clinical purity, they have evolved into distinct, hybrid, and multiplex sets of techniques—in part in response to the indigenous epistemologies of power that biculturalization has introduced into the apparatus of government. Moreover, the resonance of the millennial order with its Liberal-era predecessor suggests that Aotearoa New Zealand's unique style of neoliberal biculturalism modulated, rather than superseded, liberal techniques of a century earlier.

The final two chapters of this book lend some ethnographic thickness and specificity to the targets of neoliberal political rationality as they have been expressed, practiced, and problematized in Aotearoa New Zealand tourism. In many respects, the Treaty process meshed with neoliberal agendas such as the privatization of social responsibility, the delegation of state regulatory powers to third-sector agencies, and the corporatization of previously public services and assets. After all, it is to iwi (tribal collective) and hapū bodies functioning as investors and managers of resources that reparations are made. The process has redirected the redistributive aims of the Māori renaissance to serve capital and state interests: most iwi have understood from the outset that becoming globally competitive is the key to socioeconomic amelioration within their own communities. But the *practice* of tourism under such conditions is an infinitely more complex and inventive performance than this observation would suggest. How do Māori entrepreneurs navigate the cultural and social topography of the global? And how does the delegation of powers to tribal bodies transform the political rationality of state agencies themselves? What critics call "neotribal capitalism" has opened class divisions between those Māori well positioned to take advantage of new opportunities and those not: an instance of the well-observed neoliberal tendency to valorize the possessors of human capital, creating differently advantaged categories of "flexible" and fixed citizenship.[40] But it has also created a platform for imaginative forms of redistributive social policy within iwi and hapū: what are the limitations of economic remediation efforts undertaken, through tourism, in neoliberally stratified communities? How does the generation of new forms of value from the marketization of the cultural commons affect the ways that identity is configured and mobilized? And what calculative agencies do tourism's practitioners develop to manage this process? Finally, what are the consequences of weakened state sovereignty (deregulated flows of capital and labor across national borders, national cultures liquefied by global media saturation) for the self-determination of identities and solidarities (such as indigeneity) that have historically been defined through their dialectical entanglement with the nation-state?

THE RACIAL STATE

This battery of questions illustrates how racial, ethnic, or cultural considerations undergird every dimension of liberal statehood, governmentally understood. It is no overstatement to claim that all of liberalism's most fundamental precepts found their genesis in the racial inequities of a colonizing world: freedom, which gained its consequence in contrast with slavery; reason, presumed to be the exclusive endowment of white moderns; and property, because some were taken as property or deprived of the right to hold it. The mere existence of race exposes liberalism's hypocrisy: it is a deep fracture in the principles of formal equality of persons, and the rights to undisturbed enjoyment of property and person.[41] Moreover, whereas liberal pluralism frames cultural difference as a necessary and valuable resource in the project of self-fashioning, racial discourse reveals the tacit normative limits to the self thus fashioned.[42] In practice, political intelligibility and social advantage clearly depend on conformity to certain conducts and dispositions, usually those of whiteness. Ethnic tourism, then, as the trade in cultural difference, takes place astride liberalism's greatest constitutive paradox, which it constantly threatens to expose. This is another story told by this book. Tourism, I argue, is a space in which raced subjects can hold the liberal state to its promise or lay bare its bad faith. However, insofar as tourism also operates as a significant technology of racial governmentality, it also makes of these subjects ambivalent collaborators in the racial project of the state.

Race, for the purposes of my analysis, is a cultural construction or formation: it is a fluid constellation of discourse, belief, affect, physical or linguistic repertoires, sensibilities, and signs attributed to or performed by subjects, in connection with a claim regarding biology, and in relation to specific social, political, and economic interests. Throughout this analysis, I use race to refer to whiteness as well as blackness. Race is also a social experience: an identity or worldview collectively held and acted upon, a form of solidarity and belonging, a vocabulary of self-fashioning, a vehicle for grievance, and a repository for noneconomic forms of value. Race (although conspicuously not whiteness) is also a grammar of social equality, attuned to arguments about history and structural inequity, while ironically remaining rooted in the terms of classification and exclusion. In battles for recognition and representation, or those for redistribution, race has been a strategic necessity in attempts to remediate *racism's* social and cultural costs.[43] At the same time, race is also liberal governmentality's most indispensable technology. Race is an element in the art of government, directed to the ends of welfare, economy, and prosperity—but not equality. Racial governmentality organizes and differentiates a free population through biopolitical techniques of classification and categorization, creating the conditions (through spatial management, for instance, or the deployment of culture as a resource) that dispose *certain* bodies to become productive in *particular* ways.[44]

Indigeneity, on the other hand, appears to belong to the order of ethnos rather than race, centered on arguments relating to genealogy rather than genotype, to origins and values rather than classification. Indigeneity, too, has a place in the liberal state's genesis, both as its foundational exclusion (those whose sovereignty must be extinguished to found the nation) and also as citizenship's exemplary form: the indigenous are those who belong to a place by right of origin, crystallizing claims to natural rights, antiquity, and social authenticity that are central to the liberal ethos.[45] But distinctions between indigeneity and race have seldom been clear.[46] Expedient distinctions between noble (indigenous) and nasty (black) natives have been a feature of all settler colonialisms, and the historical application of racial biopolitics to indigenous populations by states has produced racial legacies of both social exclusion and generational disenfranchisement. At the same time, while indigeneity is an identity formation organized (like race) around shared projects and principles and around historical arguments orientated toward claims for rights and recognition, it is also a uniquely postracial formation, a global imagined community (of recent origin) that determines membership based on descent but not on biology or other principles of classification.[47]

Tourism is a space in which the four dialectically related dimensions of race—as construction, social experience, grammar of equality, and biopolitical technology—converge in a highly reflexive and highly performative way. In tourism, race is imagined, taken up, rehearsed, imposed, proposed, published, narrated, embodied, witnessed, entrenched, and elaborated.[48] Tourists and toured populations form and sense solidarities, attune themselves to signs of difference and similitude, and propose arguments about racial rights and destinies. The governmental problematics assayed in tourism, moreover, are racial ones. The doing of tourism continually produces biopolitical distinctions between, for example, "national" property and "private" property, appropriating from some owners but enabling investment in other cases. It accentuates divisions between populations endowed with the entitlements of mobility and those that biopolitical management keeps in place. It publically valorizes some identities while abjecting others.

This book attempts to catch race in action, following historical struggles that take place at the nexus of shifting orders of race and political reason. Racial governmentality in New Zealand has historically been a more protean formation than in other settler colonies, setting the conditions for tourism to become a particularly volatile site of experimental performativity. With its historically high levels of intermarriage, no formal segregation or blood quantum rules, and accommodationist or assimilationist policy frameworks, New Zealand's practices of racial classification and identification have often seemed more conjunctural than deterministic. For much of New Zealand's early colonial period, whitening discourses framed Māori, on whom settlers were dependent for trade and security, as a proximate race allied to the European colonists. Later in the century, a climate of aggressive assimilation favored arguments—from both Māori and Pākehā— that Māori were in fact Aryan people, distinct from the "degraded blacks" of Australia or from other reviled immigrant groups such as the Chinese and Punjabi. In the 1970s, by contrast, urban Māori who were battling for political recognition, land rights, and sovereignty claimed blackness or an essentialized ethnic identity, invoking the racial vocabularies of civil rights and cultural nationalist movements abroad as a unifying ethos. In contemporary New Zealand, however, the majority of Māori reject racial identification, instead favoring tribal affiliation, global terms (e.g., indigenous), or honoring their mixed heritage. Many even interpret the label Māori as an artifact of colonialism's distortion of tribal identification, representation, and membership.[49] To invoke race seems to be complicit with this history, or worse, with the white backlash against Treaty gains that draws on the virulent American strain of "postracial" neoliberalism, fulminating against "race-based preferment" and dismissing Māori rights advocates as "racists." At the same time, Māori have become major spokespeople in the global ideoscape of indigeneity, influential in transnational policy bodies, in academic circuits, and in indigenous market-based development.[50]

Although these conditions are unusual, the case of Aotearoa New Zealand can tell us much about how racial biopolitics are lived and navigated by subjects on the move across and beyond the terrain of states. We are accustomed to thinking of race as a matter of sharply drawn borders, rigidly policed categories, and essential cores. Indeed, much tourism theory presents ethnic tourism as hard racism clinically realized, anchoring truth claims about racial categories and identities in the facticity of the live (staged) body and the stark subject–object divisions of the tourism encounter.[51] By contrast, race flickers in and out of view in the cases I examine here, even those of the colonial era. Some Māori performers try to slip the yoke of race and its biopolitical entailments through the play of racial allusion and elusion. Others play the signs of class or gender against those of race, while still refusing assimilation to the liberal normativity of whiteness. Where local codes butt up against and unsettle racial frameworks that tourists bring with them from other nations and geopolitical contexts, opportunities are seized, risks encountered. Between some tourists and hosts, performance produces intimations of racial similitude, becoming a fragile medium of global community and instantiating political imaginaries other than those of the state. Racial performances throughout are experiments as likely to proliferate new networks as to render stable subjects.

This holds true for the experiments currently underway as Aotearoa New Zealand brokers another paradigm shift in the globalizing order of racial governmentality. On the one hand, we are entering an era of putative postracialism, which declares race both empirically defunct and disqualified as a locus of critique, dissent, or agitation for redistributive justice. On the other hand, we are seeing the reinvention of indigeneity as a new governmental technology capable, like race, of articulating belonging and of sustaining pleas for justice and remediation (if not redistribution) on a global basis. Unlike race, indigeneity is also oriented to the production and management of new market value from previously marginal cultures. Under pressure from state apparatuses such as tourism (I ask in the last two chapters of this volume), how promising is indigeneity as a new grammar of equality, as the conscience of the state? How capable is it of nourishing the politically alternative, the dissenting, or that which does not conform to market logic? Or is the indigenous brown destined to become the new white, shedding its associations with social negativity or resistance and assuming status as a newly valorized, exotic identity commodity? What, in that case, is the cost of the demise of race?

IMAGINED STATES: PERFORMED STATES

At the root of these chapters lies a single question: what is the field of ethical action that New Zealand's tourist state presents to its citizens and denizens? In more general terms, how do actors—indigenous and otherwise—*act* in the processes of state making mediated by the culture industries? How do actors push against the racial limits to the political imagination that liberal regimes entail, their distributions of opportunity and advantage, and the conditions they impose on those who seek to access that opportunity and advantage? How do, and how might, actors act in ways that present new possibilities, new distributions, and new imaginations that transform the workings of the state?

At the root of *these* questions lies a proposition about performance as a method of studying the state. On the one hand, this book offers new tools to scholars of performance studies, a discipline that has largely shied from extending its methods to macrostructural objects such as the state (or colonialism or neoliberalism), tending to take them as the inert and unassailable abstractions against which human-scale stories of performative agency play out. On the other hand, *The Tourist State* brings the tools of performance analysis to the ethnography and anthropology of the state, which has overwhelmingly focused on governmentality's systemic organization rather than its cultural poetics.

It should be obvious by now that this book uses performance in a capacious way. Governmentality is, in the first instance, a performance theory of the state: in its emphasis on practices, techniques, and conduct, it grounds macrological political and historical processes in micrological human acts, in patterned, programmed, "restored" behaviors.[52] The art of government is, in essence, the art of performance management.[53] Yet the study of the state also demands that we attend to a broader range of performance genres: the declarative symbolizations or mundane performatives of identity, the subtle reciprocities of sociability, the theatricality of spectacle, the cunning of orature, the *communitas* of ritual, and the artful projections of self-fashioning. Some of these resemble the reflexive symbolic systems— "cultural forms about culture"—that anthropologists and performance scholars have long contended express and renew the core meanings of a society.[54] Others form the tactical domain of everyday life: the myriad ways of knowing and being, of seizing pleasure, of dwelling or moving, and of contesting or exerting authority.[55] Performance, in the context of the state, is both a resource of the dominant culture (which requires repetition, participation, and witness to uphold that dominance) and of the powerless, who use it to navigate, to inhabit, and even to trick systems not of their making.

The study of the state also demands that we flesh out the praxis-oriented analyses of governmentality, adding to biopolitics a consideration of biopoetics and adding to the managerial, disciplinary dimensions of statehood a consideration of their affective volatility and corporal grip. Performance's power to compel belief and belonging, to enlist in action, lies in its experiential, phenomenological thickness. In the flow of performance, distinctions between action and consciousness, idea and object, or sensation and subjectivity hold little sway. The state's power to capture and canalize the action, affect, expression, and energy of its subjects lies, in turn, in harnessing this power of performance. Ultimately, then, performance methods can make palpable the mutual entanglement of categories, normally kept analytically separate, on which statehood depends: policy and cultural poetics, capital intensification and racial affect, and geopolitical force and embodied expression. The result is an event- and action-centered, motile, institutional, minutely focused picture of state making at both a human and global scale.

Finally, performance attunes us to the state's *imagination*, by which I mean the state in the process of its becoming, emergence, or expression. Performance is a propositional medium: it has the power to materialize that which it imagines. What is performed is informed but not constrained by what has been (unlike representation, for example, which aims at imitation or likeness). Performance can instantiate in image and action the yet to be. Insofar as it is witnessed and ratified by an audience, realized in the bodies of its performers or in the transformation of space, it acquires a measure, albeit contingent, of actuality.[56] Theorists of the state, from Spinoza to Castoriadis, from Deleuze to Anderson, have pointed to the imagination as the socially and materially generative mechanism of statehood. By the same token, performance theorists have shown how generation rests on human acts: For scholars of communication, the narrative and verbal art of performance is a medium of human world-making and self-making. For anthropologists, performance is a form of social poiesis through which collectivities are made and remade. For linguistic philosophers, performance (or performativity) has the power to enact that which it names, be it an identity or a public, through invoking the normative force of law. On this, most theorists agree: By virtue of its temporal and participatory character, performance remains open to improvisation or accident. It is always at once an unstable, risky enterprise and an inherently polyvocal one.

It is in these qualities that performance's peculiarity as a historiographic resource lies. In allowing us analytic access to the becoming of the state, it also reveals that state's forgotten futures: the lost details, accidents, and false starts that attended its piecemeal fabrication. It is in such forgotten futures, sequestered in the most "unpromising places"—the annals of affect, the fabric of the body, and the ephemera of pleasures past—that human agency in the process of state making can be grasped.[57]

POLITICAL STATES

If this book tells a story about human, and indigenous, agency in the process of state making, it also puts pressure on the concept of agency—as resistance or as creative action *taken in opposition to* structures of domination—that has become a shibboleth in the Euro-American humanities. "There is no position *strictly* inside or outside the state," Foucauldian analysis tells us: not in the supposed creative freedoms of performance, not in oppositional movements, and especially not in culture and community, so frequently invoked as the bastions of social authenticity against the cold rationalism of the state.[58] The critical imperatives most associated with agency are also those valorized by liberalism: the adequacy of representation, the autonomy of the individual, and the "idea of a real 'private' life, which alone is authentic and genuine" and demands expression.[59]

These are also, notably, the values that much tourism enterprise espouses, as well as the values that tourism's humanist critics claim the industry most egregiously fails to honor. The critical censure of touristic commodification, for example, suggests that by exposing the privacy of culture to the publicity of the market, we imperil its authenticity and thus its value. Such structures of feeling, however, ultimately serve tourism by raising the value of that which still lies outside the market, positioning it as fodder for more exclusive consumers.

Agency, then, in this oppositional sense, allies with the interests of the state. Moreover, it has been a signature of neoliberal policy to instrumentalize even more insistently the population's agency: in Aotearoa New Zealand (as I demonstrate in chapter 4), state agencies cultivate identity as a form of human capital; branding professionals engineer belonging and authenticity as the anchors of brand value; "performance" is the reigning paradigm in policy; and finally, resistance itself is systematically commodified, its capital worth enhanced through not having been part of the mainstream, thus retaining values of freedom and difference.[60] Even the postcolonial critique of tourism has been instrumental in the tourism industry's attempts to bring Māori cultural property into the market.

Nor can the critical agency of the scholar claim a position outside the state. As a New Zealander, a Pākehā, and an expatriate, but especially as an academic, I am hailed by the governmental apparatus I analyze. A tourist in my own country and a tourist agent for it when abroad, I am also a target. No longer deemed "lost human capital," expatriates are now identified as dedicated return visitors, vital links in transnational investment networks, and the nation's most reliable advertising medium. My interlocutors in research, including those in state agencies, have addressed me as both scholar and tourist. They also consider me a potential business contact, a knowledge-economy professional with access to the lucrative U.S. university market for tourism and cultural products. The more critical my take on their work, the greater my credibility. As a Pākehā, I have felt the affective (and inevitably appropriative) tug of belonging on witnessing a Māori haka abroad and the pull of pride at Americans' inevitable paeans to "my" most marketable national asset ("I hear it's very beautiful down there!"). The national brand is forged and forwarded in my name, but it has equally forged me. Clearly, my own conducts, affects, habits of consumption, networks, and productivities are channeled by the apparatus that I critique: the tourist state has my number.

Under such conditions, agency cannot be thought of as a *way out*; rather, it is a *way through*, a passage that is also a reordering. In liberal orders, subjects are positioned with respect to a plurality of agenc*ies*, each allowing numerous avenues for action, numerous opportunities for seizing the rules. If liberty must be expressed, then the political problem—the problem of resistance—is how to tune that expression, "finding channels, concepts, or practices that can link up and thereby intensify transversal struggles into larger, collective, but discontinuous movements."[61] Resistance is an ongoing experimental struggle; the results are sometimes transitory, sometimes enduring, sometimes aligning with the interests of state or empire, and sometimes more elusive. This book, then, is a study of performance as what we might call *weak* resistance: a resistance that (like the "weak theory" espoused by Actor Network Theory exponents) sees virtue in weakness's refusal to totalize, its refusal to put a strong model before the irreducible complexity of the world it describes, and its commitment to joining those it describes in the incessant making and remaking of their objects.[62]

THE TOURIST STATE: AN ITINERARY

I begin with the obvious: the scenic beauty with which New Zealand is synonymous in the Euro-American imagination. Rather than analyze representations of landscape, I turn instead to the Liberal-era tourist state's technologies of spatial and racial management, which drew distinctions between nature sublime, the disciplined probity of urban and pastoral modernity, and the residual spaces of savagery inhabited by Māori. Rotorua, a township and spa resort planned, promoted, constructed, and managed by the state tourism agencies, brought the three together in close proximity, functioning as both laboratory and theater for the arts of government and the "conduct of conduct" (that is, citizens' reflexive work on behaviors and dispositions). Bringing together town-planning and environmental-engineering initiatives, debates over architectural reform, species acclimatization, climatology, and public health, and, finally, tourists' psychogeographical meditations on the bizarre geothermal attractions of the area, I argue that tourism's biopolitical imperatives relied on a repertoire of biopoetical performances, imaginatively rooting and elaborating whiteness through spatialized experiences of identification and disidentification with Māori.

Taking up the question of conduct from a different angle, chapter 2 focuses on the acts of social encounter, dialogic interaction, and hospitality at the core of ethnic tourism. It details the transnational career of a celebrity Māori guide, entrepreneur, entertainer, and ethnologist from the turn of the twentieth century, Makereti Papakura. Exploiting the gendered performance repertoires of late Victorian travel culture and the state's need for cultural brokers like herself, Makereti tendered for membership in a cosmopolitan public sphere of travelers that transcended the ethnic strictures of the colony. Her story, however, points to the political and geopolitical limits of this form of liberal agency, which trafficked ethnic difference as cultural capital and accessed geographical and class mobility through racial performativity. What purchase did such cosmopolitical inventions, I ask, ultimately have on the racial topography of state, empire, or global ecumene?

Chapter 3 turns from the micropractices of vernacular diplomacy to the spectacular invention of American Empire, studying the diplotouristic pageantry staged by the New Zealand government in welcoming the U.S. Fleet while it was on tour to Japan in 1908. By placing Māori entertainers center stage, the welcome affirmed both liberal assimilationism and Sinophobic nationalism, but it also created a platform for Māori participants' dissenting, strategic visions of global geopolitics, local responsibilities, racial affinity, and destiny. The soft power of culture and the hard power of military and economic force flowed on the same currents, putting Māori performers into global circulation as commentators, diplomats, and tourists in their own right, from the parks of Rotorua to the stages of Broadway and the sideshows of Coney Island, simultaneously embellishing and disturbing the coherence of American Empire's claims about race, history, and the global future as well as the spatial logic on which racial governmentality depends.

The second half of *The Tourist State* examines neoliberal transformations in contemporary Aotearoa New Zealand as they reinvent the previous century's touristic technologies of branding, spatial management, conduct, whiteness, and the traffic in (Māori) cultural property. In chapter 4, I engage with Māori tourism policy makers, entrepreneurs, and workers at the front line of the neoliberal culturescape. Whereas policy presents the cultivation of identity as national panacea—a glue that might repair the social fractures of neoliberal reform and biculturalism, and a form of capital central to the new knowledge economy and its global brand—these individuals' struggles register the discontinuities, contradictions, and lags of bicultural neoliberalism's heroic vision. New, intimate genres of tourism performance promise development opportunities to economically sidelined hapū, while sidestepping tourism's painful histories of appropriation and racial derogation. But as tourism brings new domains of culture into market systems, what pressures does it put on indigenous identities defined by the demand for privacy and control over cultural property? What forms of conduct does the state's "upscaled" vision of a depoliticized and consumer-friendly Māori culture invite (and disqualify)? And why does the persistence of older tourism performance idioms, namely racial spectacle, seem ironically to provide a nostalgic refuge from the state's new technologies of cultural citizenship?

The film industry—a crucial site of national publicity and cultural sovereignty—has been intimately bound up with Aotearoa New Zealand's rebirth as a tourist state. If Aotearoa New Zealand's collaborations with Global Hollywood beg scrutiny both for their cultural economics and their racial politics, the renaissance of domestic film in state-sponsored international coproductions also raises questions about the traffic in (and concomitant transformation of) indigeneity that underpins neoliberalization. While *Whale Rider*, the national film success story of the new millennium, puts a globally salient but politically purified Māoridom at the center of the state brand, the *Rings* trilogy locally rehabilitates, nationally locates, and globally recirculates the heroic mythos of whiteness. What conditions of opportunity do these two state-sponsored, touristically leveraged fictions present, and for whom? I address these questions in chapter 5. Between Global Hollywood and Wellywood, local codes and global *doxa*, mythic racial hyperbole and the anxious elisions of "postraciality," what becomes of the local attachments, historical claims, resistances, and habitus formerly designated by race?

Clearly, there is little polemic certainty to the arguments put forward in these chapters. Rather, they aim to present a more nuanced portrait of the involvement of minority populations in processes of liberal state making and tourism than the Hobson's choice of exclusion, resistance, or cooptation. At a moment when tourism is (still) economically ascendant, the vehicle of global visions and revitalization initiatives of marginal populations and states the world over, it remains the bad object of cultural criticism, even after thirty years of serious academic study. What we need are not critical morality tales, not ethical directives, not choruses of celebration or condemnation. Instead, we need good stories: scrupulous, molecular descriptions of the processes, pathways, and limits encountered by tourism's actors. This book, I hope, offers some good stories.

chapter 1

The State of Nature:
Governmentality, Biopoetics, Sensation

They called it the netherworld. Situated in the isolated heart of the North Island of New Zealand, the spa town and ethnic tourism enclave of Rotorua was at once a wonderland and a hellhole. The tiny settler township and the adjoining Māori villages of Whakarewarewa and Ōhinemutu were built atop an active volcanic plateau, where sulfurous steam rose from gaping cracks in the ground and luminous pools of mineral-tinted water or mud bubbled away in residents' backyards. To the late Victorian eye, it was a space in which nature was uncannily, violently present in its most elemental form, enfolded with human society in ways that fascinated and beguiled. Even as its mineral waters were enlisted to heal, cure, pamper, cook, and clean, even as the alternately grotesque and pastoral landscapes delighted the eye, nature's titanic forces seemed to threaten the tourist with annihilation at every footstep. Yet Rotorua was also a space in which colonial modernity reigned triumphant, channeling the geothermal energy, "civilizing the wilderness" of native vegetation, and erecting a thriving, profitable enterprise on their remains.[1]

The most wondrous thing about Rotorua's Wonderland was its role as model and metonym for the Liberal-era state. The township, the spa, and the tireless publicity machine that touted them around the globe were entirely proposed, planned, executed, and managed by state agents. Plans for a nationalized leisure site were first floated in the 1870s, when the waning of the wars between Māori tribes and the Crown, along with the flourishing

A souvenir postcard of Wonderland. Alexander Turnbull Library, Wellington,
New Zealand.

of tourist traffic to the Tūhourangi-owned Pink and White Terraces, suggested that thermal regions were ripe for development. State making and
tourism growth were closely entwined agendas. Eager to get a foothold in
the sparsely settled inland North Island by establishing a town to service
burgeoning extractive and farming industries, state agents believed that
tourism was not just a source of revenue in itself but would also draw the
"best kind of settler" (moneyed cosmopolitans) by bringing the "advantages
of the colony" to international attention.[2] The Thermal Springs District
Act of 1881 prepared the ground for a resort on the shores of Lake Rotorua,
committing state funds to infrastructure development, surveying the Māori-
owned land of the area, and offering lots on long-term lease to settlers and
entrepreneurs courted from as far afield as India and Canada. An experiment in native policy, the Act framed local Māori as benefactors and partners of the state: by donating the "national asset" of the springs "for the
good of the people of the world," they would gain rent income, access to
tourist traffic, and state protection from Pākehā (non-Māori) speculators.[3]

The initial scheme was a disaster, falling victim to the depression of the 1880s and the 1886 eruption of Mount Tarawera, which demolished and buried the Pink and White Terraces while leaving the environs of Rotorua largely unscathed. When it was taken up again in the 1890s, it was with a Liberal-era appetite for Māori resources and zeal for state-driven capital development. ("Scarcely a month passes," one commentator complained, "without some convention passing a cheerful resolution demanding that the Government should step in and operate some new industry for the benefit of the public.")[4] A vocal association of leaseholders and business leaders saw Māori ownership of the township lots as an obstacle to private investment; the state concurred, making the promise of further development funds contingent upon the "security" of Pākehā residents' leases. By the time a deal was brokered in 1889, Māori had little practical choice but to sell to the Crown: rent had not been paid to them, and with no other source of income or employment in the region, many faced debt and were unable even to pay court expenses for lease rehearings.[5]

Under state management, spa facilities were constructed, infrastructure created, and provision made for all the appurtenances of colonial life (a library, town hall, schools, and even a museum). With a railway link to Auckland opening in 1894 (initiated by a private firm of land speculators but completed by the state), the resort began drawing weekenders from the rapidly growing urban middle classes of Auckland as well as international travelers.[6] Private enterprise played a part, adding hotels and boarding houses, and within a few years, this "mine of national wealth" had a "proper plant" run on "modern scientific principles, to extract all possible good out of it."[7] The settler population boomed (from 914 to 1,965 between 1901 and 1905), and tourists flocked to enjoy the genteel pleasures of the spa resort (bathing, croquet, and high tea on the grounds of the sanatorium), to view the freakish thermal wonders, and to witness "the Māori at home."[8] Whakarewarewa and Ōhinemutu were also mined: although they received little of the public monies showered on Rotorua, they were touted by the state as ethnological exhibits, living natural-heritage sites, and curiosities as novel as the thermal grounds on which they stood. At the same time, their place in the spotlight of this national project made them the target of liberal reform, a pilot for "modern Māori" progress. Rotorua became a space both extraordinary and utterly paradigmatic, a space that activated both the most arcane reaches of creative imagination and the most pragmatic reflections on the processes and principles of liberal government.

As Rotorua took its place at the heart of the state, that state's body took shape around it. The Liberal era saw the spatial project of state making at its zenith, extending physical and symbolic command over the entire territory of the islands: unifying, measuring, dominating, transforming, and symbolizing. By 1908, with the completion of the Main Trunk railway line, the newly declared Dominion had an infrastructural backbone that united its provincial territories and opened the interior for intensive settlement. National space was objectified and codified by survey, which had by this time rendered every inch of the nation uniformly fungible, forming a concentration of symbolic capital in which tourism played a large part. The Department of Tourist and Health Resorts (DTHR), one author quipped, would have "every nook, river, fiord, lake, and streamlet photographed, mounted, and scattered, broadcast, albumed, enlarged, miniatured, in every conceivable shape."[9]

It was also in the Liberal era that the most vigorous assaults were made on alternative spatial imaginaries. With land for agricultural production at a premium, the state led a ruthless rush of appropriations of Māori holdings. In a nationwide pogrom of deforestation, wetland draining, and land "improvement," the indigenous landscape (and the Māori lifeways it supported) gave way to agrarian progress, making "Home" (a better Britain) of an alien land. At the same time, the enduring touristic image of the nation as synonymous with sublime, unpeopled scenic beauty took hold as the currency of a newly nationalist self-recognition and a strategy of global branding. While actual rural vistas were scorched raw and ravaged by their rapid conversion from forest to farm, postage stamps (and letterheads and trademarks) depicted serene scenes "free from all taint of nineteenth century progress."[10] An evolving Pākehā-identity mythos (for Pākehā were by now a majority-urban population) took root in this monumental landscape ideal.

SPATIAL GOVERNMENTALITY AND THE MODERN CONSTITUTION

This chapter is about the role of tourism in forging the body of the nation and the citizen bodies that were to inhabit it; it is about the relationship between placemaking and race making, and through them, of state making.

Tourism was, I argue, a component of sovereignty, enabling the young state to consolidate and symbolize its territory, as well as to open it to intervention, circulation, and inhabitation.[11] It was also an instrument of governmentality through which that state addressed itself to the productivity, wealth, and well-being of its population. I look here at tourism's role in the spatialization of policy, as it worked in concert with a range of Liberal-era initiatives to differentiate zones and to elaborate the spatial codes, economic usages, and practices of self-cultivation associated with them. I look also at the intimate work on bodies and environments, and on the relations between them, carried out under the auspices of tourism. Such recursive spatial performances by travelers and their hosts—from the most mundane micropractices of everyday life to the most arcane rituals of tourist recreation—publicly tested, modified, and sedimented the character of citizenship.

If tourism in general offers a vivid picture of the political rationality of the settler-colonial state, Rotorua tourism shows that picture under a microscope. Rotorua was both symbolically central to the liberal enterprise and practically valuable as a dedicated site of experiment and display, a laboratory and theater of state. There, tourism development interlocked with projects of housing reform, species acclimatization, social hygiene, public health, scenic preservation, land conversion, and myriad other interventions into land and lifeways. A space apart, isolated from the denser European settlement of the coasts, Rotorua also assumed an emblematic role in the state's *racial* imagination: "I was in Maoriland at last," a typical tourist of the era declared upon his arrival.[12] Because tribal systems still confounded state attempts at cooptation, and because the seclusion of rural Māori communities and the new mobility of Māori labor were proving obstacles to the state's capacity to govern, Rotorua's designation as fictive capital of Māoridom had a certain expedience. In the frame of state tourism, Māori could be "represented" as a legible and governable constituency, a benign anomaly spatially contained within the modern colony, accessible to the gaze of the state. Rotorua made Māori available not only to lend distinction to the national brand but also to participate in biopolitical modeling that bore directly on the racial character of citizenship, both Pākehā and Māori.

I build here on an established literature approaching tourism as a mode of spatial production. Tourism, these scholars argue, shapes space in obviously material ways: it differentiates regions, boosts transport infrastructure, and establishes circulatory channels (itineraries), focal points (destinations), and specialized usages, such as game lands and preserves. Tourist space is the product of both policy and performance, as what tourists *do* in a given space creates, over time, the "possibility spaces" that the environment presents for other future actions.[13] Scholars have likewise pointed to the ways that tourism produces immaterial geographies, as monuments, sacral sites, landmarks, pleasurescapes, and so on condense and express the histories, attachments, and affects that are irrevocably bound up with the experience of collective belonging or subjective identity. On one level, this is a semiotic process: tourism generates and circulates "collections of images, sounds, actions" that attach to specific places (or, in the case of tourist simulacra, supersede them).[14] On another level, it can be viscerally performative. "Tourisms of hereness," as Barbara Kirshenblatt-Gimblett has called them, privilege physical presence and the auratic power of place: storied and textured with meaning, continually reauthenticated through performed rituals that intensify spatial experience, such as mapping, witnessing, reverie, comparison, and documentation.[15] On the broadest level, tourism forges geographical imaginaries, conceptualizations of territory and its related values and practices, which form the spatial counterpart of the nation's imagined community. As it maps and differentiates places, then disseminates information about them through the circuits of print capital, tourism generates a sense of attachment to, and proprietorship over, lands and landmarks for nationals and a sense of recognition by nonnationals.

My analysis departs from this literature in two significant respects. First, I examine the geobody produced in tourism not simply as the cultural bedrock of the nation but as an element in the governmental apparatus of state. Governmentality, Foucault argued, has its object in the augmentation of the security, productivity, and health of a population. In the early modern period, it turned away from the goal of exercising authority over a territory or dominating subjects toward an ethic of pastoral care that took "the care of the natural life of individuals into its very center."[16] In its liberal articulation, this meant government at a distance: the state acting not directly on the individual but on the biological processes of the social body through techniques aimed at improving the welfare of the population. This biopolitics is animated by a "naturalist" conception of the social. Liberal governmentality envisages population as a norm-governed entity and aims to minimize direct intervention in order to allow social equilibria

(made newly apprehensible through technologies of measurement and surveillance) to function undisturbed.[17] To this end, governmentality focuses
its transformative energies on environment and infrastructure. It engineers
the conditions that dispose individuals to act in particular ways and molds
the forms of practical expertise—or conduct—that shape perceptions,
behaviors, competencies, interests, and desires and that bring the individual to bind his or her identity to the state. Tourism, I contend, is a particularly concentrated site for this spatial "art of government" not only because
it recursively cultivates specific forms of conduct but also because it understands the pivotal importance of *art* to these processes. From biopolitical
imperatives, tourism evolves a repertoire of what I call biopoetical performances, imaginatively investing the subject in forms of conduct that are viscerally embodied, expressive, creative, improvisatory, and even eroticized.

Second, I understand space itself not as the state's mute, inert foundation
but as an actor in these governmental processes. In most spatial histories
of nation, the land, territory, place, and nature are passive: they are acted
upon, produced, transformed, exploited, or represented. Here, however, I
argue that the traffic not only of bodies over land but also *between* bodies
and land was integral to the state's capacity to imagine itself in performance.
In tourism, place could be disciplined, instrumentalized, and tooled to the
rhythm of the state, but it was also an agent that might act back in ways
that became a source of sustenance, fascination, and danger. The "modern
Constitution" of liberal political thought, according to Bruno Latour, is the
move that cleaves Society and Nature, discursively "purifying" Nature of
social influence and Society of natural objects and effects. Even as this modern Constitution places Nature and Society beyond each other's reach, however, hybrids and networks proliferate between humans and nonhumans.
Moderns "mobilize Nature at the heart of social relationships, even as they
leave Nature infinitely remote from human beings; they are free to make
and unmake their society, even as they render its laws ineluctable, necessary
and absolute."[18] This foundationalist gesture illuminates the centrality of
tourism—and especially scenic tourism—to the liberal imagination. Tourism has often been seen as the apogee of liberal modernity's cleaving of
the human from the natural. In a narrative that resonates from Raymond
Williams to John Urry, tourism lends nation meaning through preserving
and packaging its natural, i.e., nonmodern, history (the heritage of its peas-
antry, for example, or its untouched natural landscapes), which becomes a

sanctified repository for values held to be culturally foundational. Meanwhile, those values are rendered transcendental, outside history, through being naturalized by tourism's aesthetic technologies. An example might be the tourist arts of landscape that frame nature as a set of timeless views to be captured and consumed by a detached spectator. Insofar as critics argue that tourism is an effective "theatrical" program of detachment, objectification, or semiotic commodification (as in, for example, the postmodern critique initiated by Dean MacCannell and exemplified by Umberto Eco), they see tourism *through* a modern lens, rather than *as* a modern ruse.[19]

Rather than accept that tourism reflects, enacts, and mourns the severing of society from nature, I suggest that we look instead to the networks that tourism practice continually creates between the political and physical body, between social subjects and natural objects. What work do those networks perform in organizing, managing, and cultivating population? Such an analysis is particularly important, given the role that race plays in the modern Constitution. To the extent that colonial racial discourse understood racially marked populations—"primitives"—as incapable of properly differentiating nature and society, it also understood them as inherently illiberal and thus disqualified from self-government. Ethnic tourism, through making a spectacle of such undifferentiated lifeways, buttresses Moderns' belief in their own rationalized deracination. Tourism, then, is part of the mechanism that yokes liberalism with whiteness, framing characteristics such as bounded, rational selfhood, productivity, and self-management as racial properties. Yet even as it cleaves (primitive, ethnic) nature from (white, modern) society, scenic tourism proliferates ever-denser networks between the two: subjecting ethnic populations to social engineering in the name of their "natural" authenticity, putting natural environments to the social uses of capital or class, and biopoetically embroiling white moderns in natural places through intervention, projection, appropriation, and sensation. Tourism fosters a complex systematicity—linking humans, territory, indigenes, and settlers, and characterized by a profoundly transformative violence—that goes by the name of the state.

THE TRIPARTITE STATE

In 1890, booster and entrepreneur Jules Joubert lobbied the New Zealand parliament to support a permanent exhibition in London promoting the colony. Although Joubert's ambitious exhibit was never constructed, it articulated with precision what would become the dominant spatial imaginary of the Liberal era, sedimented in settlement guides, tourism promotions, and ultimately state policy. The first and most prominent feature, Joubert proposed, would be a large relief model of the colony, indicating the type of land, state of settlement, and availability for purchase in each region, surrounded by enlarged models of harbors and cities "to give those at Home some idea of the size of our towns and the extent of our civilization." Next, an art gallery of notable scenic attractions and a "Tourist Court with models of the Hot and Cold Lakes" would lead to a fernery containing a restaurant serving New Zealand products. Finally, running on from the fernery, Joubert proposed "an artificial New Zealand gully, with native plants and shrubs on the banks of a rocky creek. Here, and here alone would I allow the Maori to have a place, and that only to the very limited extent of a few whares [dwellings], with natives making mats and kits, and, possibly, also, *used with caution*, as a haka [performance] troupe."[20]

Joubert addressed what the Agent General in London, William Pember Reeves, perceived as an "information deficit" regarding the colony among "the well-to-do middle class at Home." The prospective tourist and settler held "that New Zealand is a very beautiful but very barbarous country, producing gold, wool, ferns and cannibals," into which he would have to come holding "a deadly weapon in one hand and his life in the other."[21] In placing itself in the metropolitan eye, the colony had to tread the fine line between portraying a landscape that was wild and untouched and one that was arable and available; between an antediluvian paradise and a bustling, modern nation with developed amenities; between a South Seas isle with a fierce and savage race living in their natural state, and an unclaimed agricultural tract with a biddable native labor force. As much as tourism thrived on the alterity of Māori presence, the success of the colonizing effort hinged on its containment; as much as natural purity lured, so did its antithesis, modern progress.

The viability of the liberal settler-state depended on its openness to the flows of a global economy. Rather than working to establish territorial indivisibility and to secure its borders (the classic spatial agenda of sovereign statehood), the island state's struggle was first to lure capital and then to reconcile or exploit the spatial divisions that uneven development produced. Despite the founding fiction of the nation-state, no space is uniform, abstract, or unchanging; all space is a fabric woven of "simultaneous stories so far," as Doreen Massey has argued. It is radically heterogeneous, a palimpsest and patchwork of disjunctive, superimposed temporalities and localities, trajectories, imaginations, and investments, in a constant state of productive flux.[22] In the space of sovereignty's unifying mission, liberal governmentality's genius is to harness such spatiotemporal plurality, both simplifying existing spatial differentiations and producing new ones, to enable the management and cultivation of population.

These liberal "arts of separation," I suggest, were at the root of the tripartite organization of space typified by Joubert's simulacrum, segregating the islands into zones of civilization, nature, and savagery.[23] A spatial strategy of both racial containment and racial production, this tripartite organization was not simply representational, it was performative—and tourism was its primary vehicle. Each zone elicited specific practices of encounter with, attention to, and action upon land; specific protocols of consumption or investment; and specific regimes of sensation and value. These were reproduced in the tourism apparatus's massive archive of spatial knowledge. In state guides, private accounts, letters of tourists, photographic collections, articles, advertising, itineraries, state and industry reports, and countless other sources, this state construction was globally and nationally disseminated, bodily rehearsed, and ultimately, intimately naturalized.

The visitor to Joubert's simulacrum entered the colony first by way of the spaces of civilization, beginning with a panoramic model in which the land appeared laid out for the taking: classified, packaged, and vacant but for the bustling cities and the capital infrastructure they represented. The nation that beckoned was a sunny, modern, clean, and orderly place, exemplifying the three liberal virtues: productivity, progress, and prosperity. It was to be encountered through the travel genre, the performance repertoire that I have labeled civic tourism.[24] Much like its antecedent, the Grand Tour, civic tourism lighted on the advances of civilization, through witness, inspection, and analysis of a distinctly governmental cast.[25] "No Englishman," one handbook instructed, "can fail to be interested in watching the progress and observing the institutions of this flourishing Colony; and the varied industries which have already sprung up will repay study."[26] Guidebooks coached their readers in the performance of such study, recommending strolling in Auckland, for example, where one might note with admiration the "homelike" evidence of British residency: "the undulating streets; the beautiful gardens; the verdant slopes; the mansions and villa residences, with their neatly-kept walks and flower-beds."²⁷ In accounts and letters, tourists would offer inventories of social and public services, construction, industry, and descriptive tallies of town halls, libraries, prisons, schools, and museums, pointing to spatial transformations to index governmental progress. Turning to the regions, civic tourists described deforestation, Māori depopulation, public infrastructure, industrially organized farming, and the creation of game lands in the rapturous strains of the literary pastoral and in terms that unabashedly conflated racial and spatial prerogative. New Zealand, in these accounts, was a "land where the colonizing energy of the Anglo-Celtic race" had reaped its highest reward and where the visitor "cannot help being struck with its resemblance to England."²⁸ Civic tourism schooled its subjects in "seeing like the state," evacuating and translating an alien prospect that only fifty years earlier had been "infested with a race of savage tribes" but now had "become part of the civilized world."²⁹ As it did so, its itineraries, practices, and scripts schooled tourists also in the conduct of whiteness: from the arts of disciplined urban leisure to the casual auditing of progress's evidence, civic tourists rehearsed the perceptual and analytic habits, bodily dispositions, and sensations of the settlement project.

The next act in Joubert's antipodean installation took the vicarious tourist–settler into the bosom of Dame Nature, starkly differentiated from the civilization of cities and farms. In this aesthetic cartography, the forbidding and titanic grandeur of the southern alps, lakes, and fjords played the sublime protagonist, while the North Island embodied arcadian serenity in which "fruit and flowers of every clime flourish luxuriantly in the warm and perennial sunshine."³⁰ Both remained unsullied by industrial overdevelopment and the blight of urbanization. Such veneration made a virtue (and policy) of necessity: while the colony was "old in Nature," it was "young in Art" and could "point to no gilded domes and marble palaces . . . to woo the pleasure-seeker to [her] shores."³¹ Sheer expedience, however, cannot account for the dominance of nature in New Zealand's nationalist imagination or its enduring transnational currency. It is hard to overstate how ubiquitous identification with the wild prodigality of nature was: it suffused the entire range of Liberal-era Pākehā cultural production—not only tourism and publicity discourse but also national historiography, poetry, art, popular photography, and commercial design—and formed the bedrock of later nationalist movements in the arts. Domestic tourism's leisure rituals of tramping, camping, picnicking, or scenic touring were increasingly pivotal to Pākehā civil society and class identity during this era, and their popularity motivated ongoing state investment in trails, huts, and other infrastructure.[32] While travelers' accounts and settlement advertising from the very onset of European exploration and settlement clothed New Zealand's landscape in romanticist hyperbole, by the Liberal era the literary and embodied practice of the landscape ideal had become a state project. The drive to lure international tourists spearheaded this project, but it was also linked to other domestic social and economic agendas. The cult of landscape, I contend, was not merely an exercise in the forging of spatial history, an occasion for the competitive demonstration of class distinction or colonial prerogative, or an epiphenomenon of cultural nationalism's geopietic urgings, although it was in part all of these things.[33] I posit that the national veneration of nature was systemically central, even foundational, to the sovereign apparatus of state, its governmental procedures, and political, specifically racial rationality.

New Zealand's spaces of nature, like similarly revered landscapes throughout the liberal diaspora, were irremediably hybrid entities. While defined by their absolute separation from the social—their originary purity—they were systemically entwined with the social dimensions of national life, with economy, history, politics, and civil society. This "modern Constitutional" arrangement was, unsurprisingly, alien to Māori, for whom land was also a foundation of political community, but for whom the separation of human from nonhuman domains was inconceivable: fierce attachments to territory derived from the literal consubstantiality of natural and human descent. Insofar as settlers and cosmopolites were called on to ratify the putative detachment of nature—through their reverence for its purity, their support for policies aiming to preserve that purity, and their cultural and physical patronage—that performance became, in part, a racial ticket of citizenship.

In the first instance, *natural* history stood (in) for the mythos of *national* history, undergirding the sovereign right to territory in the absence of the imprimatur of autochthony.[34] All the major Liberal-era histories of the nation began with an intimate, painstaking ekphrasis of the landscape, a subtle and sensuous cartography of temperature, atmosphere, smell, and palette, as if to take poetic possession and lay the primordial ground for the settler state to come.[35] To recognize "the grandeur and the beauty of *our* scenery" as Reeves did, or as Prime Minister Richard Seddon did in his advocacy of scenery-preservation legislation, was to take up a citizenship grounded in and founded on territory: "I could wander in the bush and there conjure up old associations and scenes," Seddon opined in parliamentary debate, reminiscent "of the days when we first came to the colony."[36] A notoriously rough-hewn publican with little time (or erudition) for high cultural sentiment, Seddon modeled this technology of the citizen–self, making of himself a character in the "drama of New Zealand's history."[37]

Nature, then, became an instrument of state culture. As a vast critical literature on the subject has established, land can only become Landscape, nature become Nature—pure, unsullied, unpeopled, apart—through its elaboration by a combination of "culture, convention and cognition."[38] As Wordsworth famously wrote, "the perception of what has acquired the name of picturesque and romantic scenery is so far from being intuitive that it can be produced only by a slow and gradual process of culture."[39] The fund of aesthetic expertise that permitted the appreciation of landscape was, at least initially, the preserve of the educated elite, often competitively deployed as a mark of refinement—as in the rites of the Grand Tour, for example—or even as a badge of dissent.[40] However (notwithstanding early Romantic claims on nature as a court of appeal against the industrial capitalist state), the course of the nineteenth century saw this expertise not only democratized but also governmentalized. Enshrined within the edicts of liberal education, the realm of culture (in Matthew Arnold's formulation) became central to the logic of the state. It became an "extrapolitical, extraeconomic" site that was to mediate between the "irreconcilable group interests" of those to be represented and the formal universality of the state that was to represent them. The citizen had to "learn to be represented," and it was through learning the disinterest of aesthetic judgment by engaging with culture that this ethical formation might take place.[41] In Liberal-era New Zealand, the culture of nature was put forth as the supposedly universal ground of citizenship. But just as Seddon's scenic reverie purified the landscape and its history of Māori, that formal universality masked racial particularism.

The Liberal state worked to enshrine access to nature as a rite, and right, of citizenship, through a conservancy movement advanced under the legitimating promise of tourism profit. Nature could thus be tooled not only to the ethical formation of citizens but also to the governmental ends of managing productivity. As with the national parks of the American West or New England, the creation of a national conservation estate would, it was argued in Parliament, perform a vital economic function by spreading tourist activity and investment from urban centers to the hinterlands, augmenting infrastructure through the specialized use of otherwise unproductive geographical resources.[42] It was no paradox that the Scenery Preservation Act (1903) was driven forward by the same state agency (Department of Lands and Survey) that oversaw the wholesale conversion of forests into farms.[43] Scenic preservation was pivotal to the spatial program of settler modernity, and nature was called on both to advance commercial development and to veil the ravages of agrarian productivity. One tourism official contended that the forest, "if preserved in its primeval beauty contiguous to the railway[s], will afford a great attraction to travellers generally, and will prove a splendid inducement . . . to go by train instead of by steamer, whereas miles of burnt and blackened logs would prove a weariness to the spirit."[44]

This nature was no less a commodity than the neat parcels of the cadastral grid that opened Joubert's exhibition. Emerson famously claimed that landscape is land put to poetic rather than economic use. But if landscape avoids the demands of utility, it still bestows a capital value that is both alienable and bankable.[45] Reeves clearly recognized this when he argued that New Zealanders needed "to be fully alive to the monetary value to their nation of the scenery."[46] Landscape promised not only to preserve nature from the reach of an agrarian economy but also to enable a more encompassing and diversified economic management of the state's territory, rendering marginal (nonarable) land an asset. Dame Nature's Beauteous Gift to the Colony could be repackaged as an invisible export, but to do so required a citizenry aesthetically equipped and touristically trained to recognize its value.

The implementation of scenery preservation legislation made it patently clear that in the eyes of the state, Māori (qua Māori) did not share in this form of cultural citizenship. When Māori holdings were claimed under the Act as the "inalienable patrimony of the people of New Zealand," Parliament demanded that title be vested in the Crown rather than tribal bodies (even though such holdings were not in danger of development, being used for hunting and gathering, or retained by Māori for spiritual reasons). Nature was to be the monopoly of the state, and a people whose Society remained entangled with Nature could not be trusted to protect the foundational purity of that "patrimony."[47] In a form of state accumulation by dispossession, preservation efforts frequently displaced Māori but then nostalgically invoked the Māori past as a poetic but inevitably extinguished component of natural history.[48] Take, for instance, the government-published tour guide to the remote Urewera authored by Elsdon Best, a former surveyor, prolific poet, and ethnographer then in the employ of the state as a health officer in the region. He described a landscape "lone, and silent" where "every hill and gulch [had] its tale to tell . . . of the 'good old days,'" of a tribe (Tūhoe) who had willingly "buried the war-axe, and taken to the pick and bar and shovel."[49] The new scenic reserve that he publicized was a component of a concerted state strategy to open the hostile region to roads, capital, logging, and leisure, to convert its forests to farms and its warriors to laborers, and to inaugurate the human history that Best announced as an accomplished fact.

If, then, the pure realm of nature was entwined with myriad economic and cultural elements of the state apparatus, it was also no less a technology of racial production than civic tourism was. In explicit ways, tourism was construed as a practice in which nature could be brought to act biopolitically on the welfare of the citizen body. In the climatological arguments that suffused tourism literature, the rugged and robust national topography was already producing a physically and morally rugged and robust national character. While European eugenicists decried the decadence of metropolitan life, the colony's promoters claimed that the first generation of native-born Pākehā New Zealanders growing to maturity during the 1890s were stronger and physically more capable than their British counterparts. Where the new dominance of urban lifestyles threatened the race, the nation's spaces of nature would be the literal re-creation ground for the "fagged man of business" and "thousands of nerve-shaken, overcivilized people," a place where they might be physically and morally reconstituted.[50] "Even the Maories," one English visitor claimed, "a mere colony of Polynesian savages, grew to a stature of mind and body in New Zealand which no branch of that race has approached elsewhere."[51] As often as not, however, this new nativist subject was contrasted with, not compared to, Māori. Indolent Māori, authors claimed, plainly preferred the easier climates of the North Island.

Tourism's nature cult educed the racial virtue of the tourist–citizen through analogy with New Zealand's southern landscapes. Martin Bernal, and Richard Dyer after him, have noted that genealogies of whiteness—in particular Aryanism and the myth of Caucasian origins—locate true whiteness in "small, virtuous and 'pure' communities in remote and cold places such as Switzerland, northern Germany and Scotland."[52] "The clarity and cleanliness of the air, the vigour demanded by the cold, the enterprise required by the harshness of the terrain and climate, the sublime, soul-elevating beauty of the mountain vistas, even the greater nearness to God above, and the presence of the whitest thing on earth, snow," all secured such associations.[53] As Barthes wryly commented, the "bourgeois promoting of the mountains" had more than a dash of "Helvetico-Protestant morality."[54] New Zealand's south was likewise perceived as feral and precipitant. Mere physical proximity to the sights seemed "to encourage morality of effort" and imbue viewers with the fabled virtues of pioneer Anglo-Saxonism: discipline, enterprise, energy, and (emulating the mountains themselves) uprightness and purity.[55] "What a magnificent world in which to establish the new kingdom," Yorkshire tourist E. J. Smith declared exultantly (after a day spent fording rivers and admiring peaks), where "zeal, backbone, stamina, and grit will be confronted by unrelenting necessity, continuous hardship and long-drawn-out privation."[56] Not only hikers, climbers, and intrepid bushmen but also sketch makers, view takers, or coach passengers could participate in this racial project by mastering the appropriate aesthetic disposition and conduct.

The art of landscape appreciation was, to be sure, the pursuit of social distinction (as described by Pierre Bourdieu): individuals competed through their exertions to master both body and nature and to exhibit connoisseurship through practices of consumption.[57] Yet, promoted and enabled by policy, and articulated with other civic and economic agendas, scenic tourism was also a governmental technology that furthered the territorial and capital extension and intensification of the state. And it did so through imagining relationships between land, bodies, and peoples, through inciting and exciting spatial performances in cosmopolitan tourists and potential future citizens alike.

HETEROTOPIA MAORILAND

The third and final set of Jules Joubert's antipodean installation was revealed to the exhibition patron like the smallest figure in a set of Russian dolls: Māori performers, sequestered safely between the two slopes of a steep gully. Penetrating the heart of the country was a journey from the empirical, imperial generics of thriving colonial cities, maps, and models; through galleries of remote mountain sublimity; into the theatrical half-light of "Maoriland," where visitors as explorers found themselves immersed in a strange, primeval world, thrillingly close to its living denizens. At the time of Joubert's writing, 1890, this virtual space was assuming an actual habitation and a name in Rotorua.

Joubert's design, and the early Liberal-era publicity literature it mim-icked, responded to Māori presence by containment and mitigation: New Zealand's intractable native population constituted a potentially objec-tionable element of the national profile that, carefully controlled, might yet be tooled to tourists' paradoxical desires for familiarity and difference, abandon and control. For the Liberal state that birthed Rotorua, the chal-lenge was not simply containment but also government: how to accommo-date and instrumentalize a population that resisted assimilation to liberal (white) norms of conduct and economic behavior. The history of tourism in the area suggested a novel experiment whereby that difference could at once be enclaved, rendered productive, and transformed to bring it into inner conformity with the political rationality of the state. The experimen-tal method assayed in Rotorua was a spatial one. The state latched onto an environment as threatening, volatile, and fascinating as the Māori pop-ulation for which it swiftly became a referent. In concert with the tourism industry and tourists themselves, it superimposed the spatial accoutrements of colonial modernity alongside the older indigenous settlements, subject-ing the entire assemblage to analysis, scrutiny, invention, and intervention. The result was an intricate network—forged in the performance of tour-ism and animated by the state's transformative violence—that linked human and environmental *bios*, society and nature, territory and economy, Pākehā and Māori.

In the section that follows, I trace the friction between three spaces of touristic biopolitics in Rotorua, each a site of social self-invention, inten-sification, and affective elaboration, and each bearing on the production of racial subjects. The first of these is the spa complex built by the state at Rotorua, where the thermal features of the land were quite literally applied in the leisured reformation of white bodies. The second is the san-itary reform of Māori dwellings, labor, and lifeways in the native villages of Ōhinemutu and Whakarewarewa. The third site is the practice of land-scape tourism in the thermal reserves of the area, a ritual of racial forma-tion in which biopolitics took on an irrefutably biopoetical cast, as tourists enacted psychotopographic dramas with a thoroughly anthropomorphized nature against the background of Rotorua's regulatory excess, *making space* for the state's impossible dreamworlds and forbidden sensations.

SANITIZING SPACE, MANAGING DIFFERENCE, AND REFORMING BODIES

The state investment in Rotorua tourism was fuelled at its outset by an almost textbook agenda of biopolitical engineering. In the popular as well as the official imaginary, the development of the spa and town was a national prerogative not only for its fiscal benefit as a touristic "gold mine" to the colony but also as the precursor to a fully nationalized public health service.[58] Such a service, it was argued, would return the cripple (a "burden to society") to the ranks of the nation's "industrial army" and serve the emerging national bourgeoisie, the "fagged men of business" who would be restored by bathing and sightseeing.[59] The enterprise bore all the hall-marks of Liberal-era state making: its benefits were unevenly, and racially, distributed; it conflated capital, specifically leisure development, with pub-lic welfare; and it courted the international tourist in the guise of serving the citizen. In classic governmental fashion, the population at large was taken as an assemblage to be managed *at a distance* through techniques aimed at welfare (prosperity, health, and security) by molding forms of practical expertise or conduct (hygiene and rational recreation).[60] State benefaction, then, was always also an operation of regulation that aimed to transform individual habitus and disposition and, through them, social and economic life itself. This biopolitical drive did not emanate solely from the state but was dispersed throughout a range of civic, state, and market agencies (Māori and settler reform organizations, commercial tour-ism entrepreneurs, tourists themselves, investment lobbies, and local boost-ers, to name a few).

Tacitly recognizing the mutually constitutive relationship of space and habitus, state developers at Rotorua focused their transformative energies in the first instance on environment. The civilizing of Rotorua was to be an object lesson in alacrity and efficiency for the rest of the colony. In a scant ten years, commentators reported the township making a transition from a raw grid "of town sections covered with manuka [scrub], and long, dusty streets without a shop" to a quaint village of "nicely formed streets, neat houses, enclosed gardens and flourishing plantations," complete with every civic amenity from a telegraph office to a library to a courthouse.[61] In these early years, Rotorua appeared to tourists as an oasis in the wild interior, where visitors might feel they "had quite got back to civilisation again."[62]

In pursuit of this civilizing process, officials planned a dedicated recreation environment: a garden with elaborate plantings, drives, walks, sweeping lawns, artificial lakes, tennis, golf, and croquet greens. Conceptually and physically, these gardens were positioned as ligaments between town and spa, civic health and bodily health. To justify the magnitude of public investment in developing the Sanatorium Reserve, promoters invoked the twin mandates of security and hygiene: aesthetic technologies were to make the place "safe" for settlers and tourists, a refuge not only from a primitive and alien environment but also from the disturbances of industrial modernity. To the colonial eye, the original area had appeared a "veritable wilderness" of "barren plains and dry brown hills," "through which few dared wander, lest the crust beneath their feet should break and bring them to an awful doom."[63] Casting the native ecosystems of the region as *un*natural, the state embarked on outright environmental conquest to produce a simulacrum of late Victorian rational, national recreation space. Vast loads of topsoil were transported from more fertile areas, and the transformation of Sulphur Point (along with the two other public reserves, Pukeroa and Arikikapakapa) began. The surrounding landscape also began to assume a simulacral quality in accounts and guides. To advocates of the new resort, it offered "lake and mountain scenery which, in its way, rivals that of Cumberland, or Killarney," or the Hot Lakes District's distant namesake and touristic template, the English Lake District (an association assiduously cultivated by promoters).[64] Spatial codes of the picturesque dominated its representation as a charming arrangement of Māori ruins, pastoral landscapes, tranquil lakes, atmospheric effects, and receding hill vistas.[65]

The native aspects of nature were not so much eradicated as diligently managed: native actors, human and nonhuman, were controlled to ensure white guests the freedom to "restore" and "recreate" themselves in this foreign-made-familiar terrain. Native plants were reinstated in bordered beds: isolated, captioned, and regularly pruned. White and black swans, along with peacocks and peahens, were acclimatized by the government and roamed free, dominating the lakefront ecosystem, while the DTHR built an aviary to display native birds: weka, pukeko, kiwi, and kea (the last far from their alpine habitat). The "native" was commodified as a national asset, not a quality of locality.[66] Other acclimatization efforts reached beyond the gardens, replicating and democratizing the leisure pursuits of British gentility by introducing trout to the rivers and lakes, and game species (including deer) to the forests. The effects were devastating to both native ecosystems and native lifeways. Championed (paradoxically) by the scenery preservationist S. Percy Smith and by his successor, T. E. Donne of the DTHR, the introduced species flourished, with the trout extinguishing the indigenous species so important to the diet and subsistence economy of lake-area iwi and hapū (extended kin groups). When Māori, the next link in this network of natural and cultural interdependencies, adapted by fishing for brown trout, they faced penalties from the state for failing to procure the appropriate licenses.[67]

Even the thermal phenomena that peppered Sulphur Point—fumaroles, bubbling hot springs, and boiling mud pools—were domesticated, framed by neatly bordered gravel paths and fences. Camille Malfroy, the government overseer, engineered artificial geysers in the sanatorium grounds by feeding the outfall of a hot spring through pipes and valves to control its release "at will."[68] "Rotorua itself," one tourist wrote, "is a peaceful place, and only the two geysers give one the faintest idea that Nature, hereabouts, is letting herself loose. The very fact that even these geysers are managed by the hand of man and made to play in a special place shows that control holds sway."[69] When native bodies took a place in this environment, it was in a similarly deracinated and disciplined form. The gardens were rarely frequented by Māori, but it abounded in asymmetric hybrids of Māori ornament and Pākehā structure: tekoteko carvings (commissioned from artists at Whakarewarewa) were mounted on gateposts and finials, and the tea kiosk was named after Māori social tradition (Te Runanga, or "the gathering") and was staffed by "prettily dressed Native girls acting as attendants."[70]

At the spa itself, the state's strategies of spatial and racial ordering followed an even more marked course. Other smaller spa facilities preceded the Rotorua Sanatorium, including Hanmer Springs in the South Island,

Postcard views of the Government Gardens, Rotorua. Alexander Turnbull Library, Wellington, New Zealand.

Te Aroha (a day's journey north of Rotorua), and out-of-the-way spots like Te Puia, Parakai, and Waiho.[71] These institutions catered mainly to the domestic market: in New Zealand, as in other New World locations, spas sprang up as a "pleasure periphery" to new towns and to remote areas.[72] But Rotorua was on an altogether larger scale, with both nationalist and cosmopolitan ambitions. After piecemeal state efforts during the 1880s and 1890s to develop the facility, the newly formed DTHR took over management in 1901 and embarked immediately on ambitious plans for a state-of-the-art bathhouse, justifying the project by linking it to public health agendas and the promise of tourist revenue. By the time of its completion in 1908, it had cost £80,000, a vast (and controversial) sum even in an era of bold public works investment. If state expenditure promised that spa going would be an accessible public pursuit, its patronage suggested otherwise: as early as 1897, Rotorua had become a haven for the colony's emerging Pākehā professional managerial class. Along with moneyed visitors from the United Kingdom, Australia, and other British territories, the colony's politicians, social illuminati, upper echelons of the civil service, and wives and daughters of affluent businessmen summered at the town, looking for social opportunities.[73]

Rotorua, then, served the drivers of the colonial, nationalist, and state-making projects. Like French colonial spas of the era, it was a practical and spatial technology that aided those individuals and those projects by mediating between race and place, attachment and detachment. These French institutions, Eric Jennings has argued, were designed to impress and distance the colonized and to "acclimatize" colonials by strategically cloning a slice of France itself, replicating metropolitan architecture and selecting as sites microclimates comparable to Home.[74] Such spas prepared colonizers' bodies to inhabit unfamiliar colonial spaces and to return to metropolitan ones, while constantly marking the "boundaries of rule" between self and other by fostering a spatial culture and conduct of moral, social, and aesthetic hygiene.[75] Following a similar pattern, the Rotorua bathhouse (designed by architect B. S. Corlett, later the Inspector of Works) was constructed in English half-timbered style, bespeaking symmetry, solidity, order, and hygiene. "Clean and inviting," airy, well ventilated, and well lit, it had every feature in the Victorian decorative vernacular of leisured luxury: verandas, clean tile and wood parquet floors, natural conservatory lighting, and ornate fountains adorned with palms and ferns.[76] Statuary with biblical and classical themes peppered the interior, and the bathing rooms were fitted with luxurious Minton tiles and Royal Doulton bathtubs.[77] The building's form was integral to both medical mission and touristic appeal, providing for a kind of racial *ressourcement* that brought settlers and metropolitan visitors into alignment around the Anglo-Saxon ideal. Rejecting Greco-Roman classicism, the state-appointed balneologist wrote of the proposed "homely" spa design, "I venture to think that it will appeal more sympathetically to the eye of English wanderer and Colonial settler alike, than would the architecture of an alien race."[78] All that was to bespeak the location of the spa was a discreet design detail of the tiles proclaiming "the nationality of the baths in a pattern of fern and teatree."[79]

NATIVE SPACE AND THE MANAGEMENT OF MĀORI CONDUCT

The sanatorium was dubbed the Dominion Baths, while the reserve became popularly known as the Government Gardens. Aptly so, since the

The Government Spa at Rotorua, completed in 1908. Alexander Turnbull Library, Wellington, New Zealand.

government not only had made them but had made them in the image of its own ideals. The difference between the opulence of the spa and the poverty of Ōhinemutu and Whakarewarewa could not have been starker, yet tourism's advocates also focused their energies on the spatial conditions of conduct in these Māori villages. In doing so, they joined a nationwide chorus of reformers—state and civic, Māori and Pākehā—working to bring Māori into conformity with liberal norms. The goals of this reform movement were to instate nuclear family life in the place of extended kin groups with customary marriage and childrearing arrangements; to advocate independence, by which they meant individual land tenure and capital accumulation, rather than the communal tenure and distribution of wage income within kin groups; and to promote temperance, by which they hoped to instill temporal discipline in wage labor and self-moderation in consumption in a population more responsive to the seasonal, ritual, and family demands of their communities. With hapū and whānau (extended families) shattered in the wake of land loss and increasingly dependent on a commodity and labor economy, such calls to "modernization" also had considerable traction within Māori communities, even as many resisted incursions into customary lifeways.

Insofar as the persistence of traditional Māori landholding, communalism, and tribal life presented an obstacle to settler capitalism's deterritorialized ideal, Rotorua appeared to offer the state a fortuitous solution: in the context of tourism, visible indices of Māori difference were not impediments to progress and productivity but potential sources of profit. Under the tourist spotlight, local Māori were at once (paradoxically) enjoined to retain the distinctive *appearance* of communal life and placed under pressure to conform to the practical rationalities (and racial norms) of liberal citizenship—to act as a model for and index of Māori modernization elsewhere in the nation.

This biopolitical imperative fastened on spatial practice, drawing its moral force from concerns about public health. The villages, state officials complained, were dirty, disorderly, and a "menace to the health of the town."[80] Against the new spa's pretentions to luxury, Ōhinemutu was described as "picturesque though squalid," its buildings in a "ramshackle and frequently disgusting condition."[81] Tourists added to the chorus: "Ōhinemutu is a fascinating place, for there you could almost imagine you were far from the evil influence of the Pākehā. The women thump their washing on stones beside the creek, the brown babies are bathed in the warm pools under the willows, the old dames make their mats in the doorways of the whares. . . . Nearer, the prospect is not so alluring, for dirt and disease is rampant, and the constant cough bespeaks the prevalence of lung-trouble."[82] Like slumming muckrakers, authors of tourist accounts combined censure, pathos, and voyeurism as they described Māori clinging to outmoded traditions or being overcome by racial demoralization. Indeed, postcard studies of village life resembled contemporaneous photographs of London's East End, showing half-dressed urchins playing in the dust or smudged maids laboring barefoot over steaming kettles.

The discourse of the reform movement drew explicit equations between spatial practice and the illiberal character of Māori life. Were the one-roomed Māori dwellings dens of pestilence where stagnant air lurked and families lived in morally and physically unhygienic proximity with each other? Was the lack of light and air circulation indicated by the absence of windows acceptable, or did the houses need to be opened up?[83] It was generally acknowledged that the waste removal services were inadequate, but were these problems compounded by the "disorganization" of Ōhinemutu, which lacked clear demarcations between private and public property, and hence a clear means for attributing responsibility for cleanliness? Such concerns were not unique to the Rotorua villages, stemming in part from the emerging health service's response to epidemics (of typhoid and influenza, for example), which had taken a brutal toll on Māori communities.[84] But as in these other contexts, Rotorua reformers looked past evidence of poverty, framing a perceived lack of hygiene instead as the product of faulty organization. As the "naturally" hygienic and self-regulating systems of "traditional" society had disintegrated in the face of modernity, it was thought, reform efforts were needed to bring the kāinga (villages) into a new state of natural and healthy equilibrium, in conformity with their European neighbors. Like the dwellings themselves, Māori collectives were considered to be sluggish and festering, lacking transparency to the regulatory gaze of government. Housing reforms promised to tool such practical technologies as drains, for example, to the production of Māori as liberal citizen–subjects: they would promote privacy but also suture private units to a broader civic and state infrastructure that penetrated them, enabling both inflow and outflow. As in similar urban planning and public health discourse in the United Kingdom, what was at stake was the regulation of Māori lifeways "via the

Postcard views of Whakarewarewa life. Alexander Turnbull Library, Wellington, New Zealand.

medium of environmental regulation; to free, so to speak, a space for vital normativity through minimum standardization of the environment."[85]

What was unique about the political dramaturgy of Rotorua's cleanliness campaign, however, was its alliance of tourist aesthetics with governmental surveillance to both justify and strategize governmental incursions into Māori domains. In place of governmentality's usual analytic mechanisms of statistics or sociology, tourism's techniques of observation documented Māori life, its natural laws, customs, and norms, while tourism's material inscriptions—travel accounts, guides, and photographs—offered "knowledge, expertise, and calculation that [might] render human beings thinkable in such a manner as to make them amenable" to the intervention of administrative techniques.[86]

Governmental science and tourist pleasure converged in projects to transform spatial practice in the villages, occasionally leading to surprising alignments between Māori political imperatives, state, and tourism industry interests. In one example, the local Māori Health Officer, together with colleagues from the Young Māori Party (a reform-oriented, pan-tribal Māori political advocacy group) and the local representative of the DTHR (the de facto mayor of the town), crafted a plan to convert the dwellings of Ōhinemutu into a "model village," exemplifying a modern, hygienic, "reasonable form" of Māori architecture, thus "enormously increasing the attraction of these villages to the tourists."[87] The homes would have several rooms (separating the functions of domestic life, as well as the members of the implicitly nuclear family), numerous windows, raised foundations, running water, and drains, but their exteriors would retain the design features that made Māori whares so picturesque to the tourist eye and pleasing to their inhabitants. Desiring the prosperity promised by tourism traffic and the security promised by hygienic dwellings, Māori (it was presumed) would embrace the change.

Although it was never put into effect, the proposal betokened a world of political consequence, given the link between spatial practice and the racial analytics of governmentality. During the Liberal era, state policy in part determined Māori identity through spatial practice, not descent or self-identification: census regulations separately registered "Maoris" and "Maoris living as Europeans," with the distinction hinging on such factors as the location of a dwelling (in a kāinga or a township) and the perceived mode of dwelling (communal or private). Although criteria were not formalized in legislation but instead left to the discretion of the census officers, the narratives that accompanied district reports centered on living conditions, suggesting that "living as Māori" implied the division of social life between one-roomed family dwellings that were used primarily for sleeping and the communal outdoor spaces of the kāinga, where cooking, social interaction, domestic tasks, and other work activities took place.[88] "Living as European" implied that domestic work, everyday tasks of bodily maintenance, and so on all took place in the self-contained privacy of the family home. The adoption of liberal spatial habitus, then, quite literally threatened to assimilate Māori as a constituency in the eyes of the state; the model village, by contrast, allowed Māori to identify and be identified as Māori, without jeopardizing citizenship by failing to exhibit hygienic, spatial self-governance.

THE ART OF GOVERNMENT AND
THE PRACTICE OF HYDROTHERAPY

While governmental procedures managed, reformed, and valorized the natural life of Māori outside the spa, inside it they worked to produce the conduct and corporeality of the white, hygienic liberal subject (and state) through the often bizarrely theatrical techniques of balneological science. According to Toby Miller and George Yúdice, cultural policy produces a radical indeterminacy in its political subjects: "it finds, serves, and nurtures a sense of belonging, through educational and other cultural regimens that are predicated on an insufficiency of the individual against the benevolent historical backdrop of the sovereign state."[89] This ethical incompleteness of the subject—the sense that it had to be repaired, cultivated, and cultured by the state—was, in the case of Rotorua, also *ethnic* incompleteness. If, as I have suggested, a white body politic was educed by the spa's architecture, that whiteness was likewise the focus of continuous reformative intervention within the institution. Patient bodies were subjected to and extended by technologies aimed at regulating flow, system efficiency, and productivity, and at constructing networks between individual bodies, nature, state, and economy—networks that were at once metaphorical and material, bodily intimate and administratively actionable.

That the public understood the Rotorua Sanatorium to be the "business of the State" is perhaps not surprising, given the spa's location at the

intersection of medicine, reform, tourism, colonialism, and class formation.[90] For millennia, spas thrived as pilgrimage sites of elite leisure culture
and as the "second seats" of aristocratic and later bourgeois power, where
physical regeneration combined with social networking. To early democratized tourism, they were rituals of bodily restoration but also of calendri-
cal pleasure, rest, and revivification, from nineteenth-century rest cures to
the bracing rites of cold-water bathing. In the hands of both the French
and the English, they were important institutions of colonial governmentality, repairing bodies taxed by the unfamiliar rigors of the tropics, under
the auspices of a "nebula of racial theories, climatic and environmental
determinism, and degeneration paradigms."[91] By the late nineteenth century, many Euro-American spas also bore the much more evangelical,
reformist, and frequently eugenicist imprint of the homeopathy and physical culture movements: hydropathic or hydrotherapeutic treatment (terms
that refer to any treatment using ordinary waters) offered both spiritual
and bodily salvation from modernity's demoralization through ascetic,
purifying self-discipline. One might "wash and be healed."[92]

These strands of influence were all woven into the history of the Rotorua
Sanatorium. Its first director, Camille Malfroy, conducted extensive research
at bathing establishments in Europe and in his role as the Executive Commissioner of the New Zealand display at the Paris Exposition Universelle in
1889 (where the French featured an entire pavilion devoted to "Balneal and
Therapeutic" pursuits).[93] The appointment in 1901 of a formally creden-
tialed expert, Dr. Wohlmann, as director of the spa marked the government's
commitment to the medical philosophy of balneology, a state-of-the-art
therapeutic science that involved a highly managed regime of bathing, rest,
exercise, and the application and consumption of naturally occurring mineral waters. Balneology also extended to other means of intervention into
bodily systems: stimulation by massage, mud packs, alterations in temperature and light levels, and the application of electrical currents. While state
sanatoria in Australia were essentially penal institutions that transformed
the dangerously infirm (often also poor or transient) into self-governing,
hygienic citizens, Rotorua applied many of the same techniques to leisured
bodies: segregation, minute regulation of activity, time, and motion, and intensive instruction in bodily conduct, from how to eat to how to sneeze.[94]

Balneology at Rotorua was premised on a naturalist logic, taking bathing
as part of a holistic health regimen that addressed the moral and physical

ills of urban modernity by restoring a natural state of balance, equilibrium, and purity. Wohlmann explained,

> There is the tired business man who is beginning to find his work an increasing burden no longer borne with zest; the man or woman on whose overstrung nerves little worries begin to jar unbearably; the man whose professional problems follow him to a sleepless pillow: there is that ever-increasing multitude whose tired stomachs protest against the habitual violation of the laws of health, whose tell tale eyes proclaim the bile-laden blood, the overstocked liver, and the gorged and sluggish veins; with overworked nervous system, overworked digestive system, and underworked muscular system—all the victims, in fact, of that Juggernaut, complex modern civilisation.[95]

Balneology adhered to an ideal of systemic efficiency, theorizing medical complaints of all sorts, from gout to neuralgia, as the result of unnatural blockages of the flow of products (waste, nutrients, or fluids) within the hermetic system of the body. Its treatments claimed to make the body into a more efficient machine, expelling waste more speedily, invigorating "sluggish organs," and exciting the nerve endings of the skin to wake up "the slumbering activity of the tissues."[96] If the problems of "complex modern civilization" were figured as faults of overconsumption ("overworked digestion," "overstocked liver" and so on), the proposed cure was to stimulate circulation. Government technicians applied the most advanced developments in balneological technology to this end, investing heavily in, for example, the "mechanico-therapeutic" exercise equipment developed by Dr. Zander of Stockholm (which mathematically regulated movement to individual requirements) and ingenious electrical apparatuses that applied currents to stimulate bodily processes.[97] Visitors were prescribed a regimen of exercise, rest, and bathing, regulating both their movement within the sanatorium and the subcutaneous motion of bodily materials. Meanwhile, each spring and mud source was meticulously classified for its specific properties, be they to stimulate elimination, absorption, activity, or circulation in particular organs. The application of waters "within and without" the body (through bathing or drinking) could thus be regulated with scientific precision.

Construing health as a state of activity, productivity, efficiency, and cleanliness—perceived attributes of whiteness—meant that its cultivation

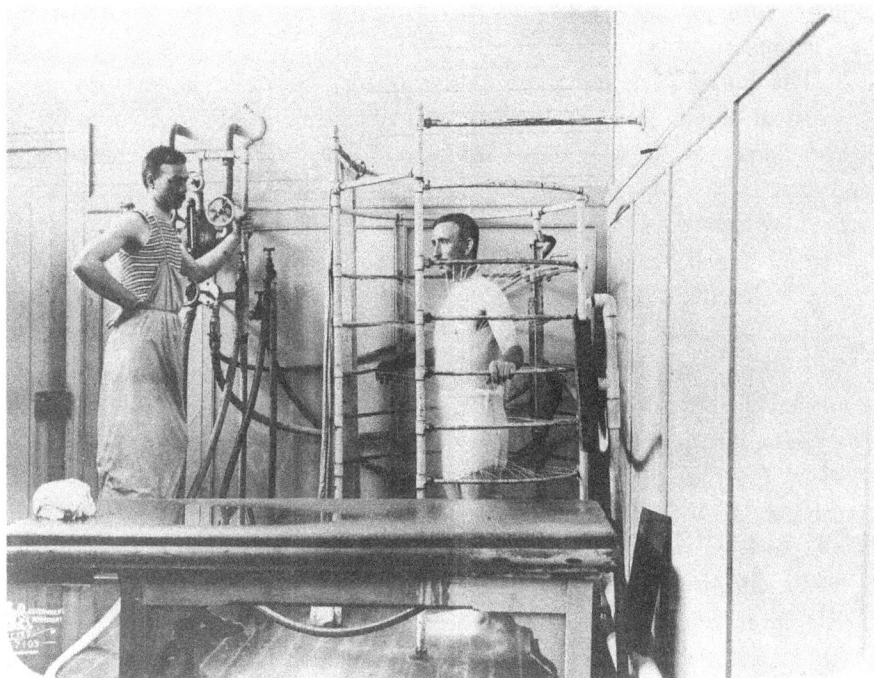

Hydrotherapy treatment at the Rotorua spa. Alexander Turnbull Library,
Wellington, New Zealand.

through leisure assumed a moral and political mandate. When publicists
quipped about the waters of Rotorua acting on "all the ills to which flesh
is heir," their meaning was intentionally double, conjoining medical to
moral and racial intervention through the metonymical association of the
physical body with the body politic.[98] Politician Peter Buck, or Te Rangi
Hīroa, who was the Māori Health Officer for the Rotorua region between
1905 and 1909 and later a member of Parliament, drew on this equation
between body and economy, between whiteness and hygiene, when he
accused parliamentarians of considering Māori "merely as an appendage
and a useless sort of appendage like a vermiform appendix."[99] While efforts
in the kāinga of Ōhinemutu and Whakarewarewa aimed to incorporate
Māori communities into the flows of the state system by rendering them
productive and removing impediments to surveillance and circulation,
Te Rangi Hīroa feared that Māori were not only regarded as vestigially

superfluous but also as a potentially dangerous repository for social and economic waste.

The biopolitical apparatus of hydropathy collapsed imperatives of personal discipline, racial hygiene, and economic vitality in a naturalist paradigm quite literally grounded in territory. "Violations of the code of health," hydropathists argued, depended on "the inherent capacity of the economy for self-rectification . . . and prefer[red] this restoration by Nature herself, to any that the highest and most recondite art can supply."[100] Recalling at once the language of eugenics and that of laissez-faire capitalism, balneology's eminently liberal philosophy concerned itself not with directly combating disease or manipulating the diseased. Instead it incited citizens to create, bodily and willingly, the conditions under which the "invisible hand" of health could naturally resume control, and it did so by bringing them into a relationship with the natural properties of the state: its waters, its mud, its air, and its light. The liberal ethos, then, grounded its practical reason in a nature from which it rigorously dissociated itself, while it constantly drew upon that same nature as both a material and metonymic resource.

Climatology, balneology's companion science, also relied on voluntary self-regulation and linkages with environmental elements to establish "natural" balance in the bodily and social organism. Determining the best venues for therapeutic relocation through an exhaustive analysis of everything from altitude and topographic features to the composition of the air, climatology's cartographic diagnostics linked racial well-being to location. As climatologists Sir Hermann and F. Parkes Weber attested, "the best climate for one race is not necessarily the best climate for another race."[101] Acclimatization science advanced in legitimating lockstep with imperial policy, documenting and analyzing its new global assemblages of human and nonhuman actors: plants, animals, humans, and geographies.[102] Could indigenes travel to the metropolis, or metropolitans to the tropics without risk to health? To what extent could exotic ecosystems be transformed into suppliers of European agricultural products? In a liberal twist on the imperial climatological rule, Rotorua's advocates argued that mobility rather than a close match of race and territory was most favorable to racial and moral hygiene.

It was thus that touristic biopolitics found a place for Māori, not as its objects but as its instruments, another weapon in its armamentarium of stimulation. "Change within and without," Wohlmann argued, "is an invariable rule of nature for the healthy organism, without which it rapidly becomes effete."[103] Whereas French spas or British hill stations replicated "Home" in the colony and thoroughly insulated metropolitan patients from environmental or ethnic difference through "ritualized, rooted and controlled" surroundings, in New Zealand practitioners extolled the spectacle of such difference as producing "excitement" to the sensory organs and causing "improved nutrition of the brain."[104] Nothing could be more of a hindrance to the process of recuperation, many argued, than "boredom and depression of spirits," and where European culture was wanting, the region's "other attractions" compensated.[105]

> The change of scene from, say, an English town to the Thermal District of New Zealand with all its wealth of weird and wonderful sights, its beautiful lakes, rivers, mountains, and forests, its geysers, boiling springs, and mud volcanoes, its Maori villages with their picturesque inhabitants, the cottages crazily and precariously perched on the brink of boiling destruction, the housewife washing clothes in a hot spring, or nonchalantly cooking the dinner in a steam-hole—all these things provide more change of scene than a mere trip to a cosmopolitan Continental spa.[106]

PSYCHOTOPOGRAPHICS AND STATEHOOD

The restorative encounter with Māori, Māori space, and Māori spatial practice, then, was one element in the battery of "techniques and inventions" of governmentality.[107] This work of leisure aligned with that of government in procedures better described as biopoetic than biopolitical. Targeting the white subject at both the biological and the "psychogogical" level, such procedures engendered habits of moral and aesthetic discrimination that bore on the racial constitution of both citizen and civil society.[108] In their visits to Whakarewarewa, Ōhinemutu, and the thermal reserves of the area, tourists trained their gaze on a nature that was, to the Anglo eye, inherently unnatural. And in their "unpleasant fascination" with those spaces, they calibrated themselves to the limits of liberal toleration of other natures, other bodies.[109] Echoing the organic metaphor of society that presided over biopolitical operations at the spa, the thermal landscape was imaged as a diseased body: contaminating, noxious, violent, and destructive.

Both set apart from and central to the quotidian spaces of the state, this nature—this other body—was a repository for the detritus of national modernity, its utopic desires, mimetic excesses, pedestrian enchantments, and erotic fantasies.

Rotorua's space of savagery might be described as heterotopic, not in the sense that it was a state of exception to the structural norm of the state but in the sense that it was integral to that state as a space of intensification and reflexivity. Tourist heterotopias of this kind make palpable everyday life itself through heightened forms of attention and attentive forms of perception. They are spaces in which society thinks system, vortexes of cultural self-invention in which "everyday practices and attitudes [might] be legitimated, 'brought out into the open,' reinforced, celebrated, or intensified."[110] Such tourist spaces are sites of a disordering that can also produce new assemblages, alternate orderings that "come into being in relation to a tension that exists between ideas of freedom and ideas of discipline or control."[111]

To Rotorua's laboratory of state, and to the spa's clinic of conduct, Whakarewarewa and Ōhinemutu were the carnival of the governmental imagination. Here nature was not the mute, passive ground, the material for and model of an idealized state. Instead, it confronted the tourist, eye to winking eye, body to bizarre body. A different genre of tourism prevailed in such spaces of savagery. Against the orderly didactics of civic tourism, tourists at Whakarewarewa approached the spectacle of society through the ludic, their observations speculative, ironic, enchanted, or playful. Where Romantic landscape tourism demanded the absence of signs of the market, here they flourished as enlivening metaphors.[112] Like the scenic reaches of the South Island, Whakarewarewa had a theatrical quality, but here the analogy was not the proscenium convention of detached objectivity, control, and contemplative absorption but the commodity form of late nineteenth-century variety theater. This was a space in which novelty reigned supreme, its thermal features enumerated by guides like the numbers on a program, in "a little valley cramfull of splendid shows."[113] Tourists abjured the disembodied, panoramic gaze of landscape tourism for a perceptual modality more attuned to the sensorium of technological modernity, delighting in immersion, immediacy, and sensations of visual assault and corporal shock, "the rapid crowding of changing images . . . the unexpectedness of onrushing impressions."[114]

Profoundly inhospitable, full of potential perils, it was an environment that willfully rejected attempts at scopic mastery. The ears were "suddenly assailed by fierce bubblings and sputterings," hissings and hammerings, while the feet battled the precariously thin crust of scorching silica and pumice that threatened to break underfoot, and eyes were blinded by clouds of steam.[115] "You never know what the wonder parts are going to do next," one tourist opined.[116] While the most ambitious of late modernity's tourism developments (the Eiffel Tower or hot air ballooning, for example) allowed tourists "to transcend sensation and to see things *in their structure*," at Whakarewarewa they were "thrust into the midst of sensation, to perceive only a kind of tidal wave of things."[117] Accounts produced a landscape animated by invisible dramas, in which the tourist was both spectator and performer: it was Dante's *Inferno*, the Brocken scene from *Faust*, or the witches' kitchen in *Macbeth*. Popular theatrical convention lent its referents. (In fact, thermal-district scenery was a star player in the two most significant nationalist theatrical productions of the era, George Leitch's *Land of the Moa* and Alfred Hill and Arthur Adams' *Tapu*.) But Whakarewarewa's sublimity could not be experienced from a theatrical distance, nor was it a space in which settler technologies of spatial sovereignty had purchase: none of the published guides provided maps, and tourists had to rely on the Māori guides who plied the reserve. Whakarewarewa was, however, not without scopic rewards. Like the other wonderland of the era, the department store, Whakarewarewa was a cornucopia of bizarre, fabulous natural objects to which utopic and acquisitory desires attached. Some aroused consumerist lust ("no feminine visitor ever looked at that sinter lace without wishing to carry away at least a scallop"), while ornamental metaphor ran amok, from the "beautiful black feathery fountains" of ash to "magnificent cathedral-like masses" of steam.[118]

Tourists described the village as a domestic utopia that inverted relations between nature and labor: no longer the inert standing reserve from which labor extracted wealth, nature was the housewife's active helpmeet.

All the ordinary cares of housekeeping are here greatly facilitated by nature. She provides so many cooking posts that fires are needless—all stewing and boiling does itself to perfection. . . . Laundry work is made equally easy. . . . One of these, which is called Kairua, is the village laundry *par excellence*. Its waters are alkaline, and produce a cleansing lather; and they are so soft and warm that washing is merely a pleasant pastime to the laughing Maori girls. No soap is required. Mother Nature has provided all that is needful.[119]

As tourists spent "many an idle hour" observing Māori work, their observations were not all as whimsical as this writer's.[120] Attempts to draw income from the thermal resources ("profiteering") by their Māori owners had long been a source of consternation to tourists, for whom the "native capitalist" was an oxymoronic affront to both Romantic assumptions about indigeneity and imperialist assumptions about rights to resources and to native labor.[121] At Whakarewarewa, the burden of blame fell on nature herself. In an ironic twist on the spa's climatological naturalism, tourists argued that the environment caused the "inveterate indolence" and degeneration of its inhabitants, whose thermal idyll had "completely demoralised . . . and unfitted them for any industrious avocation."[122] "The entire conditions of life were unnatural," another commentator concluded.[123] The irony that most of the laundry over which the Whakarewarewa women labored came, in fact, from the tourist hotels of a white resort that seemed "to be in a kind of perpetual holiday state" escaped the notice of visitors.[124]

Such "unnatural" conditions cast presumptively natural ones into relief, opening a gulf of both judgment and wonderment between tourists and the spectacle of Māori life. As rigorous as the government sanatorium was in rationalizing conduct, Whakarewarewa was full of endless novelties, irrationalities, excesses, and carnivalesque reversals of normative spatial order:

An early stroll fills the mind of the visitor with wonder. He sees hot water flowing down the street channels; he sees natural cauldrons utilised for laundry purposes; square holes, slabbed at the sides, into which boiling water pours from a natural fountain, and wherein the Maoris—men and women together often—bathe; he sees men sitting shoulder deep in water he can scarcely bear to put his palm in—the Maori complacently smoking his short black clay pipe the while. Children of both sexes are to [be] found in the hot water enjoying a bath and breakfast at the same time, their coppery mammas supplying them with 'pipis' and potatoes cooked in a natural cauldron hard by. He may also see—which is somewhat unpleasant—a dusky female figure *en deshabille*, as she is about to perform her morning ablutions, or has just emerged from her bath.[125]

In this passage, the elements have come unbound from their "natural" place, and with them the most sanctified and the most mundane precepts of quotidian conduct. Metropolitan mores (the segregation of the sexes during bathing), bourgeois spatial categories (self-seclusion during bodily maintenance), and the very rhythm of domestic temporality (breakfast and bath at the same time!) have come unstuck. Even seemingly normative givens of embodiment, such as pain thresholds, are suspended, along with liberal distinctions between publicness and privacy. Habitus is the set of embodied practices and habitual attitudes that, at the level of the everyday, unites the vectors of spatial performance—proximity, movement, tempo, directionality, and perception—in a learned system of practical mastery. It tends, as Bourdieu argued, "to impose the integration of body space with cosmic space and social space," to lend a sense of being naturally *in place*.[126] Seeing the habits of liberal life so bizarrely refracted lent them, on the one hand, a redoubled sense of normalcy; on the other, it led white tourists to experience an acute sense of their own racial and spatial alterity—their out-of-placedness.

Tourist accounts bear witness to the delicate, ambivalent experiment in ordinary affect that was a stroll around Whakarewarewa: fascination and disgust, indifference and wonder, pleasure and horror, bewilderment and desire all jostle for precedence.[127] It was a participatory drama of racial subjectification that played intimately through the senses, the point of interface between body and space. One tourist, for example, described her arrival by train in the area thus: "Besieged by a crowd of Maori children offering little baskets of hand-woven flax for sale. Such funny mites they were, in all shades of brown and pale yellow . . . and creamy-tinted maidens with fuzzy masses of bronzy hair coquettishly tied at the neck." But, the writer goes on, "insidiously an odour of extreme nastiness was creeping upon us, and with one accord we drew in our heads and exchanged eloquent glances."[128] Only much later in the narrative is the reader informed that the odor is that of the sulfurous gases pervading the thermal area, rather than that of the Māori vendors. For phenomenologists of place, sensual perception naturalizes the intimate relation between people and place ("As places make sense," Steven Feld aphorizes, "senses make place").[129] In Whakarewarewa tourism, however, they also bred intimations of difference and distance: sensuous aversion and attraction were tourists' guides as they practiced the border-work of liberal toleration, conflating Māori, their environment, and the specter of racial pollution that both seemed to pose.

At the government spa, managing corporal boundaries and regulating the traffic of material (ingestions, secretions, and mineral waters) across them was the prize of spatial discipline and racial prerogative. In the neighboring reaches of Whakarewarewa, on the other hand, such systemic equilibria gave way to proscribed sensations and violations of natural laws. A Rabelaisian "wild and grotesque disorder" ruled.[130] In this havoc of personified geography, tourists imagined bodies that could not contain their unruly passions, that could not manage their boundaries: the unleashed, animate presence of nature here represented the travesty of the civilized order, an image of "undifferentiated, unorganized, uncontrollable relations."[131] From the magnificent ejaculation of the Waimangu Geyser to the tiniest of gaseous emissions, descriptions of the thermal reserve were rife with dischargings, bubblings, stinkings, quiverings, palpitations, orifices, and protuberances. In the lush metaphor of tourist narrative, Whakarewarewa was a confusion of land and body, food and excrement, pollution and excess: "thickened fluids gurgle, and grunt, and spit out great splotches of mud-porridge" as the mud pool, a "boiling filthy sore upon the earth" struggles "in an attempt to break its bounds and cover the earth with its filth."[132] Common descriptions of the thermal district as the open gateway to the nether regions clearly had both a biblical and a bodily referent, and English names given to features at Whakarewarewa, such as the sulfur flat known as Sodom and Gomorrah, pointed in this doubled way to the repressed of the social order.

This biopoetic spatial process might be described, after Karen Shimakawa, as one of "national abjection," the constitutive movement whereby "the (racial) abject must continually be made present and jettisoned" to produce the citizen–subject and national body.[133] Affects such as repugnance or fear test the moral obligation demanded by liberal citizenship. But they also assay the constitution of the political subject itself, reminding of the fragile boundaries to that selfhood and of the inhuman materials that lie beyond. Whakarewarewa was a spatial frontier that staged a racial one, a definitional margin on which participatory performances were enacted to produce sovereign settler selfhood through playfully facing down its annihilation. These could be small spatial experiments that yielded an instant of "tremulous pleasure": daring to step on the precariously thin, hollow-sounding crust just off the edge of the path, poking a stick into a cliff of sinter to create a steaming vent, or leaping to one side as a blowhole exploded at one's feet.[134] Or they could be elaborate psychotopographic dramas, played to the experiential scripts offered by tour guides and accounts:

> This cauldron is a most interesting object, exercising over some folks a fascination which grows with every visit. It is a natural spring of translucent water, boiling hot, but soft as silk. . . . Its depth is practically measureless. You hang over its lip and gaze down, and down, into depths where purple shadows lurk . . . and wonder how long you would be getting to Gehenna if you lost your balance. Then you start back with a spasm of fear, as your eyes are suddenly blinded by a hot puff from out [of] the mist which the changing breeze has rolled your way. And then, perhaps, you leave somewhat hurriedly; but you will return again, and yet again, if you stay any time in Rotorua.[135]

The literary convention of the script is boilerplate sublime: Sensuous attraction and spellbound fascination proceed through a loss of self-possession, as if the narrator were brought into the abyssal presence of the unpresentable. Sudden shock, repulsion, and retreat follow, culminating in the renewed desire to return to the site. Other tourists explicitly expressed the thermal phenomena as spatial metonyms of psychic processes, in terms that left no doubt as to the elision of personified place and racialized person:

> I felt, as I looked down into the boiling, seething crater of one of its pools, that here I had found something human. It struck me that at last I had discovered the world's safety-valve; that the green fields, the lovely valleys, and glorious calm of the world were all in connection with this spot; that here was the other side of the earth's smile, the little hour when the preacher swears and smashes things in order that he may let off steam. Here Nature was letting off its steam . . . as fierce as a raging lion, and about as mad and uncontrolled.[136]

It was an obvious spatial twist on the Victorian structure of feeling that Foucault called the repressive hypothesis, given coherence and currency as racial theory by Freud in *Civilization and Its Discontents*: civilization tamed and introjected the destructive force of the instinctual drives, which yet remained, incompletely inhibited, submerged in the strata of quotidian psychic life, visible in the behaviors of primitive peoples or the savage turns of modernity itself. Descriptions of the "soul-shaking excess" of thermal phenomena mimicked those of Māori concert performances, suggesting that like the primeval forces contained beneath the fragile veneer of civilized space, the savage energies of the Māori were also "relieved from tension" through "violent displays of energy" in which they discharged themselves with explosive force, "their centres in a wild tumult, and their hoarse mutterings suggestive only of a scrummage of demons."[137] Meshing such disturbing intimations with dying-race discourse, one tourist confessed to a "feeling of relief" that the "hot springs, mud geysers, volcanoes and *other things of like nature* were fast disappearing. Though we would not have missed them yet they were much too uncanny to be enjoyable."[138]

BIOPOETICS: MAKING SUBJECTS, MAKING SPACE, MAKING STATES

Some were left spellbound, some were "disgusted and outraged," and others found their senses confused and "the impression upon their nervous system too deep for comfort."[139] Awed or amused, curious or indifferent, that responses to Whakarewarewa ran the gamut should not surprise: the site's role was not to resolve but to experiment with racial sentiment. In the township and spa, also, and beyond in the civic and scenic spaces of the colony, tourists' psychogeographical reveries mined proscribed racial fantasies and fears, but they also plied the more banal reaches of racialized affect: the small, mundane pleasures and comforting satisfactions of order and familiarity, the gentle elation of the fine, uncluttered view, and other such quotidian microdramas that made the project of liberal modernity literally *make sense*. Liberal life's ordinary affects were produced in tourism's intimate traffic between the body of the land and the bodies of its subjects, its congress between person and place, nature and society. Tourists' acts of touching, smelling, listening, observing, strolling, gazing, bathing, inspecting, and describing played out in concert with the state's acts of transformation, conquest, reorganization, mobilization, and instrumentalization in the work of liberal governmentality—which was always also the work of whiteness.

Tourism, then, constituted what the theory of governmentality calls a practical rationality: a form of expertise that functions as a "grid for the

perception and evaluation of things," one that "crystallize[s] into institutions" and "inform[s] individual behavior."[140] It is easy to see, for example,
how guidebooks acted as manuals of conduct, as training in regimes of
perception and aesthetic discrimination, and as protocols of engagement
with space and environmental knowledge. Scenic tourism, like the medical
procedures of balneology or the administrative sciences of public health
and city planning, consisted of "an ensemble of arts and skills entailing
the linking of thoughts, affects, forces, artifacts, and techniques that . . .
fundamentally order being, frame it, produce it, make it thinkable as a
certain mode of existence that must be addressed in a particular way."[141]
While the discourses and institutions of tourism were a crucial aspect of
this ensemble, its essence was in its practice: tourism conduct was a *repertoire* of performance, an embodied "system of transfer" that bodied forth
an environmental disposition and environmental effects through "restored
behaviors."[142]

Tourism demands that we attend to bio*poetics* as much as bio*politics*.
Whereas most studies of governmentality are preoccupied with its expert
and technical systems or with its fundamentally *necro*political violence,
tourism presses us to understand the aesthetic and affective, performative and phenomenological dimensions of practical and political reason.
To attend to governmentality's affective and sensuous force is neither to
humanize nor to romanticize but to understand its deep grip on the imaginations and passions of its subjects.[143] In particular, it gives us a purchase
on the problem of racialization that a focus on the systematicity or brutality of governmental projects cannot. While the classifications of racial
thinking can seem to conform to rational procedures (however specious
their grounds), the constitution of subjects who act and experience on the
basis of those classifications requires a level of imaginative investment that
operates well in excess of reason. In the case of late colonial New Zealand
as elsewhere, liberalism's establishment of whiteness as tacit racial norm
required the imposition of a local and specific rule of difference that established governmentality's targets: white hygiene and self-management, and
Māori discipline, surveillance, and containment. That rule was secured in
part by discursive, typological, and classificatory means but in as great a
part by the corporal intensities generated in transactions between bodies and
environment, social subjects and natural objects. These intensities expose
the fundamentally nonrational basis of political reason's racial dimensions,

its reliance on the "fluctuating testimony of the senses or the deceptive judgment of the imagination as it botches things together."[144] They also expose the fundamentally racial character of what Foucault called "technologies of the self," those techniques that "permit individuals to effect by their own means or with the help of others a certain number of operations on their own bodies and souls, thoughts, conduct, and way of being, so as to transform themselves in order to attain a certain state of happiness, purity, wisdom, perfection, or immortality."[145]

In other words, the biopoetics of tourism helps us grasp how political subjects—in particular the well-tempered, self-governing, white citizens of liberal modernity—constitute themselves through aesthetic procedures.[146] It also illuminates the mechanisms by which settler states forge intimate material and immaterial bonds between state, territory, and population— that is, how they *settle*. Tourism has long been acknowledged as an instrument in the production of nationalist sentiment, semiotically fabricating geopiety (the name that geographer Yi-Fu Tuan has given to a sense of fealty to place and oneness with environment). The touristic sacralization of space, theorists argue, substituted for organic, authentic sentiment, even as the selfsame forces of modernity that birthed the tourist worked to dissolve bonds between people and place. I venture, however, that Rotorua tells a story more interesting than this well-worn narrative of disenchantment. It tells of the creative energy, imagination, and purifying violence of liberal governmentality as it channels the affective currents connecting corporeality and territory, and as it seeks out and winnows away alternative, indigenous ways of inhabitation, all the while thrilling to and instrumentalizing the experience of spatial difference. Theorists have characterized governmentality as a series of operations upon population that takes environment as its passive ground, to be reshaped into milieus that condition conduct: as an art *in* place. The evidence of Rotorua indeed supports such a view. But it also reveals governmentality as an art *of* place, one that focuses on the animate body of the land as it does on population, working toward "the optimization of its capabilities, the extortion of its forces, . . . its integration into systems of efficient and economic controls," not least those of race.[147] While liberal mythology posits the state's foundation as a cleaving of nature from society, nature from culture, and nature from history, tourism reveals the dense, intimately networked, closely woven assemblage that unites them.

For a brief two decades, at the height of New Zealand's moment of liberal state-formation, Rotorua—a small, isolated, marginal, anomalous, recent, and sparsely populated settlement—reigned as the emblem of the nation, instantly recognizable across the British Empire as the heart of the young Dominion. I venture that Rotorua owed this status to the density of the governmental apparatus that was elaborated there: it was a laboratory of liberal statehood, not a state of exception to the national norm (a "place on the margins," as scholars have argued of other tourist enclaves) but a space of intensification, cross-semination, and invention.[148] Here and beyond, in the scenic preserves and civic sites of the nation, tourism produced the political subjects and social spatializations of state through quotidian dramas in which tourists were viscerally, affectively, corporeally invested in place, dramas that creatively allied "interests, powers, objects, institutions and persons" in the pursuit of state welfare.[149]

Chapter 2 complicates the picture I have painted here of the forms of conduct cultivated in tourism's spatial practices. Scenic and civic tourism, health tourism, and rational recreation took as their target the subject, aiming on the one hand to endow Māori with "a progressive desire for industry, regularity, and individual accomplishment," and on the other to instill in white subjects a vigilant, hygienic self-governance.[150] Ethnic tourism, by contrast, shaped cultural citizenship at the level not of subjectivity but of *inter*subjectivity, molding the tourist's conduct with respect to other citizens, whether indigenous, settler, or cosmopolitan. Ethnic tourism at Rotorua, then, was a site for the formation of the collective subjects of the liberal state, its publics. But as a practice that required the active and vocal participation of Māori, it opened a field to contest the logics undergirding Rotorua's racializing machine, to cause its arts of separation to falter, and for Māori performers to transform the tourism encounter into a negotiation of liberal *doxa*.

chapter 2

The Class Act of Guide Maggie: Cosmopolitesse, Publics, and Participatory Anthropology

At the turn of the twentieth century, the small Māori village of Whakare-warewa, at the heart of New Zealand's isolated inland thermal district, played host to tourists by the thousands. They came to soak and socialize at the spa built by the government in the nearby town of Rotorua and to sightsee, taking in the widely touted geological wonders of the region, at their most spectacular on the government reserve that adjoined the Māori village. And they came to encounter "the Maori at Home," as promised in the guidebooks and pamphlets published by the government and tour companies.

An afternoon at "Whaka" might be spent gawking at the bizarre specta-cle of the villagers living amid fumaroles and boiling pools of mud, chat-ting to the women cooking and laundering in the hot pools, or watching the children diving from Puarenga Bridge to retrieve the coins that tourists tossed into the stream below. Wait at the bridge for a moment, and a Māori woman would approach, offering (for a fee of one shilling) to guide tourists around the village and reserve. In her care, they would learn some-thing of the traditional ways of the region's people and the stories that attached to each geological feature—this pool, the place where a famous war chief met a grisly end, or that spring, valued for its curative properties. Truly discovering Māori manners, customs, and "quaint thermal lore," tourists opined, required "dealing with everything first hand," and a Māori inform-ant was considered indispensable to such self-appointed ethnographers.[1]

To round off the day, a tourist might spend an evening at Charles Nelson's nearby Geyser Hotel, enjoying a short concert of haka, poi dances, Māori song, and English glees, quartets, and parlor tunes, by a dozen Māori from Whakarewarewa, followed perhaps by a flutter on the dance floor with one of the pretty young performers. A gentleman might then adjourn to Nelson's drawing room to discourse with fellow tourists and experts, such as Nelson himself, about questions of ethnological interest or perhaps inspect the proprietor's collection of Māori curios and carvings. Discussion might turn—as it so often did in the accounts tourists wrote for friends, family, and publication on their return home—to the process of transition to colonial modernity that Māori were undergoing: what had the tourist's inspection of the village during the day revealed about "the Maori . . . as Nature and civilization have combined to make him?"[2] Colonial politics, colonial society, and not least, the conduct of other tourists—who had also been very much on display during the days' peregrinations—were all fodder for drawing-room discourse.

For a generation of postcolonial critics, ethnic tourism has epitomized the colonial apparatus of representation that enlists the colonized as performing fetishes of authenticity—"signs of themselves"—to secure racial *doxa*.[3] Tourism, they argue, lays bare the fundamental, shared structure of anthropological objectivism, scientific racism, and (neo)colonial domination: metropolitan subjects scrutinize mute, commodified colonial objects across a temporal gulf produced by a distancing tourist gaze. The resulting spectacle romanticizes, mystifying the economic and social violence of the state and enabling tourists to project racially determinist judgments that subtly, or not so subtly, legitimate that violence.[4] This account of tourism as a representational practice, however, is inadequate to the complexity of tourist sites such as Whakarewarewa. To be sure, tourism's fripperies took place there amid patent evidence of colonial devastation, which some tourist commentators attributed to the racial limitations of Māori and others blithely ignored. But in its privileging of interaction with its ethnic objects and fostering of debate between its metropolitan subjects, Liberal-era ethnic tourism in New Zealand was less a representational expression of colonial dominion than a performative "contact zone" (in Mary Louise Pratt's famous formulation).[5] Its encounters did not repress the particulars of interethnic relations in the young state but instead relentlessly produced, organized, contested, endorsed, ironized, debated, and disseminated knowledge about them, generating a fund of popular opinion bearing on questions of colonial policy. In this sense, the scene of ethnic tourism operated as a public sphere of sorts complexly entwined with both state and market: a network of voluntary association that encompassed *on fundamentally unequal terms* both Māori and tourists, nationals and cosmopolites.

This chapter examines the public sphere of tourism as an arm of the liberal state and organ of liberal diaspora. In particular, it queries the racial form such publics took, the conduct they exacted, and the paths of mobility and opportunity that they opened—and foreclosed—for Māori cultural laborers, those liminal figures, or go-betweens, positioned to manipulate the performance codes that the social art of tourism demanded.[6] Much scholarly ink has been spilled on the concept of the liberal public sphere, understood as the community of discourse in which public opinion is formed outside the institutional domain of the state, in ways nonetheless central to the experience and exercise of political belonging. Crucially, scholars have raised questions about the terms on which publics are constituted and regulated, challenging the ideal–typical model put forward by Habermas of the (singular) public sphere of liberal democracy that privileged rational critical discourse, required participants to "bracket" identity and other "private" dimensions of experience, and maintained sovereign independence from both market and state mechanisms.[7] Here, I contribute to "an alternative genealogy of modernity" by analyzing tourism *as* a public sphere and a site of sociability that privileged identity and difference as axes of personhood (and indeed, as loci for liberal self-fashioning and recognition); blurred the boundaries between private and public realms, between civic life, market, and state; and admitted forms of expression other than deliberative discourse.[8] In particular, I take up Michael Warner's formulation of "publicness" as a performative effect of address that creates a relation among strangers through the reflexive circulation of discourse. Insofar as individuals respond to that address, they take up provisional membership in a public. Such a public, Warner argues, is a form of "poetic world making" that imagines into being the "life world of its circulation" and proposes a repertoire through which its members might in turn perform their social placement within that world.[9] A public in this sense is not only responsive to but also productive of difference, generating expansive networks of individuals (and potentially institutions) that respond to, take up, and recirculate its experimental projections of political personhood.

As utopian as this conception of unrestricted, creative, participatory civics seems, especially for minority subjects, Warner emphasizes that a public can only become "political" (in the sense that the opinions it generates can be brought to bear on state policy) insofar as it is able or willing to adapt itself to the forms of expressivity and hierarchy of faculties that characterize the state. But what if, as in the case of Rotorua, the context in which a nonnormative public flourishes is one taken in some way to *represent* the state? What if the networks such a public generates reach deep into the state apparatus, linking private actors to public officials? And to what degree are the expressive repertoires that are the normative social idiom of the state's most privileged classes open to appropriation: to mimicry, mutation, improvisation, and in particular, ethnic manipulation? To what extent, then, can minority acts or enunciations within such provisional publics become political speech?

While chapter 1 examined governmentality's recursive work on spatial conduct, this chapter examines conduct of a different kind: the codes of civility that constituted the state's normative, privileged social idiom, securing and expressing mutual recognition and moral obligation between members of the liberal political community. Conduct of this kind was likewise a performative medium, manifest in the minutiae of social interaction, the formalities of hospitality, and the intimacy of embodied encounter. During the rise of liberal democracies, "conduct" became synonymous with the social bearing of the "respectable classes" who formed their most politically enfranchised caste; the demonstration (or withholding) of reciprocal respect through conduct was the coin of membership.[10] Conduct, then, was neither neutral nor invisible, least of all in the context of tourism, in which encounters between strangers took place out of defining social contexts, placing a burden on the legible signs of caste, affiliation, and belonging. "Caste and creed and clothes go for nothing in the baths, and democracy is as prevalent as it should be," one tourist joked of the spa at Rotorua, pointing to the ways in which tourism both functioned as a social leveler and focused attention reflexively on performances of social stratification.[11] While the "genus tourist" scrutinized itself, however, it also scrutinized Māori, who in turn scrutinized their visitors and—sometimes artfully, sometimes unwillingly—presented themselves for scrutiny.[12]

I argue here that the practice of ethnic tourism offered Māori guides a novel tactical field. In ethnic tourism's acts and arts of embodied encounter, dialogic exchange, narrative improvisation, self-presentation, and hospitality, guides could appropriate these repertoires of conduct, countering the spectacle of racial difference with claims to affinity, confronting social exclusion with the assumption of civic membership, and meeting colonial surveillance with the gaze of reverse anthropology. Attending ethnographically to the specifics of these encounters reveals those fleeting moments in tourism when race operates not as a factitious fixity, determined by colonial discourse, but is instead porous and unstable, hostage to the vagaries of class and gender, and open to strategic manipulation at the same time as it is circumscribed by the brute realities of prejudice and structural inequality.

I approach these issues by detailing the career of a celebrity Māori guide, entrepreneur, entertainer, and, later, published anthropologist in her own right. Makereti Papakura—also known as Guide Maggie—worked at Whakarewarewa between 1893 and 1911. She was in many respects an exceptional figure, but she was also an exemplar whose legacy helped establish Arawa guiding tradition as a form of cultural diplomacy. Makereti exploited the gendered conventions of late Victorian travel culture, in which individuals tendered for social advancement through demonstrating a mastery of conduct. Through a finely calibrated performance of Māori modernity and self-cultivation, Makereti claimed membership in a cosmopolitan public of travelers, a global bourgeoisie that transcended the ethnic strictures of the colonial nation-state. But she also crucially *proposed* a public that redefined the terms of liberal recognition. Her community of address— those who numbered themselves among "Maggie's friends" or followed her doings in social columns and travelogues—took indigenous expression not as a disqualification but as a form of social distinction. This valorization of Māori difference, I suggest, bore (however indirectly) on the state, for which Makereti was also a de facto representative, occasional critic, and ambivalent adjunct.

Makereti's career (which began in a remote village, brought her into the orbit of the global community, and ultimately took her to live in London and Oxford) makes clear that liberal public spheres can never be understood as purely national in character.[13] This chapter concludes with a discussion of the implications Makereti's story holds for scholarly debates around cosmopolitanism. Cosmopolitanism, this story suggests, can be understood, not as an individual disposition or endowment, a political project,

Guide Maggie on the reserve at Whakarewarewa, ca. 1908. *Auckland Star* Collection. Alexander Turnbull Library, Wellington, New Zealand.

or a global social fact, but as a performative repertoire, appropriable even by those in positions of immobility and isolation. But what normative limits does the relationship between class, conduct, and transnational civil society impose on membership or expression? It is tempting to interpret Makereti's remarkable career as a triumph of indigenous agency in a cosmopolitan key. Yet to the extent that that agency was enabled by liberal mechanisms, it was also constrained by them: what were the terms of racial intelligibility and individual exceptionalism that determined Makereti's global mobility and membership, and what were the political costs of living by those terms?

GUIDE MAGGIE: A LIFE ON THE CIRCUIT

By the time of Makereti Papakura's birth in 1872, Māori tour guiding was already an established tradition in Arawa territory. The Tūhourangi proprietors of the village of Te Wairoa had insisted that visitors be accompanied by one of their number on the trek from the village to the Pink and White Terraces, the geological marvel that drew tourists to the as yet unsurveyed and uncolonized interior of the nation. In time, gifted bilingual interpreters such as Kate Middlemass and Sophia Hinerangi became guides not just to the territory but also to the culture and history of the area; these "personalities" were frequently mentioned by name in tourists' accounts. When tourist traffic recovered after the Tarawera eruption in 1886 destroyed the terraces, this tradition was sustained at Whakarewarewa, where several of the guides (including Guide Sophia) relocated. While there were some notable male guides, the work of guiding at Whakarewarewa fell largely to women, by dint of indigenous traditions of hospitality but also because of their availability for casual, seasonal labor close to the village.[14]

Makereti, then, joined a lineage of culture brokers prized for their skill as raconteurs and entertainers, but her reputation rapidly eclipsed that of her forebears. It was not so much *what* she did as a guide, which for the most part differed little from many of her peers: She greeted tourists and led them around the village and reserve, naming the thermal features and recounting the stories attached to them. She showed them some of the important houses in the village, talking about the "uses and customs" of her people, their arts of carving and weaving, and how they lived their lives in this unusual environment. She led her fellow villagers in performing concert programs at the Geyser Hotel in Whakarewarewa or the Assembly Hall in the township. She entertained with anecdotes and answered as native authority the questions tourists posed. It was not so much *what* she did; rather, it was *how* she did it. By the end of her guiding career, she was a tourist attraction in herself. She was a legend not only for the graciousness of her hospitality, her personal distinction, and her genteel charm; she was also a legend for being a legend. She crafted a role without equivalent in the colony: national and international celebrity, cultural ambassador, industry entrepreneur, published author, entertainment professional, and society hostess.

Makereti's savvy as a publicist and networker was beyond compare, as was her acuity in the arts of self-presentation (covered in depth later in this chapter). But her fame was due, at least in part, to the historical conjuncture at which she rose to prominence. Makereti's reign as "uncrowned queen of the thermal regions" (from 1893 through 1911) coincided almost exactly with the Liberal era that made Rotorua an epicenter of (trans)-national attention, governmental experimentation, and national aspiration. For Rotorua's patrons—the wealthy, independent, largely British or Commonwealth travelers and the weekenders drawn from the rapidly growing urban middle classes of the colony—the state-made town was the puppet capital of an imagined nation, "Maoriland." It was a brand of national distinction and a premonition of Pākehā (non-Māori) modernity: a paradise of rationalized, democratized leisure and a paragon of state-of-the-art civic planning. It was also the public testing-ground of liberal strategies in racial governmentality and the only place in the "two worlds" of this ethnically bisected nation where tourists (either urban New Zealanders or international visitors) were likely to rub shoulders with Māori.[15] Makereti's guiding performances, then, took place on the spotlighted stage of a national theater.

Like Sophia Hinerangi before her, and not unusually for her time, Makereti was of biracial heritage, one of three children of Pia Ngarotu Te Rihi and William Arthur Thom, an Englishman, land court interpreter and clerk, and former soldier from the colonial militia that had prosecuted the Land Wars against other North Island iwi (extended kin groups).[16] Her prestigious Māori lineage on her mother's side allied her to both Tūhourangi and Ngāti Wāhiao, two groups that had historically been associated with the tourism industry and held much of the land on which the principal attractions were located. She was raised by Māori relatives in Whakarewarewa and the nearby village of Parekārangi, spending time also at the village school in Ōhinemutu. At the age of ten she was sent to Willow Bank girls' school in Tauranga, then spent a year with a private governess, and finally spent three years at Hukarere College, a state school for Māori girls that offered a broad academic curriculum and training in domestic duties, fitting its students for the gendered work of racial uplift prescribed by Māori reform movements of the era and for the assimilation to European custom favored by mission and state bodies.[17] Although she entered her five years of formal schooling without a single word of English (by her own account), she was an able student, and her education continued as she began to guide and learned through observing her patrons. By the time tourists began recording their encounters with the fetching young guide in the late 1890s, she was eloquent in English, proficient in French, well read, and "finished" enough to hold her own in colonial society. At the same time, her early childhood and close ties to her Māori whānau (extended family) ensured her mastery of her tribal genealogy, lore, and history and her expertise in Māori song and movement forms.

Options for young, schooled Māori women of the time were limited: return to one's kāinga (village), to marriage and participation in the mixed subsistence and agricultural day-labor economy, marriage to a European, or domestic service with a European family. Makereti chose to return to Whakarewarewa and began work as a tourist guide, one of the few occupations that afforded a modicum of financial independence (although income from guiding was unstable and usually the supplement rather than the mainstay of a family's wages). She resided in the village nearly continuously until 1912, spending a brief period in Wairoa (in 1891) after a short-lived marriage to a European named Francis J. Dennan, by whom she had one child, William Te Aonui Dennan. She divorced the father in 1900, and her son was largely raised by close relatives, in the custom of whāngai (intrafamily adoption), before being sent to boarding school. Certainly, her tourist patrons had no knowledge that she was either divorced or a mother.

Celebrity came to Makereti when she was chosen, along with the then-elderly Guide Sophia, to guide the Duke and Duchess of Cornwall and York around the thermal wonders at Whakarewarewa as part of their Royal Tour of 1901. Before this occasion, the archival record of her guiding life is slight: there are a few extant photographs of her as a young woman and a handful of cursory references to her in tourist accounts. After the royal visit, the record is voluminous. The barrage of publicity surrounding the tour made her a household name in New Zealand and circulated her image, blessed with the royal seal of distinction, throughout the popular press of the empire. Six years later, her renown was so great that postcards from abroad addressed to "Maggie, New Zealand" would find their way to her, there being "only one Maggie in the Dominion."[18] On the covers of illustrated weeklies, in the social columns, at civic and state events, as the author of her own travel guides, and as the subject of innumerable photographic features, postcards, and souvenirs, Guide Maggie was a ubiquitous presence. The elements of her class act were set: her representative status, her mastery of conduct, the mise-en-scène within which she staged her domestic and cosmopolitan accomplishments, the networks she sustained with state agents and global social elites, and her deft navigation of the treacherous waters of racial identity.

Makereti confirmed her status as the international face of Māoridom in 1911 by leading a troupe of Arawa performers to the coronation festivities in London, where they took up residence at the Festival of Empire (at the Crystal Palace) and the Coronation Exhibition (at White City, Shepherd's Bush) and performed at mission and philanthropic functions and on the variety circuit. It was this final venture, I argue later, that pressed home the social and geopolitical limits of her class act, making the second half of her career a marked departure from the first. Returning to England in 1912, Makereti married Richard Staples-Brown, a well-to-do Englishman whom she had met some years previously as he toured New Zealand. Taking up residence at his Oxfordshire estate, she abjured her former public life and the carefully groomed projection of ethnicity that had accompanied it. Mrs. Staples-Brown became a "home student" in anthropology at Oxford University in 1926 (after having divorced in 1924), and her thesis on Māori life and customs, which was near completion when she died suddenly in 1930, was published posthumously as *The Old-Time Maori*—the first published book-length Māori-authored ethnography. At her own request, Makereti was buried at a small church in Oddington, near Oxford, her grave marked with a simple wooden cross. At Whakarewarewa, she is memorialized by a large marble edifice in the center of the village, now a required stop on the contemporary guides' itinerary.

THE UNCROWNED QUEEN:
CELEBRITY AND REPRESENTATION

At the height of her fame, Makereti assumed a role in the Pākehā public sphere that might be cautiously described as representative. The state appointed Rotorua as the symbolic capital of Māoridom, and the guide's role as "uncrowned queen" of this capital meant that she was the public face of Māori for many international visitors, including the guests of state and the political commentators for whom Rotorua was invariably on the itinerary.[19] Entertaining the heads of the Australian Chambers of Commerce, British admirals, cardinals, field-marshalls, premiers of the Australian states, and visiting governors general, Makereti was the front line of the state's hospitality: both articulate and politic, she was considered "well able to represent both the European and Māori races in New Zealand."[20] She was representative also in a mimetic sense: one "could not find a finer specimen or a better exponent," authors declaimed as they invoked her personal accomplishments to index the potential of Māori as self-governing liberal subjects in the making, giving her individual qualities as racial proofs.[21] "Maggie is a highly cultured lady," wrote the *Toronto Globe* in a photo feature on the guide, "and writes and speaks the English language as fluently as if she were a Briton born. The Maoris are, as a tribe, the most intelligent aborigine people yet discovered, and are adopting the ways of civilization with great avidity, in fact many of them showing almost phenomenal intelligence and ability in the management of their affairs."[22] I should be clear that Makereti was without representative status in any conventional, political sense of the word. She was active in civic life (for example, in philanthropy, temperance movements, and voter organization), and by virtue of her "sheer force of brains and personality" and her close relationships with Department of Tourist and Health Resorts (DTHR) officials, she was a dominant—if not uncontested—force at Whakarewarewa.[23] But she did not possess, especially as a woman, any formal authority to speak *for* her community in pan-tribal contexts.[24] To the press, however, Makereti's celebrity was in itself a form of political action—she was "doing much for the Maori race."[25]

As I argued in chapter 1, Rotorua tourism solved, in the form of a practiced fantasy, the Liberal-era state's ethnic conundrum: it reconciled "schemes of a one-way history: progress, development, modernity" with their "negative mirror image" of Māori underdevelopment and tradition by endowing the latter with new value as a heritage attraction.[26] In the person of Makereti, liberal Pākehā also imagined resolutions to other issues: how to *represent* Māori in a way consonant with principles of consensus and toleration, and how to do so in the face of the brute facts of Māori dispossession, distress, and resistance, especially given the complexities of rapidly changing tribal leadership structures. What better candidate than an unelected representative, a celebratory figurehead, and one who seemed to foreshadow so optimistically the becoming-modern condition of Māoridom?

Makereti's media profile was part "client native," part Pākehā wish-image, to be sure. The sphere in which she reigned—the illustrated magazines, ladies' journals, and travel features of the Pākehā and foreign press—was largely oblivious to the preoccupations of other Māori leaders during this era: stemming the state-driven tide of land loss, combating laws eroding the infrastructure of Māori communities, and grappling with the symptoms of widespread poverty, from catastrophic infant mortality to hunger and disease. Yet the arguments about Māori capacity for self-management, self-betterment, and self-cultivation that commentators drew from her representative example were close to those made by other Māori politicians and public figures of the era working within the Liberal apparatus.

Liberalism's compact cut two ways: if the liberal public sphere made demands on her compliance, she made demands on the recognition and respect it promised. On tourism's unlikely stage—so often a site of ethnic and sexual exploitation—Makereti advanced Māori claims to civic rather than formal juridical citizenship, to a social standing not granted to Māori as denizens of a Pākehā state. In the "soft" realm of social praxis rather than the "hard" one of political power, she charted a line of flight from the poverty and prejudice that dogged the dispossessed Arawa in Whakarewarewa. Yet whether, as a representative, she was an exemplar of Māoridom or an exception to it was a question left unresolved in tourist discourse.

CONDUCT, PERFORMANCE, AND
THE POLITICS OF MANNERS

For the chirpy English tourist Alys Lowth, New Zealand in 1906 was a veritable Eden where all were well paid, honest, and prosperous, food was cheap and plentiful, and the natural splendors were untiringly splendid. Not all, however, was picture-perfect about the colony: she declared her "preconceived ideas of what a Maori proper should be like" ("soldierly-looking men and graceful, houri-eyed women") to have been "sadly disabused" since she had met them.[27] The Māori she encountered en route were (Lord forbid!) middle aged, half "Europeanized" in attire, and worst of all, unkempt. They were, in short, not romantically primitive but disappointingly proletarian. Guide Maggie, however, did not disappoint.

> [She] has a most captivating voice and manner, and is a great favourite, especially with the Australians, who feted her tremendously when she visited Sydney. She invited us into her *whare*, or hut, which to our surprise was furnished in European style as a bed-sitting room, divided by a tall bookcase filled with all the modern works of fiction and travel, and a reed curtain. And here she entertained us for over an hour, showing us pictures and photographs, telling us tales of travellers she had met and happenings in her experience. And then her sister Bella came in, and played the accompaniment to Maggie's singing of Lord Henry Somerset's "Echo." Her voice was so sweet that we asked her to sing again, but Warbrick [our guide] suggested that it would be too late to see everything if we lingered any longer, so we spent the rest of the afternoon looking at boiling mud-pools and geysers, and so on. But none of these orthodox marvels were half so astonishing and certainly not nearly so pleasing, as Maggie the guide. Who would have expected to find culture and accomplishments in a Maori village? But it seems that most of the Maoris are educated now.[28]

Refined, charming, talented, and unimpeachably modest, Makereti was for Alys Lowth a fount of romantic traditional tales that gained "additional charm" by being recounted "in her sweet musical voice."[29] Like her whare, Lowth seemed to suggest, Maggie was Māori to the outward eye but European in spirit: reassuringly familiar, while delightfully novel. Lowth's patronizing surprise—"Who would have expected to find culture and accomplishments in a Maori village?"—swiftly translated into a new-found recognition of the admirable accomplishments of Māori modernity, tout court.

When William Baucke (also known as W. B. Te Kuiti, a columnist for the *New Zealand Herald* and sympathizer with Māori causes) visited Maggie in 1908 at her home in Whakarewarewa, he also found himself "sadly disabused," but not by the guide. "Maggie the ubiquitous, the guide, the magnum opus of quaint thermal lore, the vital germ of every scheme to make of holidays a memory," he trumpeted, "a hostess in her humble, spotless home—oh! Incomparable."[30] His disgust found its target instead in the "gaudy tinsel stuff" of ethnic tourism itself, a cheap theatrical trick mounted on the ignominy of Arawa poverty: "all this poi, haka, penny-diving, and toying with the vast capacities of a noble race," he wrote, "is making of Rotorua a squalid Raree-show, a sordid menagerie!" The people were "prepense kept poor, and made daily poorer, lest they wax fat and of a noble manly independence refuse to be further exploited." For Baucke, tourism exposed the condition of a people "with us but not of us," denied dignity and justice by the systematic violation of both Treaty guarantees and promises of citizenship. In both accounts, Makereti sailed above the fray, even as she played a part in the "squalid Raree-show," even "half Europeanized" as she was. But how? Makereti's surprising currency lay in the manner of her self-fashioning—or, more simply put, in her manners.

Throughout her professional career, the popular press consistently focused on class-codified aspects of the guide's self-presentation: her grace of deportment and gesture, graciousness, fashionable attire, elocution, and qualities as a conversationalist elicited constant commentary. She "has a regal dignity and condescending courtesy that quite impresses. Her diction and voice are both charming. She speaks in sentences, and uses dictionary words, and her face is a delight to watch, so expressive in its comeliness," one typical tourist noted.[31] Regardless of whether she appeared in the "latest Paris fashion" that she donned when traveling outside of Whakarewarewa, or "dressed in a short skirt, a brown jersey and a man's coat . . . her manner [was] that of a gentlewoman."[32] Many commented on her "catholic and cultured taste," listing as evidence the contents of the bookshelves in her whare where Dickens, Burns, Twain, and Longfellow rubbed shoulders with Orientalist and imperialist mainstays such as Omar Khayyám's *Rubaiyat* and William H. Prescott's *Conquest of Peru* and with up-to-the-minute American commentary such as Winston Churchill's *Coniston*.[33] Many others, like Lowth, remarked on the intelligence of Makereti's conversation and on her skills as a pianist and vocalist. But dominating tourists' impressions were the much more ephemeral signals of physical and verbal conduct: the mannered poise of her greeting, her "natural" smile and attentive expression as she rose and received visitors "with the charm and grace of an English lady."³⁴ That these elements of Makereti's self-presentation were so consistently remarked on suggests not only how heavily racially coded they were—the graces of an English lady possessed by a Māori wahine!—but also the deliberate way in which she exhibited them as a kind of social pedagogy.

While it might be tempting to read Makereti's self-presentation as a form of strategic colonial mimicry, it is better understood as an act that drew on a crucial performance repertoire available to all members of liberal polities, including indigenous denizens: *conduct*. A capacious term encompassing embodied codes of gesture, bearing, expression, and costume, as well as the complex verbal and spatial protocols of hospitality, conduct in the nineteenth century was a set of techniques for negotiating status relationships between strangers, for projecting and assessing claims about identity and allegiance. Conduct was the indispensable social medium of the West's dynamic market democracies and was (especially as it was disseminated through the conduct book) linked to the class habitus of its aspirant "middling types." In the heterogeneous public spaces of nineteenth-century urban life, when new social mobility posed the problem of class categorization, conduct's codes of self-presentation and interaction both ensured the recognition of one's peers and prevented embarrassing confusion with one's inferiors. Similarly, in the milieux of a democratizing tourism industry (as well as in the social spaces of colonial circulation), conduct helped to make strangers socially legible in the moment of encounter and in the absence of determining context. Underpinning it was a political philosophy of social relationships that emphasized liberal toleration: conduct's standardization of behavior expressed the mutual respect in which citizen-subjects held each other in an inclusive, meritocratic polity.³⁵

The culture of manners was also patently race matrixed, in dialogue with the physiognomic, kinesthetic, and oral codifications of racial classification. Conduct was felt to progressively chasten Rousseauean nature to produce the corporal and emotional self-discipline central to liberal citizenship, containing the unruly excesses of the primitive.³⁶ This capacity for self-government, in both senses of the term, was ostensibly legible in micropractices of proxemics, expression, attire, and deportment.³⁷ It was against violations of these practices that visitors chafed when they railed, like Lowth, against the "unkempt," "unwieldy" bearing of Māori they observed or, for example, when they condemned the "vulgarity" of tourist haka.

In an exchange of letters in the *New Zealand Herald*, an anonymous English "visitor" decried such spectacles: "To see two dozen men and women making horrible facial grimaces and twisting their bodies into ungraceful (or disgraceful) attitudes was something to be remembered with shame."[38] To the author of the letter, such practices disqualified their performers from civic membership: "*If we are true friends to the Maori*," he declared, "let the haka be at once relegated to the limbo of obsolete heathen barbarities." Māori would willingly become "graceful," another suggested, to assert themselves as legitimate claimants for their "treaty-confirmed rights."[39]

Contrary to contemporaneous codes of theatrical and scientific realism that saw gesture and expression as inalienable, innate components of racial personhood, conduct both marked intrinsic difference and begged amendment.[40] As much as it stabilized racial and social divisions, its being an *open* repertoire of performance also militated against determinism. Conduct operated as a strategic resource for advancement across social strata—

Makereti poses on the porch of her home, Tukiterangi. Price Collection. Alexander Turnbull Library, Wellington, New Zealand.

leveling as well as leveling up. Indeed, if the price of admission to spheres of social privilege was through bourgeois self-regulation, the pedagogic industry that developed around etiquette proposed that it might be learned, rather than guaranteed through wealth or birth: "There is no longer any question of admission 'by ticket only.' . . . Good behavior is everybody's business."[41]

HOSPITALITY, SOVEREIGNTY, AND RECIPROCITY: MAKERETI "AT HOME"

Not only scrupulously observing such "good behavior" herself, Makereti also made similar observances on the part of tourists a condition of their visit, embedding guests in a social contract of mutual recognition and deference that played on class solidarity as a court of appeal against the divisive hierarchies of race. Her first gambit was to offer her services to tourists in a way that maintained her social standing as their peer, not their hireling. Rather than wait near the entrance to the village with the other guides and solicit business from visitors as they approached the gates, Makereti, once her celebrity had ensured her drawing power, waited for tourists to approach her by calling on her "at home" in her whare and requesting her company on their tour or by making an appointment with her in advance by mail. With her growing influence in state circles, the staff of the DTHR offices in Auckland or Wellington would issue letters of introduction to the guide (as they had for Alys Lowth). Makereti also kept herself informed of visitors of note to the region (including journalists and other authors), leaving elegantly penned *cartes de visite* at their hotels inviting them to call on her at their convenience or to dine with her at the Geyser Hotel.[42] Such social rituals of introduction set a tone of drawing-room politesse that prevailed over the subsequent encounter, as did the pains taken by both Makereti and her clients to distance the engagement from the taint of market relations: rather than having money change hands in person, a "small appreciation of gratitude" or "expression of thanks" might be discreetly mailed after the tourists' departure from Whakarewarewa.[43]

Scholars have critiqued tourism's frequent recourse to the analogy of hospitality as euphemizing a grossly unbalanced economic and social relationship, in which hospitality is, more frequently than not, compelled.[44] The thrust of Makereti's strategy, by contrast, was to reframe the hospitality of tourist entertainment as both voluntary *and* reciprocal, rather than purchased or coerced. To lay down the laws of hospitality, as Derrida reminds us, is a sovereign deed: "It is always about answering for a dwelling place, for one's identity, one's space, one's limits, for the *ethos* as abode."[45] The (singular) law of unconditional hospitality, he argues, marks the ideal of cosmopolitanism, but the myriad ways in which hospitality is offered, withheld, or made conditional in practice are the mark of cosmopolitanism's politics. Tourism's (pseudo)hospitality is usually offered on the terms dictated by the market or state. This was certainly the case in New Zealand, where the state assumed the sovereign prerogative of hospitality on land that had been alienated from its Māori owners, turning Māori into cultural laborers delivering hospitality on its behalf. The Liberal era even saw moves to establish a state certification and licensing program for guides at Whakarewarewa that would have enabled the DTHR to regulate both the content and conduct of Māori hospitality. Makereti, significantly, claimed exemption from this program, calling on her high-level state patrons to support her appeal.[46]

When Makereti claimed the right to lay down the laws of hospitality at Whakarewarewa, then, it was a politically charged gambit. And lay down the law she did: her observance of the spatial, gestural, and conversational codes of bourgeois politesse set clear expectations that her social standing would be recognized (as she recognized that of her guests) and that privacy, property, and person would be respected. Like the Māori tradition of manaakitanga (hospitality) and its rites of welcome, the liberal conduct of hospitality established social boundaries and negotiated allegiances, determining limits to guests' behavior.[47] The stakes were high: the expectation of reciprocity displaced other status-compromising performance frames that tourists brought to the visit.[48] On the one hand, tourists came primed on the philanthropic practice of visiting the poor and on slumming ethnography in working-class entrepôts—whereby they were encouraged to "inspect" the whares of the village "and their people"—a ritual that conflated class adjudication and racial surveillance.[49] For one tourist, Māori men "looked like the Mexican greasers"; for another, Whakarewarewa appeared "much like a Negro suburb in an American town." For yet another, the kāinga invited allusions to the working towns of the British midlands, with its "groups of women in dresses of showy prints, smoking pipes, and laughing and behaving very much like a lot of factory girls out for meal time."[50]

On the other hand, tourist expectations were conditioned by the racial spectacles of ethnological show business: the native villages of metropolitan World's Fairs and themed attractions, in which objectivist, often eroticized, display conventions mitigated physical proximity with less literal forms of distance, buttressing racial typologies and social divisions between audience and object.

In contrast to such practices of touristic consumption that gave license to pry, gawk, and judge without regard for the feelings of their objects, Makereti held her charmed guests to strict standards. Her clients felt little of the objective impunity that theorists of the tourist gaze impute to metropolitan pleasure-seekers. When she found herself the object of racial spectacle, she countered by making her guests the object of each other's, and her, class scrutiny. Tourism is from one perspective a private act of consumption; from another, it is also intrinsically public: collectively undertaken and socially witnessed. Tourists accrued cultural capital as their exploits circulated through the networks of print capitalism (in published travel accounts, social column reportage, and so on) and as they themselves circulated through the de facto salons of tourism's public sphere—hotel drawing rooms, geographical society lectures, and the attractions themselves—where the competitive arts of social placement took place.[51]

This fact lent the guide a strategic advantage. For example, Makereti's elocution was constantly remarked upon as an accomplishment that placed her favorably in a spectrum of class and colonial identity as speaking "*naturally* in a well-bred English manner."[52] During an era in which the first glimmerings of a distinctive New Zealand vernacular were greeted as a sign of the cultural and moral decline of that "better Britain's" Anglo-Saxon stock, the guide's English was perceived to be "more refined than nine-tenths of the Pākehā visitors" and to be "entirely free from faults like those so often charged against colonial speech."[53] She mobilized elocution tactically to position herself in cosmopolitan society: "Maggie told me a good story. She was guiding a party of tourists from Great Britain over the wonders of Whakarewarewa, when one brilliantly-dressed lady said, 'Why, Maggie, Hi declare you speak Hinglish halmost has well as hus.' Maggie said if she could not speak better than that lady she would not attempt it at all."[54] Although Makereti might not have publicly humiliated this brilliantly dressed lady in person for her supercilious comment, she invoked the story to enlist other clients in a coalition of the *genuinely* well-bred, as opposed to the merely pretentious. Trumping racial condescension with class disgrace, it was a monitory tale, warning other tourists of the public shame to which they would expose themselves were they to violate the compact of hospitality. When the tourist–author of the anecdote reprised Makereti's performance in the papers, she ratified the ideal of an unostentatious cultivation that was the natural property of "high-caste" Māori and their metropolitan social peers. "It's breeding that counts," she opined in one interview, obliquely countering those thinkers for whom "breeding" was a matter of blood quantum: "If he is a gentleman we Maoris respect him."[55] Hers was an appeal to globalized liberal ethos, an open social system premised on ideals of reciprocity and respect but also of fierce competition. Tourism, as Makereti construed it, was a cosmopolite sphere of social arbitration to which access was determined through conduct, in which behavior rather than blood mattered, and in which, moreover, Māori might act as arbiters.

POSSESSIONS, PLACES, AND PUBLICS

I have suggested that the discursive and social forums established by leisure travel (travel literature, hotel drawing rooms, and so on) housed publics of a kind: like the eighteenth-century salons analyzed by theorists of liberal civil society, they were communities of knowledge production, critical reflection, and sociability, organized independently of the state yet bearing on its business, locally enacted yet extending through broader networks. In seizing on the freedoms and political potency of this publicness, however, Makereti modified the ideal–typical model of the public sphere imagined by such theorists: she insisted on conduct (as opposed to rational critical discourse) as the leveling medium of interaction, admitting—indeed privileging—ethnic expression as its currency. Her circle could be seen as part of an alternative genealogy of salon culture such as that described by Seyla Benhabib (in her analysis of Hannah Arendt's account of Rahel Varnhagen): it was an elite, intimate social forum hosted by a cultural outsider and woman, a "curious space that is of the home yet public, that is dominated by women yet visited and frequented by men, that is highly mannered yet egalitarian," and that is governed by ideals of "self-revelation and self-concealment" rather than the "transparency and visibility" valued in the spaces of the polis.[56]

At the center of Makereti's guiding performances was a salon of a quite literal kind: her whare in the village of Whakarewarewa. First Tukiterangi (an ancestral house, given to the guide by her mother in 1907) and later Tuhoromatakaka (commissioned from master carver Tene Waitere) served as a forum in which she entertained and as a crucial element in her self-presentation.[57] There the guide would receive tourists or return after a tour of the village to continue her exegesis on Māori life and customs, often entertaining guests deep into the evening with song, story, and conversation. Both houses were built to traditional Māori design: they were single-roomed dwellings with a rectangular floor plan, entered from a front porch area by a single door. They had sloped roofs, carved panels on the exterior, and painted ornamentation on the beams of the interior.

However, there was little else that was traditional about these dwellings. Although, historically, Māori socialized and slept in different buildings, Tuhoromatakaka enclosed a "bed-room, library . . . and sitting room" in the one space, divided (in some reports) by a flimsy reed curtain. In photo features, postcards, and tourist accounts, the neatly kept interior of the whare juxtaposed quality European furniture—a writing desk, tallboy, piano, bed, and well-filled bookcase—with Makereti's extensive collection of taonga (valued possessions), including carved treasure boxes nestling in corners, cloaks draped over chairs, and weaponry propped against the walls. The decoration similarly hybridized Māori and European elements: the walls were lined with photographs of Makereti and her fellow villagers (many produced for the tourist market, others commissioned by the guide herself) and autographed pictures of the illuminati that she counted among her circle. Venerated tupuna (ancestors) took their place in decorative *métissage* alongside photographs of international celebrities, politicians, and royalty. Other walls were graced with tukutuku (flax weaving) panels, and the supporting poles were carved with ancestral figures. In all, the whare was declared a "model of comfort and elegance" that both resembled and represented its owner. [58] Just as Makereti was described as "a quaint medley of ancient and modern," her home was "a quaint medley of Native and Pākehā . . . where drawn-thread work is side by side with beautiful native carving."[59] "Like a little Maori house without," the whare was "almost a lady's boudoir within."[60]

The whare was the indispensable mise-en-scène of the guide's self-presentation. Makereti was frequently photographed in the space, often at

Makereti pictured in her whare, Tuhoromatakaka, in a newspaper feature. *Auckland Star* Collection. Alexander Turnbull Library, Wellington, New Zealand.

work at her writing desk or posing in the front porch area—pictured as proprietor, woman of letters, and artist in her home. The *Weekly Graphic and New Zealand Mail,* for example, published an illustrated feature showcasing Tukiterangi, complete with wide-format photographs and descriptions of its contents that recall both a review of a museum display and the discernment of a *Better Homes and Gardens* interior-decorating feature: "The interior . . . is tastefully adorned with rare mats, carvings, and Maori implements, which are viewed with great interest by all who are privileged to inspect them. The floor is covered with Whariki mats, and over the beds and chairs are kiwi, korowai, and other mats."[61] The image of the house traveled on postcards and accompanied articles in the illustrated press, and it traveled literally *with* the guide: when she journeyed to Sydney in 1910 and to the Festival of Empire in London in 1911, Tuhoromatakaka went also, and when journalists interviewed her at the New Zealand International Exhibition in Christchurch in 1906 (where she took up residence in a replica thermal village that had been constructed in the fairgrounds by the DTHR), it was in her "charming cottage."

Despite being referred to as her "boudoir," there was little that was purely private about the whare. While Makereti was the uncontested gatekeeper of the space, it operated on the one hand as a place of business and on the other as a quasi-diplomatic forum for intercultural dialogue, subject to the same ideals of conduct—manners, hospitality, respect, and reciprocity—that governed her interactions with tourists. The opening of Tuhoromatakaka was one such diplomatic affair, as well as a tourist entertainment in its own right, with a guest list of locals, tourists, Māori, and Pākehā dignitaries (including the premier of New South Wales, Sir John See) that numbered nearly three hundred—a number that was taken to represent "the esteem in which [Maggie] was held." Whaikōrero (ceremonial speeches) by Māori participants "alluded to the affection that existed between the Pakeha and Maori," and both parties improvised spontaneous expressions of interracial bonhomie: the European chorus of "For They Are Jolly Good Fellows" being answered by a Māori "war cry in appreciation," and displays of poi and haka being followed by European dancing until dawn. On another occasion, a visiting British admiral, Premier Sir Joseph Ward, his deputy and Minister for Native Affairs, James Carroll, and other members of Parliament were the guests of the guide at her whare.[62] The diplomatic performance protocols that accompanied such widely publicized visits (such as formal "addresses" and the singing of the national anthem) resembled the exchanges of greetings, prayers, song, and dance were the lingua franca of Māori intertribal diplomacy, offering opportunities to establish status and consolidate alliances.[63]

The guide's whare was a wholly modern invention: a space both public and private, linked to the business of both state and market. Unlike the salon, it intersected with parliamentary politics. Unlike marae (Māori centers of community government), it privileged women's participation. It was also arguably the closest thing the colony had to a bicultural forum. To participate was to engage in the play of identity, to mark and witness difference; there was none of the purported cultural neutrality of the ideal–typical public sphere. Even the structure itself argued for a culturally inflected liberal ethos. The architecture spoke of social intimacy, holism, and tribal mana (prestige) but also of economic dynamism, individualism, and social hygiene. For Pākehā, the single-room cottage was the nostalgic spatial analogue of gemeinschaft, the home as sanctuary and refuge from modernity.[64] Yet for health and reform activists of the Liberal era, the wharepuni (sleeping house) was emblematic of the ills of "Maori communalism": a dark, dangerously constricted space where unreformed Māori lay in indecent proximity, vulnerable to both physiological and moral infection. They called for the whare to be "opened up": like Tuhoromatakaka, it would be ventilated, enlarged, and lifted from the ground but also configured to ensure the privacy of its newly individualized inhabitants.[65] The guide's whare, with its refined and disciplined domesticity, rose above this contradiction, exemplifying Māori modernity without sacrificing its nonmodern intimacy.[66]

At the same time, an imprimatur of domesticity deflected the surveillance that accompanied both tourism and reform with protocols of hospitality that "bound together propriety, privacy, and property."[67] Much travel practice of the era followed what David Spurr has characterized as the "trial of penetration into the interior spaces of non-European peoples."[68] For the visitor to Tuhoromatakaka, however, any such quest ended in an ironic reversal. Penetrating beyond the authentic exterior—by invitation only— one was greeted not with a revelation of "backstage" authenticity but with a staged hybridity that addressed the visitor's gaze with unguarded candor.[69] Like the celebrity home features of the contemporary magazine press, the space invited identification rather than judgment.[70] It was a tantalizing combination of domestic rectitude, fashion-conscious modernity, and primitive chic:

> High on a hill stands the cottage of Maggie Papakura, the bright and charm-ing priestess of the place. . . . Modern Maori, indeed, with her piano, her bicycle, her photographs and autographs; her French slippers and English furniture; her trinkets and luxuries; her telephone and her books. Such books—books of poetry, travel, and romance, with that jewel, "The Rubaiyat of Omar Khayam" at the top! We marvel. Here, verily, has civilisation civilised.[71]

In a social landscape in which women were positioned as custodians of class comportment, the domestic competencies of consumption were arts in which strategic possibilities of advancement were concentrated.[72] Tuhoromatakaka distinguished Makereti as a consummate, indeed *expert*, connoisseur. The guide and her guests often described the whare as a "museum."[73] Like early cabinets of curiosities, the collection enhanced its owner's prestige through arousing in others the "envious longing for pos-session," while its objects remained firmly in her epistemological and cul-tural control.[74] Tuhoromatakaka's contents were not inert commodities to be categorized or collected by metropolitan observers, Makereti's presence as docent, curator, and hostess made clear. Introducing each item by name, she would detail its history in her family and its venerated role in her com-munity.[75] Whereas museums and "native villages" tend to represent the living as dead, Makereti's performances asserted the continued vitality of Māoridom and its sovereign, inalienable rights to its cultural property.[76] At the same time, the guide accrued cultural capital through her aesthetic expertise and her enviable wealth of possessions.

GLOBAL NETWORKS, LOCAL INFLUENCE, AND EXPERT KNOWLEDGE

Theorists in the Habermasian tradition judge the public sphere efficacious only insofar as it operates independently of market and state. But existing liberal publics rarely conform to this ideal–typical model; indeed, the more associations they form with noncivic entities, the more politically vital and actionable they are. The publics of tourism are no exception. Makereti's

salon was a node in a complex network that linked state actors, cosmopolitan civil society, transnational markets, domestic and foreign media, tribal
structures, local government, and anthropological knowledge brokers.
Infinitely more complex than the dyadic bonds of patronage or clien-
telism, with their simple exchange of obligation and service, the pathways
of this network offered Makereti the opportunity to translate her gifts as a
cultural performer into a means of mobility, security, and advancement.

In the first place, the guide, with "her charming personality, foreign connections, autograph book, little house, education and refinement," traded
in the currency of celebrity, positioning herself within a transnational
cognoscenti that brought together culture workers and political society.[77]
Alongside autographed portraits of the Prince and Princess of Wales and
the Premier, Dick Seddon ("a great friend of herself and family," whom
they knew "as well as any of their own people"), were those of actress Grace
Palotta and music-hall doyenne Marie Hall, soprano Madame Carreno,
and pianist Ignacy Paderewski.[78] All had been Makereti's guests: The Pol-
ish pianist she dressed in Māori costume and taught the haka ("a very
different performance to that which the artist usually gives"). Madame
Carreno and the men of Whakarewarewa exchanged performances in a
concert organized by the guide.[79] And hanging beside the photographs
of these luminary alliances that included journalists, artists, authors, composers, military leaders, businessmen, and politicians were those of the
guide and her whānau. Makereti's links to celebrity certainly paved the
way for her own international forays, but the degree to which they led to
tangible advantages for "her people" can only be the territory of specu-
lation. Makereti's claim to be able to call upon the Premier himself for a
favor for her kāinga was never put to the test.[80] But this is hardly the point:
such claims were acts of social, and implicitly racial, self-articulation that
were efficacious insofar as they were witnessed and repeated by the public
to which they were addressed.

Makereti's mobilization of tourism's networks, however, was concretely
at work in her interface with the rapidly expanding state apparatus at
Rotorua. The guide stepped into the gulf between established Māori leaders such as Mita Taupopoki (a rangatira, or leader, of the Ngāti Wāhiao at
Whakarewarewa) and a Pākehā establishment intent on capitalizing on
Māori culture. Such an enterprise required cultural brokers like Makereti:
bilingual, business savvy, and fully literate in European codes of cultural

value. T. E. Donne, head of the DTHR, was at the center of Makereti's actionable networks. He became a lifelong friend and professional associate, and their correspondence shows their exchange of information, business, and favors over the course of her tenure at Whakarewarewa and later in England. From his first action as head of the DTHR, appointing Makereti as guide for the Duke and Duchess in 1901, Donne relied upon her to put forward "the best face" of Māoridom, to organize "the Maori presence" at state events, and to keep him apprised of affairs in the kāinga. In return, he was a great publicist on her behalf, delivering prestigious contacts and business connections, and acting as official state guarantor of her authority at Whakarewarewa.

Charles Nelson—amateur ethnographer, founding member of the Polynesian Society, trader in Māori "antiquities," author of tracts on Māori origins and customs, and the proprietor of the Geyser Hotel at Whakarewarewa—was another valuable link in the guide's network of influence. Although never in Nelson's employ, Makereti acted as the house guide of his hotel: she received select guests, dined with them (often in the company of Nelson), performed with her troupe in the hotel ballroom, and provided tours of the attractions Nelson sponsored (for example, the carved house, Rauru). It was an advantageous business partnership: the Geyser was one of the premier hotels, and her uninhibited access to its communal spaces and clientele would have helped her marshal both patronage and press. Her relationship with Nelson also gave her access to another kind of salon: the hotel drawing room and library in which foreign tourists, civil servants, and nationalist culture workers (including journalists, composers, and Nelson's colleagues from the Polynesian Society) came together in conversation regarding both Māori culture and matters of state.[81]

Tourist discourse of this era closely shadowed the concerns of colonial anthropology: delineating "types," determining the extent of and capacity for civilization, and scrutinizing customs, from food cultivation to religious beliefs. Whakarewarewa's guides were crucial informants, and it is apparent that they took a broad range of approaches to the task, from the folkloric virtuosity of Guide Sophia to the outspoken improvisation of one tourist's elderly guide, who (on the pretext of explaining the female moko, or tattoo) entered into a lengthy disposition on the benefits of female suffrage.[82] A vernacular rather than a pure science, touristic anthropology was not so much a quest for ethnological fact as a ringside seat in

A postcard image of Makereti with Rauru, the whare whakairo (carved house) belonging to Charles Nelson at Whakarewarewa. W. A. Collis Collection. Alexander Turnbull Library, Wellington, New Zealand.

the drama of colonial governmentality: "The country is mapped, taxed, stocked with sheep, and sold, stolen, organized, and labeled British; but anyone who wants to see the transition period—to me always so exciting—had better make haste. The dissolving view of the Maori out and the whiteman in can only be once shown. It is now going on, and, like other dissolving views, it is no sooner begun than it is ended."[83] Rotorua, then, was a picture show of incipient modernity rather than a portrait of doomed or embalmed tradition. Tourist ethnography circulated, moreover, together with other discourses that were auxiliary to the state: settlement literature and tracts of political commentary, for instance, in which tourist testimony was liberally quoted.

Makereti intervened into this discourse as both object and subject of expert knowledge, with a hauteur that defied those skeptical of the liberal capacities of the race. As a spokesperson in exegeses on the "Modern Maori," which peppered the pages of the national press, but also as an author in her own right, she painted a picture of Māori life that countered every slight in the catalogue of censure so frequent in tourist accounts. Her souvenir *Guide to the Hot Lakes* told of disciplined, industrious village life with none of the laziness, dirtiness, and disorder imputed so often to Whakarewarewa residents: "There is a Maori Council in the village. The Maoris are very temperate and never stay about the hotel for the sake of a drink. The parents encourage their children to go to school, and join them in their many games. There is a very good school at Whaka., and you cannot bribe any of the children to stay away."[84] Elsewhere (in a British publication), alongside such paeans to discipline, self-governance, and "moral self-culture," she extolled the virtues of Māori communalism: "There are no Maori poor and no unemployed. Nearly all Maoris are landowners, and if they are not, the tribal feeling is too strong for a Maori man not to work. . . . It often reminds me of the spirit of an English cricket team, in which no one is forced to do his best, but none the less always does."[85] Summarily dismissing the specters of so-called Māori landlordism and Māori communalism, which the Pākehā land lobby (and many tourists) claimed left Māori ill-disposed to productive labor, the guide linked land title to industry and self-discipline, and self-discipline not only to liberal individualism but also to tribalism. Education, hygiene, temperance, and industriousness—all the "multiform tactics" that produced liberal citizen-subjects and made them productive—were the *natural* property of Māori.[86]

It was a sales pitch, to be sure, and one that flew in the face of patent evidence of Māori poverty on the tourist circuit. But it was also a passionate defense of the sovereign integrity of the Māori community, mounted in a sphere in which such sentiments were seldom heard.

THE RACE OF CLASS AND THE
MANAGEMENT OF GENDER

For tourist ethnographers, the relative purchase of nature or nurture on racial "type" was likewise put to the test in Rotorua's assimilationist governmental projects. Will the Māori, they asked, "advance to meet the realization of English ideals or relapse to an almost irresistible reversion to type?"[87] Makereti's interventions in tourism's public sphere claimed, in discourse and deed, that the Māori "type" was already the English ideal, countering the state's technologies of racialization with appeals to class. The "natural" proclivities of the "high-caste" Māori, she declared, were those of the "English country gentleman," as evidenced in the performance of conduct: hospitality, sincerity, dignity, "quiet force of character," and a cultured, high-minded antimaterialism. This appeal distanced Māori both from a colonial elite characterized (for its critics) by a social crudity and grubby materialism ("sheep and gold, gold and sheep," as poet and parliamentarian William Pember Reeves phrased it) and from the "lower types" of the Pākehā population with whom Māori would be lumped in the state's proletarianizing vision.[88] Against the force of liberal assimilationism, she could appear both a proud racial "patriot" (like a "Jew with his eye still on Jerusalem," as one tourist put it) and the intimate equal of genteel cosmopolites from around the Anglo-Saxon world.[89]

This dimension of Makereti's class act was also clearly self-interested. It was further enabled by the guide's appearance as a biracial individual, seeming to stand both inside and outside the identity she interpreted for tourists, at once model native and objective observer. It was hard for tourists to get a racial "fix" on Makereti: her features strongly reflected her father's Anglo heritage, while her olive skin suggested otherwise. She was described as "a cultured gentlewoman whose colour is as light as that of a Spanish high-born dame."[90] Makereti herself often performed a narrative gloss in which Māori either resembled European peoples ("not darker than the Italian" and "in features . . . strangely European") or were their distant kin, drawing on a monogenist discourse of origins that had long been popular ethnological wisdom in the colony.[91] Māori were, in one version, the lost tribe of Israel, and in another (more frequently argued in the late nineteenth century), Aryans who had taken a migratory route across India into the South Pacific.[92] These kinds of "whitening" discourses were common in the Polynesian Pacific, figuring island women as a racially proximate (yet exotically different) sexual resource for colonists. But they were especially common in New Zealand, where they buttressed assimilationist policy by suggesting that Māori already had much "in common with English sentiment" and by distinguishing them from the "degraded and hideous blacks of Melanesia and Australia" (a distinction that Makereti seemed to endorse).[93] In the guide's preferred variant, Māori were in fact Celts, "two branches of a family that were separated in the early ages of the world's history."[94] The origin narrative lent cultural (and political) distinction without racial disqualification, locating Māori on the margins of Europe's field of interlocking nationalisms rather than within the dichotomous racial discourse of empire.[95]

Yet even as the guide pandered to imperial hierarchies, her class act diverted the racially determinist, typologizing force of touristic ethnography. To be part of the public that Makereti proposed was to recognize racialization as at least in part, or potentially, a performance—an art of allusion or elusion—and race as a malleable and fungible asset of personhood. Tourist accounts show the guide tactically navigating the terrain of racial signification with skill and playful delicacy, code-switching between society matron and Māori maid; racial effects seemed to flicker about her. Even the bewildering range of names by which the guide was known in her lifetime (Guide Maggie, Margaret Thom, Margaret Dennan, Maggie Papakura, Makereti, and Margaret Staples-Brown) suggests the lability of her racial identification.[96] The "Papakura" moniker was apparently a name she gave herself while at work guiding a group of tourists who (having been introduced to her as "Maggie") asked what her "real" or "Maori" name was. Standing near a geyser named Papakura, she replied with its name, yoking her professional identity to the territorial legacy on which her livelihood depended. A ludic response to the demand for a specific performance of racial authenticity, the act both sated and deflected that demand, affording the guide a degree of privacy and control over the property of personhood.

The other remarkable quality of Makereti's class act was its explicit valorization of *bi*cultural identity in colonial civic life, a rarity in the Pākehā public sphere. The guide's biracial heritage was no anomaly in this era— the colony had a long history of marriage alliances between Māori and Pākehā—nor was her mixed parentage a secret to tourists. On the contrary, it loomed large. Linking biracial appearances to national futures, the "half-caste" woman was a paradigmatically Liberal-era icon, figuring a national consensus brokered through interracial desire, the promise of "a new and insistent race that would make the future its own."[97] This "Romance of Two Worlds" was endlessly recapitulated in landmarks of nationalist literature, theater, and opera, predictably posing the woman (passive, virgin, and alluring land) as the ingress for European adventurers.[98] As Apirana Ngata put it, Pākehā felt that mixed-race children held the promise "that there may be added to the all conquering, all devouring Anglo-Saxon, a fresh strain of blood . . . a fresh element of strength."[99] It was a blatantly assimilationist paradigm: while biraciality was lauded by nationalists, biracial progeny were rarely accepted into Pākehā families, and bicultural practice was roundly castigated, with even Māori reformers arguing that "living as neither European nor Maori" was the root cause of health, social, and economic ills.[100] Guide Maggie, however, refused to surrender either pole of identity: in her stories, her conduct, and the character of her whare, she insisted that the "Romance of Two Worlds" she represented exemplified "the *best of both* worlds," admitting the custom of both cultures as marks of status and taste.[101]

Femininity posed challenges to the guide's claims to social standing and liberal respect akin to those of race. Her response was similar, relying on the tactical expedience of performance to deflect invasive or compromising demands on her privacy and self-possession. As a single woman who spent much of her time in the society of men and whose striking figure, face, and ability to charm were the instruments by which she made her livelihood, her position was delicate. Like the actress or prostitute, she was an object "of desire whose company was purchased. . . . Patrons bought the right to see [her], to project their fantasies on [her]."[102] Tourism could often be an intimately embodied transaction, as when Makereti danced with clients at the conclusion of concert-party performances. The language of many accounts (such as this one, published in a British illustrated gazette) left little doubt as to the double jeopardy of race and gender: "Many of our race are delightful dancers, but here was the poetry of motion, upright as a dart, the conventional corset never known, untiring limbs and body, a mass of hard, brown coloured, satin-like healthy flesh ready to dance all night and the next day too if required."[103] The history of ethnic tourism has always been shadowed by that of sex tourism, in which gross disparities in wealth and power led to expectations of sexual hospitality—doubly so in the history of Pacific tourism, where the fantasy of the uninhibited South Seas maiden, like the virgin islands she metonymized, affirmed white potency and promised cultural renewal.[104] Early tourism at Te Wairoa was dogged by rumors of prostitution, and periodic decency scandals still rocked Whakarewarewa during Makereti's tenure.[105] Whether such goings-on were actual or imagined, soft primitivism was an integral part of Rotorua's destination image: the ubiquitous genre of "Māori belle" photography featuring young women draped in traditional garments ran the gamut from chaste allure to supine, bare-chested availability.

Given this context, the guide's ability to maintain a public image of irreproachable respectability and sexual self-possession—even as she "beguiled" tourists with her "languishing glances"—seems remarkable.[106] Her early marriage and son were never mentioned, nor were any romantic interests imputed to her until the engagement to Staples-Brown. (In fact, she privately considered the newspaper announcement of that engagement to be an unconscionable intrusion on her privacy.)[107] "I do not care to marry," she was once quoted as saying: "My work is my life."[108] For that livelihood to be sustainable, that life had to be both available to tourist fantasy (being unmarried helped) and preserved from tourist advances.

Her trademark image was a key factor in this balancing act.[109] In postcards and photographic features, she dressed in a gathered cotton skirt hanging to just above the ankles, bare feet or walking boots, a high-necked white cotton blouse, a tiki adorning her neck, and either her signature scarf tied around her head or her hair falling neatly in two simple braids. She appeared in folkloric rather than primitivist idiom, in the character of the peasant matriarch, her dignity and "quiet force of character" resonating through association with land and ancestry. It was an image that cried shame at tourists' prurient fascination. In a scrapbook in T. E. Donne's papers is a hand-penned cartoon, "The Thermal Regions, Rotorua, During the Christmas Holidays." A horde of monocled Englishmen lean over their canes to leer at Makereti, whose figure is a photograph pasted into

A postcard portrait
of Makereti with her
signature headscarf.
Donne Papers.
Alexander Turnbull
Library, Wellington,
New Zealand.

the pen-and-ink scene, gazing serenely out of the picture frame.[110] The
cartoon is richly suggestive of the way in which Makereti negotiated her
compromising visibility through conduct, her pose at once a stereotype of
exotic femininity and utterly unassailable. "To strike a pose," Craig Owens
has argued, "is to present oneself to the gaze of the other as if one were
already frozen, immobilized—that is, *already a picture*." Posing in this way,
he suggests, has a strategic value. Like the eyes on the wings of a butterfly,
the pose is an apotrope: confronted with a pose, the gaze itself is immobilized, its power reflected back on itself.[111] As the guide curtly stated in a
letter to the editor of the *New Zealand Herald*, on the subject of the alleged
indecency of the haka: "Of course, anything is vile to evil-minded persons,
and I can but say to these individuals 'Honi soit qui mal y pense.'"[112]

COSMOPOLITICS, COSMOPOLITESSE, AND
THE CULTURE OF TRAVEL

Tourism's rhetorics of display, scholars argue, immobilize and transfix their objects, freezing them in time and space, a tendency ironically referenced in Donne's cartoon. Immobilization is not simply a representational effect of commodification or exoticization, however; it is also a structural effect of tourism's codes of social distinction. Leisured mobility accrues value in part through distinguishing cosmopolitan tourists from those whose mobility is curtailed through being too poor, too bound to wage labor or local lifeways, or too backward to desire to travel. The "class consciousness of frequent travelers," as Craig Calhoun has wryly called it, demands a cast of less-privileged locals to remain reliably *in place*, neatly intersecting with the spatial mandates of ethnogovernmentality.[113] Tourism is, however, a market system. Like any market system, it opens up new networks and paths of circulation that can catch all (not just the privileged) in their orbit, albeit in unequal measure. It is precisely this inequality, the discrepancy of mobility—as much liberalism's signature as its promise of freedom—that I examine in this concluding section.[114]

To this point, I have argued that conduct, the medium and currency of tourist sociality, formed the ground of reciprocity between guests and hosts. In the hands of Makereti and her public, these reciprocities became ways of thinking and feeling political community beyond the state and its ethnic strictures. They evinced the kind of "world-mindedness" that is often called cosmopolitanism: a heterophilic consciousness of shared humanity, an acceptance of plural loyalties, and an embrace of diverse cultural experiences as resources for self-fashioning. In recent criticism, theorists have pinned hopes for ethical globalization on the recuperation and valorization of such cosmopolitan sentiments, suggesting that supranational experiences of "conviviality" and mutual obligation might be translated into something resembling a transnational civil society, and from thence into political institutions. I need not, I think, rehearse the critique of this cosmopolitan theory here: the complicity of cosmopolitanism with global capital; the "weak" nature of such bonds in comparison to those of ethnic or national belonging or in the face of ethnic or national prejudice; and the fragility of universal rights or the potential of political institutions embedding such rights to undermine the struggling independence of decolonized states.[115] Most intractably, the critical literature on cosmopolitanism has failed to account for the divergences between voluntarily mobility and forcible displacement by economic or political circumstance or between the cosmopolitan experiences of individuals of different national, class, ethnic, or religious origin. A battery of attempts to theorize cosmopolitanism "from below" (vernacular cosmopolitanism, discrepant cosmopolitanism, working-class cosmopolitanism, and postcolonial cosmopolitanism) have paradoxically affirmed that the claims of a progressive cosmopolitan politics are "performed from the perspective of first world modernity."[116]

Ultimately, the flaws of the cosmopolitical promise are those of liberalism itself, not least those inherent in the politics of recognition that form its foundation. Advocates argue that the cosmopolitan disposition (an openness toward "divergent cultural experiences" and the capacity to mediate cultural boundaries) begets the empathies, identifications, and allegiances through which subjects develop a sense of moral obligation toward one another, recognize "the Other within oneself," and thus create the basis of transnational civil society.[117] But toleration is premised on normative limits to what counts as worthy of recognition: What counts as culture (and not, say, moral failing)? Who counts as a politically viable subject (and not as the object of state discipline)? These limits, which Elizabeth Povinelli has called the "cunning of recognition," are sounded in a different register than the overt conflicts of belief or custom that so concern liberal theorists such as Kwame Anthony Appiah.[118] More often affective than rational, more subliminal than conscious, they are limits that have everything to do with both race and class.

Viewed through an ethnohistorical lens (an approach largely neglected by theorists of cosmopolitanism), a story such as Makereti's can tell us much about the discrepancies of cosmopolitan experience. It can also illuminate the field of agency available to an indigenous woman and the tactics by which she might traverse the topography of the global by using a cunning of her own. Indeed, Makereti's discovery was that *performing* the cosmopolite conduct, entitlements, and class disposition of the tourists she encountered could be a way to *claim* the recognition entailed by cosmopolitan privilege, with its social access and epistemological prerogative ("the habit," as Henry James had it, "of comparing, of looking for points of difference and resemblance, for present and absent advantages" between races).[119] In the latter half of her life, she was also to claim cosmopolitanism's literal freedoms of movement. While governmental initiatives of the Liberal era, from census to schooling to the surveillance of social welfare programs, worked to bind Māori spatially as minority subjects of the state, Makereti's unbound networks of global affiliation, and the global entertainment economy in which she participated as a tourism worker, lent her a line of flight from the state itself.[120] In navigating the race- and class-scapes of other nations, however, her carefully fashioned "worldly disposition" encountered distinctly mundane limits. Her freedom came at a cost both personal and political, one that ultimately pointed to the limits of a strategy founded on liberal, individualist, cosmopolitan principles.

SLIPPING THE YOKE OF STATE: INDIGENOUS REVERSE TOURISM AND VERNACULAR DIPLOMACY

As Makereti frequently noted in interviews, her placement at the hub of the tourist circuit in Rotorua gave her access to "the best" of global society. Ultimately, the social currency (and funds) she accrued enabled her to travel herself. She undertook highly publicized journeys to Australia in 1903 and again in 1909, where she was entertained by politicians and civil servants, enjoying the reciprocal hospitality of her "friends." As befitted her status as de facto representative, she was treated as a state visitor, even receiving free passes on the railways. "If I had been the queen," she declared, "they could not have entertained me more."[121] In a classic performance of civic tourism, she visited Darlinghurst Gaol in Sydney, escorted by W. P. Crick, Minister for Lands, along with the Governor of the jail. She also toured the mint, the telephone exchange, Government House, and the Parliament buildings (where Premier Sir John See and his wife, also "friends," were "very kind to us").[122] Reports of her success in Australian high society were published in the New Zealand papers, along with her travel diary, which was reprinted as a booklet that (like the vanity publications of her elite clients) she could distribute to her circle.

Makereti was a cultural ambassador for the Pākehā state as much as for Māori. When she visited an Aboriginal reservation and reflected on the quaint customs of the "Blackfellow," she not only borrowed the mantle of white imperialism and class prerogative but also dignified New Zealand's nationalist punditry, which distinguished the colony from its neighbor by boasting of its superior native race and magnanimous native policy. In claiming the citizen's right to free movement in and out of the nation, however, she was once again the exemplary exception. Māori could and did travel a great deal within New Zealand: kin ties linked whānau across districts, and visiting (for funerals, for example) was a socially and politically important practice. But while Māori had legal rights to freedom of movement, state policy and Pākehā public opinion castigated the illiberal habits of traveling Māori. James H. Pope (Inspector of Schools and a reform advocate) was not alone in railing against the excesses of hui (gatherings): overconsumption, the disruption of work discipline, transmission of disease, encouragement of vice, and waste (by which he meant communal expenditure rather than individual investment of capital).[123] In the eyes of the state, leisure travel was a right and a rite of citizenship that, correctly performed, evidenced and cultivated forms of conduct associated with a capacity for liberal self-government; Māori did not qualify. (Such structures of feeling no doubt lay behind ubiquitous tourist commentary on the supposedly uninterrupted leisure and lassitude that prevailed among the residents of Whakarewarewa.) Likewise, while Māori traveled abroad with some frequency (often as members of entertainment groups such as the one that Makereti would take to perform in Sydney and London), these journeys were also controversial. Paternalists feared, sometimes with justification, the exploitation of Māori performers by unscrupulous promoters, but more often concerns were that Māori "may be made vicious by traveling to other countries, and the junketing which accompanies it, and that any habits of industry they may have formed may be destroyed."[124] Such journalistic hyperbole betrayed Pākehā anxieties about the weak grip of the state's ethnogovernmental techniques on Māori bodies. But behind the stifling paternalism lurked a deeper fear: where the spatial arts of government are countered by liberal rights to mobility, racialization falters as a strategy for managing population.[125] No longer bound to and by the state, Māori might enjoy access to other publics, other memberships, other frames of racial and class intelligibility.

Makereti retorted (in debate and in deed) that the benefit of travel was "an educational gain," enabling her people to understand other modes of life.[126] Tooling heterophilic cosmopolitan discourse to the rallying cry of racial uplift, playing to paternalism, and deftly skirting governmental imperatives regarding both land and labor, she argued for the prerogatives of transnational membership as much as those of national citizenship.

When, in 1911, as the crowning act of her reign at Whakarewarewa, she headed a venture taking forty accomplished Arawa performers to London as national representatives, they journeyed under this legitimating banner. But how well did the guide's class act travel? How well did her harmonization of class and race weather the passage beyond the state to which it was so finely calibrated? To what extent was she able to maintain the delicate balance of respectability and exotic femininity, of class normativity and racial patriotism, that had ensured her success at home? And to what degree could that bravura act be extended beyond her own celebrity to secure the mana of her people?

The troupe traveled to London, supported by a business syndicate with which Makereti had contracted, to take part in George V's coronation celebrations and to perform for a summer at the Festival of Empire at the Sydenham Crystal Palace. While they were not officially representing the state at this civic-sponsored exhibition, they traveled with the sanction of Makereti's associate Donne, who (having moved on from his position at the helm of the DTHR) was acting as the commissioner of the New Zealand exhibits at the festival. The enterprise was reported at home as a patriotic triumph, and the doings of "Maggie's Maoris" were followed in the social columns. In the British press, likewise, the guide held court in features devoted to the "Maori Queen's" opinions of British society, while her troupe made a series of well-engineered public relations coups: when they joined the Henley Regatta in a carved war canoe, for example, or baptized a newborn in a dawn ceremony by the Thames. In their reconstructed village on the grounds of the Crystal Palace, they demonstrated their arts and crafts, performed songs and dances at appointed hours, and went about their "daily life" for the edification of Londoners. It was, in a symbolic sense, an embarrassment to the colonial state. In the official New Zealand pavilion, a series of narrative murals staged Māori consent to British annexation and then wrote them out of the subsequent triumphal progress of nation building. Meanwhile, from her outpost at the other end of the Crystal Palace grounds, Makereti lectured fairgoers on the autonomous dignity, history, and accomplishments of modern Māoridom, and she was feted at the ladies' clubs of Sydenham and Dulwich.

While the charming matron was a temporary star in London's crowded entertainment firmament, somewhat more tawdry struggles took place behind the scenes. As the troupe embarked on their journey, the British

Home Office had telegraphed forbidding them to travel: such ventures were in violation of recent Colonial Office policy not to allow "natives to be trafficked" to the metropolis for the purposes of entertainment or exhibition. The New Zealand High Commission pointed out the limits to the state's powers over the group: these were "independent business persons," they protested, and Māori were "in no way comparable to other natives" (an argument that Makereti's own well-publicized exceptionalism supported).[127] Making explicit the relationships between mobility, liberal rights, economic agency, and race, the terms of the exchange were a yardstick of the racial predicament the group would find themselves in, as well as of the potential humiliation attendant on involvement in the culture industries of the great imperial metropolis. Were they cosmopolitan reverse tourists, globe-trotting businessmen and women, cultural ambassadors, and free citizens of a liberal state? Or were they itinerant ethnological labor? Improperly trafficked colonial property? Did they command recognition as fellow subjects, or were they the hapless objects of exotic spectacle?

The performance frame argued the latter. Living conditions in the Māori village at Crystal Palace were far from comfortable, and the business conditions were worse. As the only native village, it was an outlying anomaly, tellingly situated next to Hagenbeck's zoo and symbolically away from the national pavilions and the "All Red Route," the mini railway that linked them. The unusually hot summer and equally hot competition among London attractions meant that business was slow at the Crystal Palace: even with twice-daily concerts at the Crystal Palace Theatre, the group's take at the turnstile must have barely fed them. After several weeks, they transferred their operation to entertainment magnate Imre Kiralfy's Coronation Exhibition at White City, a massive, purpose-built theme park and permanent exhibition complex in west London.

White City was a potlatch of whizbang rides and exotic sensations, packaged with the exonerating gloss of imperial patriotism and educational benefit. It was also London's ethnological show-business center: Natives everywhere! its ads brayed. Human "exhibits" from Sudan and Dahomey performed as part of in situ displays akin to those of zoos, while Londoners ogled the "savages" nervously from behind partition fences.[128] Business was better for the Arawa troupe; they performed on White City's variety stage as well as in their reconstructed village. But the new venue lacked the civic imprimatur of the Crystal Palace, and their contract offered no protection from the drudgery of entertainment labor: rather than the two shows they had initially anticipated, they found themselves performing six to eight times daily.[129] The long hours and lack of privacy must have severely tried Makereti's pride and patience, not to mention the sheer numbers of British punters: not the elite bourgeoisie she could confine her attentions to at home but working-class and middle-class thrill-seekers primed on the promise of savage spectacle.

Nevertheless, at the conclusion of the summer season, the group elected to stay on, trying their luck on the variety stage, assisted by Rangiuia, a Māori musician who had set up residence several years earlier in London. It was an ill-advised plan. Earning a living in variety performance was difficult, even for established and well-connected artists, and a group of their number was economically unviable. They did a brief stint at the Palace Theatre, but the act's novelty soon wore off on London's blasé audiences, and the group was forced to ask the New Zealand High Commission to help pay for their repatriation.[130] Despite a whirlwind celebrity turn in Australia on the journey back, their return to Whakarewarewa was an undignified and little-celebrated affair, especially for Makereti (who was held accountable for the financial catastrophe and for the decision of several group members to stay on in the United Kingdom).

Whakarewarewa must have held little appeal for the ambitious guide on her return: Donne, her collaborator and impresario at the DTHR, was gone. Instead, she was left to contend with the officious and culturally ignorant Supervisor and the Engineer in Charge at Rotorua. Moreover, the financial precariousness of guiding life at the kāinga and the constant vigilance it demanded against the slights of a life as a spectacle must have worn on her after her experience in the United Kingdom. The delicate balance of Makereti's class act—between exotic allure and the normative claims of fraternal respect, between racial pride and class conformity, and between public celebrity and irreproachable privacy—had proven to be a solo show, possible to sustain as she traversed the racescapes of other states, but only alone.

When she returned to the United Kingdom the following year, it was as a private British citizen: the newly married Mrs. Staples-Brown. Her life in London and Oxford for the next eighteen years—her time as a society matron, her divorce from Staples-Brown, and her work as a student at

A portrait of
Makereti as
Mrs. Staples-
Brown, ca. 1913.
Donne Papers.
Alexander
Turnbull
Library,
Wellington,
New Zealand.

Oxford University and collaborations with the Pitt Rivers Museum—was largely one of guarded privacy. In this life, her new salon (the "Māori Room" at her Oxford home) was closed to press and public, her performances undertaken only for a select few. Except for a brief trip back to New Zealand in 1926, she next emerged into the public sphere with the posthumous publication of her thesis in anthropology, *The Old-Time Maori*. From her isolation in Oxford, as a scholar, she reached back to represent Māori, acting as a guide of a different kind. The book was, in some sense, a testament to the unresolved predicament of her guiding career. By turns nostalgic and distantly objectivist, generously intimate and guarded, she fiercely defended her ancestry's integrity against the affronts of white scholarly ignorance. The idealized, functionalist Māoridom she conjured was guided by the invisible hand of moral law, undisturbed by the depredations of colonial modernity, and irreproachable in its claim on a reader's respect. It was an irreproachability that the contact zone of tourism—shot through with social risk, class competition, racial derogation, and epistemological violence—could never afford.

ON NOT CONCLUDING

Like many celebrities, Makereti was something of a chameleon, a screen for the projection of others' desires—even more so after her death. Scholars have tried to make a feminist exemplar out of someone whose fame depended on being "pretty, graceful, charming and seductive" and to make an ambassador for Māori out of someone who proclaimed the inevitability of assimilation, was a willing mouthpiece for the government whose policies hastened it, and praised the British with almost sycophantic ardor.[131] The archival record of her life conforms ill to the values of contemporary indigenous historiography: she was quick to elevate Māori above the indigenes of other nations and could even be condescending toward her own people. Indeed, I have been asked by readers of this account to denounce Makereti as an Uncle Tom, "client indigene," or social climber, to seek out Māori who did (there are none), or to search for stronger exemplars of resistance to touristic exploitation.

This impulse to cast a historical figure like Makereti as hero or villain in contemporary scholarly drama is problematic. It is not just that such histories serve the political interests of present readers: all histories do, including this one. It is rather that they unreflexively judge her by the same liberal, individualist, statist criteria of political agency against which she was pitted in her lifetime: the principles of representational adequacy and efficacious action. Instead, they should query the conditions that produce a range of agencies, in specific historical and governmental conjunctures. If we resist this impulse to judge on liberal terms, we allow these figures to tell subtler, more textured stories, stories *about liberalism itself.* Makereti's story, my account suggests, says volumes about the tactical options that liberalism presents to those go-betweens caught on the cusp between being liberal citizens and racial denizens, about the fractal and porous line between race and class, about tourism as a social art, and about how an institution that derogated and exploited indigenes could be occupied by one of them as a site of mobility and advantage. Makereti's story tells of the contested processes of racial constitution in cosmopolitan solidarities and the receptivity of liberal public spheres to cultural arguments, even to racial dissent. It tells, finally, of the limits of such arguments and dissent: Makereti's art was tactical, not strategic—it could secure no territory, gain no permanent ground.[132] The mana of her celebrity could never be fully extended to a collective, no matter how capacious the languages of representation that the guide mobilized.

That class act, however, was no less remarkable for all its limits. Makereti's performance of cosmopolitan entitlement as the cultural property and natural inclination of Māori diverted the state's racializing impetus at its most publicly visible, in Rotorua's proving ground for policy. While systematic expropriation proletarianized the Māori population, public opinion conferred on them a range of class and racial pathologies (laziness, poor discipline, dirtiness, profligacy, immorality, and lack of ambition) that formed the pretext for ever-greater governmental intervention. Makereti's guiding performances appealed, by contrast, to transnational memberships that competed with national racial formations. Against paternalist intrusion and state surveillance, she asserted the need for respect and privacy; against the Hobson's choice of assimilation or derogation, Makereti posed a kind of elective hybridity that modeled access to the "best of *both* worlds"; and against the picture of Māori at Rotorua as atavistic spectacle and embarrassment to settler modernity, her performances presented Māori tourism workers as travelers, diplomats, cultural polyglots, and ethnographers of cosmopolitan culture.

By insisting that Māori relations with their uninvited guests be adjudicated by the observance of conduct, Makereti and the guiding lineage she helped to found staked a claim to cosmopolitan entitlement, class kinship, and full membership in transnational modernity, a claim that was ratified with the performance of each genteel encounter. And each encounter provisionally refashioned tourism as a site of interracial civility (rather than economic contract or colonial imposition), policed by the threat of shame and the carefully managed pleasures of social competition. The fundamental tenet, as described to me by veteran Whakarewarewa guide Dorothy Mihinui (trained by Makereti's sister, Bella), was "like begets like . . . treat people how you like to be treated."[133] Nineteenth-century conduct was a creative repertoire for self-fashioning across class lines, but guides' actions argued that it also had the potential to refashion the social field, from the level of the gesture upward. Commonplaces such as "like begets like" veil a world of political strategy.

Makereti was acutely in step with the liberal ethos of her moment but was out of joint with the ethnic resurgence of the 1920s to 1940s, in which pan-tribal solidarities formed a class bloc, forcing recognition of their collective interests by the state. If the guide has become a beacon to contemporary scholars (in a growing stack of popular histories and theses), it is perhaps because her life only begins to make sense as something to celebrate in the wake of the neoliberal turn. Māori tourism policy (as I argue in chapter 4) now follows the line of flight Makereti charted, privileging intimate reciprocity between hosts and guests, normalizing class privilege to mitigate racial antipathy, and refiguring ethnic difference as cultural capital: a fungible resource that can be strategically invoked and profitably circulated within a global economy. It would be anachronistic to call Makereti "bicultural" (yet her life was in part a public experiment in how to live biculturally), and even more so to call her "postracial." Yet there was much in her performance of race that resonates with the actors I describe in chapter 5: her tactical mimicry of whiteness, the combination of racial allusion and elusion, the invitation to identification, and the resistance to definition.

If the past, as Paul Ricoeur wrote, is a "cemetery of promises which have not been kept," then Makereti's story is a testament to the unkept promises of liberal modernity, to its stubborn limits, and to the cunning required to hold others to its guarantees.[134] The guide's act left no mark on the enduring edifice of policies and institutions that we call the state. Yet the myriad, often ephemeral networks, tactics, identities, itineraries, loyalties, and reciprocities that performances such as Makereti's produce are as much a part of the practice of state making as the harder domains of policy, security, and interstate diplomacy that I examine in subsequent chapters. Ultimately, what we make of her political significance rests on what we make of performance itself. Performance, as its most insightful theorists have noted, is a form of poiesis that works in a subjunctive register to materialize fleetingly what it imagines. The "as if" of the performance frame becomes the "like this" of the accomplished performance. Lent witness and the bodily participation of an audience, performance's subjunctive can, albeit provisionally, become more than a potentiality: it can take the form of a practiced reality. The selves fashioned, and the temporary and conditional "we" of that audience, can become a space of potentiality in which new subjectivities and new social formations are immanent.[135] Makereti's performance shows us, not a cemetery, but a reservoir of unfulfilled futures—not all of them felicitous—that demand admittance into the archive of a newly bicultural state.

chapter 3

Translation, Transnation:
Theatrical Politics and Political Theater
in the American Pacific

In 1840 the British Crown signed a treaty with representatives of Māori tribes to officially establish British dominion in the islands of New Zealand and pave the way for systematic colonization. In the same year a new figure, "the New Zealander," made an appearance in a review by Whig historian Thomas Babington Macaulay printed in the *Edinburgh Review*. Macaulay's subject was the continued dynamism of the Roman Catholic church, which "may still exist in undiminished vigour when some traveller from New Zealand shall, in the midst of a vast solitude, take his stand on a broken arch of London Bridge to sketch the ruins of St. Paul's."[1] The image became a touchstone for imperial pundits, cited endlessly in editorials, histories, travel, and publicity literature. It mattered little that these words actually belonged to the *German* historian Leopold von Ranke (cited in Macaulay's review of his work), or that Macaulay was perfectly unconcerned in this essay with the future prospects of New Zealand, which he invoked as one might Timbuktu or any other unimaginably distant place.[2] It mattered even less that, given the usage of the term in 1840, Ranke and Macaulay probably imagined their New Zealander to be Māori: all the more a register of epochal change through being a figure of racial disorder. What mattered about Macaulay's mythic New Zealander to the pundits who invoked him was that he seemed to stamp the motherland's seal of approval on a vigorous young nation and its progeny, destined for prosperity and global significance: "New Zealand is the outpost of the British

Empire and its epitome," one typical guide wrote. "Some writers seem to indicate that one day it will be its centre."[3]

"That New Zealander of Macaulay will surely never die," complained British humorist Frank Richardson in 1906, a year in which New Zealand was on the brink of becoming a Dominion—a significant, if titular, step on the road toward independent nationhood. He continues with the image of two New Zealand tourists of the future, who disembark from an airship, speaking Esperanto with a German accent. "This is a very uninteresting place," says Hans, while Gretchen looks in her Baedeker and discovers that they have landed in London.

> "But there are nothing but ruins about," exclaims Hans in amazement. Gretchen, with that accurate knowledge characteristic of the New Zealand girl, tells him that London used to be the capital of the British Empire, but that the British gave up their army and navy out of a spirit of economy and spent the proceeds on education and religion. "It was not always like this," she explains. He asks her if it is true that New Zealand was once part of the British Empire. "In the dark ages," she admits: "But the Liberal Government gave back New Zealand to the aborigines. They gave back India to the natives, South Africa to the Dutch, Wales to the Welsh. They even wanted to restore Ireland to the Irish. But they wouldn't have it as a gift." "What an extraordinary nation!" reflects the New Zealander sadly, "Let us go back into the airship." Gretchen makes a mute request for a kiss. "I'd never have wasted a single minute of our honeymoon here, darling," she says, "If it hadn't been for Macaulay!"[4]

Macaulay's New Zealander was, by the turn of the century, a cipher of global modernity, an undecidable figure invoked with equal parts amused delight and monitory alarm, whose prodigious mobility heralded the overturning of geopolitical order. In fact, Macaulay's tourist was for Richardson and many others the harbinger of a specific revolution: the supersession of empire by a global order of autonomous, postcolonial nation-states run on liberal principles of social democracy. Suggestively, the often-repeated parable troped tourism as an index of both imperial prerogative *and* national sovereignty. The rite and right of touristic looking was a performance of imperial and racial privilege, doubly so when tourists displayed economic advantage in gazing upon the superseded, the quaint, and the primitive. To be a nation toured in this way was compromising enough, but to be the dullest offering in the Baedeker of the future was the ultimate national humiliation. Was this to be the fruit of Britain's failure to invest in imperial defense when German, Russian, Japanese, and even American interests jostled for a piece of her Pacific territories? Was the cost of supporting sovereign statehood in erstwhile colonies the surrender of one's own sovereignty? Would such surrender also cede racial prerogative? And how did the seeming trivialities of tourism get tied up with such monumental geopolitical prognoses?

For global small fry like New Zealand, concern over compromised sovereignty mingled with intimations of opportunity. When Thomas Cook and Sons travel agents opened a bureau in Auckland in 1888, the paper of record quipped that it was something of a "derogatory splash" for a nation to be so honored.[5] Yet tourism had already taken up residence at the heart of the young nation's rituals of state. Over the ensuing two decades, it would become an integral dimension of the state's diplomatic idiom and the instrument of its self-promotional politics, both international and domestic. Diplomatic missions and state visitors traveled the routes charted by the tourism apparatus and enjoyed state and Māori hospitality at Rotorua. The many guests included touring British royals in 1901; the officers of the Imperial Army in 1907; representatives of the Commonwealth's chambers of commerce in 1908; countless Australian ministers; and political commentators from J. A. Froude or Henry Demarest Lloyd to Alice Egerton, the Duchess of Buckingham and Chandos. Witnesses of and occasions for the state's self-staging, these political tourists' published accounts wove into the story of state the voices of the citizens they encountered on their travels.[6] And they wove that story into still grander narratives of empire, Commonwealth, modern government, and racial destiny. Such accounts took on trajectories of their own through sale and circulation, prompting yet more journeys, yet more stories of state. But how did the medium of tourism shape the idiom in which the state could be imagined, in particular its racial idiom? What avenues did it offer for Māori to intervene into that work of imagining? And what was the fate of the national symbolic cast abroad: what racial figures and articulations of sovereignty could travel, and how were they transformed by their journey?

SPECTACLE, TRANSLATION, AND IMAGINATION: FROM REPRESENTATION TO PERFORMANCE

In this chapter, I take up the relationship between tourism and statehood within the broader frame of global geopolitics. I am curious about the ways in which the affects and governmental *effects* of race are, at the same time, produced and disrupted by systems of mobility such as tourism. I am interested also in how race itself moves, the rhythms to which racial subjects and structures of feeling circulate globally, transforming in the process. The link between circulation and sovereignty is, I suggest, both constitutive and unsettling: the social imaginaries, political communities, and subjectivities of liberalism are both made and unmade in circulation. Modalities of performance, in particular translation and spectacle, are crucial to this process. They do not simply *represent*, and thus stabilize, existing formations: they can also propose trajectories, affinities, or correspondences. Spectacle and translation are expressive rather than representational media, materially constitutive of the worlds they imagine, precisely through their capacity to both navigate and generate circulatory momentum, cutting across local, domestic, and global contexts.[7]

Imagination is a significant term in this critical, and political, turn from representation to performativity. In Benedict Anderson's much-cited theorization of nation as "imagined community," imagination named the process through which the most intangible, barely perceptible, or not yet existing relationships between disparate peoples were first made perceptible and then ultimately rendered material in the nation form, through the reflexive circulation of cultural forms (novels and newspapers, for example).[8] For thinkers such as Dipesh Chakrabarty, Charles Taylor, and Arjun Appadurai, imagination describes the means by which we grasp the still less apprehensible connectivities and collectivities of the global social order, forming intimations of solidarity that in turn mediate collective lifeways.[9] Some of these imagined relations with strangers are transitory or minor, while others acquire enormous institutional force (in, for example, diasporic communities, trade alliances, or protest movements). Regardless of their outcome, according to Edward LiPuma and Benjamin Lee, these "social imaginaries" are all bound up with "cultures of circulation," systems of reflexive circulation and exchange—of money, information, people, and commodities— that both depend upon and produce the forms of sociality that characterize global modernity.[10]

Imagination, in the words of Cornelius Castoriadis, is the "unceasingly and essentially undetermined (socio-historical and psychical) creation of figures, forms, and images" that compose the institution of society.[11] Like all forms of creation, it has its techniques and arts. Translation is one of these: an art of the road, a staple of diplomacy and trade, and a necessity of travel and tourism. To be translated is to be transported, to be borne across: transmitted, transmuted, transfigured, transacted. Traduced. *Traduttore, traditore*, as the Italian proverb goes—translator, traitor. The inherent ambivalence of translation at the same time promises the mutual legibility of distinct cultures and attests to their mutual opacity. It pretends that kernels of meaning might be carried whole and safe across what Gayatri Spivak has called "the spacy emptiness between two named languages" and threatens that such essential meaning might be forever lost in translation.[12] Translation names the fidelity of power's replication over time and space (as in *translatio imperii*), but it also points to the intractable obstacles (the resistances of difference and distance) to any empire's spatial and temporal continuity.

As Naoki Sakai has observed, the *representation* of translation as the effective communication of meaning between two autonomous, unitary, stable tongues operates as a powerful fiction in the political discourse of (inter)-national modernity. In purifying the heteroglossic complexity of actual social speech, the representation of translation is a "theory" that consolidates diffuse, contested, moving, and heterolingual communities into homogeneous, territorialized populations (an operation, of course, that readers of Anderson will recognize as the foundational gesture of nation formation). The representation of translation, then, produces the solidarities it presumes, through staging absolute difference (spatial, linguistic, and ethnic) and enacting the ritual of difference's mediation.[13] Whereas the *representation* of translation purifies, however, the *performance* of translation proliferates. In what follows, I trace how the state's work of defining and mediating (inter)national difference through translation became the occasion for Māori dissent from, and creative negotiation of, those same solidarities. Far exceeding the merely linguistic, translation operated as a mimetic repertoire that generated intimations of affinity and identity as well as of antagonism and discord.

In the same vein, I address the role of spectacle in the production of liberal social imaginaries, sovereignties, and subjectivities. My interest in spectacle may seem counterinstinctual: spectacle has long been vilified as a quintessentially *il*liberal modality, one that imposes rather than proposes or persuades. Such critiques date from spectacle's ascendance as the hallmark of nineteenth-century aesthetics and register its pivotal importance to capitalist modernity. Colored by a distrust of popular politics and its dynamic entanglement with market and social processes, early critiques took spectacle as the negative mirror image of theater's ideal role as a political medium: with its material quiddity and plenitude, spectacle anaesthetized the dramatic imagination and (in eschewing rational critical dialogue) eclipsed political impulses toward decision and action "in which men in general try to change their condition."[14] For Frankfurt school analysts of the twentieth century, spectacle epitomized the art of distraction in an age of display: extending the fetish character of the commodity, it masked the social relations of production, stunting processes of political recognition or resistance. All politics had become spectacle, all spectacle had become perforce political, they argued: an eclipsing, violent system of representation-as-reification that distorted the very ground of human experience and sociality. In Guy Debord's formulation, the spectacle of the state—diplomacy, warfare, and patriotic pomp—is but one specific instance of this encompassing condition. Tourism, of course, is another, thought by many following him to epitomize the spectacle's qualities of inauthenticity, false consciousness, dazzling superficiality, and a paradoxical longing for the lost "Real."

Contesting this well-rehearsed narrative of modernity's disenchantment, I take spectacle not as representational but as performative, as a form of "poetic world-making" that works across the terrain of fantasy and materiality.[15] In my account, spectacle welds the hard power of military geopolitics to the soft power of the culture industries; it embodies the projective, performative energy of capital, that which animates desire by picturing the desirable.[16] Far from hypostatizing the image of power (or, indeed, race), spectacle gives it circulatory momentum: it generates networks, connections, collisions, impurities, localisms, sensations, and intimations of political pasts, presents, and futures. This does not mean that spectacle is innocent of political hegemony. Spectacle's scale makes it an obvious vehicle of dominant imaginaries, especially those of the state. But its need for participation and witness also makes it an inherently open system, unstable and porous to the imaginings, actions, and investments of a range of agents.

In what follows, I detail the workings of translation and spectacle surrounding an act of military-diplomatic tourism—the trans-Pacific tour of the U.S. Fleet and its welcome by the New Zealand state in 1908—and its theatrical afterlife on the stage and streets of New York. In particular, I follow the interventions of Māori actors, both political actors and theatrical ones, from the Government Gardens of Rotorua to the New York Hippodrome, tracking the stagings of interstate, intercultural, and interracial encounter in which they participated. The Fleet's tour stood at the vanguard of what Michael Hardt and Antonio Negri have called Empire: a globalizing geopolitical regime predicated on circulation, communication, and mobility. Empire, in their definition, is a "decentered, deterritorializing apparatus of rule," the extension and consolidation of a liberal model of sovereignty (and biopower) on a global basis, under the signs of fraternity and peace.[17] Empire in the Progressive era was not an objective fact but the horizon toward which geopolitical developments aspired: a vision of a universal republic, a network of powers and counterpowers suspended in perfect equilibrium "under the direction of a single conductor."[18] Significantly, the mechanism of this new global order was not only U.S. military power but touristic exchange: the Fleet's welcome juxtaposed representations of travel and colonization, theatrical performances by and for tourists, and acts of cultural diplomacy of a particularly performative stripe. It was, ultimately, an event not only thematized by global mobility but also active in promoting and producing it.

CONVERGENCES, TRANSLATIONS, MIGRATIONS

Late on a Saturday afternoon in 1908, in the small government town of Rotorua in the central North Island of New Zealand, Admiral Charles Sperry of the U.S. Navy confronted an unaccustomed spectacle. Mita Taupopoki, a leader of the Tūhourangi and Ngāti Wāhiao communities, paced before him dressed in a cloak of bird feathers, brandishing a short bone club in one hand and a long carved wooden spear in the other, speaking with great animation in Māori. Mita was a master of the Māori political art of whaikōrero, or oratory, a fundamental component of the Māori protocol of welcome enacted in honor of the fifty visiting American naval officers, who sat on a dais fingering their neatly printed programs. In whaikōrero, the paramount men of the host and visiting groups exchange highly formalized addresses, paying homage to each other's ancestral lineage, recounting genealogical and historical connections between the two groups, and acknowledging the occasion or mission that has brought them

VISIT OF ADMIRAL SPERRY TO ROTORUA, AUCKLAND. AN OLD TIME MAORI WELCOME TO NEW ZEALAND'S WONDERLAND. AUGUST 15, 1908.

A TALE OF WARRIOR DAYS. AN OLD MAORI CHIEF AT ROTORUA ADDRESSING ADMIRAL SPERRY. AUGUST 15, 1908.

This grand old chief presented the Admiral with the spear, which he is shown holding aloft, remarking: "With this weapon we used to kill men; therefore I give it to you—a man of the sea—as you may have occasion to kill men. When you see it first put this mat (removing the one he was wearing and laying it at Admiral Sperry's feet) around you.

VISIT OF ADMIRAL SPERRY TO ROTORUA. A POI DANCE BY THE WAHINES IN FRONT OF THE NEW BATH-HOUSE.

THE VISIT OF THE GREAT AMERICAN BATTLESHIP FLEET TO NEW ZEALAND, AUGUST 9 TO 15, 1908.

Mita Taupopoki addresses Admiral Sperry and parliamentarians at the Government Gardens. *Auckland Weekly News.* Courtesy of Auckland Public Library.

together. The illustrious chief wished to welcome the travelers on behalf of his Te Arawa people, the broadest tribal formation with which he was affiliated. "Welcome to our distinguished visitors who are sprung from the same lineage as the Anglo-Saxons and our King, Edward the Seventh," he began. "We especially welcome you because the Maoris are a seafaring people and in the olden days, when your ancestors were hugging the coasts, they sailed in canoes all over the Pacific Ocean. Long before Columbus discovered your country or Leif the Red touched upon its shores, our tribe came to New Zealand in the Arawa canoe from which we take our name."[19]

Mita Taupopoki's words were rendered in English by Peter Buck, or Te Rangi Hīroa (Rotorua's District Health Officer), who stood at the end of Mita's speech, presenting "quite a contrast to his fellow countrymen in their nakedness & weird costumes; he was dressed in a swell English frock coat & tall silk hat."[20] He interpreted for the benefit of the honored guests, assembled parliamentarians, townsfolk, and colonial gentry, and the national papers in turn rendered Buck's translation thus:

> The Maoris at one time owned the Pacific. All of it was Polynesian territory once. Their Maori ancestors were the first owners of this land. . . . In the early days they were navigating the deep sea, while the Anglo Saxon races were hugging the coasts in their own countries. Further, the chiefs recognized that the Americans were upraising the prestige the Maori enjoyed. They welcomed them because once they (the Maoris) themselves were navigators and seafarers.[21]

The speech, it seems, was a translation in more than one sense: a translation between tongues, yes, but also one between peoples, aiming to express their "central reciprocal relationship."[22] The old man translated Māori into American English through claiming a similarity of intention, an echo or "reverberation" between indigene and alien, host and guest: both were "races" of master mariners, sovereign in their own lands and over the Pacific; both were colonists and voyagers, each of whose achievements (separated by five hundred years of history but brought into correspondence by this historic meeting) "upraised" the prestige of their counterpart. Such a translation served both to differentiate and to affiliate the two peoples, both to define and to authorize them.

This remarkable diplomatic convergence was also, I will argue, the site of a trenchant historical irony. In one significant sense, the ceremony itself was a translation: a solemn and efficacious Māori ritual transformed into a colorful sideshow to a geopolitical, racial compact between the colonial state and American power that eclipsed Māori interests. In another—and equally valid—sense, it was the subversive culmination of the tour's riot of intercultural performance, one that undercut the cultural diplomacy of Empire by publicly testing its claims to transparency and reciprocity. The difference between these two readings, crucially, hinged on the tension between the *representation* of translation and its *performance*.

PACIFIC PURPOSE, SPECTACULAR MEANS

The officers were representatives of the so-called Great White Fleet, sixteen state-of-the-art battleships from the U.S. Atlantic navy, en route from Virginia to the western Pacific Rim in a spectacular act of symbolic diplomacy. A classic Rooseveltian "bully tactic," the Fleet's tour was also a performative proposition of something that might be called the American Pacific, an Imperial geopolitical formation never fully realized but violently incipient over the course of the late nineteenth and early twentieth centuries. Extending American manifest destiny's westward thrust, Theodore Roosevelt responded to domestic instabilities and impatient corporate capital with aggressive expansionism.[23] By 1906, after the forcible annexation of Hawai'i, and amid the bitterly contested military occupation of the Philippines, there was a perilous balance of power in the Pacific. American diplomacy struggled to manage the ambitions of Japan's imperial modernity in the wake of the Russo–Japanese war, which had left the Japanese effectively occupying Korea while Manchuria—vital to the competing commercial and strategic interests of Britain, Russia, and the United States, particularly in relation to the "open door" of China—remained only marginally independent. Meanwhile, at home, the backwash of capital expansion and modernization in Asia (the much-vaunted "opening of the East") increased immigration, which met with virulently Sinophobic labor and legislative activism. The Exclusion Acts bundled together Chinese, Japanese, Korean, and Filipino immigrants under a common yoke of discrimination, outraging the governments of their nations of origin. In 1906 the situation reached a crisis point, with a mutinous California legislature passing legally questionable acts that excluded Japanese from property and educational rights, in violation of international treaty provisions. A paranoid Roosevelt, goaded by the "yellow" press, was apparently convinced that Japan not only harbored territorial ambitions in China but was also plotting eastward expansion over the Pacific.

The result was the global tour of the U.S. Fleet: a spectacularly theatrical political solution designed to symbolically establish U.S. naval command of the Pacific, simultaneously placate and threaten the incensed Japanese, and demonstrate to the Californians that something was being done. The deeper motives behind the tour have been hotly debated by scholars, all the more so because the tour itself was never debated but rather was executed by presidential fiat. Economistic arguments are weak: the vast Far East market was, in real terms, a mirage, and most other countries in the tour's compass (including Australia and New Zealand) had neither economic nor strategic importance to the United States at this historical juncture.[24] Roosevelt himself probably gave the most coherent rationale when he retrospectively glossed the tour as not directed at any power, nor even as managing volatile alliances between Russian, German, British, Chinese, and Japanese interests in the area. Instead, he saw the tour as projecting a more general policy far into the future: to affirm the legitimacy of U.S. naval presence in the Pacific, to win domestic support for military investment, and (most significant, in his eyes) "to impress the American people" with an awareness of themselves as the dominant global force in the Americas and Asia-Pacific. As a journalist from the *London Times* proclaimed, "a spectacular display has valuable uses in impressing the masses, who will remember the sight for years, and draw important political deductions therefrom."[25]

The gesture was in a sense a public rehearsal, an attempt to bring into being that which it imagined by materializing it in performance and inviting its ratification by an audience of participating witnesses.[26] At a moment when the frontier of U.S. sovereignty had seemingly run up against its spatial limits, Roosevelt-era foreign policy turned to a form of Empire based not on the right of occupation but on the right of intervention, secured by "a very strong feeling of a community of material interests."[27] The seed for this American Pacific, this "curious sort of protectorate" (as Sperry termed it), had been planted fifty years before by another American show of naval force in a Japanese harbor, when Admiral Perry (Sperry's predecessor) "opened" Japan to global trade and Western modernity.[28] To political commentators of the era, the mimetic *translatio* between the two tours underscored the epochal yet inevitable historicity of this dawning Empire of commerce. To our contemporary eyes, it exposes the ways in which the expansion of liberalism, founded on a professed faith in "the brotherhood of man" and "respect for the differing opinions and the possessions of others," rested not only on the absolute freedom of capital but also on a foundational violence that compelled nations into the "bonds of good neighborhood."[29] In the words of the adage that followed the Fleet throughout the English-speaking Pacific, "preparation for war means universal peace."

With the symbolic excess of Progressive-era pageantry to the fore at every level of planning and execution, the battleships set sail on a monumental tour. Painted in white and gold for the occasion, and tellingly dubbed the Great White Fleet, the boats departed from the Jamestown Exposition, which marked the tricentennial of European settlement in the United States.[30] Making America's "entry onto the world stage" with self-conscious theatricality, the Fleet circumnavigated South America (construed as a protectorate under a reinterpreted, post-Panama Monroe doctrine) and then pushed westward into the American Pacific, pushing with it the frontiers of America's imagined community.[31] The Fleet played its part as hero in a spectacular melodrama that presented a forceful argument for national and transnational racial solidarity on the one hand and imperial advancement on the other. It was a material performative, "realiz[ing] the magnificence of the ideal it represented."[32]

This Empire of commerce, the tour proposed, might be accomplished through the frictionless yet controlled mobility of capital, information, and bodies across a Pacific smoothed for the free movement of the imagination. It promised to erase linguistic and racial resistances to mobility through establishing an "unbroken line of English speaking countries" around the globe, united in "commerce and vigour."[33] Localities were translated into mobile signs (each battleship was named after a state of the Union, so the tour literally took Tennessee to Tokyo) and mobile signs into continuous spaces of information flow (Sperry proudly announced that he took the Fleet across the globe's vastest ocean without once falling out of wireless contact.) It was a fantasy of uninterrupted communication, faithful replication, and limitless circulation. Likewise, the circulation of information *about* the tour took place on a scale rarely before witnessed.

The accounts of Franklin Matthews (correspondent for the *New York Sun*) alone reportedly reached thirty million readers in the United States, first as syndicated dispatches and later as a best-selling volume. Part travelogue, part political commentary, part puff piece for Roosevelt's global vision, Matthews's account, together with those published in other venues, whipped up a frenzy of "Fleet Fever" in the United States. That in turn created a fad for naval fashions, produced record profits for Rand McNally, generated massive public demonstrations of support, and democratized the prerogatives of global knowledge.[34]

Tourism was both medium and message of the tour's American Pacific order. Just as the State Department later promoted tourism during the Cold War, those in command felt that training the sailors (and their proxies, the American public) in the arts of leisure travel would generate a sense of command of global space, of cosmopolitan civility, and establish a benign but undeniably forceful presence abroad.[35] In Hawai'i, while the Admiral consolidated the agreement for a naval base at Pearl Harbor and manufactured the consent of deposed queen Liliuokalani, a citywide spectacle established the aura of sensuous sentimentality and the commodity codes (lei-bedecked hula girls and surf-riding crooners) that would later become synonymous with America's distant, Edenic extopia.[36] In letters home, Sperry bragged about how quickly his men were acquiring the habits of leisure travel, hiring guides, and seeing the sights. These were, he wrote, "cleanhanded, clear headed young Americans, quick witted and out to see the world with all the interest and ten times the sense of a party of Cook's Tourists."[37] The claim was explicitly political: "they are as representative a body as Congress," Sperry crowed, citing the "mutual enlightenment" to be gained from coming into contact with thousands of other people living under democracy. The ties of common material interest, touristic amity, consumption, and communication born of these vernacular ambassadors' travel would forge a "natural alliance far stronger than any written treaty of alliances—and less offensive."[38]

STAGING NATION, SEEKING SOVEREIGNTY

Despite its monumental goals, the spectacle of the Fleet's tour—in the nature of all spectacles, whether touristic, military, or political—was open in form, an available language in which diverse claims to recognition could be put forward and multiple agendas advanced. For the New Zealand and Australian governments, uncomfortably situated between their imperial obligation to honor the terms of the recent Anglo–Japanese entente and domestic climates of ardent Sinophobia, the tour offered the opportunity to acknowledge an identity of interests with U.S. policy in the Pacific.[39] Furthermore, the independent Dominions were increasingly unsure of the British naval capacity, and political will, to secure the South Pacific against competing European imperial interests in the area (in particular, the German threat). In welcoming the Fleet, Australia and New Zealand could flex their newly formed independent nationalist muscle—and hedge their security bets—by pursuing diplomatic relationships outside the British Commonwealth, all without the risk of actual strategic commitment.

The reception of the twelve thousand men and five hundred officers in both countries was a costly, spectacular civic and state investment saturated with political and racial significance. Bunting, ceremonial arches, illuminations, addresses, galas, regattas, and seemingly endless speechifying were the lingua franca of this projected global order, in which American naval power underwrote the "freedom" of the Anglo-Saxon Pacific and the "mingled destiny" of its peoples. "Now, Uncle, let them all come," cried the diminutive figure of New Zealand in welcome to the towering Uncle Sam: "Brown or yellow, we'll keep a white flag over our lands!"[40] The contours of this subjunctive world order were, again, not only those of race—the "ties of tongue and blood and colour" called upon by both parties as a bulwark against the yellow tide—but of tourism, with an itinerary that clearly prioritized leisured pleasure over statist diplomacy. This was particularly the case in New Zealand, where the government had put its weight behind the burgeoning tourism industry, recognizing the "multiplier effects" of publicity and development that accompanied it. "Every man is going to be an advertising medium for possibly fifty years to come," a parliamentarian argued to justify the state's massive investment in the welcome.[41]

Placed in the hands of the Department of Tourist and Health Resorts (DTHR), the welcome was conducted with an eye to capturing future traffic. The seamen were issued with free postcards and postage, and with DTHR-produced booklets extolling the prosperity, progress, and natural beauties of the colony. Meanwhile, Sperry and his officers sojourned at the tourism capital of Rotorua as the government's guests (declining an invitation to the actual capital, Wellington). They saw the sights, opened the new Dominion Baths, and enjoyed the entertainments laid on for their benefit by Māori performers in the pay of the state. Thanks to the rapturous reports of the tour correspondents (borrowing liberally from DTHR materials), millions in the United States vicariously enjoyed the entire episode.

In an orgy of symbolic excess, New Zealand's spectacular self-staging proclaimed symmetry, equivalence, and perfect translation between the two sovereign nations. Portraits of Sir Joseph Ward (the New Zealand Prime Minister) and Roosevelt hung together on Auckland's buildings; the battleship and the war canoe were anchored side by side in newspaper illustrations; the eagle and the kiwi greeted each other on souvenir crests, flags intertwined; and no one could detect the slightest "clashing notes in the cry God Save the King—Hail Columbia."[42] The serial semiotics of the liberal national idiom (to each nation a flag, bird, and anthem) provided the ground of mutual recognition between hosts and guests.

Much like whaikōrero, the transnational rhetoric of popular diplomacy summoned correspondences in lineage, deed, reputation, and history to bond the parties. As the New Zealand government put it, the two nations were united in their interest in "the cause of national welfare," pursued through pacific techniques of liberal government, while their citizens shared the colonial virtues of "courage, rectitude, and self reliance" in the winning of their respective frontiers.[43] (That the American visitors seemed to consider New Zealand part of their own domain—"Newest America," where once it was "Better Britain"—went politely unremarked upon by their hosts.)[44] The nations were also symbolically yoked through a rhetoric of kinship that had endless permutations. (England was the mother, Columbia the daughter taking responsibility for the Pacific's defense after England's abandonment; both were "sons of the Mother of Nations," distant cousins reunited, and so on.)

The resort to kinship made explicit the extent to which claims to transparency and understanding that figured in the representation of translation rested on a fundamentally racial logic. Again and again, "ties of tongue and blood and colour," of "common race and common interest," were called upon to cement the allegiance of "this great Anglo-Saxon family," yoked in "fraternal pride." Again and again, such imagined kinship was buttressed by the threats of imagined Asiatic aggression and an impending global race struggle centered on the Pacific.[45] The "interests of the world," parliamentarians claimed, were "bound up with those of the white race," who, with their passion for liberty and individuality, were in the vanguard of evolution.[46] "One race, one destiny" read the banners fluttering in the Auckland wind: "We realize today that a great bond now exists between us, that of perfect understanding, perfect trust, and greatest of all, perfect friendship."[47] This proposed Empire of sentiment rendered translation obsolete: absolute transparency of communication and community might be achieved through resort to a universal language that transcended them both, a language grounded in a contract between tongue, genealogy, race, and reason.

THE VENTRILOQUIST STATE

New Zealand, then, spoke with a voice that on the one hand marked its national difference and on the other claimed cultural, genealogical, racial, and intentional affinity with its addressee. Every national language (postcolonial critics remind us) is already a stabilizing translation that belies the heteroglot, contested character of national origins; its further translation threatens to expose this fact.[48] As I have argued in previous chapters, the New Zealand state's self-articulation was a ventriloquist act that presented Māori as the mark of international distinction—a trademark, essentially— and as the settlers' surrogate, lending Pākehā (non-Māori) the mantle of romantic autochthony despite their fifty short years of habitation.[49] It was in this ventriloquist spirit that the state's published greeting could announce, "In the tongue of old Maoridom we greet them 'Haere-mai! Haere-mai!,'" that the arches over the Auckland wharves could be emblazoned with "Haeremai ki Akarana" (Welcome to Auckland), and that the official gifts (such as caskets, plaques, and illuminated addresses) could bear images of chiefs, tiki (ornamental carvings representing humans), and Māori weaponry.[50]

It was also in this ventriloquist spirit that Māori were actively discouraged from arranging their own welcome and accompanying address, lest an unsanctioned impression be given to the visitors.[51] In fact, the Māori King, Mahuta, who had not been invited to join the official welcome, even though he was technically a member of Parliament at the time, and who had been barred from representing Māori in an independent welcome to the American visitors, staged his own spectacular *coup de theatre diplomatique* that clearly exposed the divisibility of New Zealand sovereignty. Traveling

Cartoon commentary in New Zealand papers on the visit of the American Fleet. *Top left*, "Duett Amici," *Weekly Graphic and New Zealand Mail; top right*, "Kiaora Goodbye," *Auckland Weekly News; bottom left*, "Uncle Sam," *New Zealand Free Lance; bottom right*, "Te hongi," *Auckland Weekly News.*

An arch of welcome.

up from his seat in Waikato with the Kīngitanga's magnificent waka (ceremonial canoe), Taheretikitiki, he met the anchored Fleet in Auckland Harbor in an irresistible photo opportunity—the battleship and the war canoe!—and delivered ceremonial greetings to the nonplussed admiral. State officials were rankled but powerless to stop him. The state spoke with a forked tongue to the Americans: its language *contained* Māori political expression, both including *and* attempting to regulate it. At Rotorua, Te Rangi Hīroa's performance of translation threatened to rupture this non-consensual national voice, exposing the paradox of Māori bodies borrowed and burlesqued to revitalize Anglo-Saxon domination.

Te Rangi Hīroa was a founding member of the Young Māori Party, a parliamentary and professional network that worked across the liberal state apparatus and existing tribal power bases to forge the economic, social, and political structures of a hoped-for Māori modernity. His whaikōrero was consonant with the discourse of this movement: while traditional oratory drew on the tribal preserves of proverb and genealogy, this new pan-tribal whaikōrero was a paean to a supranational spirit of cosmopolitanism, which it posed as the natural inheritance of the Polynesian race. Moreover, by presenting Māori as prior colonizers, it appropriated and deformed the tenets of Anglo-Saxonism, which took the colonizing energies of "the white races" as evidence of their racial superiority. While Ward, the Premier, publicly lauded Māori as "a race alike naturally courageous and dignified and now dwelling in permanently harmonious relations with *us*," Buck (a state agent) usurped the collective subject—the *we*—of the national enunciation.[52] "Poetically enough," one paper had it, "it was suggested to the visitor further that they had embarked, as it were, on the Arawa canoe. [By means of this ceremony of welcome] they were one with the Arawa people, one with the Maori race—with the people of New Zealand."[53] Rhetorically eliding tribe, race, and "the people of New Zealand," the dedication obliquely but publicly embarrassed the state's assumption of an Anglo-Saxon "people of New Zealand" on behalf of whom a welcome was performed by "their natives."

Given such oratorical cunning, it might come as a surprise that Mita Taupopoki was not lauding the nautical prowess of his race at all. He was, in fact, waxing lyrical in Māori about the lamentable state of the drains in the village of Whakarewarewa.[54] He had taken the opportunity of the epochal state occasion to needle the officials of the DTHR—all of whom

were present, trussed up in their ceremonial finery—about their responsibility to the Māori villages over which they were the appointed managers.
(Several of the department officials were competent, if not fluent, in Māori;
the Premier, members of Parliament, and cohort of reporters were not.)
This fact puts a different complexion on the enthusiastic response to Mita's
speech that issued from the Māori onlookers, some of whom, according to
the newspaper reports "could not resist 'chipping in' from time to time,
dancing brief hakas and interjecting encouraging remarks [*in English*] as
bits of the speeches floated up to them." "Hear, hear!" "Good boy!"⁵⁵

It was a loaded issue that Mita contested. The state honored Sperry by
choosing him to ceremonially open Rotorua's new spa, which had been
bankrolled by taxpayers to the tune of forty thousand pounds. This was an
astronomical sum for the era, doubly so on top of the thousands already
invested by the government in the town itself and in the modern electrical, water, and waste systems about which the Premier bragged so loudly
that afternoon in his own speech. Rotorua was held up as an object lesson
in Liberal modernity to the American public, with commentators such as
Matthews extolling the prosperous, industrious, and healthful environment produced by a combination of generous public provision and settler
entrepreneurialism. Yet the neighboring Māori villages, Whakarewarewa
and Ōhinemutu, under the governance of tribal committees, had received
little assistance, despite the local economy's dependence on them (and their
picturesque premodernity) to attract visitors to the region. Mita Taupopoki's improvisational cunning confronted liberalism's global aspirations
with its abjectly local shortcomings, asserting itself against the statist representation of translation (and the unified national public it presumed) by
playing to linguistic heterogeneity. His performance mapped the political
field, measuring—in units of shame, indignation, and hilarity—the distance between an oblivious state (whose bad-faith surrogate exhibitionism
exploited and excluded Māori), the Young Maori Party's accommodationist pan-Māori leadership, the settler community, and struggling hapū (extended kin groups).

DISSEMINATION, (DIS)SIMULATION

Mita's semipublic dissent from the dramaturgy of the occasion, however,
was perhaps not solely directed toward domestic quibbles. The planning of

the reception had prompted a heated parliamentary debate about the politics of Roosevelt's proposed global order. To what degree could (or should) American constructions of liberal political justice—specifically those pertaining to race—be translated transnationally? How might New Zealand manage the tension between the reciprocal claims of national sovereignties and the not so reciprocal dictates of the Imperial compact? A week before the arrival of the Fleet, Apirana Ngata, MP for Eastern Māori, challenged Parliament on the claim that the stars and stripes symbolized "political freedom and human fraternity," given the treatment of "the Indians and others" in America.[56] Rotorua chiefs had discussed the matter at a meeting and concluded unanimously that they would take no part in the celebrations. It was only through the exercise of unfair pressure by government representatives, Ngata stated, that they had been induced to participate.[57] By contrast, what for Ngata was a matter of moral principle and transnational race solidarity was for Te Rangi Hīroa a question of the right of Māori to represent and be represented as national subjects in the global sphere: "Any welcome extended to an outside country, in which the Maoris were not given the opportunity of co-operating, would not be representative of the desirable unity of the two races. It would be a direct insult to the Maoris, and belittling them as an, apparently, unimportant factor."[58] The Pākehā MPs, however, understood the problem as the state's sovereign control over the ethnic terms of citizenship: would the American color line travel the Pacific with its military might? If so, on what side of it would Māori land, and what capacity would the New Zealand state have to assert its own principles of ethnic conduct?

In Ward's eyes, the claims of national sovereignty trumped those of Imperial prerogative and marked a limit to translation. The American officers would be obliged to treat "our natives" with respect, according to New Zealand custom and law, he argued: "We are not going to transfer New Zealand into the interior of America."[59] Te Rangi Hīroa, again speaking in favor of a high Māori profile at the diplomatic events, suggested that racial translation could be managed—and racial effects produced—*through performance*:

> We know that the Americans are prejudiced against coloured people, but that is in America, where they are of negroid-descended [*sic*] from generations of slaves, whom the Americans bought and sold. The Maori people are

of Caucasian descent, and should not be identified with the objects of American aversion. The Maori welcome is the highest honour the Maoris can confer upon the visitors. We venture to think that the American officers will realize that the ceremony is dignified and impressive, and according to the traditions of a race which is not unworthy of being greeted on terms of perfect and equal brotherhood.[60]

Buck's platform was clear: racial categories were noncommensurable and racial stigmas nontranslatable; whiteness was the condition for cosmopolitan community and the extension of liberal recognition; and performance was the medium through which Māori could lay claim to it. In the event, Sperry took his lead well (although he may well have thought the ethnological theory of Caucasian Māori fanciful, and he privately believed that the entire exercise was a result of Ward pandering to the Māori vote): "You are, like us," he addressed the Rotorua tribes, *"members of this great Anglo-Saxon family*, now extending in all directions over the Pacific."[61]

The fears expressed by Māori and their allies in Parliament were revealing of the stakes of Empire, and of Imperial tourism, for fourth-world peoples. What if racial kinship were not recognized, making the performance's dignity illegible to its addressees? Would the surrogate circumstances of the ceremony, in which the tribe both did and did not speak for itself, contaminate its solemn performative with the taint of theatricality? In their rush to interpret the unfamiliar ritual, would the Americans settle on the familiar, degrading analogue of showbiz barbarism? One MP wanted to "prevent any exhibition by the Maori people for the delectation of these American visitors," while Ngata resented that "on every possible occasion we are asked to trot out our Maoris to be exhibited for the entertainment of tourists." Buck countered firmly, "The demonstration is not a series of show items, arranged by any official, but a Maori welcome from the Arawa tribe, arranged by a council of the chiefs . . . such as our ancestors would have done in welcoming the distinguished representatives of another tribe."[62]

What transpired was both theatrical *and* performative, so double-tongued as to confound any simple translation. In contrast to the vast, representative gathering of Māori tribes who greeted the Duke and Duchess of Cornwall and York in Rotorua in 1901 (which had elicited broad and eager participation from Māori eager to mark their relationship to the

Crown), the elders who addressed the American officers were waged performers. Their gifts were not tribal heirlooms, invested with ancestral mana,
but souvenirs manufactured for the occasion by craftspeople at Whakarewarewa and paid for by the government. The proceedings followed formal
Māori protocol but were concluded by a show every bit as showy as any
feared by the parliamentarians: a model pā (fortified village) had been constructed on the green in front of the bathhouse, and the 150 Māori (from
nine local tribes) staged an invasion, mock fighting each other with traditional weaponry and feisty haka. The welcome was at once exotic entertainment and diplomatic contract; symbol of native consent and cipher
of indigenous intransigence; heritage reenactment of a feudal, superseded
past and contemporary political ritual of state; dignified demonstration of
statesmanship and carnivalesque romp; a site of simulation and dissimula-
tion. It was, in short, an event that played on the cusp between the representation of translation and its performance.

THE MIMETIC EXCESS OF
IMPERIAL BURLESQUE

Everywhere, the mimetic exchanges prompted by the tour overspilled the
terms of the state's representation of translation. Sperry found himself uncomfortably translated in Rotorua when Guide Maggie Papakura draped
him in a ceremonial cloak and bade him hold the weapons the Māori leaders had given him. "In a trice," the papers suggested, "Admiral Sperry lost
his identity, sinking it into that of a pakeha chief."[63] The performative gesture was a hybrid of tourist idiom (a standard element of the Rotorua tour,
in which the visitor was dressed in Māori garb and photographed as a pantomime chief) and Māori diplomatic protocol (important visitors were often
gifted with valuable and storied cloaks, in order to symbolically assume the
mantle of mana lent by the tribe welcoming them). But it also evoked,
with an acute mimetic irony, the connections between prior exploratory
or colonizing performances and the Americans' Imperial enterprise. Like a
hyperbolic amalgam of Cook, Cortez, and Kurtz, Sperry became an embodied sign of white colonizing energy so transmuted, traduced, and refracted
by its translation as to travesty its referent. Translation, as Walter Benjamin
argued, makes a language foreign to itself, sending the sign on a journey
from which it cannot return unchanged.[64]

Beyond Rotorua, also, rallies of parody and homage, improvisation and impersonation, flew between guests and hosts, settlers and Māori, hyperbolizing differences and ironizing affinities between them, and returning compulsively to the central theme of the diplomatic drama—race. On the dais of the Assembly Hall in Auckland, the members of Parliament (assembled at a state banquet in honor of the visitors) performed a "rousing" haka to conclude the speeches, and the gesture was parodied in a newspaper cartoon picturing the leaders of the nation clad in tribal garb, their august bellies bouncing to the martial rhythm. In an adjacent cartoon, four honorable MPs were dressed as a Yankee barbershop quartet, wearing top hats emblazoned with the stars and stripes. Auckland glee clubs actually serenaded the embarking sailors at the wharf with touching renditions of "Louisiana Lou" and "Give My Regards to Broadway." Some American journalists reported that Sperry was greeted at the Rotorua welcome "by a Maori chieftain who embarrassed him by shouting 'Bully!' through a bucktoothed mask of Teddy Roosevelt."[65] Again, the papers joined the mimetic fray, picturing a chief's head—a cartoon hybrid of a minstrel Roosevelt and a Māori chief—with the caption "Kapai all te same, Roosevelt!" ("Thanks all the same, Roosevelt!" in mock pidgin).[66] Such performances of translation laid bare the gaudy, showbizzy bad faith of the Imperial enterprise, exposing the New Zealand state's eagerness to debase its own mana and to pimp Māori for the chance to share in wealth and global dominance.

THE GREAT WHITE FLEET AND
THE GREAT WHITE WAY

The immediate political dividends of the tour for U.S. interests in the Pacific were uncertain. Historians have argued that it precipitated rather than prevented a global arms race, that it antagonized rather than pacified a delicate international balance of power. The U.S. welcome in Japan perhaps even gave diplomatic cover to Japanese expansionism, the very outcome it was designed to forestall.[67] For New Zealanders, the event—in stark contrast to the landmark 1901 Royal Tour—was quickly forgotten, warranting barely a footnote in histories despite its momentous scale and impact on civic life (Auckland declared a citywide holiday, and Parliament sessions in Wellington were suspended for nearly a week). The nation's brief dalliance with the American Empire is now a forgotten future of the past.

"KAPAI ALL TE SAME ROOSEVELT!"

"Kapai all te same Roosevelt!": a cartoon from the *Auckland Weekly News* pictures Roosevelt as a Māori chief, in minstrel pose.

In America, however, Roosevelt's "great show" seized the public imagination at a moment in which the achievement of an American-dominated global order, anchored in the Pacific, seemed at once glimmeringly possible, entirely imminent, and continuously imperiled. It aligned with an evolving regional imaginary: the American Pacific.[68] A compounded genealogy of projections of and into the Pacific, the American Pacific was, from the outset, markedly theatrical and singularly spectacular: from the exalted, elemental brutality of primitive accumulation in Melville's "dirty, yet somehow vast and magical Pacific" to the hedonistic, surf-licked South Seas narrated by Margaret Mead, Robert Flaherty, and numberless touters of tourist pleasures.[69] It encompasses both the ambivalent pluralism of Cold War Broadway's *South Pacific* fantasy and a contemporary infatuation with the "friction-free" flow of capital and entertainment commodities through the polyglot urban nodes of a dramatically compressed "Asia-Pacific," facilitated by Asia-Pacific Economic Cooperation (APEC).[70] An ongoing "act of wary social fantasy," the American Pacific has functioned as an enduring spatial figure of Euro-American self-identity, a sublime vision of illimitable expansion carried on currents of hyperbole, paranoia, passion, primitivism, arcadianism, Orientalism, and sheer sleaze.[71]

Like Edward Said's Orient, this geographical imaginary was textured, animated, and organized by a logic of race.[72] But Orientalism was binary in form, whereas the American Pacific was triangulated, multiform, even rhizomatic. Orientalism was a practice of representation, an apparatus of discursive command that legitimated the material operations of imperial geopolitics before and after the fact. In contrast, the American Pacific performatively constituted its geopolitical projections through mobility itself, through journeys—actual and virtual, actualizing and virtualizing—in both hemispheric directions. Unlike the hermetic and self-referential spectacularity of Said's Orient, this materially dynamic quality made the American Pacific more porous to the unauthorized imaginings and to the transitory and often unpredictable solidarities generated by American Pacific peoples on the move.

If Roosevelt's goal was to "impress" the American people with their new identity as a global elect, he manifestly succeeded. The United States embarked on a nationwide festival of global imagining—Fleet Fever!—that registered most powerfully in the communication and entertainment industries, those desiring machines and information networks that gave shape to American Empire and its subjects. The taste of an American Pacific offered by the spectacular tour parlayed into a taste for Oriental and Pacific adventure with a naval theme in the mammoth melodramas offered at the New York Hippodrome the following season.

The Hippodrome loomed on the front line of America's consumer, entertainment, and information revolution, a hinge between the vernacular entertainment of the nineteenth century and Global Hollywood's interpellation of a mass subject.[73] The largest theater in the world, or so publicists claimed, this "palace of the people" boasted an auditorium of over five thousand seats and a stage that could (and regularly did) hold a ballet corps of four hundred dancers, fifty horses, ten elephants, and sets of an opulence and scale that defied the turn-of-the-century imagination. It was touted by its army of publicists as a "national and nationalizing" theater, one that in its affordable service to the New York masses epitomized both the benefits and entitlements of consumer, corporate democracy. Heralding the onset of the "department store style of theatre," it also exemplified the frictionless flow of mass production itself, manufacturing and distributing fantasy at an economy of scale.[74] The Hippodrome's stock-in-trade of exotic melodramas promised imaginative transport to a dream-world of superabundance, pleasure, and enchantment that all could buy, ranging from the Orient to Mars, from ancient Atlantis to a gloriously global science-fiction future: "You went into the Hippodrome in the sunlight, and when you came out there were stars in the sky. But you had lived in those hours through a lifetime of adventure. You had been to foreign lands, at the circus, under the sea, in a balloon."[75] The enterprise's mastermind was the father of Coney Island, Fred Thompson, who had made his first million at World's Fairs, the other landmark on the entertainment horizon of Empire that similarly united tourism and theater in the transcendent figuration of global space. In a scenic profusion of robots, monorails, blimps, balloons, and box-kite planes, technology and transport were yoked together under the rubric of cosmopolitan fantasy.[76] The Hippodrome's nexus of industry, entertainment, and communication promised— like the Fleet's tour—to usher in a national modernity that was affective, inclusive, and expansive rather than hermetic, territorial, or homogenizing like the sovereign modernity of old.

In this spirit, the Hippodrome also commandeered the cachet of the circus, both in its name and in the spectacular centerpieces of its programs.

As cultural historians such as Janet Davis have argued, circus perform-ance's exaltation of freedom, mobility, and exotica placed travel at the core of both its attractions and its mode of production. Circus was a metonym of, model for, and force behind not only the corporatization and depro-vincialization of America—with tours closely linked to the expanding rail-road and communications network, linking the productive breadth of America—but also its imperial ambitions. Traveling circus acts brought the spectacular diversity of Empire (as well as its race, gender, and labor poli-tics) to the nation's doorstep. At the same time, they were instrumental in the domestic extension of Empire's mobile frontier. (The affinity between the technologies of entertainment and expansionism was made explicit when the War Department adopted the traveling circus's regimented en-campment operation as a model.)[77] The Hippodrome localized the mobile energies of the circus in the urban topography of New York, its "global sen-sory blitz" consolidating "the nation's identity as a modern industrial soci-ety and world power."[78] As Hardt and Negri argue, the communications industries "integrate the imaginary and the symbolic within the biopoliti-cal fabric, not merely putting them at the service of power but actually integrating them into its very functioning."[79]

THE WORLD ON STAGE AT THE HIPPODROME

In its few brief years of commercial success and public acclaim, the Hippo-drome was a barometer of the temporal rhythms of American modernity. Capturing the ephemeral figures of fashion and news as they circulated in the nation's mediascape, its productions were constantly in step with the preoccupations of the emergent mass public they addressed, and in address-ing, helped to conjure. The 1909 season was no exception. Its two featured melodramas, *Inside the Earth* and *A Trip to Japan*, playfully revisited the political events of the preceding summer, bizarrely refracting the current affairs, fervent aspirations, and recent history of the American Pacific, as if in a hall of fun-house mirrors.[80]

The first of these, *A Trip to Japan*, was a lurid confection revolving around a nefarious plot to steal U.S. military secrets and sell them to the Japanese. When the *Siege of Port Arthur* had been staged at the Hippodrome some years earlier at the conclusion of the Russo–Japanese War, public opin-ion had favored Japanese pluck and courage against the imperial muscle of Russia. In the spirit of the times, the fascination with japonaiserie and Japanese military modernity persisted in *A Trip to Japan*, but it was matched by a simmering suspicion of the newfound ally's political and territorial aspirations. The plot follows the fortunes of shipbuilder Hiram Dixon, who has built a submarine for the U.S. Navy, to be tested by Lieutenant Dick Gordon, also the suitor for Dixon's daughter Dolly's hand in marriage. Unbeknownst to either of the men, the plans have been stolen by Dixon's manager, Sharpe, who has constructed two additional submarines to sell to the Japanese government. Under cover of a touring circus, traveling at the behest of the Mikado to entertain the American Fleet on its arrival in Japan, the two craft are secretly dispatched to Tokyo. There the plan is uncovered and (after a spectacular chase scene, armed combat with Japanese gangs, and the conflagration of a teahouse) all is set to rights.

Symptomatically, the melodrama's crisis is precipitated by an unauthorized crossing of commerce and military force, when Sharpe (the Yankee entrepreneur on the make) plots with Japanese businessman Yamamora to sell the craft.[81] The play's outcome suggests that these kinds of global flows need to be channeled to their legitimate ends by state regulation: the threat is allayed by the heroic intervention of Gordon and his sailors, while the culprits are punished by the Japanese government, which promises to restore the illegally obtained submarines to the inventor. In classically melodramatic mode, legitimating revelations of paternity and the narratological and juridical closure of heterosexual union seal the resolution: Mary (the tightrope-walking belle of the circus) is proved to be the daughter of the American consul himself; she can thus happily wed Tom Dixon, the inventor's son. Meanwhile, the U.S. government's (fortuitously telegraphed) approval of the submarine design leaves Gordon free to marry Dolly Dixon. Uncle Sam hastens and blesses the unions, which occur against the backdrop of the Fleet's triumphantly spectacular welcome in the Japanese ports.

Of course, the scale of Hippodrome productions and the absence of amplification technology meant that only the scantest details of the plot were communicable to the audience by dialogue. Instead, the plot operated as a loosely hinged vehicle for patriotic spectacle. As a component of the communication apparatus of Empire, the Hippodrome specialized in the production and manipulation of affects, and it did so in perfect harmony with the press and state sponsors of the previous year's diplomatic spectacle. Hit chorus numbers such as "Every Girl Loves a Uniform" and

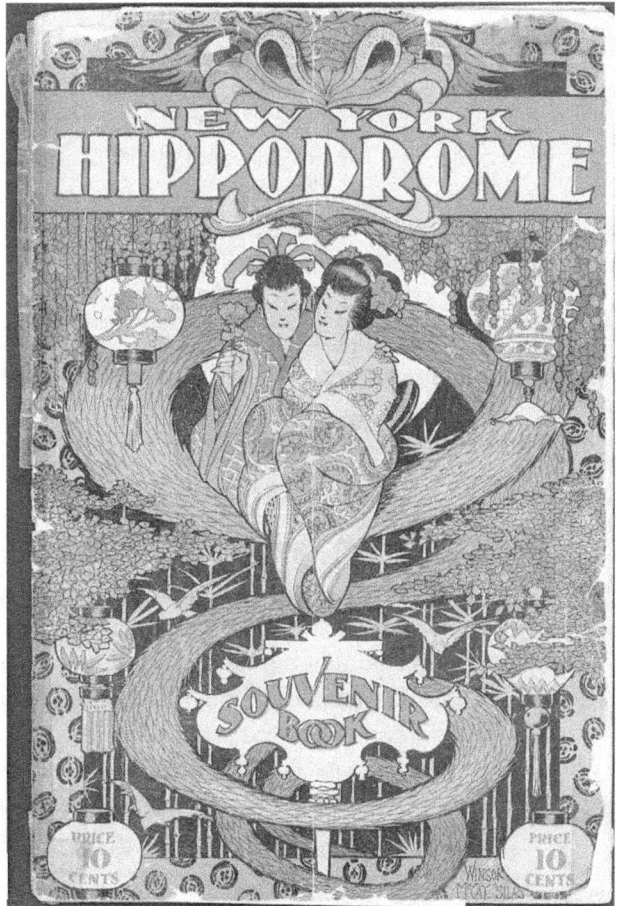

Postcard of the New York Hippodrome (property of the author) and the souvenir program cover of *A Trip to Japan.* Alexander Turnbull Library, Wellington, New Zealand.

"Our Navy's the Best in the World" were sung to the sight of a ship weighing anchor in the Hippodrome's onstage tank, a naval procession staged against the backdrop of the illuminated New York skyline, and a scenic montage of smoke-tossing battleships on the open sea.

Even more marked, however, was the theater's presentation of opportunities for virtual tourism. The scenes included a stage replica of the Mikado's palace, elegant teahouses with scores of dancing geishas and lantern ceremonies, and street scenes of Tokyo, for which the stage directions note, "merchants sell their wares, people enter to buy goods, sailors come on in rickshaws, American tourists in sedan chairs, sight seers and circus performers."[82] Proof positive that tourism was a creature of the industrial imagination as much as a practice of actual travel, the Hippodrome productions participated in its déjà vu semiotic economy, whereby a site or sight achieves destination recognition through the repeated replication of its image.[83] "The wonder of the trip," one regular declared, "lay in the fact that every place the group visited looked exactly as one had been led to suppose it ought to look."[84] For the Americans who saw their surrogate doubles on stage, touristic prerogative segued seamlessly, and with interpellative force, into the busy scene of global commerce and military advancement. Seizing on the symbolic capital of the previous year's actual events, the chorus numbers were rife with Fleet tour catchphrases, from the cry of the sailors ("For guns or rollicking / For fight or frolicking / Our Navy's the best in the world") to the declamation of the circus workers, foot soldiers of the culture industry: "We're going away to far Japan / A jolly good time it is going to be. . . . We ought to win a big success / We'll try to do the best we can."[85]

While the actual mediated melodrama of the Fleet tour ended with a triumphant welcome in Japanese ports and the rapprochement of the Root–Takahira Agreement, in the Hippodrome the Eastern threat was ritually disarmed not so much by the heroic machinations of the state as by the mass production of scenes of military might and by offering Japan to the virtual tourist gaze as a site of leisure, pleasure, and entertainment. The principle of the freedom of capital enshrined in the Root–Takahira agreement was echoed in the freedom of movement celebrated by the show's characters: the world they inhabited was penetrable, navigable, and available, suffused with the fungible sentiment and manufactured goodwill of tourism. The lyrics of the final chorus, in unalloyed touristic cliché, announced the extent to which this affective tourist capital could be appropriated and circulated: "Fair land of Japan! / You've a beauty no other possesses, / You're quite ichiban, / And their happiness here, / Each with pleasure confesses. / *You'll ever remain, / In the heart of each maiden and man!*"[86]

While *A Trip to Japan* closely followed the arc traced by the Fleet's spectacular tour, the second melodrama on the Hippodrome's bill conjured another American Pacific territory through the force of sheer fantasy. This territory was no less receptive to the American imagination. In fact, *Inside the Earth* unfolded as a fantasy of ultimate penetration: touristic, commercial, and bizarrely literal. The short melodrama was an old-fashioned blood and thunder fantasy classic, with none of the songs or circuses or tongue-in-cheek flair of *A Trip to Japan*. It followed the adventures of American miners in New Zealand, which it figured as a far-western outpost of Empire, inhabited only by friendly Māori tribes and a few doughty Yankee entrepreneurs. Guided by a fifty-strong force of Māori whom they have befriended, miner Dave Allen and his colleagues venture into the center of the earth to rescue one of their womenfolk, who was abducted by the Sun King and his dwarfish henchmen and imprisoned in his magnificent stronghold. With the Freudian suggestibility promised by the melodrama's subtitle ("A Fantastic Play"), the Sun King not only inhabits a city in the nether parts of the netherworld, "a city where the sun never shines" (as the program tellingly notes), but also appears as a misplaced Aztec, attended by dwarves who speak no English but are apparently fluent in Māori. In other respects, the racial coding of the narrative is entirely predictable: the Māori warriors dutifully promise to follow hero Dan Willoughby "wherever he shall lead them," and the mission resolves into a quest to rescue "the white woman," Rose Allen, whom the Aztec king intends to force into marriage.

The headliners were the fifty Māori performers contracted for the season and "imported" from New Zealand by the Hippodrome management: migrant touristic labor and ethnic commodities from this new node in the American Pacific's transnational network. The show opened on a scene of festivities in a Māori village, advertised in the press as "the splendor of the antipodes, the home life and customs of savage peoples from distant climes . . . faithfully portrayed."[87] Reproducing the performances enjoyed by the Fleet officers a year before were many of the same Māori entertainers who had hosted them. The performers reprised popular numbers from the variety program that, as part-time tourism workers, they might have performed for tourists on the stage of Rotorua's town hall.[88] They demonstrated Māori "sports and pastimes," chants, dances, and speeches of welcome (karanga, haka, and whaikōrero), followed by poi (a song and dance form performed by the women, involving twirling balls of flax on long strings, to both percussive and visual effect). Most famous, however, was the haka, the unique chant and rhythmic posture dance that Hippodrome publicists described as a "war dance," misnaming it to evoke the familiar evolutions of stage Indians in U.S. melodrama. In every one of the season's 447 performances, the haka interludes that punctuated the pursuit of the Sun King's dwarves brought down the house, bestowing on the New York audience the self-same spectatorial rewards of South Seas tourism that the sailors had enjoyed the year before.

In a gesture that closed the distance between the soft politics of show business and the hard politics of military imperialism, between virtual and actual tourism, high-ranking naval officers were invited as honored guests to witness this simulacral translation of their diplomatic act. They were in New York harbor for the Hudson–Fulton celebrations, commemorating both the three hundredth anniversary of Henry Hudson's "discovery" of the Hudson River and the one hundredth anniversary of the first successful steamboat by Robert Fulton, replicating in a domestic frame the Fleet's triumphalist celebration of unhindered mobility and the conquest of space as rite of whiteness.[89] The cries of "banzai" and "hangey" that greeted the Māori on stage from a mingled audience of sailors and New Yorkers—the broadened public witnessing and affirming this machine of expansionist, techno-commercial command—were read as a study in international harmony. "Peace is built this way," the papers confidently declared.[90]

TE HAERE KI AMERIKA:
A DIPLOMATIC MISSION, A TOURISTIC PLEASURE

The performers were mostly Ngāti Whakaue residents of Ōhinemutu village in Rotorua, assembled under the supervision of Frederick Bennett, the future Māori Archbishop of New Zealand.[91] Many were likely involved in Bennett's Mission Choir, which performed weekly in Rotorua for tourist and local audiences, presenting variety programs of ethnographic tableaux, Māori song and dance forms, and religious and popular song (in both

Māori and English). The choir also toured the country to raise funds for various reform efforts related to the work of the Young Māori Party (of which Bennett was a prominent member) and as ambassadors for the liberal Māori modernity proposed by that body: temperate, industrious, disciplined, and self-governing, secure in Christian probity but also deeply grounded in Māori values and history. The group's ethnically inflected liberal virtues were clearly legible in the repertoire choices, polished ensemble work, and conduct of the troupe in (and out of) performance. So, when Apirana Ngata organized the Māori Congress, a major conference in Wellington the year prior to the tour that aimed to put the party's strategies for Māori development in the public (and parliamentary) eye, the Mission Choir's evening performance was not mere entertainment but formed a crucial part of the program's argument.

A publicity still of the Māori performers at the New York Hippodrome. Photograph, R. H. Burnside Collection. New York Public Library.

The traveling performers took this image of a disciplined and vigorous Māoridom abroad on a new Māori mission—a mission in equal parts diplomacy, tourism, exploration, and good (show) business. The descendants of these performers, many of whom still participate in the unbroken tradition of Arawa cultural and touristic diplomacy established by their forebears, spoke eloquently to me of the group's likely motives in their travels.[92] Some of the party told reporters in New York that they were there to enjoy a "vacation," and curiosity and adventure no doubt played a part for many of these reverse tourists. Likewise, experience in America would have been understood as advantageous to the iwi (extended kin group), not only in publicizing Rotorua as a destination to the Americans but also in enriching concert-party work back home through exposure to different audiences and other performers.

Most significantly, however, the trip was seen as an ambassadorial responsibility and opportunity. An announcement in a Māori newspaper describes the trip as the fulfillment of a reciprocal agreement made with the visiting Americans: the party was to have their passages paid for and would be welcomed by the Americans as they had welcomed the visitors the year before. "This is a momentous occasion for Te Arawa to be embarking on such an illustrious journey," the article declared.[93] For a community that understood their participation in tourism as representing Arawa mana and vitality, Te Haere ki Amerika (the journey to America) offered an opportunity to garner international recognition. As a descendant of one of the group's leaders put it to me, "Our people saw the future. The pathway was to tell the people of the world that we were alive, that we were more than primitives."[94] No matter what lens of prejudice or ignorance may have tainted the Americans' perception of the group, this leader argued, they would have borne this mana with them, made manifest in the ihi and wehi of their performance (the intensity of presence and the awe, fear, and excitement it inspired in their audience). It was a message of vitality, modernity, and relevancy that the New Zealand state's ventriloquist welcome of the year before had manifestly failed to deliver; the group grasped the opportunity to forge new connections, unencumbered by the biopolitical constraints that reigned at home.

Some indication of the gravity of this kaupapa, or mission, was given by the choice of leaders: Kiri Matao and Kiwi Te Amohau. Kiri Matao was a woman of formidable mana, sixty-six at the time of the tour and a well-established force in and beyond the Rotorua region (she died in 1913).[95] Kiri Matao was no stranger to high-profile diplomacy: she was known as the Duchess, having charmed the Duke of Edinburgh on his visit to Ōhinemutu in 1876. She had also led the haka pōhiri (the welcome haka) for the Duke and Duchess of Cornwall and York in 1901. Unusually for a woman—a mark of her exceptional status—she was trained in the art of the taiaha (a fighting staff, brandished in battle and in ceremonial display) and on occasion performed the wero (challenge). Te Kiwi was indisputably a rangatira, a leader, called te ahi rangatira, the shining light of all the iwi of Te Arawa. He was a prominent figure in the church and (as the son of Paora Te Amohau) a descendant of an illustrious political lineage, who displayed all the gifts of his rangatira status. He was, for example, a master carver—Tunohopu, the magnificent ceremonial house (whare whakairo) he carved still stands in Ōhinemutu. If some in Rotorua had been skeptical about the venture (these American entrepreneurs came with no guarantee of their intentions), the choice of leaders indicated that the mana of Arawa would be upheld.[96]

The previous half-century had seen numerous international forays by Māori performers mostly to Australia and Britain, where their status as the native race "belonging" to the New Zealand state or the Crown was an established fact for their audiences. The context of American Empire, however, allowed the group to assert a different political character. One paper quotes Kiwi Te Amohau explaining, "'The Maoris are the only people England ever fought and did not conquer'—and he added diplomatically, 'except the Irish and the Americans.'"[97] So successful was he in enlisting American's recognition of an autonomous Māoridom, with these strategic appeals to American patriotism and antimonarchical sentiment, that when Ward, New Zealand's Premier, visited New York only a week later, he had little choice but to endorse the American press's assumption of Māori rangatiratanga, or absolute chieftainship. Ward was briefly in New York on his return from the Imperial Conference in London (where the topics of debate had included the future of the Commonwealth Pacific, defense commitments, imperial communications, and the possibility of federating the Commonwealth settler states). Echoing Te Kiwi's words with uncanny precision, the press reported Ward stating that "these, his . . . constituents" were "the only unconquered race in the world, for while Maoris have engaged in many a terrible warfare, they have never yet been overcome."[98] The statement was a subtle embarrassment to a politician whose assimilationist government's reputation rested on its claim to have "managed" the "native problem."

URBAN PERFORMANCE FROM
BROADWAY TO CONEY ISLAND

The group had slipped the yoke of race's biopolitical entanglements—at least those binding them to the New Zealand state. But what other racial topographies did it navigate in its journey? How did its projection of ethnic signs and sentiment translate? The group was indeed a perplexing amalgam of exemplary liberal conduct—exhibiting civility, self-moderation, and all the virtues usually attributed to normative white subjects—and ethnic defiance, in their evident martial prowess, claims to unceded sovereignty, and the pride with which they wore the badge of their culture in the Imperial city. Meanwhile, the cosmopolitan savoir faire they exercised as tourists and their coding as stage personas broadcast yet other contradictory messages.

For reviewers of the Hippodrome season, the semiotics of ethnological show business, circus primitivism, and stage exoticism became hopelessly confused as they grappled with this novel spectacle. Were the Māori savages, primitives, or exotics? The *New York Press*, for example, described them "wearing animal skins" (against all visual evidence), while others drew on Orientalist conventions. The *New York American* described the men as "clad Salome fashion" (presumably with reference to a biblical stage-Orient of bare chests, skirts, and spears).[99] To seasoned showbiz hacks, the Māori presence seemed to release a new infusion of theatrical capital and skilled labor into circulation, detached from its ethnic value: it was not their native authenticity but their accomplishment as performers that provided an "object lesson" to chorus directors everywhere in grace, precision, and rhythmic accuracy.[100] Poi was even seized upon as an alienable performance commodity and appeared in subsequent Hippodrome seasons divorced from its Māori origins.[101]

The unsettling effects of racial translation were more marked outside the bounds of the theater itself, as the momentum of this circuit between theatrical politics and spectacular theater propelled its ethnic properties into a second life in the civic spaces of the metropolis. The Hippodrome productions imagined for New Yorkers their diplomatic, military, and commercial presence in the Pacific, inviting them to witness and ratify that imagined world order through their participation as virtual tourists. Yet as much as the Hippodrome's spectacularity stabilized and enframed the American Pacific, it also *mobilized*, inaugurating new forms of interpenetration, collision, encounter, and alliance—producing the American Pacific as a space of circulation, enacted on the stage of New York's urban topography.[102] Surreal South Seas scenes made New Yorkers tourists in their own city as Māori "spontaneously" performed in the streets, museums, and meeting halls of Manhattan for an audience of journalists and passersby, and their performances were dutifully reperformed in a local press well managed by the Hippodrome's public relations machine.

The theater's opening publicity gambit was to stage the Māori performers' arrival in the metropolis as an act of reciprocal tourism. Ten of their number had been detained in quarantine in San Francisco and arrived in New York to join their compatriots by a later train.[103] The two groups greeted one another near Madison and Forty-fourth, in front of Saint Bartholomew's church, carrying ceremonial weaponry and dressed in traditional mats, cloaks, and piupiu (flax skirts). Their passionate display astounded New Yorkers. They performed a haka in greeting to each other, followed by tearful embraces and hongi (touching noses), making the astonished commuters "drop their cocktails" and the baggage wranglers of Grand Central Station stand stock-still in their tracks.[104] As they proceeded through the city, "at intervals . . . they shouted their war cries and shook war clubs and spears at the surprised inhabitants of Manhattan." Yet they also smiled "amiably" and shook the hands of spectators in a "cordial . . . *Anglo Saxon*" way.[105]

Seated in two sightseeing automobiles and accompanied by an American brass band, the Māori took in the sights of New York City, from Grand Central Station to Dreamland and Luna Park, while New Yorkers took in the sight of the strangers and assessed the physiques of their menfolk ("stalwart and of a bronze color").[106] In a wry play on the cosmopolitan fantasy of reciprocity that underlay touristic diplomacy of the era, it was unclear in these exchanges of gaze who was the tourist and who was the spectacle. At intervals during the season, other events—spectacles begotten of spectacles—brought the Māori visitors into the metropolitan field of vision. These included a visit to the American Museum of Natural

History for an emotional reunion with alienated tribal treasures. In another example, a regal Waapi Tungi Yates was seated on the podium of a major suffrage meeting at Carnegie Hall alongside Emmeline Pankhurst and Harriot Stanton Blatch, as an exemplar of voting womanhood (New Zealand women, Māori women included, had won the franchise in 1893).

Yet perfect reciprocity could only remain elusive given the force of the United States' own racializing apparatuses. These sights simultaneously democratized the benefits of the American Pacific's new cultural economy and theatrically contained a minor reflux in the global flows initiated by the incorporation of New Zealand into the American Pacific, by framing the events as spectacular, savage anomalies in the heart of civilization. Moreover, the metropolitan journey the Māori made also intersected unpredictably and ambivalently with other regimes of racial logic. What were New Yorkers to make of the Māori visitors' encounter with the Filipino performers resident in an ethnological exhibit at Coney Island (the Hippodrome's sister site)? Was this affinity or difference, solidarity or distance? The newspapers reported that the party was "especially interested" in the Bontoc exhibition and that "arrangements" were under negotiation to locate the Māori at Greater Dreamland the following summer, "in a reproduction of their New Zealand habitation."[107]

Such reports characterized Māori as at once spectators, actors, exhibits, and entrepreneurs, conflating racially assigned roles in ways that destabilized the geographical imaginary that practices of exhibition worked to secure. (It is worth recalling, for example, that Jamestown—the highly symbolic point of origin for the Great White Fleet—also sported a Filipino exhibit, orchestrated to endorse the American civilizing mission in its new colony.) Were readers to understand the "exhibits" in those native villages as, like Māori, migrant theatrical labor on the circuits of Empire? Or were Māori, like Filipinos, trophies of imperial conquest? The accounts unwittingly illuminated the messy middle ground between the two species of competing imperialism.

On other occasions, the Māori performers' status as entertainers and tourists sat uncomfortably with their theatrical roles. One paper attributed the difficulty they had in finding lodging to the barely tamed savagery they exhibited onstage. It may have had much more to do with the ambiguity of their racial classification as migrant laborers in the segregated accommodations of New York City.[108] The Māori performers were quick to recognize the gravity of technologies of racial categorization and to adopt the same strategies of exception that Te Rangi Hīroa had done before the Fleet officers. "The only thing that can rouse Maori to the old savage instinct," one paper remarked (rhetorically classifying them in the same gesture as it troubled that classification), "is to mistake them for 'colored people,'" adding that they appeared to compromise if compared to Indians or Filipinos.[109]

Outside the determining frame of the state, race itself seemed set in motion, intimating affinities, connectivities, and differentiations that encompassed the breadth of the new geopolitical purview of Empire. The press's taxonomization of Māori ranged from a "bronze color" (distinguished from American Indians by the absence of a "red tint"), to "café au lait color" ("almost like the Japanese"), to "very light colored, almost white."[110] On the one hand, this was a classic example of *translatio imperii*, the "colonial quotation" that naturalizes imperial expansion by encompassing the newly discovered within the domain of the already known and already othered.[111] On the other, it proved the force of global liberalism's norming impetus. They were at once assimilable and already assimilated, indigenous and exotic, but (the press insisted) quiet, temperate, and church-going. Waapi apparently began to receive marriage proposals in numbers, while the other girls became quite fashionable and took to the New York dating scene.[112]

Ultimately, however, the press's confusion demonstrates not only how protean and pervasive such classificatory frameworks were but also how little purchase they had on subjects on the move across the terrain of Empire. The racial axes of the American-Pacific imaginary were constituted not through spectacle's power to definitively *locate* the subject in a given grid of racial, spatial, and geopolitical relations but through its mobilizing force. This was an inherently performative process: the nomadic, theatrical acts of the performer–tourists across the already theatricalized terrain of the city produced its putatively immutable racial facts. The racial topography of the city was forged in these transversal, theatrical crossings, its social imaginaries produced in tourist acts and actualized in the imaging of spectacle: "They looked like Broadway until they put on their mats and brandished their spears for a photograph, and then they were as wild as Coney Island."[113]

The presence of these unclassifiable strangers was also a litmus test of the global translatability of American Empire's liberal commitments. Was seeing Waapi Tungi Yates and Kiri Matao on the stage of the suffrage meeting an uncomfortable reminder to a women's movement that had recently renounced its commitment to black women's suffrage? Were they the sign of a truly international solidarity of sisterhood? Or a cry of "silent reproach" to white America, pointing out that even the brown savages of the South Pacific enjoyed a prerogative of citizenship not permitted to the educated echelons of Yankee womanhood?[114] The press posed an answer: tourism, they seemed to suggest, would precipitate the formation of global ideoscapes, which would hold liberal ideals to account, even as travelers' trajectories through New York's urban spaces traced the inevitable, and uncomfortable, refluxes between the national metropolis and the American Pacific. One feature in the *World* recalled Macaulay's famous "New Zealander" of the future. Remarking on the urbanity of the Māori women attending the meetings, the journalist quipped that Macaulay's tourist "may now be replaced by the figure of a Māori suffragette skirting Central Park New York in a taxicab, taking notes for a magazine article on the ruins of a bygone social system by which the American Woman once suffered in bondage as 'wife,' 'mother' or married slave."[115] Macaulay's mythic tourist once more yoked anxieties regarding race to those surrounding sovereignty, indexing tourism's complicity with intimations of global liberalism's peril and promise.

SPECTACULAR POLITICS, SPECTACULAR PRODUCTIVITY

These visions of Māori suffragettes, entrepreneurs, tourists, and flaneurs belied the claim to triumphant, mythic clarity made by the tour of the Great White Fleet. The spectacular idiom of the Fleet's tour had tacitly acknowledged that representational stabilization was not only impossible but also inappropriate to the emergent dynamic of the Imperium. Indeed, the performances examined here—the welcome, the tour, the Hippodrome's melodramas, and the urban performances—were born of a system of circulation (touristic, theatrical, economic, and human) that they momentarily crystallized and lent a further refractory momentum.

In the performance sequence initiated by Roosevelt's grand gesture, we see the lineaments of what later scholars would call fluid modernity, the smooth space of capital flow imagined by the totalizing project of global liberalism.[116] We also see a stark reminder that technologies of race formed the pathways of that flow. Racial affects and effects bound the social imaginaries, the connectivities and collectivities upon which states and citizens acted, and they composed the field of forces—the affinities and attractions, the repulsions or blockages—through which bodies, information, and capital moved. If tourism operated as a generative and motive technology of this system, performance was its more general medium. No easy conclusion, however, follows from this observation: tracing performance through American Pacific circuits reveals not only the classificatory authority of such social imaginaries as race but also their frangible, labile, and porous quality. Performance analysis lays bare how mobilities and agencies are racially circumscribed, but it also points us to the navigational tactics and nomadic acts through which subjects traversed the terrain of Empire, and occasionally even to the places where they jumped tracks.

This chapter's attention to performance genres of translation and spectacle has labored to refine our understanding of this process's liberal dynamics. Translation, as Homi Bhabha has argued, "is the performative nature of cultural communication. . . . The sign of translation continually tells, or 'tolls' the different times and spaces between cultural authority and its performative practices."[117] Just as every mimetic enunciation is a translation, every translation is also a mimetic enunciation, a sign of the theatricality necessarily produced by bodies (and capital and ideas) on the move. In line with the majoritarian, territorial myth of the nation form, the global regime of liberal modernity takes as its translational premise an ideal of equality and ultimate transparency between distinct languages. It holds that each nation is bounded, unified, unique, static, and commensurable with every other nation.[118] Translation is both generative of this imaginary and, in turn, erodes it; it puts meaning in motion, making every statement and every gesture available to misperception, deception, or a multitude of divergent conceptions. In the words of Paul de Man, translation "puts the original in motion to decanonize it, giving it the movement of fragmentation, a wandering of errance, a kind of permanent exile."[119] And as figures such as Te Rangi Hīroa (or Mita Taupopoki, Admiral Sperry, Kiwi Te Amohau, or countless others) show us, the subject of translation, the one who translates, is a "subject in transit," a performer who navigates and shapes the textured, often treacherous terrain of power between worlds in motion.[120]

Rethinking translation in this way, with an eye to spaces of dissent, digression, or even just faint disturbance produced in performance limns an alternative understanding of communication and community in Imperial modernity. The small acts of transmission and traduction at the core of vast geopolitical movements are not mere accidents of history to be set against a transparently stable international, translational ideal. Instead, they are key to understanding global modernity's geopolitical imagination differently: as a mobile and fractal process, a racially motivated process, with performance—exigent, ephemeral, subjunctive, productive, and transformative—at its heart.

Likewise, spectacle's centrality to the globalizing processes I have detailed demands that we understand it as a productive and dynamic force rather than dismiss it as reification or delusion. Spectacle is machinic rather than monumental, multivocal rather than monologic, not hegemonically totalizing but a mobile cultural formation vulnerable to the intransigence and momentum of the subjects it produces. The American Pacific needed spectacle, which fostered a taste leveled across lines of class and education, enabling a newly inclusive national solidarity—a solidarity that might be "grasped with the senses."[121] Its circuits crucially depended not just on the production of desire for the foreign commodity but also for the elsewhere itself, enacted through its virtualization and penetration by a subject at once consumer, actor, and audience. The tourist was this point of ingress into the phantasmagoria of the global scene, a conduit of imperial aspiration: the "lucky tar" welcomed by Māori in New Zealand, the New York bystander treated to a haka, the Māori traveler seeing the sights of Broadway, or the stage tourist in his rickshaw on the set of *A Trip to Japan.*

The Hippodrome season and the performances that preceded and succeeded it represent a pedagogy of imperialist and globalist progress through mobility. The process was palpably performative: in forging new connectivities between peoples and places, the here and the elsewhere, spectacle also forged a circuitry between the actual and the virtual. In materializing the imaginary, it imagined other materialities. It was affectively and effectively real, deriving its cultural power not only from its scale, its assault on the senses, or the institutional force that impelled it but also from its production of pleasures and from those pleasures' production of social collectivities. Above all, spectacle was in motion, overspilling the spatiotemporal borders of its stage, making visible the interplay between the forms of circulation—militarism, tourism, migration, and trade—with which it was enmeshed. Spectacle, at the dawn of the American Pacific, did not mask the social relations of imperial modernity; it constituted them, in their monstrous triumphalism as well as in their impure, chaotic motion and their permeability to localisms, collisions, displacements, or deceits.

The chapter that follows traces the ambivalent persistence of touristic spectacle as both a vehicle of the state's ventriloquist self-promotion and a medium for Māori claims in the global sphere. A century later, aspirations and anxieties surrounding sovereignty—national and cultural—still play out in the spectacular performances of tourism. Meanwhile, neoliberal policy has taken an anti-spectacular turn as state agents push for the invention of more intimate, interactive, "authentic" modes of performance in tourism. Aiming to establish new pathways for global circulation, these neoliberal modes of performance stand in stark contrast to the demotic, porous, liberal idiom of spectacle. They give rise not to collectivities but to new subjectivities (such as indigineity) that promise to supersede the sodalities and strictures of race while capturing the cultural productivity of citizens on behalf of the general welfare. But at what cost? And to whom?

chapter 4

Trafficking Race: Policy, Property, and Racial Reformation in the Tourist State

"All around New Zealand, a lot of Māori stories help us define this place and understand it, and where people have taken that up, it's made all the difference to the visitor. You'll come for the scenery, but you'll take away something else." So begins the narrator of *The Tourism Edge*, a twenty-minute promotional documentary produced by Tourism New Zealand's (TNZ's) Māori development team in 2005, intended for use by Regional Tourism Organizations (RTOs) and at industry conferences. TNZ is the state body that (in partnership with industry) coordinates and advises marketing efforts across the country and produces international publicity campaigns. *The Tourism Edge* is a part of a broader policy effort by this recently biculturalized state agency to help industry reimagine the shape of ethnic tourism, still dominated by formally staged attractions: concert-style performances, demonstrations, and themed cultural centers. In warm, chatty tones, it paints a picture of a different modality of ethnic tourism—intimate, immersive, and dialogic—that is not so much about "seeing the Māori" as "seeing through Māori eyes." What Māori have to offer to New Zealand tourism, it suggests, is not exotic entertainment or racial spectacle but the experience of a relationship with cultural difference. Either in the immediacy of the tourism encounter itself or in the broader domain of branding, Māori culture, the narrator bluntly claims, will "add value" to your business, transforming a mere commodity into an experience: "Adding even a small dimension of Māori culture gives that business a real edge."

Superimposing Māori-themed graphics over resplendent photographic panoramas, *The Tourism Edge* promises to harmonize national branding efforts, making Māori the key point of difference, paradoxically foundational and supplemental to the national (implicitly natural) experience: "New Zealand's biggest appeal is the natural landscape, no question—but what can Māori add? It's the history. It's where New Zealand began. If you haven't experienced that, you haven't experienced New Zealand."

For many Māori, within and outside the industry, the policy shift signaled by *The Tourism Edge* is long awaited and welcome. The video issues an implicit demand that Pākehā (non-Māori) publicly recognize the centrality of Māoritanga (Māori culture and lifeways) to the national symbolic as a core identity, not an exotic addendum or tradable ornament. In a post–Waitangi Tribunal era, when Māori enjoy newly assured rights over cultural property and tribal assets, it promises that they can participate, *on their*

The upscale aesthetic of *The Tourism Edge* linked Māori interpreters to landscape values.

own terms, in Aotearoa New Zealand's largest foreign-exchange-earning industry. It pictures a tourism industry informed by Māori values, particularly those pertaining to tribal rangatiratanga (self-determination, sovereignty, ownership, and control) and taonga (treasures, valued property). This would be an industry capable of communicating the experiential richness and complexity of Māori modernity to the visitor, not one presenting the hypostatized image of a confected, primitive "tradition." Māori would stand to benefit from this industry not only as entertainment labor but as entrepreneurs, sole proprietors of a cultural patrimony newly construed as "cultural capital." For other Māori, however, *The Tourism Edge*'s propositions more likely invite distrust: for generations of critics and activists, tourism epitomized the rapacity of Pākehā capital, intruding on indigenous lives, appropriating indigenous culture, trafficking it in deformed and demeaned versions, and all the while promoting the spectacle of happy, dancing natives to tacitly bless the state that robbed them.

This chapter details these far-reaching changes underway in Aotearoa New Zealand tourism, the political rationality that undergirds them, and the tensions and risks that attend them. The state's efforts promise not only to transform ethnic tourism, leaving behind the industry's former colonial dynamics and drawing Māori into a neoliberal economy replete with its own dangers and promises. They also promise to inflect *all* the nation's tourism with indigenous values. Such a move might prove a model for indigenous peoples the world over who look to tourism as a tool for development and cultural remediation but who fear for their cultural safety. It might also prove to be neocolonial business as usual, all the more insidious for the intimacy it promises with those who stand to be exploited. As far-reaching as such policy transformations may be, however, I suggest that ethnic tourism in New Zealand is the midwife of a much more fundamental change: a shift in the constitution of ethnic selves and solidarities in the neoliberal state. The lineaments of this shift are legible in a policy artifact such as *The Tourism Edge*.

The producers of *The Tourism Edge* are well aware of the residual distrust of tourism in Māori communities. In encouraging Māori to release cultural property into the market, to actively offer stories, language, and design elements for adoption by the broader Pākehā tourism sector, it allays fears about appropriation by embedding tourism's transactions in the thickness of social reciprocity. As the Māori proprietor of one guided-tour and homestay business states on the video, "It's not about exploitation. It's not about giving away anything, because you can't give anything away without your permission, I guess. But it's certainly about sharing and making a connection with other people." Pākehā, likewise, are encouraged to approach the trade in culture as a relational procedure that respects Māori cultural sovereignty: "It's important to see this as a mutual exchange—the stories, the heritage, the knowledge. The guardians of these things are the Māori people themselves, so it makes sense to speak to the right people."

It is not surprising that political and ethnic differences over tourism should focus on property. Indeed, debates over indigenous political recognition have historically, and globally, coalesced around claims to property rights as the proxy of human rights. Classical liberalism conjoined property, personhood, and sovereignty, and it did so in the context of both slavery and imperial expropriation. It defined its implicitly white subject as that man to whom the state guaranteed the right to "property in his own person" (Locke), while relegating its objects (indigenes or slaves) to the status *of* property, or while arguing that they were incapable of properly exploiting property (lands, goods, or their own labor capacity) and were thus best relieved of it. Liberalism, as Cheryl Harris has powerfully argued, understood whiteness itself as the "quintessential property for personhood," an attribute (like human capital or an individual's earnings potential from education) from which a subject could expect to accrue advantage.[1] Property and whiteness both, then, represent sovereignty delegated from the state to the individual. The irony is that insofar as indigenous groups have succeeded as claimants for rights to property (as they have in post–Waitangi Tribunal New Zealand) or have secured the right to "invent and image the race to which they belong" and thus to raise its property value, they have also faced expectations that they will participate in the entrepreneurial *and* racial norms of white liberal subjectivity.[2]

It is little surprise, then, that *The Tourism Edge*, in heralding the anxious birth of a new entrepreneurial Māori subject, also urges the dissolution of old ethnic differentiations. In the sharing of stories, music, and hospitality, the video's spokespeople argue, the host must "get to the heart of our guests—share who they are," cultivating a sense of *identity with* visitors. Toward the end of the video, the Māori proprietor states, "It's very touching to my European guests especially, because they have a strong sense of who they are. And they know who they are in terms of their indigeneity,

I guess. And they're coming to meet another indigenous people of another land, and so there's that connection. . . . Our hearts have met." Even a decade ago, such a statement—claiming a common "indigeneity" with a European tourist—would have been unimaginable, let alone promotable in a Māori- and state-produced policy instrument, so grounded was post-colonial Māori politics in the ethos of ethnoracial solidarity. However, in the context of contemporary agendas shared by Māori leaders and the neo-liberal state (regional revitalization, knowledge-economy excellence, and global competitiveness), ethnoracial identity frameworks premised on difference and exclusivity have outlived their usefulness. *The Tourism Edge* suggests, first, that certain ways of acting and feeling for other global subjects that are practiced in tourism (namely, identification) are more valid than others (the marking of difference); and second, that new economic value might flow from cultural commons (ethno-racial culture) that had previously been repositories of social negativity and resistance to both state and market. While *race*, then, becomes newly unthinkable, its porous, fungible, and valorizing heir, *indigeneity* (like the whiteness of old) has new currency as a property of the entrepreneurial subject.

This is a charged moment, presaging the surrender of closely defended political practices, passions, and positions. Pierre Bourdieu was neither the first nor the last to observe neoliberalism's tendency to systematically dismantle solidarities, be they unions, regionalisms, or racial and class blocs such as that formed by Māoridom for much of the twentieth century.[3] Others have detailed the neoliberal drive to enclose the cultural commons and bring the most intimate recesses of social, indeed political, experience into the domain of the market. The imminent danger, they argue, is the eclipse of loci that foster dissenting democratic alternatives and competing forms of value to neoliberal capital. For indigenous critics, the threat has particular trenchancy. Neoliberalism's incursions on tribal social and economic resources accelerate the processes of "accumulation by dispossession" in place since the colonial era and make political recognition contingent on the performance of standardized, valorized, and often individualized forms of identity and tradition that offer little resistance to capital's mandates.[4] Such processes seem doubly insidious when, as in Aotearoa New Zealand, they champion values such as self-governance, community, partnership with (rather than domination by) the state, and cultural rather than techno-cratic operating principles. Thus, neoliberalism adopts and co-opts the very terms on which indigenous struggles against colonialism have been waged. In Aotearoa, Treaty principles of rangatiratanga mean that state agencies form relationships with "responsibilized" iwi (extended kin group) bodies operating as the "third sector" agencies on which decentralized, downsized neoliberal states classically rely to deliver services that were previously the domain of public welfare.[5] Although maintained at arm's length, these relationships are nonetheless a conduit for the ethos, techniques, and even languages of the state to enter Māori communities, channeling collective energies away from opposition and into projects of "capacity building," "social entrepreneurship," or "adding value."[6] The liberal arts of racial separation, classification, and discipline are now outmoded; in their place this new regime of ethnogovernmentality creates the conditions by which Māori (with other New Zealanders) come to understand themselves as free but responsible to become "globally competitive" and to deploy an instrumentalized "culture" to that end.[7] The revolution in the tourism industry epitomizes this transition.

Even as *The Tourism Edge* incites its audience to perform ethnogovernmentality into being by crafting forms of ethnoracial conduct that look starkly unlike those of the previous generation, the video is also clearly addressed to the persisting racial dispositions of that generation. The desire to leave behind the old exploitations and exclusions, the rigidities and rules of race, to reap new benefits as proud entrepreneurs of a rich ancestral legacy chafes palpably—one suspects, painfully—against anxieties about the renewed alienation of property and the compromise of cultural sovereignty. This chapter concerns itself with precisely the frictions of this moment, with how people live torqued between the racial formations and subjectivities of settler welfare democracy and an incipient, putatively "postracial," order of the neoliberal state. Just as tourism was the site at which the former state most potently declared its racial (and racist) logic, it is now one of the key spaces in which this new state is being forged. It can, then, illuminate the "structures of feeling" of the neoliberal state in the making, the tension between residual, dominant, and emergent ways of experiencing cultural citizenship and between official culture and the practical consciousness of raced subjects.

I begin by examining cultural policy in Aotearoa New Zealand over the last decade, drawing on interviews with over two dozen policy analysts, state agents, Māori promoters, entrepreneurs, and managers who play a crucial role in brokering relationships between Māori constituencies, the market in culture, and the state.[8] Theorists argue that policy is performative: it works to bring into being the order of things it articulates. But policy also produces the conditions for particular kinds of performances: the frameworks, incitements, institutions, and beliefs about individual and collective betterment that create fields of possible, and profitable, action. I trace the policy moves that made culture central to the political rationality of Aotearoa New Zealand neoliberalism (as an attribute of its citizenry that could be cultivated, instrumentalized, and invested in by the state toward the end of improving national welfare) and thus turned tourism (the trade in culture) into its model technology. I go on to show how this centrality of culture provided Māori the opportunity to converge with, and indigenize, the changing national symbolic, the "languages [and logics] of stateness" that are produced and circulated in tourism.[9]

In the second half of this chapter, I engage with the performances elicited by policy in a concrete way. Since the turn of the twenty-first century and the beginning of state efforts to harmonize Māori tourism with the changing national brand, the contrast between residual Keynesian and emergent neoliberal policy idioms has been paralleled by a perceived contrast between two performance forms. The first of these, formally staged "concert-party" performance, is considered outdated by state tourism agents; its theatrical and populist aesthetic (forged in the colonial era of racial spectacle) is out of keeping with a sophisticated, entrepreneurial, upmarket image of Māori modernity. Meanwhile, policy favors a new generation of dialogic, interactive experiences of indigenous culture and heritage, such as those described in *The Tourism Edge*. I have dubbed this paradigm FIT tourism after the target consumer that market research has identified: the Free Independent Traveler (covered in detail later). Although FIT experiences are every bit as performative as their concert-party counterparts, FIT tourism is claimed as more "authentic" by virtue of its nontheatrical character. FIT performers are brokers and leaders of postneoliberal economic renaissance in their communities and the public imagineers of bicultural statehood abroad. But for Māori who must perform this act, "the tourism edge" can be a tightrope: they aim to secure Māori access to the benefits of tourism growth but must also sidestep, even heal, the painful histories of dispossession, appropriation, and racial derogation that Māori associate with the state's earlier promotion of tourism. It is in performance that this work is done; the boundary between marketable cultural material and exclusive tribal property, public and private, self and other, is constantly forged anew as tourism workers craft "cultural product" from lived experience through strategic choices of excision, selection, and narrative art.

Drawing on interviews and fieldwork with new-generation Māori tourism operations, along with performance analysis of older-generation concert tourism productions, I examine how performers navigate the fractures in bicultural neoliberalism's heroic vision. How do tourism workers understand the risks and potentials of brokering tribal futures through tourism? What occurs when the residual racial expectations of international tourists conflict with emergent articulations of Māori modernity and Māori tradition? How do Māori respond to pressures to detach indigeneity from race and to sanitize and depoliticize ethnic life, bringing it in line with neoliberalism's implicitly bourgeois norms? And why does the persistence of older tourism performance idioms seem ironically to provide Māori with a space of refuge from the state's new demands on cultural citizenship?

At stake here is an understanding of neoliberalism, not as a form of centralized power or fixed accomplishment, but as a dispersed set of precepts, arts, practices, and techniques of government, at work within, below, and beyond states. Governmental biopolitics, I have argued, finds its deepest purchase on subjects and socialities through biopoetic performance. Analyzing such performances, we can pose what Foucault understood as the most significant question facing analysts of governmentality: *what kind of tactical field, what specific agencies, does it present for ethical action?* It is a question, I contend, best answered in the specificity of ethnographic analysis, which can attune us to the singularity—and most importantly, to the inherent heterogeneity and incoherence—of a given neoliberal order. To recognize the ways in which other value systems, other modalities of conduct, endure in the midst of neoliberal governmentality's evolving future is to recognize neoliberalism not as an instrument of rule but as a field of struggle.[10]

POLICY, PERFORMATIVITY, AND
THE RISE OF THE CULTURAL STATE

Knowledge based industries are New Zealand's future. Many of them will be predicated on, and marketed, using our national identity—an identity which successive governments have paid only the most cursory of policy attention to. Cultural capital is an undeveloped economic resource. It is also an essential condition of humanity.

—RUTH HARLEY

For the half-century following World War I, inbound tourism numbers remained consistently low, with the scant state resources devoted to the industry spent maintaining infrastructure for the domestic rites of (largely Pākehā) leisure: hiking tracks, national parks, and so on. When a slump in agricultural exports coincided with the onset of jet travel in the late 1960s, however, tourism first presented itself as a possible economic recovery mechanism. The state stepped in as primary investor, and New Zealand entered the mass tourism era as a stopover on trans-Pacific flights. Travel companies offered package itineraries that paired the natural splendors of fjords or alps with the "Polynesian mystique" of Rotorua (where the state had intervened to spruce up the facilities and to regulate and routinize ethnic tourism offerings) and pitched it to a majority-Japanese clientele primed by the soft primitivism of U.S. marketing of Hawai'i.[11] When the neoliberal reforms of the mid-1980s demolished agriculture- and forestry-based regional economies, tourism was again identified as a growth catalyst that would address regional unemployment. Indeed, while the rest of the economy stagnated, tourism grew, becoming the highest foreign-exchange earner in 1988–89.[12] Impatient and newly influential industry leaders mounted an assault on the Fordist legacy that they believed hampered tourism growth: the strong regulatory climate (from licensing laws to labor protection legislation), a low appetite for investment risk, and a national antipathy to service work. Meanwhile, the Tourism Department went the same way as many other government units in a political climate increasingly hostile to public service. It privatized, outsourced, or divested many of its functions (such as travel offices and film services) and restructured along the public–private partnership model, with a new Ministry of Tourism overseeing policy analysis and Crown lands, and the Tourism Board, weighted by industry representatives, overseeing publicity and providing strategic-development advice.[13] (The Tourism Board was later reformed as Tourism New Zealand in 1999.)

With the *Destination New Zealand* report in 1990, the lineaments of a new state approach to tourism began to form, but it was not until *Strategy 2010* (published in 2001) that the global policy vision sought by industry pundits emerged. Helen Clark's fifth Labour government returned tourism to its Liberal-era role as a prominent instrument and expression of the state's political rationality. No longer a minor service industry, tourism was to be flag bearer for a new knowledge-driven economy, steered by a pro-active state that had abandoned its dependence on primary commodity production and "moved up the value chain in everything."[14] In this new state ecology, investment was to be concentrated in education, research and development, public infrastructure, and enterprise incubation to cre-ate "high value, sophisticated and specialized" products in the information and communication, biotechnology, and creative sectors. At the same time, Clark's "third way" policies aimed to reinvent progressive social democracy in the key of neoliberal economic rationalism: Aotearoa New Zealand's style of government would be collaborative, compassionate, inclusive, sus-tainable, and above all bicultural, while remaining "responsible" to market imperatives.[15] The principle of cultural citizenship, which Clark's admin-istration understood in two complexly intercalated senses of the term, uni-fied this vision. On the one hand, the state acknowledged its citizens' right to participate in public life while honoring, expressing, and demanding recognition of their cultural affiliations, even those not historically norma-tive to the idiom of the state (what political scientists call a "politics of recognition").[16] On the other hand, it hailed its citizens as creative, innova-tive, and communicative, productive not in capacity for labor (the "indus-trial army" that politicians served a century earlier) but in sociable life as generators, bearers, managers, and transmitters of what became known in the new policy vernacular as "cultural capital" (pace Bourdieu). Aotearoa New Zealand after neoliberalism, then, became a state that no longer posi-tioned culture outside the domains of politics and economy (as, for exam-ple, a zone of social authenticity or a court of ideological appeal). Culture in this new epistemic framework was instead a primary economic and governmental resource orchestrated *by* the state and bearing on the pro-ductivity *of* the state through the conduct of its citizens. Culture is to the neoliberal, in short, what labor was to the liberal: a component in a regime of biopower.

This impetus positioned tourism—the trade in cultural knowledges, materials, and experiences—at the core of the state's operations. In tour-ism, the citizen was no longer simply a stakeholder but also now the basis of a product "that is made up of not only every element of scenery in New

Zealand and every activity but also, in fact, every New Zealander."[17] Tourism literalized the neoliberal cultural state's construal of the individual as a "flexible collection of assets" and site for investment.[18] Without the incitement to perform, however, cultural capital is an asset latent in the citizen. Cultural policy, the hallmark of Clark's administration, offered this incitement: it created the conditions designed to bring citizens to discover, deploy, and circulate cultural capital in a global market, simultaneously serving the subject's self-interest and the interest of state welfare.

Cultural policy—the "institutional supports that channel both aesthetic creativity and collective ways of life"—has been a core feature of high-liberal governmentality from its nineteenth-century inception.[19] For the Keynesian policy makers of twentieth-century liberal diaspora, culture was a public good that legitimated the enlightened authority of the state and was charged with "evoking the nation and educing the citizen," a public subject amenable to self-governance, rational consumption, class harmony, and civic participation.[20] Culture was a political technology that worked not through the top-down application of power but through the benevolent promulgation of desire and commitment.[21] This much remains true of neoliberal policy. The distinction between the neoliberal approach and its liberal forebear lies in the convergence of domains of governmentality previously held discrete and the unifying dominance of market logic in all of these domains. They include the regulation or promotion of artistic production and mass communication; the definition, preservation, and management of the state's heritage and history; and interventions into the anthropological domain of culture (the "whole way of life") through instruments such as taxation structures or educational curricula.[22]

Aotearoa New Zealand has been among a cluster of nations to lead this charge, with the growing cultural sector integrated under a "whole of government" policy framework that created linkages between arts, tourism, sports and recreation, media, and design, bringing them into dialogue with trade, industry, education, and export agencies. Clark's first term as Prime Minister and (significantly) Minister for Arts, Culture, and Heritage saw a slew of initiatives designed to measure, spur, support, or manage the cultural activity, attitudes, and ambitions of New Zealanders: the Cultural Revitalization Strategy, the Cultural Well-Being Program, the Cultural Statistics Program, the Growth and Innovation Framework, and the all-encompassing *Heart of the Nation* report. Like Blair's "Cool Britannia" campaign or the "Creative Nation" platform in Australia, Clark's strategy was a third-way effort to reconcile Keynesian sentiments with neoliberal precepts by posing culture as an underexploited export, a driver of knowledge-economy innovation, and a domestic social good. What distinguished this experiment was its emphasis on social well-being, which it allied with economic growth, positing "an inclusive and cohesive society as the building block" for an innovative economy and looking to culture to secure this cohesion. In these governmental moves, culture became what George Yúdice calls an "expedient."[23] It formed the invisible infrastructure of the information economy to come: an "aid to connectivity," standardizing interaction modes and expectations across networks of productive cooperation and communication.[24] It also compensated for the demise of the former state, creating social cohesion despite waning political participation, absent welfare provision, employment insecurity, weakened class collectives, and other communitarian traditions being steamrolled by reform.[25] The culture that touristic biopolitics took as its object was paradoxically both a resource targeted for exploitation by capital and a refuge for civil society from the ravages of that same economic system.[26]

One prominent prong of the state's cultural campaign was an unflagging project to discover, publish, and celebrate a distinctive "national identity." This might seem an untimely project for a supposedly postnational, postidentitarian era, but the quest for national identity was expertly fitted to the new, postneoliberal political rationality in which tourism took pride of place. First, policy analysts argued, national identity was the content of the national brand, "projecting what is unique about this country" to earn recognition and global market share. Identity was, like culture, a form of capital, a "primary cultural asset [and] driver of creative processes," part of an "extended value chain" that began in the recovery of heritage and ended in the market.[27] Second, it functioned as a unifying fetish, a "new type of 'glue' between New Zealanders," from which citizens might draw the pride, confidence, common purpose, and sense of self-determination that would be the foundation for growth.[28] (This "identity" was far from essentialized: policy statements described it in terms of both roots and routes, as continually reinvented, internally differentiated, and even contested—it was, nonetheless, still singular.)[29]

Labour's cultural policy machine presented the erosion of liberalism's protective firewalls between market, state, and civil society as a new kind of synergy, offering up the cultural commons to capital with glib optimism. Policy documents argued that a "symbiotic" relationship existed between the creative industries (those industries that trade in intellectual property) and culture at large (defined as all creative expression and communication "where profit or commercial gain is not a primary motivator"). Culture's purpose was to generate raw materials (intellectual property, creative skills, and energies) to feed the creative industries.[30] The subject of this ideal biopolitics, the creative individual, would move between economy and community without tension or alienation, to the ultimate benefit of the general welfare: after all, policy argued, creative industries employ people simply "doing the jobs they love."[31] Tourism became pivotal to the policy vision in part because it promised to make this cultural citizenship available to all those who shared in the capital of Kiwi culture, not just the creative class. Yet this halcyon vision held significantly different implications for Māori. Those same liberal firewalls had historically enabled a countercolonial politics for Māori through which their communities could resist the alien values of both capital and state. To many Māori, the call to surrender cultural goods to the market, in the interests of the state, resembled processes of appropriation and expropriation as familiar as colonialism itself.

The state could not compel Māori compliance with this new cultural ecology: under Treaty principles, all policy initiatives affirmed the autonomy of iwi and national Māori agencies ("things Māori should be devolved to Māori"). Yet the encompassing framework shaped the conditions within which any Māori venture in cultural commerce could flourish. Policy statements posed Māori as bearers of a unique reservoir of cultural capital that they might profitably mobilize in a value-added economy and that was invaluable to the distinctiveness of national identity. Māori, however, faced unique challenges in embracing the cultural opportunities touted by the state. Well before the Clark era, the Māori-authored 1986 report *Māori in Tourism* sought Māori economic recovery on Māori terms, but it pointed to the legacy of racial discrimination that stood in the way: lack of access to development capital, low levels of business expertise and education, and lack of representation within tourism-industry and state bodies.[32] A visual essay that prefaced the report, however, suggested that the biggest stumbling block would be the distrust and damaged Māori cultural confidence stemming from the Pākehā state's historical assaults on cultural sovereignty in the name of tourism. Twenty pages of sexually exploitative

"Māori maiden" posters, condescending slogans, inappropriate souvenirs (often violating important cultural principles), and campaigns that blatantly appropriated the work of Māori artists made the case with irrefutable clarity. When a second report, *He Mātai Tāpoi Māori*, was issued in 2001, little had changed: Māori were found to be underrepresented in industry and state bodies and in higher-wage tourism employment; their businesses were smaller, undercapitalized, and faced challenges in securing finance; and their needs were invisible in industry or state research. Moreover, despite wholesalers reporting unmet demand for Māori products, many Māori were reticent, exhibiting what the report's authors called "low cultural confidence," in part stemming from the ethnocentric posture of the industry.[33] In the report of the Māori Tourism Advisory Group in *Strategy 2010*, the tone of impatience was palpable. They called for retrospective remediation (utu) to clear the way for involvement, and for a deeper awareness of Māori cultural property values: "The industry needs to develop ways in which to support control by Māori over Māori culture and the use of its symbols, language, images and practices beyond that as a tourist asset or marketing tool."[34] But could the neoliberal cultural state—on which recovery hopes were pinned—incorporate Māori in a way that the erstwhile liberal state had not? The state's initial moves were not promising in this regard.

REMAKING THE TOURIST, REMAKING THE STATE

In tourism's policy-managed transition from Fordist service industry to post-Fordist, experience-economy adjunct, the task of reimagining tourism workers (as nonalienated entrepreneurs of their own culture acting in synergy with the state) began by reinventing the figure of the tourist. The post–Gulf War recession and Asian economic crisis of the 1990s saw damaging declines in the industry's huge U.S. and Japanese markets, but these years had also seen significant growth in independent youth travel, ecotourism, and adventure tourism.[35] A small and remote nation—expensive to get to, with a minute publicity budget—could not reliably compete in mass markets. To do so would also risk squandering its primary assets: its unspoiled natural beauty, exclusivity, and the casual, friendly openness of its people. Moreover, the mass model, which concentrated traffic in a few locations over a restricted season, benefited offshore agents and a few already highly capitalized carriers (such as hotels and coach lines), but it failed to address the patent economic need of the moment: filling the void left in regions eviscerated by the decline of agricultural markets and state industries. Inspired by the success of adventure tourism, policy strategists focused on drawing not *more* tourists but *higher yield* tourists: those who would stay longer, spend more money on a wider range of more expensive products, visit at all times of the year in a range of locations, and be return visitors.[36]

Thus was born the Free Independent Traveler (FIT), also called the Interactive Traveler, the ideal tourist modeled by policy analysis and courted by policy measures. Educated, affluent, and autonomous, the FIT was imagined as coming from New Zealand's traditional markets—the United States, the United Kingdom, Australia, or Germany—or from the cosmopolitan class of any number of other countries. Drawing on global industry research suggesting that tourists were seeking more active, qualitative experiences, the ecologically minded FIT embraced nature not as a spectacle but as an immersive environment in which to participate. Above all, the FIT would seek exclusivity, educational and cultural experiences, and bonds of intimacy and identification with those who delivered them.[37] FITs would do considerable web-based research before arrival, and (although a small demographic) they were technologically savvy market leaders who would circulate information about the destination widely among equally affluent and educated networks. The FIT, this human invention of policy, is the paradigmatic subject of an immaterial economy: a communicative agent in a durational relationship with the state and its human and natural assets. As in the Liberal era a century earlier, the tourist state's ideal consumer was also its ideal citizen. This citizen, the FIT profile suggests, was also implicitly English speaking, wealthy, and white.

The second prong of tourism's experience-economy makeover focused on the national brand. Even more so than the sale of a commodity, the provision of an experience requires enduring and wide-reaching networks to facilitate continuous information flow. *Strategy 2010* called for strengthened feedback loops between tourism policy makers, promoters, and producers (ensuring that the marketing message closely aligned with actual tourist experience) and enhanced cross-sectoral partnerships (linking museums, arts agencies, and tourism bodies to develop high-yield cultural products, for example). The most crucial network, however, was the nation as a whole. Given New Zealand's small scale and isolation, unified and consistent branding was essential: the only viable marketing unit, analysts agreed, was the nation itself. Further, if the product were the experience of immersion in a unique cultural environment, the performers of that environment—whether tourism workers or the citizenry at large— would have to be similarly unified and consistent in the celebration of *"our* culture" (emphasis mine). Tourism, more than any other arm of the cultural state, aimed to secure the welfare of the population through inciting citizens to continually cite, elaborate, and communicate their state of nationhood. The distinctive content of that identity, however, had first to be discovered and symbolized by the state.

While the valorization of cultural interactivity might have opened new doors for Māori participation in tourism, the monocultural character of the national brand initially devised by state agencies seemed to close them again. The first serious rebranding efforts in 1993 introduced the idea of a national "personality," Brand New Zealand. It melded pastoral and natural images (clean, green, and pristine) with signifiers of the new: new technology, youth, experimentation, and achievement. The campaign rejuvenated old Pākehā topoi of a virgin wilderness that could be mastered by the keen energies of capital to express the perverse ecstasies of what Ulrich Beck has called "risk society."[38] "Adventure tourism helps New Zealand to become a nation of calculated risk-takers . . . dynamic leaders," the Tourism Minister opined.[39] A decade later, Saatchi's landmark 100% Pure campaign (which I treat in more detail in chapter 5) brought to the fore yet another core neoliberal value: freedom.[40] In tune with the softer, market-friendly social democracy of new Labour ("contemporary and sophisticated, innovative and creative, spirited and free"), it was no more aligned with bicultural values than its predecessor.[41] Initially devised without thorough Māori consultation, the brand still imagined the state in a resolutely Pākehā idiom, marrying deracinated neoliberal futurity to a resuscitated colonial-nationalist primordialism with distinctly racial (one might even say eugenic) overtones, again linked to the purity of landscape. At the same time, research was pointing to the clear demand of FIT tourists for indigenous experiences and for a more distinctive, peopled quality to the brand: the peripherality of Māori seemed increasingly like a missed marketing opportunity.

THE VISION AND CHALLENGE OF
MĀORI TOURISM

At the time of the 2010 strategy's drafting, newly capitalized tribal bodies (especially Ngāi Tahu) were investing in major adventure-tourism holdings. But despite extraordinary Māori entrepreneurship elsewhere in the economy, there were few small businesses outside the Rotorua region that could provide the intimate cultural engagement the FIT sought or that would enable Māori, as the report suggested, to "empower their own development" in accordance with whānau and hapū (extended kin group) values.[42] Following Treaty principles and report recommendations, Māori appointments were made to major state agencies, and Māori Regional Tourism Organizations (MRTOs, with relationships to hapū, education, and development bodies) were created to parallel existing RTOs.

Policy's performativity inheres in its capacity to produce asymmetric networks—feedback loops, essentially—through which state-level macrostrategics and the microenvironments in which actors operate bring pressure to bear upon one another. In the first years of the new millennium,

100% PURE NEW ZEALAND

While early campaign images depicted an unpeopled natural landscape, later iterations populated these scenes to emphasize the interactive possibilities of New Zealand tourism. Tourism New Zealand.

these new Māori appointments and bodies began to weave these feed-back loops, allowing the language of the state to enter Māori communities, linking neoliberal analytics to the self-articulation and rehabilitation of struggling tribal economies. "The way to achieve security is to beef up the quality of our operation," one MRTO leader told me: "The profit motive is the only way we can ensure that we can employ and develop more of our people." "Best thing is to create an environment in which [Māori businesses] can become innovative," another state agent argued, "through raising the profile and commercial value of indigeneity." Such language ("security," "environments for innovation," and "raising the commercial value" of identity) imagines a thoroughgoing transformation of expectations, aspirations, and understandings of political agency for Māori actors, understandings newly aligned with market logic and brokered by tourism.

Ultimately, however, the work of Māori representatives in state agencies transformed not just the conditions of possibility for Māori tourism but also the state's self-symbolization. When I began talking with Māori appointees at TNZ in 2003, the question that dominated their work was how to intervene into the 100% Pure New Zealand brand, then in its first flush of success. "They tell me our number one product is landscape," the Māori liaison for TNZ argued, "but we're pitching the country, not a product! Why is the landscape not *part* of the culture? Why can't we pitch Aotearoa rather than New Zealand?" The TNZ marketing machine took the un-peopled image of landscape as the national product (a dominant trope for more than a century of New Zealand tourism, as I argue in chapter 1). Relying on racial spectacle—Māori carving, warriors, maidens, or haka (rhythmic posture-dance) performance—the approach positioned Māori as a hypostatized, representational supplement to "New Zealand." Māori representatives objected not just because it entrapped them in an artificially inert "tradition" (about which more later) but also because it restricted Māori access to tourism to providing a limited range of cultural commodities, namely staged entertainment. Moreover, while such racialized images evoked curiosity, they invited no attachment: Māori were ineluctably separate from the idea of New Zealand that the visitor was invited to "feel a part of."[43] What Māori advocates imagined instead was selling, not the image-commodity of nature ("New Zealand"), but the experience of immersion in a "living landscape" in which the cultural and natural are integrally related ("Aotearoa").[44]

To do this, Māori appointees had to imagine a new, postrepresentational organization of the tourism industry itself, porous to indigenous ways of sensing, perceiving, and acting—even acting institutionally. "How do we build a brand that includes Māori, not as the bolt-on, but *across everything we do?*" a TNZ Māori liaison subsequently asked. Taking 100% Pure "to the cultural level" would mean transforming the brand from two dimensions to four, serving both Māori cultural perspectives and FIT proclivities by mobilizing an entire sensorium to evoke a vital intensity that escapes representation. Tourism workers, TNZ's General Manager of Development proposed, would draw on tactile, aural, olfactory, and affective associations to allow the visitor to "engage with difference—not just watching, but understanding, being a part of it." "Here's a picture of a mountain," the Māori liaison explained to me, "it looks the same to you and me. But actually I see *an ancestor.* How can you see through my eyes?" Ultimately, the work of selling an experience pertained not just to tourism providers but to the state apparatus itself: the task it posed for policy makers and publicists was a deep kind of national-identity work, "trying to get outside ourselves, see ourselves . . . put your finger on the intangible."

Between 2003 and the present, the 100% Pure campaign was modified to bring Māori into the national picture, but the process of *institutional* reimagination underway was much more encompassing. TNZ modeled and responded to new Māori cultural tourism products, engaged marketers in debates about how to pitch Māori products, conducted sustained research on Māori cultural tourism, and extended strategic and data-sharing relationships with a range of units (from Te Puni Kōkiri to the Tourism Industry Association and the Department of Commerce). The brand was coming to operate, as Celia Lury suggests, as a medium in itself: mediating supply and demand by organizing relationships, networks, and information flow between consumers and producers, between the different (ethnic) elements of the (national) product itself, and between the inside and outside of the (national) corporation.[45]

Throughout these transformations, Māori in state agencies were emphatic that performance should be the "core of tourism." The success of Māori in the industry, and of the industry as a whole, would rest on the intimate interface between tourist and tourism performer, on "raising the bar on the interpretive experience."[46] "Māori have a great product, just by being themselves," an MRTO director told me. But to allow tourists to truly encounter te ao Māori, the Māori world, providers and marketers would need to communicate in ways that reached beyond the purely icon-ographic to the phenomenological depth of affect, habitus, and spiritual experience. TNZ agents seized on Māori performance competencies as a primary resource, in effect enlisting Māori creative and expressive conduct biopoetically into the state's biopolitical regime. In 2006, a Māori General Manager at TNZ told me of being at an industry convention in the United States and showing American wholesalers a popular TNZ image of a hongi (pressing noses in greeting) between two children. "What comes to mind?" she asked. "Cute," said one. "Eskimo" said another (speaking worlds about the way such iconography can be assimilated into generic racial typolo-gies). She then told them the story of the creation of Hineahuone, the first woman, by Tane, the god who formed her from clay and gave her the breath of life. She talked of the ways in which, among her own Ngāpuhi people, this greeting was now a most sacred dimension of hospitality, bond-ing two people by bringing together their heads, where the life force is con-centrated, and mingling hau (the breath). She held the image up again, again asking for associations: "spiritual," "meeting of minds," and "con-nection of cultures" came the replies, as the audience physically reacted to the image, inclining their bodies toward it in resonance. "Māori can use story to create that link," she explained. "This is the real strength of Māori tourism," an MRTO manager told me, "enabling people to tell stories. As an oral culture, a lot of Māori have this skill without knowing." This was not simply replacing visual with verbal representation. Story, kōrero, is understood as an art of presence, bodily engaging listeners: a good kōrero will raise hairs on the back of your neck; its ihi (power, force) can be sensed. Kōrero (usefully for tourism) places a premium on the experi-ential, inviting tourists to coexperience but leaving the authority to nar-rate and share in Māori hands: "You really have to live it and breathe it to explain it."[47]

Māori tourism operatives also called on kōrero—a deep ligament between people, past, and place—to inflect the construct of national identity pro-posed by the state campaign, invoking Aotearoa as a land cloaked in story to counter the erstwhile New Zealand (the natural, unpeopled, unstoried paradise). The New Zealand Māori Tourism Council (NZMTC) devised a promotional framework building on the poetics of whenua (a word mean-ing land, home, and birth) in which the islands' creation story (shared by

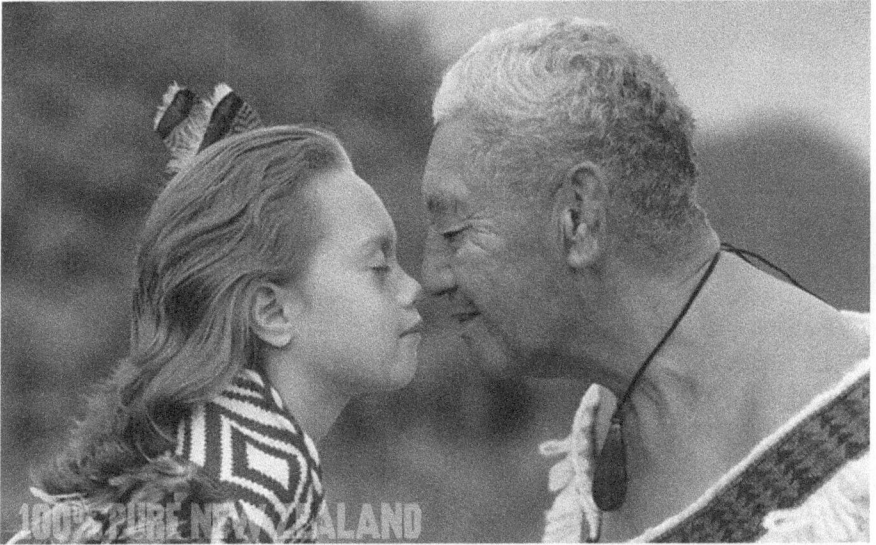

The hongi greeting, from a recent TNZ campaign. Tourism New Zealand.

all iwi) anchors regional origin stories, allowing each MRTO to thema-
tize copromoting attractions within its territory. Rather than presenting
Māori as an undifferentiated minority collapsed into or supplementing a
totalized 100% "New Zealand" identity, the campaign images a bicultural
nation-space alive to the claims of tribal rangatiratanga: each iwi, hapū, or
whānau can find its own touristic performance idiom, and in that idiom,
mana (prestige). It also supports the dispersal and diversification of Māori
products—and tourism development opportunities—outside the enclave
of Rotorua, challenging the spatial logic of Māori containment and isolation that has endured since its Liberal-era inception.

TNZ, NZMTC, and their subsidiary agencies have become, in a sense,
experimental sites: institutional spaces devoted to the collaborative invention, symbolization, and communication of a (bi)cultural state and to the
cultivation of conducts appropriate to it. They operate in a bicultural compromise of economic necessity. Bound by Treaty obligations and drawn to
the "point of difference" that Māori offer, the Pākehā-dominated apparatus
has given ground. Limited by scale but attracted by tourism's opportunities
for a global profile and local development, Māori have had to mesh with the

broader national campaign. Meanwhile, the languages of state and Māori have converged. Two key principles of conduct have anchored all state tourism policy statements since *Strategy 2010*, taking up residence at the heart of tourism's, and thus the state's, political, cultural, and economic rationality. These principles take Māori names: kaitiakitanga and manaakitanga. Kaitiakitanga is "sustainability," in the state's neoliberal parlance, but also guardianship, a generational responsibility to preserve and manage a living natural and cultural birthright that is the ground of well-being. Manaakitanga, "the art of hospitality," is translated with a distinctly liberal cast as seeking "common ground upon which an affinity and sense of sharing and respect can grow," forming a "unique kinship between the two cultures."[48]

This bicultural, neoliberal concord is far from absolute. Māori agencies also insist on rangatiratanga (the right of Māori to determine their relationships within tourism), whanaungatanga (the collective basis of Māori enterprise and its commitment to tribal development), and utu (the active redress of past wrongs by the state)—an affront to neoliberal norms of compliance, individualism, and blindness to history.[49] Nor is it entirely novel. The new story of national identity leaves intact the modernist, even neoprimitivist, division of symbolic labor that has defined state tourism since its Liberal-era inception, whereby white New Zealand offers cosmopolitan familiarity and modernity, while Māori offer historical depth and difference:

> There are two equally marketable New Zealands. One is modern, innovative, and 100% pure in adventure, landscape, lifestyle. It's urbane, multicultural, and the people generally speak English—like many other destinations the world over. The other destination is unique: it's Māori, spiritually connected to the landscape. . . . It offers mystique and the promise of a spiritual connection with a tribal society still in touch with culture and tradition.[50]

To what extent, we might ask, has this state-level change truly transformed tourism discourse or tourist perceptions, or for that matter the dispositions of Māori being called on to take up this new form of entrepreneurial cultural citizenship in support of Aotearoa's brand experience? What of those being asked to traffic their cultural capital and to create the affective global networks through which that capital might move?

THE THEATER OF TOURISM AND THE
NEOLIBERAL PRACTICE OF LIBERALISM

Cultural policy is a statement of intent, gesturing always toward new sets of relations, identifications, faculties, and forms of value and citizenship that it struggles to bring into being.[51] But it also addresses itself to the past, to the intransigence of old orders that it seeks to transform or to practices evolving along trajectories at odds with its prevailing rationality. Given that the impetus of Aotearoa New Zealand tourism policy is the incitement to perform, it is no surprise that this tension between emergent and residual forms should play out over the particulars of performance. Before turning to FIT tourism (the state's imagined future), I want to address the performance practice that it is pitted against in the policy mind: staged ethnic entertainment, identified with the era of mass tourism and with the racial politics of the welfare state. My analysis of both sites is preoccupied with the entangled problematics of property and of race, an unresolved schism of the neoliberal transition. For if recent policy's postracial language of "kinship" and "common ground" works to counter the divisive force of racialization, racial difference remains a motive force for tourists, and racial inequity remains a stubborn fact of the social and political landscape for tourism providers—one that they must navigate daily in their performances. Likewise, although the analogy of "guardianship" and gift exchange supplants that of ownership and purchase, tensions around cultural property rights nonetheless abound.

Historically, the colonial state's failure to respect Treaty-guaranteed rights to property, tangible and intangible, marked the racial lines that defined Māori as subjects unworthy of liberal recognition, respect, or privacy. It was this breach in the uniformity of citizenship that made battles over property the flashpoints of Māori resistance. In disputes over state confiscations of property or over the appropriation and disrespectful performance of the haka by Pākehā, Māori exposed the liberal state's (racist) failure to live up to its own (race-blind) principles, simultaneously tightening the bonds of racial solidarity that would enable them to wage the future struggle for recognition. Now, as new dimensions of the cultural commons are drawn into the information-economy market, many fear that colonial expropriation will be replaced by a new and more insidious form of appropriation, again eclipsing Māori rights—and with them Māori rights to identity.[52] Staged attractions, I argue, use newly traditional Māori modalities of performance to manage such anxieties, manifesting an aesthetic of nostalgia not for the authentic premodern primitive (as much tourism criticism would suggest) but for the racial certainties of preneoliberal politics.

While formally staged attractions such as concert-style performances, demonstrations, and cultural centers still dominate the ethnic tourism market in Aotearoa New Zealand (in both revenue and numbers of tourists served), state agents see them as less amenable to the upmarket demands of the Free Independent Traveler. The FIT seeks opportunities to be hosted in natural rather than stage-managed settings and to interact freely with individuals from the host culture. Staged attractions are not intimate in this way, nor do they reflect tribal diversity or modern Māori lifestyles; at best, "they tick the box for a certain demographic," as one agent told me. The fact is, however, that the state has little control over this thriving and largely Māori-run industry niche.

The hāngī-'n'-haka sector of the industry (as it is affectionately known), ranges from regular concerts staged by hotels and followed by a "traditional" meal (the hāngī) catered by the hotel kitchens, to events arranged by Māori communities using marae (community center) facilities. Similar entertainment, with or without food, is also offered by resident or visiting cultural groups at specific attractions (such as the daily performances at Auckland Museum or at Te Puia in Whakarewarewa). As in the Liberal era, Rotorua remains the enclave where most of these businesses are concentrated and where the vast majority of tourists go "to experience Māori culture." What makes hāngī-'n'-haka attractions easy to advertise, package, and deliver, as well as reliably profitable, is precisely what makes many in state agencies uneasy. They are a routinized mass entertainment medium: one business can cater to anywhere from twenty to over two hundred people several times a day, expanding and contracting with variance in seasonal visitorship. They are also a recognizable genre of product that can be described with ease and folded into a range of itineraries, catering to backpackers and coach-package tourists, English speakers and non-English speakers alike.

Ethnic tourism of this sort is highly semiotically legible. As a generation of postcolonial critics has argued, it forms a chain of metonymy whereby the face of the tattooed warrior (or the smiling maiden) stands in for the performance form, while the form stands in for the culture as a whole. Or rather, it stands in for the *race*, because (as Jane Desmond has contended) these kinds of performances spectacularize corporeal difference, grounding a range of racial discourses in the purported facticity of the performing body.[53] In short, it commoditizes culture—producing it as "a sign of itself," objectified and inert, hypostatized and hyperbolized—and positions patrons as the arbiters of an authenticity based not on a deep understanding of cultural ethos but on the performers' consistent observance of the conventions of primitive realism. (Tourists, for example, feel entitled to critique performers for wearing contemporary watches or for being too European in appearance.)[54] Māori appointees at TNZ and the Ministry of Tourism broadly concur with the spirit of such arguments: the staged attraction, they hold, is a thin medium of cultural experience, distancing audience from performer and detaching static signs of culture—the "stereotypes," as they call them—from the lived, contemporary specificity of iwi and hapū ethos, territory, and history.

Many in planning and policy dismiss hāngī-'n'-haka tourism by describing it as "old" and "outdated." The terms mark the form's double time-lag: On the one hand, it stages Māori culture as heritage, thus culturally anterior, frozen in time, and nonmodern (what Johannes Fabian famously called the "denial of coevalness").[55] On the other, there is the aesthetic antiquation of the genre itself; as I argue later, the concert party is a living archive of performance conventions past. The adjectives used by less politic observers—in the arts, museums, and academia, and by FIT demographic tourists themselves—betray as much distaste as critique: "same old, same old," "tacky," "clichéd," and even "embarrassing." This distaste is in part class antipathy (to a product both overtly mass-produced and popular in aesthetic), but it also marks a deep discomfort with the racial interpellation that these spectacles enact. Separating the viewing, paying subject from the performing, native object who is paid to please, hāngī-'n'-haka performances can feel like the most blatant expression of colonial exploitation. (As one "right on" white English tourist put it to me when I asked whether she would go to a Māori performance during her stay at Rotorua, "It would feel wrong—there's just something about being an ethical tourist.")

Yet the form not only persists but flourishes despite pressures to surrender to the neoliberal (relational, experiential, exclusive, and individualized) future of FIT tourism. And it continues to enjoy considerable support from the Māori community it supposedly demeans. There are practical reasons for this, other than its sheer profitability: it provides both regular and seasonal work in a region with disproportionately high (and disproportionately Māori) unemployment, often to individuals on the margins of the labor market (students or middle-aged women), drawing on existing resources of iwi and hapū life (the shared performance repertoire that allows workers to cycle in and out of groups with minimal rehearsal).

Performance analysis, however, reveals other reasons why ethnographic entertainment might be thriving in Aotearoa's current moment. The concert-party form on which it is based articulates a finely tuned political posture for Māori performers and non-Māori audiences alike, fitted to the residual racial dynamics of the liberal state as well as to the unresolved, emergent tensions of the neoliberal one. It holds in dialectical tension racial pride and postracial irony, (trans)national intimacy and indigenous privacy, while balancing state demands on Māori (to offer hospitality, display identity, and render cultural commodities fungible for the national cause) with Māori demands (for control and ownership of culture and for recognition).

For this claim to make sense, some explanation of the genre and genealogy of concert-party performance is necessary. A tourist troupe usually consists of roughly equal numbers of men and women, from about eight upward, who perform in presentational convention: the performers face the audience from a stage or podium area, most often at first arrayed in regular lines with the women to the fore. Any given program will consist of a sequence of shorter items performed in the Māori language and combining movement (most often in unison) with song or chant, performed either a cappella or accompanied by guitar. The items range from waiata (part-song) and poi (a part-song accompanied by the percussive and visual effect of twirling fist-sized balls of flax, beating them against the hands and body) to haka (the famous rhythmic posture-dance and chant). While the movement is usually nonrepresentational, the content of such items varies enormously by occasion: they might be narratives, addresses, celebrations, love songs, lyrics, challenges, or prayers, ancient or contemporary. Few groups, it is worth noting, would share especially significant, sacred, or treasured taonga in a tourist context. While dexterity, grace, athleticism, and power are valued, the form emphasizes the cohesion of the ensemble rather than the soloist's talent, and performers are almost invariably accomplished nonprofessionals rather than self-identified artists.

This genre of performance, kapa haka, has a prominent place in bicultural public and political life in Aotearoa New Zealand. It has been the mainstay not just of ethnic tourism but also of Māori intertribal and state diplomacy for over a century. Today, kapa haka groups perform at state welcomes, parliamentary occasions, openings, and national and international events, from the Commonwealth Games to the Venice Biennale. They also perform on marae grounds at hui (meetings, gatherings), community or school events, pan-tribal festivals and competitions, and innumerable other occasions, formal and informal. The format is a supple vehicle for generating and expressing solidarity and mana, supporting collective ventures, and representing tribal, institutional, or national entities, but also for critique and dissent.[56] The exchange of performance between visiting and host parties was a fundamental component of precontact Māori protocols of welcome, in which groups could articulate intent and disposition by drawing on the rich poetic, musical, and gestural language offered by expressive forms. While there were other contexts in which the performing arts were practiced, these exchanges on the marae ātea (the cleared ground in front of the wharenui, or the main meeting house) proved particularly responsive to the evolving political needs of postcontact iwi and hapū.

It was this diplomatic DNA, as well as the form's legibility to Pākehā audiences, that made concert-party performance a natural medium for reformist Māori of the Liberal era searching for ways to strengthen fragmented, demoralized iwi and hapū and to present a disciplined, united face to the Pākehā establishment. The massive Māori welcome for the Duke and Duchess of Cornwall and York in 1901, the New Zealand International Exhibition at Christchurch in 1906–7, and the Māori Congress meetings in Wellington in 1908 were all moments at which concert-party performance spoke with a powerful, if ambivalent, political voice. On the one hand, kapa haka underwrote the claims these events made to the liberal state's legitimacy, through staging Māori participation and assent. On the other, they allowed tribes to engage in spirited displays of mana to each other but also to Pākehā audiences (many of them tourists). The marae ātea is the domain of Tū, the god of war, and Māori performance scholars speak of his spirit of competition and pride informing the evolution of kapa haka.[57] With uniformity and precision unison work as newly valued aesthetic properties, these performances provided crucial proof to the Liberal-era establishment of Māori capacity to collectively organize and represent themselves as a pan-tribal bloc, differentiated by iwi and hapū. Moreover, the disciplined Māori subject of kapa haka performance—much like that of Siegfried Kracauer's "mass ornament"—was felt to mark the race's fitness for the demands of military and industrial modernity.[58]

Concert-party performance, then, was a "newly traditional" instrument and expression of cultural sovereignty, and as I argued in chapter 3, such associations were not lost in tourist contexts.[59] The touristic form of kapa haka began as an organic (and highly profitable) dimension of Tūhourangi hospitality at Te Wairoa before the Tarawera eruption made the performers refugees at Whakarewarewa. Later, in Liberal-era Rotorua, troupes not only performed in the hotel drawing rooms but also held regular concerts in the town hall, with a mixed audience of tourists, Māori, and Pākehā from the township community. Concert-party performance was syncretic from the earliest periods of contact, borrowing from English hymnody and popular song and making imaginative use of European instruments. Adventurous Arawa impresarios added to the repertoire, performing traditional items together with glees, "coon songs," popular religious and parlor songs (in English or translated into Māori), whaikōrero (oratory) demonstrations, stick games, recitations, and mimetic elements such as legends or scenes narrated in tableaux (for example, "life in the village," or the workhorse romance of Hinemoa and Tutanekai, "the Māori Hero and Leander"). Bearing traces of variety entertainment, amateur choral performance, ethnological show business, and the jovial, interactive bonhomie of British pantomime and music hall, the form held for Europeans both the comfort of familiarity and the frisson of difference.

Yet undergirding it all for Arawa performers were the kaupapa (mission) of diplomacy and solidarity and the mark of mana. When state agencies worked to revitalize and routinize Rotorua tourism at the onset of jet-age mass tourism in the 1960s and 1970s, tensions between state or industry perspectives and this Māori philosophy of performance (also a cultural engine of the then-flourishing Māori nationalist renaissance) were palpable. When the new, Pākehā-owned township hotels that began to stage performances during this era wielded influence over aspects of convention, costuming, and casting, Māori community members chafed: if performance were an expression of rangatiratanga, of autonomy and sovereignty, then any foreign manipulation of those traditions was an insult to mana.[60] Today, the work of tourism performance remains far from alienated entertainment labor. While some describe their work merely as "a good job" or can often seem uncommitted in performance, many current and former entertainers have talked to me of their "special responsibility to those who've come before and those who'll come after" to uphold the Arawa "tradition of excellence in the presentation of Māori culture," often in the face of concern about cultural commodification from other Māori. As one former Ngāti Whakaue performer with ten years on the hotel circuit explained, "'Here come the Arawas,' they say. But I loved it, 'cause I'm really proud of the culture. I love it deeply and love sharing it. Everybody makes comments about 'the plastic Māoris'—there's a lot of envy from other iwi— they don't have that tradition."

IMMERSIVE THEATER
AT TAMAKI MĀORI VILLAGE

With most of the major operations now under Māori management, recent touristic reinventions of this living tradition blend the concert party's ritual aspects with immersive, story-focused staging techniques that aim to provide not just a performance but (echoing TNZ's language) an "experience." I have chosen to focus here on one enterprise: Tamaki, the aggressively marketed behemoth of the Rotorua hāngī-'n'-haka scene. My reasons are several. First, there is the sheer scale, success, and industry influence of Tamaki's Māori-owned and Māori-run tourism venture, which baldly flouts state wisdom about politically acceptable indigenous representation in tourism. Second, Tamaki not only preserves this century-old performance tradition but also constantly repackages and innovates it, consistently expanding its operations, often drawing on Ministry of Tourism research and rhetoric (such as the storytelling emphasis). Yet the product they offer could not be further from Ministry recommendations: neither intimate, nor interactive, nor tribally or locally specific, their shows are explicitly theatrical, highly routinized, mass-market events relying on primitivist conventions of ethnographic entertainment that date to the World's Fairs of the nineteenth century, even as they experiment with new technologies of theatricality.[61] I argue, however, that Tamaki is no relic: instead, its sheer success reveals the contemporary limits and resistances to the cultural state's displacement of ethnoracial politics.

Tamaki Maori Village, South Pacific's gateway to
the world of ancient Maori and proud warriors.

The Tamaki Tours brochure, 2007. Tamaki Tours Ltd.

With truly Taylorist efficiency, Tamaki processes more than eight hundred
guests a day at four shows every afternoon and evening in their purpose-
built entertainment complex on the outskirts of Rotorua. For upward of
NZ$105, tourists purchase a four-hour-long package, which begins when
one of Tamaki's fleet of customized buses picks them up at any of Rotorua's
hostels or hotels and whisks them off to the Tamaki visitor center in the
township. There they receive a handout detailing, glossary fashion, the traditional components of the evening's entertainment and are funneled through
an immersive installation that evokes the originary Māori migration to
Aotearoa. Scenic, audio, and video elements take them back to a village in
Tahiti, where they overhear an old man telling his grandson why his people
must leave the shores of their ancestral homeland and embark for a distant
island. When they emerge, visitors are in (virtual) precontact Aotearoa. They
follow a winding path through a hall filled with lush fern growth, burbling
streams, waterfalls, the din of birdsong, and brightly colored placards pertaining to dimensions of "Māori culture." There the next stage of the journey

begins: another migration in which cheerfully drill-sergeantish emcees organize visitors into "tribes" and usher them onto "waka" (migratory canoes—
here, winkingly, buses) that transport them to Tamaki Maori Village.

With a jovial bus driver on mike at the helm, the twenty-minute drive
leaves time for important tribal business—the election of a "chief" from
among the tourists—and a briefing on the wero, or challenge, that will
greet the visitors on their arrival at the village. When the buses pull up at
the forested compound, with its spiked wooden ramparts, a suspenseful
wait begins in a gravelly forecourt inside the fence. Finally, announced by
the sounding of a conch trumpet, three athletic, tattooed warriors emerge
from the inner set of ramparts to challenge the visitors. They threaten the
visitors with flourishes of the taiaha (fighting staff), nimble footwork, and
intimidating expressions, impressing with their martial prowess, goading
the "chief" into accepting the challenge by picking up a taki (dart) placed
on the gravel. The challenge accepted, the warriors retire into the inner
compound, leading the way for the visitors into a village: a forested con-
geries of whares (dwellings), theatrically lighted and roped off from the
pathways where the tourists circulate. There, some twenty costumed performers simulate the daily chores of precontact Māori (such as weaving,
cultivation, and making fire) and some more-sensational practices (such as
the moko, or tattoo), occasionally answering patrons' questions but mostly
observing the fourth-wall convention.

After fifteen minutes of viewing the village, the visitors are seated in a
"meeting house," its architecture and decoration are cursorily explained to
them, and the concert begins. In around forty minutes, twelve performers
work through a bracingly paced series of numbers, punctuated by an emcee's
glib, sound-bite explanations of performed gestures. ("The wiri represents
the shimmering of light in the early dawn." "The long poi was only ever
performed by women of high rank looking for a mate." "Sit back, relax,
take heaps of photos, and enjoy the show!") From there, visitors are gently
ushered to a dining hall, where they enjoy a buffet that is, they are assured,
prepared hāngī-style in a "traditional Māori earth oven"—an unpreten-
tious, meat-and-potatoes repast containing nothing that would puzzle the
middling Anglo palate. After dessert, visitors move seemingly organically
out into a courtyard area, where they have ample time to shop for souvenirs at the advertised "craft market" before assembling for a final warm
farewell from their hosts and boarding the buses back to the city.

The Tamaki brothers, the two founders of the company, are controversial in and beyond the Rotorua industry. They are not Arawa, nor local to Rotorua (nor to Auckland, nor Christchurch, the other two urban sites where they have recently opened new facilities), and thus they work outside the strictures of tribal authority. They are also the charismatic founders of the successful Destiny Church, an American-style procapital evangelist movement that stands accused of intolerant conservatism, attempts to skew the political process, inappropriate uses of Māori traditions, and preying on the hopes of those Māori left behind by the rising national tide of prosperity. Mostly, however, it is the sheer, shameless scale and corporate ethos of their tourism operation that offends, as well as its kitsch borrowings from American theme-park hospitality (Oahu's Polynesian Cultural Center is a palpable influence on the operation). There is a world of difference between Tamaki and the ad hoc, community-based, cheerful, often ragged performances at Whakarewarewa Village, for example. By industrial standards, Tamaki Maori Village is a perfect product: slick, utterly consistent, efficient, and professional. As one of the most reliable employers in the region, it has its pick of performance personnel, and their work is tightly scripted, well rehearsed, and technically robust. Visitors get what they expect; they go away happy. What commands my attention about Tamaki, however, is that Tamaki has ridden the wave of knowledge-economy resurgence with a product so consistently dissonant with the ethos of neoliberal policy as to seem like a deliberate counterargument.[62]

ETHNOGRAPHIC BURLESQUE, VERNACULAR DIPLOMACY, AND RACIAL RECOGNITION

In the first instance, the geopolitical imaginary undergirding Tamaki performances is the modernist imaginary of nation and race, in sharp contrast to recent FIT policy for which the highly individualized tourism encounter represents the meeting of global ecumene and indigenous locality (mediated by the managerial state). Tamaki Maori Village itself is a pure simulacrum, grounded in the kind of abstract, homogenous spatiality that made the idea of nation thinkable. In te ao Māori (the Māori world) there is no abstract space: all land is genealogically linked to the specific peoples who inhabit it and who are responsible to ancestral mana to uphold custom.[63] In the abstract space of the state, however, as in the marketplace, valorization happens independently of history and locality. Tamaki has constructed such a space, and with it, its own imagined community: its wharenui (meeting house) is named not after an ancestor but in honor of the performance enterprise itself, Te Rōpu Whakaoho (which the emcee translated as "our family," but which literally means "the group that startles, arouses"). The gesture allows Tamaki to avoid the sort of tensions between community and commercial values that have plagued many marae-based attractions. (It observes few customary protocols, for example. Even bans on food and smoking seem pragmatic rather than observances of tapu, the rules pertaining to the separation of different categories of practices and objects.) It also means that there are few concerns about the unauthorized use or trade of cultural property, which here belongs not to an ancestral group but to a corporate (read commercial) entity. Likewise, while Tamaki's newer attractions base themselves in "traditional storytelling," they tell stories about fictional tribes, the sole property of company imagineers. As a consequence, what Tamaki offers is the stark opposite of "authenticity," as construed by Māori advisers in TNZ: as one explained to me, to be authentic, the tourism experience should not simply be delivered by Māori but should "take place in a natural environment with interpretation by tangata whenua, or someone with local experience . . . there needs to be a relationship between the interpreter and the place—people talking about their own connection and own family."

Instead, the voice that Tamaki Maori Village speaks in is unabashedly one of ethnos rather than tribe or, for that matter, state. That is, it claims to speak for a coherent ethnoracial entity, a "nation" in the nineteenth-century or Herderian sense of the word. The emcees and drivers welcome guests to "this beautiful country of Aotearoa," inviting them in the racial first-person plural to enjoy the hospitality "*we*, the Māori people," offer. Whereas Te Puia and many other Rotorua mainstays are increasingly careful to specify their emphasis on performance, ambassadorship, and hospitality as a distinctively Arawa tradition, Tamaki has no such qualms: their presenters appoint themselves as "proud ambassadors of *our Māori culture*," and they even own the domain name maoriculture.co.nz. Their usage of the term "culture" lies at the opposite end of the semantic spectrum from that of the fifth Labour government's policy framework. It is not a fungible currency of national unity and global prosperity; instead, what the emcees reference is the inalienable common property of a collective—the perceptually verifiable, unifying root of their difference. It is, in fact, a usage much closer to "race."

The performance conventions clearly evoke race: the uniformity of "traditional" costuming, the temporal mise-en-scène of premodernity, and the ferocious dance (haka) as racial metonym. Even with the wide phenotypic variation of the performers (unlike Hawaiian lu'au, Māori producers do not select for racial appearances or body type, despite customer expectations), the interpretive frame is explicit: the experience is to be educational, and the object purchased is evidence of ethnoracial difference. "We hope that you have now learned more about our people," the emcees conclude.[64] At the same time, Tamaki scripts playfully ironize the racial typologies of those same performance conventions, in what Barbara Kirshenblatt-Gimblett has called the ethnographic burlesque: wry jokes about Māori "warriors" appreciating hamburgers, television, and beer abound in the improvisations of emcees, while the prowess of the national rugby team is a constant point of reference in explanations of ancient custom.[65] The performers' warm generosity makes collaborators of the audience, as if to suggest that the primitive mythos is a joke that all share: race here is neither rallying cry nor mystique nor stain but a comfortable fact of national life, known through benign stereotypes such as sporting prowess or a predilection for junk food. (It is a welcome relief, at times, for both performers and some audience members, for whom the transparent silliness of the primitivist conventions at play can be embarrassing.)

Despite this equivocation, Tamaki's mobilization of race as the basis for factional solidarity is clear. Racial recognition is the political metaphor at the core of Tamaki's dramaturgy, which immerses the visitor in a feel-good fantasy of liberal reciprocity, built on the model of Māori manaakitanga, in which two distinct and sovereign peoples—Māori and non-Māori, visitor and host—meet in mutual respect. The moment the visitor is picked up in the Tamaki bus, the process of consolidating the visitors' "tribe" begins: the drivers demand that all join together in bellowing the Māori greeting "kia ora" in reply (an interpellating gesture that, like the Hawaiian "aloha" catchphrase, is repeated with numbing regularity). The range of languages among the visitors is no obstacle to the production of this temporary solidarity. Traditionally, the pōwhiri (welcome) ritual defines the meeting parties through the demonstration and respectful witness of each group's mana and peaceful intent, the guests symbolically consenting

The performers at Tamaki Maori Village pose in the forecourt, as they do at the conclusion of the pōwhiri. Tamaki Tours Ltd.

to abide by the hosts' protocol. The Tamaki drivers likewise coach their new tribes, only half ironically, in the performance of respect in the face of cultural difference: you may think this looks peculiar, you may think he's joking when he brandishes that taiaha, but you had better carry yourself like a chief, or you won't be on the bus home with us! (In a recent incident at Tamaki, a performer of the wero, or challenge, head-butted a Dutch tourist he felt was behaving disrespectfully toward the proceedings. While commentators were quick to chalk the reaction up to "cultural fatigue syndrome," it might be taken to indicate the opposite: that these protocols remain charged, even in their most commercialized and burlesqued form.) Awash in manufactured sentiment and *communitas* ("You are one with us, now," the visitors are told at the end of the evening), and having eaten and talked together at shared tables, few visitors notice that the hosts have melted away behind the scenes, preparing for the next "tribe" to arrive. On the bus home, warm with amity, the visitors nationally reaggregate in an "it's a small world after all" globalist spirit, in a driver-led sing-along of a medley of national anthems.

The experience of Tamaki Maori Village affectively reinforces the most basic of shared liberal nationalist ideals: toleration, curiosity, and respect. But its binary model also draws the lines of control over cultural material, together with the lines of identity, with uncompromising clarity: the boundaries between public and private domains, guest and host, front stage and backstage, those aspects of culture to be shared and those to be retained, are etched as sharply as the fortified fence that walls the complex.[66] What the visitor has entered into is a transaction in the analogy of a relationship. As one former Tamaki manager explained to me, "The whole thing is performance. You've paid for it, you'll walk away with it—that's the proposition. It's about presenting a product. . . . It's based around the concept of time limit—the expectation that you will deliver a certain depth of culture in a certain format." Of course, any transaction is a relationship, a *temporary* relationship *between equals*, entered into for mutual benefit, at least in the ideal imagination of classical economic theory. The same manager noted the consumer habitus of many Tamaki patrons, who are not motivated (like the FIT) by "discovery" or "connectivity" but by a respect at once mercantile and cultural: "You know what's best to share and what we need to know. So give it to us." Pragmatically, the temporal and spatial containment of such enterprises limits the intrusion of tourist traffic on community life, and its commodity structure protects against the touristic appropriation of either unpaid cultural labor or cultural property. The agency to determine the boundaries of cultural commerce lies with those accountable (and, here, Māori) individuals who "know what's best to share."

Ultimately, Tamaki's approach cuts to the core of the political imagination sustained by ethnic tourism. It offers the nostalgic comfort of liberal belonging to clearly demarcated, symmetrical solidarities, neutralizing the normative white subject's encounter with difference through choreographing the performance of recognition as hospitable reciprocity between equals. It is well established that ethnographic attractions of this kind attempt to render the compact of race innocent, detaching it from historical narratives of economic and political violence and producing it as semiotic artifact and spectacle. Colonialism, in precontact Tamaki Maori Village, is an unimagined future (or a forgotten past), and the visitors are interpellated as allies and equals, not imperial sons and daughters. The irony that Tamaki

reveals in this formula is that, in the context of neoliberal cultural governmentality, the mere fact of staging race in theatrical tourism comes to
seem, quixotically, like the refuge of an oppositional politics. The contrast
of ethnographic entertainment with the logic of the experience economy
and its touristic correlative, FIT tourism, is obvious: While the former sees
a bounded service transaction, the latter sees an ongoing, bidirectional relationship between consumers and producers. While the former produces
and addresses complementary solidarities, the latter takes the individual as
its target (and project), apprehending identity not through representation
but through coexperience. While the former secures cultural property and
privacy in the bodies of performers, the latter is premised on its circulation
as communicative capital. Finally, while the former adheres to race as its
organizing principle, the latter sublates race in an ideal of cosmopolitan
(and class) commonality, by means of a new assemblage of conducts and
values that it calls indigeneity. This, I suggest, is both its promise and its
danger.

FIT TOURISM: CULTURAL HOSPITALITY
IN AN EXPERIENCE ECONOMY

FIT ethnic tourism is hard to define in part because it is deliberately un-
codified: it operates not by creating cultural products but by "adding value"
to quotidian recreational activities, imbuing them with "the Māori dimension." It might take the form of an adventure-tourism operation that explains the Māori history of its site to visitors; a spa that uses Māori methods
of massage; a guided bush walk in which tangata whenua guides (Māori
genealogically linked to the locale) explain traditional methods of bushcraft, food-gathering, and medicinal uses of plants; a high-end winery that
serves traditionally influenced food; or a bed-and-breakfast that displays
Māori art and greets visitors in the Māori language. The value added, however, more often than not inheres in the art of interpretation: those performances in which workers select, narrate, and explicate details of Māori
life to their patrons, in the individualized, conversational interaction prized
by FIT advocates. These are, like concert-party performances, transactions
that bring elements of cultural property into market systems, but they do
so in the more fluid, improvisational, and ephemeral medium of sociable conduct. "They take people and share culture in an intimate way," a

FIT business owner and frequent consultant to Tourism New Zealand explained to me. "It's tangible. You can grab it and see it, interact with it, become part of it—it's deliverable. It's not a song and dance but a people we can show."

Unlike concert-party performances (which trade in the representation of stabilized cultural commodities), FIT tourism is a potentially limitless form of identity production conducted at the border of market and ethnos: as iwi and hapū lobby for a slice of the tourism pie, one MRTO head told me, they will have to "discover their own identities," looking to their own stories to ask what they have to share—"are we comfortable to commercialize that in an appropriate way?" FIT tourism blurs the frontstage–backstage distinctions that undergird the confident stridency of an enterprise like Tamaki: the boundaries between zones of cultural privacy and commercial exchange, self and other, and producer and consumer that marked the biopoetics of Fordist-era tourism. In the discourse promoting FIT tourism, such structural distinctions, and the racial difference with which they are aligned, are trumped by an ideal of imagined global community: the transaction is refigured as a sharing of experience and a meeting of like peoples newly linked in an ongoing relationship. Meanwhile, the work of managing the circulation of property and marking the boundaries of cultural privacy and ethnic identity is refigured as a technology of selfhood performed by the tourism laborer: "You're not being asked to compromise," one Ministry of Tourism appointee explained to me (recalling the words of Makereti Papakura from a century earlier), "just to be yourself."

In analyzing FIT tourism, I again have chosen to focus on a single operation, one that occupied a privileged place in the touristic network linking state, industry, and Māori agents. This company, Potiki, was a model and poster child for the state's Māori tourism development initiatives: the business grew in symbiosis with their policies and publicity strategies, drew on their research, and was aided by their business-development programs. Its proprietors deliberately kept a finger on the pulse of policy developments and were likewise closely watched by those in Wellington, who sent them a constant stream of international journalists and agents. They were a regular feature in upmarket travel journals, general-interest magazines, and the Māori press, in which they were a beacon of successful, small-scale cultural entrepreneurship. And they were active in supporting similar enterprises, keeping networked with Māori tourism providers around the nation.

The company was started in 2003 by two women of Ngāpuhi descent now in their midthirties. After spending a few years working in Māori arts nonprofits and women's health organizations and training in adventure ecotourism, they joined forces to build a business that would fill a conspicuous gap in Auckland's tourism market. Between 2003 and 2010, the business offered tours of Greater Auckland that introduced clients to urban Māori and Pasifika lifestyles, to Māori custom, philosophy, and ecological practice, to contemporary and traditional arts, and to the Māori history of the area. In 2010, the company divided into two separate operations: Potiki Adventures retains the title of the original enterprise and focuses on adventure or ecological tourism informed by Māori values, while the other director has founded Mōhio Tours, which continues the urban and cultural tours on which I focus here. The daylong tours are intimate, interactive, and highly responsive to the interests and motivations of the guests, who are taken in groups of no more than ten with an articulate, informed, and open guide (either the proprietor or the small but growing number of colleagues she is bringing on board as the business blossoms). They are deliberately upscale, their clientele affluent, highly educated, and interested in indigenous culture, ecological and social issues, and high-end shopping for contemporary Māori art and fashion. As an ethnographer and a scholar of tourism, I was closer to the rule than the exception for their clientele: educated, English-speaking, white-collar professionals who are culturally curious but uncomfortable with the practice of mass ethnic tourism. Most are affluent and from affluent nations. (Although she found it difficult to generalize, the proprietor estimated that the majority of her customers are from the United States, with significant numbers from England and other European nations.) Taking travelers off the beaten track to places frequented more by locals than tourists, the tours offer them the opportunity to assuage curiosity and gain cultural access, in the company of someone who feels more like a peer than a service provider.

The tour begins with the guide picking visitors up at their hotels in a company SUV or minivan. Itineraries vary but might include a trip to Maungakiekie, where museum displays give insight into precontact Māori lifeways; also known as One Tree Hill, it is a former Ngāti Whātua fortification of enormous historical, political, and spiritual significance and is now a park in the middle of Auckland. Other possibilities include shopping for jewelry or souvenirs at the hip boutiques run by Māori artists in

Kingsland; a walk along Karekare Beach and into the rainforest preserve, with an explanation of the medicinal uses of plants along the way; or enjoying a snack from the takeaway at Piha Beach while watching the surfers. A day trip on the weekend might also include some time in the Polynesian suburbs of South Auckland at the massive Ōtara market and a few hours spent kayaking in Goat Island Marine Reserve, followed by fish and chips on the beach. The essence of the tour's experience, though, is the interaction with a guide: visitors are instructed to ask about anything that piques their curiosity, and conversation flows freely throughout the day. The guides' detailed and frank answers are nondidactic, never sound scripted, and situate the limits of the individual speaker's knowledge and authority carefully.

These tours for individual travelers were the core of Potiki's mission but only part of its business—the less lucrative, more vulnerable part. They would also customize expeditions for delegates to conferences or organize events for cruise-ship passengers on commission from other tourism providers. The business catered equally to corporate hospitality and the global education industry. Potiki hosted student groups from wealthy U.S. preparatory schools, for example, organizing residencies at an urban marae, where students learned Māori arts such as taiaha and undertook a joint visual arts project with local children. (So close are the global linkages between higher education and FIT indigenous tourism that, in my encounters with other FIT businesses, I have often found myself being "pitched" to by proprietors who assume that I am scouting for international programming opportunities for my U.S. university.)[67] In keeping with the kaupapa (the Māori philosophy or mission) of the business, they also lent their support to Māori communities, partnering with a school marae in an underprivileged neighborhood of Auckland to provide opportunities and funding to its students. In the eyes of Potiki's proprietors, this close linkage between capital and community is a quintessentially Māori ethos (not the anathema that postcolonial critics assume it is): wealth flows out of the richness of whanaungatanga (togetherness, family, community) and should ultimately flow back.

Potiki and its successors flourish under a quintessentially knowledge-economy model: the product itself is infinitely flexible, relying not on material infrastructure but on the human and cultural capital of its proprietors. Circulation, meanwhile, is not solely organized around a vertical producer–wholesaler–consumer model but is predominantly fed by horizontal networks of ongoing, communicationally rich relationships between the providers and publicists, commercial agents, cultural institutions, other businesses, other cultural producers, state agencies, customers (institutional and individual), and communities.

IMAGINING THE INDIGENOUS

If the unspoken premise of the staged attraction is the liberal dyad of racial recognition, Potiki's FIT tourism turned the question of *who* or *what* to recognize into a complex story that took, in one way or another, much of the day to tell. On a tour I took with Potiki in 2007 (discussed throughout this section), my guide delicately cleared the ground for this story by disarticulating the phenotypical impression of race from Māoriness, and Māoriness from nonmodernity. "So," Melissa began once I and another guest were settled in the car, "you probably know from our publicity that Potiki is about giving you a sense of the urban Māori experience—the kinds of lives that indigenous Māori people like me live in a city like Auckland. In the process, I'll be telling you a bit about the Māori history of the area." An unfamiliar tourist would be unlikely to visually index Melissa—with her fair skin, her middle-class Kiwi accent and affect, and her casual but hip aesthetic suggesting a young professional on a day off—as Māori. The only visible marker she offers is a magnificent tiki pendant around her neck. Throughout the tour, in response to our questions or to illustrate other points, Melissa described her own background in detail, lending texture to how identity is lived through time and across contexts in a becoming-bicultural state. The child of a part-Māori (Ngāpuhi) mother and a Pākehā father, she was brought up by her mother identifying largely as Pākehā, but she lived in rural Northland, where the majority population is Māori and where taha Māori (Māori ways) permeate the operative norms of many social institutions. She did not fully "engage" with her "Māori side," as she phrases it, until tertiary education gave her the opportunity to study Māori art: she has experienced her Māori identity, then, not as a given but as a process of discovery, inquiry, and spiritual deepening that she shares with tourists.

Race, however, remains part of the interpretive frame clients bring to the encounter. When I asked what the most common questions she gets from tourists are, Melissa replied wryly, "Americans always ask for statistics": "What percentage of the population is Māori, and where do they live, and what's the life expectancy and education levels, and all that stuff. It was funny. After a few times I had to go and look it all up." While Tamaki's customers look to the corporeal facticity of race as the guarantor of the encounter's value or authenticity (I have been told by several fair-skinned performers in similar troupes that the most frequent client question is, "Are you really Māori?"), Melissa's clients seek to map Aotearoa New Zealand's racial topography through classically governmental, biopolitical analytics of population. If asked, Melissa will address the structural legacies of discrimination, and such issues drift into the conversation as the SUV drives through tracts of state housing on the way from boutique to beach, but this is not the focus of the tour's discourse. Likewise, the politics of Māori resistance is a palpable, if covert, presence in the urban landscape and thus on the tour. When we climbed Maungakiekie, for example, we visited one of the symbolic flashpoints of the sovereignty movement, the stump of a tree planted by colonists on a site sacred to Māori and felled by an activist in 1994. When we passed the Harbour Bridge, it was difficult to avoid mention of the protests that halted traffic only a couple of weeks before our tour, when the Harbour Authority refused to fly the Māori (Tino Rangatiratanga) flag alongside the New Zealand flag on Waitangi Day.[68] Melissa is cautious, however, of being too outspoken. She is not sure, she tells me quietly, how the company's relationship with TNZ would fare if they got a reputation for stridently antistate leanings.

Melissa's task is common to many FIT providers. FIT interactivity must work at the same time to displace the determinist, factitious hold of racial logic over tourist interpretations and to downplay the challenge that race (with its historical and class baggage) presents to state claims to bicultural consensus. In the place of race, FIT tourism installs indigeneity, a discourse of identity that is being mobilized in national tourism policy and practice as something between an emergent structure of feeling, a brand, and a knowledge-economy value. This shift from race to indigeneity represents a significant change in the political rationality of state, for which tourism practice has become a laboratory. Unlike race, which is a biopolitical technology of categorization operating through empirical epistemology (the supposedly hard facts of phenotype and genotype), indigeneity—as construed in FIT tourism—is brought into knowledge experientially as a constellation of attachments, sensitivities, awarenesses, and conducts that evoke links to place, past, and lineage. It is not a medium of allegiance or solidarity (like the abstract, representational community of strangers described by nation, ethnos, or race), nor is it a political claim on the state (as scholars such as Ronald Niezen have argued regarding the political use of the term). Instead it operates through a nonexclusive, largely nonessentialist principle of affinity.[69] Indigeneity, in this policy-fueled reinvention, is less a discourse of difference than (increasingly) one of similitude, invoked to offer the tourist access and attachment. Crucially, whereas race is a device by which states distribute resources and opportunity, indigeneity is being newly identified (as my reading of *The Tourism Edge* at the beginning of this chapter suggests) as a locus of value in itself: the property of specific subjects but widely available for empathic participation, and a space through which capital might flow on these currents of empathy. In particular, it is often discussed as a compensatory supplement to the deracinated, disenchanted, neoliberal subject known as *Homo economicus*. In an increasingly rootless world, as several state tourism representatives told me, indigeneity's gift is to revivify, redimensionalize, and respiritualize our sense of place and thus of belonging—an effect that cannot be lent by the simulacra of ethnographic entertainment or the distanced, generic gaze of landscape tourism.

It is easy to dismiss this promise to reenchant modernity through purchasing access to otherness as a form of global neoprimitivism. On one level, it is exactly that. It is also easy to see the expedience of indigeneity for a retribalizing society in a postracial climate: for many Māori, the category "Māori" is an artifact of colonial biopolitics that lumped disparate tribes together and has no relevance in a postcolonial age that honors rangatiratanga. But indigeneity is also an evolving, complex, and contested technology of subjectivation and a located form of political community that deserves serious critical attention. As it is proposed and practiced in FIT tourism, indigeneity entails for tourists the experience of an unbinding but ideally durational attachment to place and people. Privileging material contiguity over abstract membership, it issues a call to responsibility—that is, to respond affectively and to care about (implicitly, to care *for*) those places and peoples. This discourse, crucially, is not imposed from outside Māori culture but evolves in dialogue with the development strategies of Māori themselves, representing a foothold of Māori ecological politics in the domain of the cultural state. An example from Potiki's tour serves to illustrate.

Melissa's tours are successful in attuning their patrons to the temporal and cultural textures of the places they traverse. As we walked on Karekare Beach, Melissa's comments illuminated the space: It is one of quotidian recreation (she and her Auckland friends hike there) and of global mediation (it features in the spectacular opening scenes of Jane Campion's 1993 film *The Piano*). It is also a place saturated with history, the site of a battle between invading Ngāpuhi and Ngāti Whātua in the early nineteenth century so brutal that some of Melissa's Ngāti Whātua friends refuse to come here because they think it still reeks of death. We enjoyed an informal lesson about kaitiakitanga, guardianship or caretaking, by watching her attend to the beach by picking up stray pieces of litter or seeing her harvest leaves to make medicinal tea, taking care not to disrupt the growth pattern of the shrub. At one point, Melissa asked us to close our eyes and turn our faces into the wind. Then she told us the first story of the place where we stood, its creation story—of Papatūānuku and Ranginui, earth and sky, locked in a passionate embrace that was rent by their impatient children (the winds, forests, and seas), thus giving birth to our world of struggle, strife, and loss. Melissa did not emote or dramatize; she told the story *as fact*, in clear, measured sentences, inviting us to feel the mauri (life force) and wairua (spirit) of the elements around us, the land that we touch and that touches us.

This moment, Melissa later explained to me, is the core of her vision for her company. She recalled improvising the gesture at the conclusion of a retreat she ran for at-risk Māori youth to learn bushcraft skills, believing that the greatest gift these rootless kids could receive was a sense of connection to ancestry and land, to their indigeneity. It was a gift she felt might also be welcomed by the ecologically conscious cosmopolitan tourists who were coming in increasing numbers in search of a more profound experiential engagement with the place they were visiting, in search (as one other promoter put it to me) "of their own indigeneity," a contiguous, sensed attachment to place and past. Without exception, every FIT tour I have experienced offers some similar embodied microritual of attachment: joining in a karakia, or prayer, to the ancestral guardians of a particular place; rubbing a mauri stone to invest it with your spirit; or crafting an object from flax and committing to take it back to your own home and ancestors. These are simple, often sentimental, lessons in Māori cosmology and eco-practice. The gestures also clearly mesh with the mandates and logic of a cultural economy, issuing on invitation to a return visitation. The affective

On tour with the Potiki Urban Māori Experience. Courtesy of Melissa Crockett, Potiki Tours.

substance of such experiences forms a network—in this instance between Potiki, its ecopolitical commitments, the land on which it thrives, the local community it serves, the international community it courts, and the state—through which future business and exchanges might flow.

PERFORMING THE LIMITS TO CULTURAL TRAFFIC

Indigeneity is an open system, available for and porous to global traffic. While Māori in FIT tourism retain performative, and thus proprietorial, privileges in the sharing of cultural material, the cultural economy in which they work is often at odds with the claims to both privacy and property that constituted racial recognition under the former liberal regime. As the chair of the newly formed Māori committee of the Historic Places Trust (a TNZ partner) told me, "We have to revise Māori ideas of history—getting away from the possessiveness and defensiveness—and start looking at it as *human* heritage." Making this shift from exclusive possession to universal gift, from race to indigeneity, however, is a labor (frequently an uncertain and painful one) for the tourism workers who must daily determine the limits of capital's reach and the boundaries of cultural privacy. The question of what to share is a constant topic of discussion between her and her colleagues, Melissa tells me: each of them has stories of moments when that thin membrane between public and private knowledges is tested and shame, unease, and intimations of danger take hold. For one of her colleagues, an hour spent with clients in the Māori collection of the Auckland Museum changed tenor when she found herself watched by two older Māori patrons in silent censure. She wondered whether she was speaking too deeply of her hapū connections to the taonga. Where exactly had she crossed the line from cultural pedagogy to cultural profligacy?

The tour guide's work is peppered with brute reminders that whatever claims policy might make for the universality of indigeneity's human heritage, the market privileges the *exclusive* possession of property, and its laws do little to protect collective minority interests. Appropriation is a risk as old as colonialism itself; what is new in FIT tourism is that the work of defining and defending the boundaries of sovereign possession and privacy is a work of performance in which property is always in solution, dissolved in the messy thickness of copresence and real-time improvisation. Melissa herself recalls driving with a client who engaged her in conversation about

Māori decorative arts, referring frequently to an interior decorating business she intended to set up in the United States, with a Polynesian aesthetic. As the conversation progressed, Melissa realized with alarm that the persistent client was fishing for a brand name for the business. What, she asked, was the word for "home," for "house," for "dwelling"? She asked as if, were Melissa to cooperate with her inquiry, it would constitute a kind of permission. Melissa felt profoundly uncomfortable. Te reo, the language, is a taonga: a treasured, living possession that connects Māori with ancestors. It cannot be owned, neither should it be appropriated; instead, it must be nurtured by its kaitiaki (custodians), living Māori. As innocent as the woman's inquiry might have seemed (she could, after all, have looked the words up in a dictionary), alienation of the cultural commons represents a palpable threat to Māori entering the global economy, a threat that can, quite literally, assault the ground of identity. After recounting this episode, Melissa mentioned the example of Moana Maniapoto, a Māori R&B singer who tried to release an album in the United Kingdom only to find that her name, Moana (meaning "sea"), was a registered trademark belonging to someone else. Melissa described the chill that came over the space as she sensed cultural danger; it was a communication from the animate matter of place and the ancestors who are consubstantial with it. To work in Māori tourism, she said, is to attune yourself carefully to these voices.

Alongside this boundary-work, however, another way of thinking about the relationship between property and identity is flourishing among Māori in tourism, a way more consonant with Māori understandings of knowledge as "an energy, not a thing," and property (taonga) as an element in the sustained temporal and global extension of relationships. In this framework, indigeneity's value is not a finite resource but deepens and propagates in the context of its touristic performance. The argument resembles the claims of autonomous Marxists such as Maurizio Lazzarato: in an immaterial economy, knowledge is no longer governed by the laws of scarcity assumed by classical economics; rather, the more it is shared, the more its value is enhanced.[70] In being used, it is not used *up*; instead, it is rendered more legitimate, more productive of further knowledge, relationships, and subjects. This theory runs against dominant vernacular and academic ideas about tourism's Midas touch: that, once drawn into touristic circulation, the original object of value loses its scarcity (or exclusivity) and thus its aura. One manager gave the example of a half-day tour in the Whirinaki Forest:

Because the forest is such an enigmatic being with so much stuff in there, you can continually talk about stuff, picking up on the environment as a prompt, layering on the cultural dimension. . . . It comes back to how strong the culture is in the person, how energetic they are in continuing to give. . . . The culture's language is getting stronger in people delivering tourism. Māori will be in an added-value position vis-à-vis their non-Māori competitors. . . . It has to do with wairua [spirit]—it has to be there, and it has to grow.

Others talk of plumbing ever-deeper strata, or awakening a sleeping taniwha (supernatural guardian), to describe the ways in which surging cultural pride in Māoridom is deepening the wellspring of culture drawn upon in tourism. And like this speaker, in doing so they often yoke Māori concepts (for example, the reservoir of spiritual, ancestral energy that is wairua) to the state's neoliberal terminology (the competitive mobilization of identity to add value). Indigeneity as property is imaged as a fountain rather than a fortress: generative, illimitable, and augmented through links with partners and profit, rather than a finite, imperiled resource that must be both protected from and deployed in the market. This is so little like the old equation between sovereignty, property, and privacy that proponents search for other analogies than the commercial transaction— the gift or barter, for instance—to describe the tourism relationship, in the process leveling structural distinctions (and perforce class and racial distinctions) between consumers and producers. The contrast with the transactional relationship evoked and exemplified by Tamaki could not be starker.

THE TOPOGRAPHY OF OPPORTUNITY IN A CULTURAL ECONOMY

How tenable is this horizontal, postracial, identity-economy ideal, given the legacy of inequality bequeathed to Māori by the colonial state? Where FIT tourism's goals of intimate equality succeed, I venture, it owes that success at least in part to the establishment of class—with its specific capacities and conducts—as the normative ground on which consumers and producers meet. It is little secret that creative economies favor the professional-managerial class, even as they trade on the rhetoric, and capital, of multicultural inclusion.[71] The emerging economy of FIT tourism is no exception. Potiki again offers an instructive example. Its clientele were tourists of means ("high yield" in Ministry of Tourism parlance), and Potiki's most frequent tours catered to their consumer habitus, "adding value" to what a specific, highly culturally capitalized (and not majority-Māori) class fraction of New Zealanders also do on the weekends: go for nature walks and scenic drives, eat at swish cafés, and visit galleries and boutiques. Further, there are class barriers to entering the FIT economy. A FIT business, while it may not have high start-up costs, has a complex business model; to establish one means drawing deeply on reservoirs of social, human, and economic capital—before cultural capital even enters into the equation. Melissa describes her work as more of a vocation than a business: Potiki was built at enormous cost (years of low cash flow, borrowing from friends and family, sleeping on couches, and burning up enough hours to make supporting dependents entirely inconceivable) and drawing on resources (of business and marketing savvy, education, connections, confidence, and creditworthiness) that few would be able to muster. Then there are the performance competencies that the work demands: the subtleties of conduct that (as Makereti Papakura knew) lend confidence and authority in cosmopolitan circles. Concert-party performers are clear that they draw their performance presence from whanaungatanga, the power and courage of the collective, but FIT guiding is an individual endowment. According to one FIT adventure-tourism operator, representing a Māori enterprise that claimed to have tried and failed to apprentice Māori guides from the socioeconomically depressed working-class region in which it was located, "it takes a very particular kind of person to do this work."

The class distance between the Māori communities that generate the cultural property traded in FIT tourism and those cosmopolitan social spaces through which it flows is another fracture of the cultural state that brokers such as Potiki must mediate in their performances. One particularly poignant anecdote serves to illustrate. Melissa found herself approached by a visiting cruise ship's agent with a request for Māori cultural entertainment. Being no fan of the hāngī-'n'-haka industry, she suggested that, rather than contracting to one of the several Māori troupes that perform regularly for tourists around Auckland, the agent should try something more original. Potiki worked with a marae attached to a local elementary school, which trained an accomplished troupe in an original and impressive repertory; at the same cost, the cruise could hire these students, get a fresh, exciting, authentic, and high-quality (if nonprofessional) performance, and support an underresourced community. She prevailed (a testament to her marketing skills), and arrangements for the concert were made. When the time came for the children to board the ship at the dock, however, their parents moved to follow them, to support the kids in their concert's kaupapa, its mission. These men and women were dressed in work clothes from the factories, supermarkets, and warehouses where they were employed, looking tired and tough. The group's mere embodied presence, let alone their customary conduct—laughing, chatting, and loudly cheering their kids on—would have been wildly incongruous in a cruise-ship ballroom filled with middle-aged, moneyed, dinner-dressed Europeans. Melissa described to me her hasty attempts to head off disaster, to persuade the group that they would need to support their tamariki (children) in spirit from their cars on the dock. Most obliged, understanding the social delicacies of the moment. But one kuia (female elder) dug in her heels: if the kids were welcome, why wouldn't she be? This was their custom, and she didn't see why they should change it. It was an excruciating moment; Melissa, of course, could see her point. If the tourists wanted to see authentic Māori modernity, why did it have to be edited to preserve their class sensibilities? In the end, the woman made her symbolic stand, sneaking onto the ship and standing quietly in the back of the room where the children performed, her arms crossed in defiance.

Tamaki Maori Village or its like would never face a conflict of this nature. Ethnographic entertainment is a mass medium with no pretentions to class exclusivity, its conventions a shared contract that protects the privacy of tribal life by offering tourists engagement not with the fullness of cultural personhood but with the façade of a clearly defined role. FIT tourism, on the other hand, blurs community and commerce, interlarding spheres of social production with the market in ways that play across the terrain of class privilege. In doing so, it accentuates the gulf between the socially resourced and those positioned as cultural resources, those subjects entitled to bear, generate, and circulate identity capital and those from whom it can only be selectively mined. For an indigenous body, conduct, or custom to be endowed with value in the economy of the cultural state, this last example suggests, it must (like the child) be unmarked by the twin stigmas of race and class.

FIT tourism's practitioners find themselves caught in a trenchant set of tensions: between making Māori culture "deliverable" and honoring tribal demands for privacy, autonomy, and control over cultural property; between the state's upscale vision of a sanitized, privatized, depoliticized, and consumer-friendly Māori culture and vital tribal performance cultures shaped by working-class habitus, anticolonial struggle, exclusion, and poverty; and between the freedoms and gifts of a borderless, fluid, and limitless neoliberal economy of culture and the needs of those to whom neoliberalism's golden promises appear most disingenuous. "Would you do it again?" I asked Melissa, following up on the story of the children on the cruise ship. "In an instant," she replied. "Absolutely. We raised more money for that school in one evening than we could in twenty jumble sales." To navigate these tensions, to evolve these kinds of calculative faculties: this is the ethical work of Māori tourism and the price of Māori development in a cultural state without social guarantees.

PERFORMANCE IN A NEOLIBERAL KEY

Ministry of Tourism statistics show that the number of FIT businesses is growing, but FIT ethnic tourism remains a small sector of the market. By and large, it does not serve backpackers (for whom the expense is prohibitive), non-English speakers, or package tourists (especially the growing Chinese market). Nor does it appeal to the domestic market: Pākehā New Zealanders are rare clients of Māori cultural tourism operations and are frequently resistant, critical, or dismissive.[72] Given its low turnover, the archetypal FIT business is vulnerable: as one promoter quipped, "Heidi and Fritz once a week just aren't sustainable." Why, then, the cheerleading from policy quarters? The state's investment in FIT tourism is, I argue, performative rather than pragmatic. The actual number or profitability of FIT ethnic-tourism businesses is of less consequence than the ways in which, under current policy, the techniques, conducts, dispositions, and discourses evolved in FIT tourism are coming to inflect *all* tourism practice. In doing so, tourism is imagining and rehearsing into being the (bi)cultural state.

Under the auspices of FIT-focused policy, the state has recalibrated the national brand, attuning it to Māori difference. It has created value out of Māori modernity, enrolling third-sector agencies to bring it into the market *on Māori terms*, yet aligned with the interests of national prosperity. It has cultivated the communicative capacities and conducts of its subjects, encouraging them to generate and sustain (trans)national networks and endowing them with new ways to understand, value, and deploy the experience of cultural life as capital. In making capital out of culture, it has changed the relationship of property to individual and collective personhood, inducing a mutation in the racial character of citizenship. And it has offered a space of mediation or translation between racial solidarities forged in the era of anticolonial and class counterpolitics and its new, desired subjects: entrepreneurial, cosmopolitan, cultural citizens. FIT tourism, in short, tools racial subjects to "postracial" neoliberal governmentalities. Tourism is by no means the only space in which this kind of cultural state making work occurs. Nor is this work entirely new: we can see echoes of Liberal-era patterns in the neoliberal appropriation of Māoridom as a bulwark against the "loss of cultural distinction that is a consequence of market fundamentalism" or as a way to legitimate the state's new progressive, pluralist vitality by performing consensus around neoliberal principles.[73]

The new generation of ethnic tourism can, however, help us understand two important things about neoliberal governmentality, less legible in other arenas. The first is the centrality of performance to the cultural processes of neoliberalization and to the refiguration of political agency under neoliberal governmentality. Critical consensus tells us that neoliberalism represents the "marketization of everything" in ways especially hostile to the values represented by culture. Its ideal subject, *Homo economicus*, is a rational utility maximizer, detachable from the web of cultural associations that sustain both community and resistance. Public or cultural goods are only good in the sense that they can be transformed into private property. Neoliberalism, in this analysis, is capital's enclosing of the final remaining commons—the cultural commons—thus curtailing the possibility for an independent civil society that might fuel dissent against or present alternatives to market mandates. Yet any analysis of actually existing neoliberalism, especially in its third-way incarnation, demonstrates that cultural qualities (difference, affect, expressivity, relationality, and attachment) are not merely ancillary or instrumental to the post-Fordist means of production; rather, they are its central value. The experience economy values goods not for their usefulness but for their capacity to capture customers through connecting them to experiences (branding). It aims not to transform raw materials but to transform "the production and manipulation of affects" that sustain networks, teams, and other forms of cooperation between minds.[74] As is clearly visible in FIT tourism, it is not that culture is being "turned from a communicative process into a set of commodities" but that the commodity is being turned into a communicative cultural process.[75]

If culture is both fuel and fabric of neoliberal economy, performance is the machinery that makes it go. Diverse theorists of post-Fordist production have long seized on performance as its metaphor and model: For Lazzarato, the material production cycle (production–consumption) is replaced by an "aesthetic" one (author–reproduction–reception). For Paolo Virno, culture (also known as the general intellect) is the "score" that the virtuoso worker performs. And for Michel Callon, in the "economy of qualities," the product is an ongoing performative process of relation between producer and consumer, oriented toward the manipulation of human attachments.[76] FIT ethnic tourism demands a particular *kind* of performance, clearly distinguished from its theatrical predecessor: improvisational, nonmatrixed, narratively generative, and site- and community-specific, it is a live exchange of affect and information potentially productive of enduring and extensive social and spatial relationships yet reliant on existing ones. It is a world-making activity. As a collaborative performance enacted in real time, it is emergent, porous, and inevitably contested.

Performance analysis of FIT tourism makes explicit what remains implicit in other sectors of the neoliberalizing culture industries: that the marketization of culture is not a fait accompli; instead, it is an ongoing and open-ended *process*. That process is both enacted and resisted in the daily ethical practice of culture workers like Melissa. That this kind of performance should be so pivotal to Aotearoa New Zealand's neoliberal transformation demonstrates the necessity of biopoetics to the biopolitical regime of the cultural state. It is also indicative of the ways in which neoliberalization has transformed the ground of political, and particularly indigenous, agency such that engaging with tourism, and thus with global capital, is identified by many as the best means to advance and sustain Māori communities in a way consonant with kaupapa Māori. While there is reason to be skeptical of this new intimacy between kaupapa and capital, it is easy to see its promise. First, the new tourism's performative mode locates ethical responsibility in the hands of individual actors embedded in the thickness of social (even ancestral) networks. Second, FIT performance is a process by which political alternatives can and do enter the domain of the state. It introduces priorities, languages, dispositions, understandings, faculties, and a "diversity of calculative agencies"—including indigenous ones—into the market and hence into the state's canons of value. The market, and by extension the state, can no longer be regarded as "that cool, implacable, impersonal monster which imposes its laws and procedures." Instead, "it is a many-sided, diversified, evolving device which . . . the actors themselves contribute to reconfigure."⁷⁷

Whether this new construal of agency results in substantive political gain for Māori or in the redistribution of advantage and opportunity beyond current inequalities remains to be seen. The answer may well depend on the ethnic topography that replaces racial governmentality. Again, the analysis of FIT tourism offers insight. One of neoliberalism's animating fictions is that racial inequity will disappear if the politics of racial solidarity (along with its structural and class analysis and the demand for recognition and remediation of historical wrongs) is abandoned in favor of individualism. The result is to naturalize a range of old and new inequalities while robbing us of a language—race—with which to name them, giving us a dizzying rush of promise in its place: freedom, growth, opportunity, mobility, and competitiveness. Moreover, neoliberalism, as has been widely noted, establishes the endowments of middle-class white conduct as the normative ground of citizenship, defining those who do not conform as deficient in the eyes (and accounts) of the state, responsible for their own exclusion from opportunity and profit. The cultural state is no exception to this rule: in turning cultural difference into entrepreneurial opportunity, it has its own cunning of recognition that differentiates capitalizable diversity from forms of difference that constitute a market liability.⁷⁸

Tourism exposes the subtle technologies through which culture is selectively capitalized, cultivated, and circulated and the markers of value and valuelessness attached to specific conducts and subjects: it attunes us, in other words, to the practice of race in a putatively postracial order. It is in this touristic space that the figure of the indigene has emerged as a paradigmatic subject of the cultural state: endowed with richness of difference, rooted cosmopolitanism, and holism but unmarked by the (racial) stigma of social negativity.⁷⁹ Tourism produces, then, a new (old) order of exclusion, drawing lines between noble and nasty savages, acceptable indigenes and other Others.⁸⁰ However, what touristic relics like Tamaki also make abundantly clear is that the cultural materials accumulated in an era of ethnoracial-class identity—and made durable in racial structures of feeling, dispositions, perceptions, and bodily practices—are incompletely subsumed into the regime of the cultural state. What happens in the cultural state to the remains of race, to its persistent legacies, discourses, and habits? And how does indigeneity fare when facing the forces of global racialization? These are some of the questions I take up in chapter 5.

chapter 5

Altered States: Global Hollywood, the Rise of Wellywood, and the Moving Image of Race

Tourism and cinema, it has been argued, are natural companions. Twin components of the industrial machine of public imagination, both promise escape, pleasure, and all the sensations and prerogatives of mobility.[1] From the outset, film offered experiences of virtual travel, cashing in on the modern fascination for motion and the hunger to "bring things 'closer' spatially and humanly," if only by their likeness.[2] Tourism, meanwhile, found in film a promotional idiom and instrument that turns places into destinations, and destinations into bundles of affect, story, image, and sensation that circulate globally, inviting the audiences they touch to travel in turn. Just as the roving eye of the camera moves through spaces at once fictive and real, in tourism we travel a fabric of interwoven times, stories, significances, and material spaces. (For all its emphasis on presence, tourism never takes place entirely *in place*.) Both cinema and tourism, then, choreograph motion, and in doing so, both produce pathways for future traffic (of ideas, persons, and images) and the spaces through which that traffic passes. Finally, and most fundamentally, both popular cinema and cultural tourism are pedagogies of a kind, their actors representing forms of conduct, value, and personhood—often racially encoded forms—to be taken up or judged by a public. What my previous chapters have argued of tourism might equally be claimed of cinema: it offers scripts for inhabiting and traversing places, for making knowledge about and wresting value from those places and the persons who dwell there. And it occasions

performances of collective and individual selfhood for an audience composed of both outsiders and those selves in the making. It should be little
surprise, then, that both cinema and tourism are institutional assemblages
in which states are deeply invested.

If we understand cinema and tourism as kindred "technologies of the
truth," however, questions follow.[3] What kinds of places and forms of personhood do they privilege? Which stories do they endow with value? In
giving form to a collective imagination, do they circumscribe the imaginable? In forging paths, do they delimit who moves where, and how?
Moreover, for whom and by whom are their ficto-realities crafted, and on
whom do they bear? If cinema globally circulates racial forms and figures,
for example, those forms and figures are surely shaped by the conditions
of their global circulation. The rest of this book has suggested that the
live, performative immediacy of the tourism encounter provides a forum
for the contestation of racial definitions, albeit a conditional one. But can
the same be said for the disembodied commodity form of film, for which
the authors of those definitions include not just local actors, writers, and
creatives but also multinational corporations, foreign focus groups, and
global investors of all kinds?

Such questions take on an additional trenchancy when small markets
and producers engage global economies of scale. Here, being "globally
competitive" can necessitate state investment and policy support, with the
paradoxical result that (much like tourism) cinema is called on to be the
expression of a state's culturally sovereign identity at the same time it is
being pitched to please a global audience. Meanwhile, the state's cultural
sovereignty is continually compromised by those same global economic
pressures. This predicament is compounded for substate solidarities, such
as Māori, struggling for cultural sovereignty autonomous from the state,
as well as for a foothold in a global economy still patterned by the logic of
racial inequality.

This chapter chronicles the past decade of film production in Aotearoa
New Zealand, where the neoliberal economic renaissance detailed in chapter 4 propelled a convergence between tourism and cinema. It focuses
on two cinematic landmarks: first, the *Lord of the Rings* trilogy. Here, a
state-sponsored explosion of runaway production (in which major Hollywood studios locate production abroad) yoked state film, tourism, and
trade agencies to build culture-industry capacity, earn foreign revenue

from underutilized human capital and national assets, and harness film's "place differentiation" effect as part of a national rebranding campaign. The country was cast as "Home of Middle-earth," a place of infinite scenic beauty in infinite variety, available to the global adventurer and the global imagination—a place, moreover, that offered little human resistance to the signally modernist racial logic of Tolkien's fantasy. The second is *Whale Rider*, director Niki Caro's internationally successful feature film of 2002. Here, a new state-administered domestic coproduction policy was to enable New Zealand to "tell its stories" (with the aid of foreign partners) and again brand itself abroad through realizing its "cultural capital" in mobile, fungible form. That the stories told and the capital realized in *Whale Rider* derived from Māori culture was, I argue, no coincidence, nor was that choice a simple reprisal of the appropriative moves of the colonial era. Ecstatically uplifting and auratically pure, the film posed indigeneity—in the radiant person of its young star, Keisha Castle-Hughes—as the aspirational emblem of a new raceless but rooted citizenship. These films were, I contend, flip sides to the same neoliberal coin, precise articulations of the racial conditions of global success, mobility, and viability in a putatively postracial world.

In the first section of this chapter, I read the racial and spatial figures of these films against the public discourse and policy machinations surrounding their production, attending to the mutually constitutive processes of filmmaking and state making, mediated by touristic imperatives. A defining feature of Aotearoa New Zealand's cultural state, the cinematic apparatus can be analyzed as a network that brings together local, state, and global actors, ideological and economic investments, powerful fictions, and equally powerful neoliberal political processes. This network shapes the ways in which tourists and nationals travel, encounter, value, and in turn shape nation-space and the ways in which the nation's symbolic, spatial, and human properties circulate globally. In the second section of the chapter, I examine one such channel of circulation: the cinematic tropes that enable Māori performers and stories to travel the racialized pathways of the global mediascape. Throughout, I track a seemingly contradictory phenomenon: the ascendance of indigeneity in domestic coproduction as a valorized category linking personhood, place, and political futurity (*Whale Rider*) and the concurrent revitalization and relocalization of racial melodrama (with its exaltation of whiteness and excoriation of black villainy) by Global Hollywood (*Lord of the Rings*). That both public discourse and national policy understand these impulses as entirely compatible is, I suggest, symptomatic: it marks the ultimate nullification of race as a dissenting idiom of political community and cultural citizenship that can call to account the liberal conscience of the state.

It is ironic that postracial structures of feeling should flourish in a state for which ethnic recognition is (under biculturalism) a defining mandate. Put bluntly, my proposition is this: Aotearoa New Zealand's quest for success in a global neoliberal knowledge economy that privileges certain forms of cultural capital, affects, mobilities, and subjects has placed limits on the spectrum of identities, political expression, and conduct valorized by the state. We might understand the screen (with Toby Miller) as "the newest component of sovereignty, a twentieth-century cultural addition to ideas of patrimony and rights that sits alongside such traditional topics as territory, language, history, and schooling."[4] But if a state's capacity to contain, manage, and symbolize its population through racializing procedures is in part secured by such technologies of cultural citizenship as the screen, how is the state itself transformed in an era of runaway production and multinational partnerships?

Neoliberal biculturalism, then, is an inherently paradoxical state. Even as Aotearoa New Zealand promotes the cultivation of "national identity" in film, its commitment to knowledge-economy success has meant both launching deterritorialized cultural commodities and services into the global market and making the nation-space porous to other stories, other patrimony, and other construals of rights, in particular those represented by Global Hollywood (arguably its own sovereign entity as well as a component of U.S. sovereignty). As the nation negotiates its uncertain position in the new global division of cultural labor, film makes visible such collisions and collusions between sovereignties: national sovereignty, cultural sovereignty, sovereign individualism, and the sovereignty of capital. This chapter is an effort to understand how this far-reaching process subtly shifts conditions of dwelling, belonging, and citizenship—how it alters states.

Ultimately, this is an argument about the fundamentally liberal mechanism by which racial formations are bound to those of sovereignty, while sovereignty in turn is cut across and compromised by the transnational mobility of capital, population, and ideas—including the ideas of liberalism itself. This ambivalence lies at the core of what I have been referring to as postraciality. On the one hand, postraciality is a neoliberal ideology (or neoconservative myth-wish) whose pernicious local effects in the United States have achieved a global currency with the take-up of U.S.–generated strategies of governmentality and the penetration of sovereign states by multinational corporate capital. It represents an assault on collectivist politics by an absolutist conception of individualism and opportunity: it declares obsolete the "restrictive" sodalities of race identity, discredits race-based critiques of actually existing inequalities, and forecloses political alternatives grounded in race-based analysis. On the other hand, postraciality names an observable neoliberal phenomenon: a "crisis of racial meaning" induced by changes in global political economy.[5] Rapid global flows of population and capital mean that processes of racial subjectivation, affiliation, and recognition take place on an increasingly global scale, while sovereignty-compromised states are less able to effect racializing procedures within their populations. Within states, weakened public or democratizing instruments (such as education), widening wealth gaps, and ubiquitous precarity often make class appear as much a determinant of the distribution of opportunity as race (although whiteness and privilege are as complexly intercalated as ever).

These postracial conditions and ideologies throw up new figures of the racial imagination: commentators across partisan lines hail the proliferation of hybrid, flexible, or liminal identities (as if racial mixing were a novel phenomenon), and icons such as Barack Obama become foci of both reactionary racial hysteria and revitalized liberal idealism, occasioned by a world in which race will not stay in place. Notably, South Pacific indigenes occupy a privileged semiotic role in the liberal imagination of a postracial future, a day—which Henry Louis Gates Jr. looks forward to—when "we [will] all look Polynesian."[6] Meanwhile, ethnogovernmental techniques and quotidian racism continue powerfully to shape lives, aspirations, and apprehensions. Indeed, one of the speculations of this chapter is that postracial structures of feeling not only veil the continued hegemony of white privilege but also prompt the invention of new forms of whiteness less aligned with phenotype or genotype and more aligned with criteria of value, affects, and mobility of use to the neoliberal state. Cinema makes these forms available as objects of identification to a broader constituency while leaving racial stigmatization intact and rendering structural inequities illegible. The recent global currency of indigeneity, which I suggest is central to trends in both tourism and cinema, could be seen as an example of this.

Critiques of postracial ideology are now legion, yet (after Paul Gilroy's *Against Race*), so are arguments that race is an inadequate or flawed conceptual foundation for a politics to come. The following does not advocate for the rehabilitation of race, nor mourn its passing. It is rather an inquiry into the persistence of racializing procedures *after the demise of racial politics.* What is the place of race in the global civil society brokered by the transnational entertainment industry and "the dispersed and diverse forms of transnational allegiance and affiliation" it enables?[7] How are the social spatializations of racial categories changed with the penetration and transmogrification of a state's territory by cinema's transnational imagination? How do communities invested in the production of racial fantasy live, instrumentalize, or imagine away the contradictions between local codes and global *doxa*? And what becomes, in this arguably postracial moment, of the local attachments, historical claims, resistances, and habitus formerly designated by race? Tracing the motile networks of the culture industries, my account attempts to capture the poetics of a state poised between the eclipse of one biopolitical mode—both an instrument of state violence and a vehicle of social resistance—and its emergent successor, yet to be fully imagined.

A BRIEF HISTORY OF
AOTEAROA NEW ZEALAND'S CINEMATIC STATE

Film was recognized in the Liberal era as a valuable instrument of publicity, and it fell under the authority of state tourism agencies for the majority of the twentieth century.[8] State documentary film production focused overwhelmingly on tourist tropes and locations (with Rotorua featuring prominently), prompting the British filmmaker John Grierson to complain in 1940 that "national film" in New Zealand resembled a "cinematic Sears Roebuck catalogue." Meanwhile American producers came in search of "canned" scenery that their state sponsors vainly hoped would "be labeled 'New Zealand' when it reache[d] America."[9]

Narrative film was a latecomer on the national scene: it was not until 1972 that it became a candidate for the state support it needed to survive (in fact, only three domestic feature films were produced between 1940 and 1972). Under the aegis of a new agency, the New Zealand Film Commission

(NZFC), cinema was at first a Pākehā-dominated field. (Māori documentarist Merata Mita jokingly called it the "White Neurotic Industry.")[10] It was plagued by the problems of a scale industry in a tiny market: talent left for better opportunities abroad, while small budgets and inexperienced artists meant low production values and few resources to compete with the promotional muscle of Hollywood, either domestically or abroad. Significant international success came finally in the early 1990s with a suite of films that (thanks to changes in the structure of independents in Hollywood) distinguished themselves in the art-house market: Jane Campion's *An Angel at My Table* (1991–92) and *The Piano* (1993), Peter Jackson's *Heavenly Creatures* (1993), and, significantly, *Once Were Warriors* (1994), a Māori-written feature that broke all New Zealand's domestic and international box office records.[11]

National film's success, however, arrived at the same time as the Keynesian policy structure that had supported it flagged in the face of early 1990s neoliberal reform. The virtues of national culture were no longer self-evident in the eyes of the state, and film pundits were forced to craft new and economically instrumentalist rationales for investment. Over the course of the decade, two not always compatible arguments found favor. First, film was of value to the national brand: cinema generated a deep, lasting, and targeted international recognition that no promotional campaign could approach. Second, film gave underutilized raw assets (locations) and labor (production services) new export value: as home to *Xena: Warrior Princess*, *Hercules: The Legendary Journeys*, and a growing list of other productions, New Zealand was a beneficiary of the globalizing Hollywood trend toward runaway production, which increased from 7 percent to 27 percent of total U.S. screen expenditure between 1990 and 1998.[12] By the end of the 1990s, policy makers were coming to see film as more industry than art, aligned again with tourism and trade as an arm of the state's formative creative-industries strategy.

It was the mammoth triumph of the *Rings* trilogy, however, that "fundamentally changed the game" with regard to the way the state saw the screen, now as a major player in an economic renaissance on neoliberal terms.[13] The New Zealand production budget alone represented a major impact on the economy: over 74 percent of the US$330 million budget was spent in New Zealand, on around five thousand vendors and three thousand employees, from leatherworkers to taxi drivers and from coffee importers to IT specialists.[14] The project indirectly transformed local economies (raising house prices or fostering new business enterprises, for example), while in the world of film it raised industry capability, upskilled the workforce, and marketed the nation abroad as a competitive production base.[15] According to a 2002 government report on the subject, Jackson's filmic colossus "changed the aspirations of our filmmakers" and "the way the film world views New Zealand."[16] In 1998, when Peter Jackson purchased the Tourism and Publicity Department's old Film Unit facility in Wellington, it was the only full-range postproduction service in the country and was on the verge of being sold off piecemeal to foreign investors, victim to the hard bottom line of neoliberal reform, potentially sounding a death knell for the domestic film industry. When, three years later, Jackson reincarnated it as The Film Unit Ltd.—part of his state-of-the-art "Wellywood" facility servicing the most ambitious film project the world had known—the irony was replete. This irony was not lost on the state: in a slew of reports, initiatives, task forces, and ministerial mandates, it identified both domestic and runaway film for the first time as a driver of cross-sectoral economic growth, a success story of privatization and the judicious marriage of entrepreneurial initiative and state cultural investment. (The NZFC had sunk some NZ$5 million into Jackson's first four features; the state got a handsome return.)

Lord of the Rings also advertised and epitomized another serendipitous marriage: that of scenic sublimity and technological triumphalism. As such, it was an ideal vehicle for the state's national rebranding campaign, positioning New Zealand as a lean, green, efficient economy, no longer a hidebound pastoral backwater but a leader in job-rich, high-skill, high-value knowledge industries (biotech and telecommunications), creative entrepreneurship (design and film), and luxury cultural commodities (wine, food, and above all, tourism). "New Zealand: Home of Middle-earth" (a New Line–licensed tagline developed in partnership with TNZ) yoked the brand values of "New Pacific Freedom"—"contemporary and sophisticated, innovative and creative, spirited and free"—to purity of landscape.[17] The films' "place differentiation" effect was more precisely keyed to TNZ's ambitions than any campaign they could have designed: Jackson effortlessly refreshed tourism's century-old colonial stock of landscape imagery, infusing it with an aura of pristine primordialism along with hypermodernity, adventure, heroic discovery, and (as I will argue later) whiteness.

The Prime Minister devoted NZ$16 million over four years to promotional activities that encouraged a new interpenetration of the filmic imagination and the national interest, public agencies, and corporate entities. The government hosted lavish release parties at embassies around the world (starring New Zealand food and wine); TNZ's website was given over to virtual site tours; promotional features aired on travel channels in key markets, starring *Lord of the Rings* actors as well as state agents as spokespeople; and private-sector companies leveraged opportunities (for example, Air New Zealand emblazoned its planes with film stills). The impact was profound: visitor numbers were up an average of 20 percent in each of the years following the release of the films, cementing tourism's status as New Zealand's top export-earning industry. While other factors contributed to these figures, TNZ's surveys indicated that *Lord of the Rings* loomed large: 89 percent of visitors knew of the films and were aware of the film's association with New Zealand.[18] International touts were gratifyingly on-message: according to *Condé Nast Traveller*, the films were but the trailer; the real event was the country.[19]

RUNAWAY SOVEREIGNTY

Film creates culture, builds identity and markets that identity to the world. . . . Those stories and the voices, characters and landscapes which constitute them give expression to our identity. They create culture. The successful exhibition of our films builds a sense of identity in the viewers—and the sale of the films overseas markets New Zealand to our trading partners.[20]

Despite such success, leveraging the films in this way highlighted the inherent tensions of runaway production between the beleaguered cultural sovereignty of an economically vulnerable state and Global Hollywood's cultural and political clout. Witness the following comment from a begrudging Australian columnist:

Peter Jackson may be the fush and chups frontman, but the film is as Yankee as baseball. New Zealand has trouble financing a proper football team; international blockbuster movies are way out of its league. What we are left with is the pathetic sight of our Kiwi cousins boasting about how great the scenery looks. The Government is even pumping what remains of its Budget

into an advertising campaign to tell the world about the national role as an
extra. It's sad, really. And desperate. Imagine Bikini Atoll advertising itself as
a nuclear superpower and you can see what I mean.[21]

Thanks to Jackson's insistence on local postproduction, design, and crew-
ing and on the cast's support in putting New Zealand at the forefront of
publicity, the *Lord of the Rings* movies could be described—and indeed,
formally recorded—as New Zealand films. But film production in the
pattern of *Lord of the Rings* seemed set to become what this columnist
hinted it already was: a service provision to U.S.–based multinationals
attracted by the weak currency, generous tax incentives (which substan-
tially subsidized *Lord of the Rings*, with New Zealand taxpayers bearing
the risk), and raw assets of a cheap, deregulated, un-unionized but skilled
and English-speaking labor force, good telecommunications and supply
infrastructure, and relentless, eye-boggling scenic beauty.[22] At about half
the cost of comparable production in the United States, the advantages to
multinationals were obvious—at least until the scenery became too recognizable to viewers or the country's "hewers of wood and carriers of water"
got too expensive.[23] *Lord of the Rings* posed a policy conundrum much
debated in the national press. How could the country attract longer-term
and less-intermittent (or exploitative) investment? How could it handle
production companies that believe they "are entitled to work outside the
standard bureaucratic controls"?[24] How could it capture quality employment opportunities (in postproduction, design, and acting) for nationals
yet prevent local talent nurtured on these projects from fleeing the country
for better wages, bigger opportunities, or something like regular employment? How could it secure the place-differentiation and spin-off benefits of
each project, ensuring that audiences and investors associated New Zealand
products with New Zealand? Could it avoid undermining domestic production by forcing up prices and crowding out cash-starved small fry?

These were the familiar pitfalls of global outsourcing, taking a cultural
turn. Ultimately, these public debates suggested, New Zealand's new shoot-
'n'-scoot celebrity threatened a crisis of cultural sovereignty that was also a
crisis of national differentiation. Runaway production imperiled the capacity of the state to symbolize itself in the transnational arena, the ability
of its citizenry to participate in that process, and the control of either over
the circulation of their human and intellectual capital. If, as Ruth Harley

(NZFC chair) argued, "film creates culture" and its "voices, characters and landscapes . . . give expression to our identity," then what were the national consequences of *Lord of the Rings*, given, first, that it created a culture of *global* genesis, and second, that its reorganization of the screen industry potentially compromised domestic expression? More specifically, what were the racial consequences? Critics of Global Hollywood have warned that its global monopoly promotes a global monoculture that roughly maps onto the ideological dictates of late-liberal U.S. corporate capitalism, emptied of local content, contest, or contradictions. That monoculture is matched by a production machine primed to "render bodies that are intelligible and responsible to the New International Division of Cultural Labor."[25] In the case of *Lord of the Rings,* such laboring bodies were, not surprisingly, racially coded: New Zealand's highly skilled but underunionized and low-waged workforce was reportedly described by film executives as "Mexicans with mobiles."[26]

The bodies cinematically rendered by the films, however, had no less marked racial qualities. One might go so far as to argue that in the past ten years Aotearoa New Zealand has been transformed into a cinematic export processing zone for American modernity's lost racial certainties. *Lord of the Rings* stages a Manichaean struggle of light against dark, in which the "race of Man" bests Saruman's monstrously hybrid multitude, and the implications are writ large in a design aesthetic that pits blond elves against dreadlocked, tattooed, cannibal Uruk-hai. Peter Jackson's follow-up act, *King Kong,* matched its mythic budget with equally mythic racial hyperbole, softening the original's argument about miscegeny by sympathetically humanizing the ape, but leaving the odious spectacle of Skull Island's blacked-up, miscreant savages entirely unrevised. In these cases and others—New Zealand–filmed *The Last Samurai* and the *Chronicles of Narnia,* for example—Hollywood's distant satellite has manufactured fantasies of race at an economy of scale.

THE TROUBLE WITH MIDDLE-EARTH

Despite the protests of Tolkien and Jackson apologists, reading the *Lord of the Rings* trilogy critically through the lens of race is like shooting fish in a barrel.[27] Tolkien's tome was a self-consciously ethnonationalist effort to forge a "mythology for England," which he thought lacking in a purely indigenous tradition.[28] Cobbled from Greek, Roman, Norse, Finnish, Celtic, and Old English literatures, his Middle-earth was a densely layered composite of European histories and folklores that lent primordial resonance to British modernity's cultural nationalist topoi (its pastoral romanticism, for example). However, the trilogy's melodramatic construction of a homeland that must be defended against an alien, hostile intruder by an alliance of nations was capacious enough to lend the books enduring and broad appeal in an incipiently global age. Sauron's embodiment of pure, ruthless power read clearly to the trilogy's Cold War fans, just as its nostalgia for the lost values of agrarian localism or "practical-ethical wisdom" resonated with 1960s counterculture, which saw in the evil wizard's project the "soulless calculus of profit-and-loss" of hyperindustrial capitalism and militarism.[29] Its perceived pertinence in an "age of terror" should not, then, come as a surprise.[30]

What *Lord of the Rings* illustrates with almost blinding obviousness is the way in which this heroic vision of liberal internationalism is bonded to its bad faith with respect to race. Middle-earth is presided over by an ethos of liberal toleration, in which elves, dwarves, and hobbits live in their own isolated, separately evolved communities and treat each other with detached curiosity.[31] But the limits to toleration are etched in repugnance: the Uruk-hai are pictured literally emerging from muddy abjection, and it is through battling this specter of the *racial* deject that *ethnic* enmities (for example, between elven and dwarfish folk, as with the Legolas–Gimli friendship) are resolved and social harmony regained. Ultimately, the "age of Man" is established by the spatial containment of Mordor's alterity: its inferior breeds, slave-race hybrids, and primitive throwbacks. With Jackson's creed of fealty to Tolkien's idea, the filmic result was (from a racial point of view) ludicrously overdetermined: armies of swarthy, oliphaunt-riding Southrons and slant-eyed, beturbaned Easterlings swarm like dehumanized cockroaches over the ramparts of Helm's Deep, while the radiant elves look like a host of pre-Raphaelites, the nations of men resemble the Aryan Brotherhood, and the dark hordes of Mordor appear as benighted grotesques.[32] Casting choices followed predictably and unquestioningly. While men or elves of color were unimaginable to the designers, orcs or trolls of color were not. The only Māori actor in a named part was Lawrence Makoare as Uruk-hai prototype Lurtz, a gesture that was doubly symptomatic because it was unnecessary: under pounds of prosthetics, Makoare

attested, not a millimeter of his skin was visible. His racial phenotype
was the typecast foundation overwritten by mythic racial hyperbole. (In
his other role in the films, as the spectral Nazgûl king, the ethnic erasure
was complete: his body was literally invisible.)

At the broadest level, the films mythologize whiteness. Tolkien's tale
was forged in the crucible of the white imperial imagination, drawing on
the same primordial repertoire (of classical, Norse, Norman, Saxon, and
Celtic lore) that helped British nationalists calibrate the nativist compass
in the midst of accelerating imperial expansion, class conflict, and domestic diversity. Likewise, the films celebrate all the classic tropes of imperial
whiteness: its masculine, homosocial, heterosexual, muscular, and world-
girdling ways, animated by rationales of judicious government and secured
by the purging of degeneracy. The echoes abound: think of the Romanesque
detail of Minas Tirith, the "white city" of men, or consider the Caliban-
like Gollum whose incapacity for self-rule has distorted his very body.[33]
The deployment of this cultural material by a blockbuster with such transnational apparatus and appeal, however, points to the newly *global* availability of white entitlement as a locus of fantasy identification at the farthest
reaches of the liberal diaspora, reinvigorated through sentimental and epic
spectacularity.

The feared third-worlding of Aotearoa New Zealand's fledgling culture
industries never transpired: the economy and the currency rallied; Jackson
poured his profits into building high-end postproduction facilities and
subsidizing local producers; and state policy, while touting the beautiful
locations, also pitched the nation's first-world infrastructure and the "innate
creativity" of New Zealanders—the nation needed to be competitive, they
argued, not cheap.[34] But such fears also receded in part because throughout the several years of *Lord of the Rings's* production and sequential release,
New Zealanders increasingly experienced the films not as a Hollywood
imposition but *as their own*. The extraordinary global success of Jackson's
enterprise became a wellspring of national pride in a pride-starved, economically battered nation: the new New Zealand was possessed of territorial, technological, and human assets the world desired and was capable
of realizing a triumphant fantasy. However, insofar as the films inspired
national identification with the ideal self of global capital—an identification consummated most emphatically in tourism—they also entailed a
pact with whiteness that was dissonant with the claims of biculturalism on

the sovereign national symbolic. It is to this tension between transcendent racial narrativity and immanent racial struggle, between mythological history and a painfully unresolved national past, that I turn in the following section.

TOURING MIDDLE-EARTH:
100% PURE COLONIALISM

Lord of the Rings "put New Zealand on the map," pundits and politicians claimed, with the kind of colonialist repetition compulsion common in Ringish circles. But whose map? What pathways did it chart? And what other systems of figuring space and statehood did this map overwrite? Over the release period of the first two films, TNZ repositioned the nation. The state that had gone by the Liberal-era tagline "Home of the Maori" was now a destination on a different kind of global fantasy periphery: "Home of Middle-earth." The agency's website (also under the banner of "100% Pure New Zealand") offered virtual tours in which the vicarious traveler was incited to acts of exploration, discovery, and wonderment akin to those of Frodo and Sam as they traversed Middle-earth, or to those of the location scouts, designers, and cast as they "found" the sites described in the books. In rapturous interviews, the films' promoters waxed lyrical against backgrounds of supersaturated natural sublimity. "Middle-earth really does exist," Ian McKellen exhorted. "You will find it in New Zealand!"[35] The country's timeworn touristic topoi were reactivated through technological augmentation and kinaesthetic intensification, what Claudia Bell and John Lyall call the "accelerated sublime," in which consumption and subjectification occur not through pictorial capture but through embodied motion and immersion.[36] The films themselves produced this cinematic velocity, complementing their CGI-enhanced hyperpictorialism: mountains leapt, plains sprawled, and shots had the viewer plummet like a bungee jumper into deep ravines.[37]

The TNZ campaign cannily (and uncannily) recapitulated both the marketing and ecological interventions of the colonial era detailed in chapter 1 through pitching the nation (to tourists and future runaway ventures) as a natural *multum in parvo* where one could find the Swiss Alps, the Norwegian fjords, and the British Lake District—all the (Saxon, Nordic, and Celtic) spatial correlates of whiteness—within fifty miles of one another.[38]

These colonial hauntings of *Rings* discourse were both endemic and unintentionally ironic. If the bucolic Shire was "found" by Jackson's scouts in Matamata, it was because it was *made* there a century ago by colonists laying waste to native forests and displacing Ngāti Hauā to forge an imagined Shropshire of yeoman farms and agrarian stability that no longer existed in industrializing Britain. Much of Matamata was made by one colonist in particular, Josiah Firth, author of the booster mytho-history *Nation Making, a Story of New Zealand: Savagism v. Civilization* and one of the lobbyists behind the Rotorua railway.[39] In the wake of the wars that devastated the region in the 1860s, this state maker marshaled government agencies, the promise of tourism dollars and global investment, British pastoral nostalgia, "savage" mytho-history (appropriated and romanticized), and military force to transform this tract of Aotearoa into Little Britain, the ultimate "immersive simulation."[40] When, in 1999, the New Zealand Army offered its soldiers at cut-price rates (so much for sovereignty) to hew the set of Hobbiton into the obdurate Matamata hills, the irony of the moment was lost on commentators. Jackson's design team, state makers of another generation, planted the reshaped hills in a meticulous reconstruction of an English country garden, intervening with the new tools of "ecological imperialism" (digital grading and CGI) when nature did not cooperate.[41] The farm where Hobbiton was realized now offers tours of the stripped site, complemented by a "sheep farm experience" that uses the touristic currency of the film to rehabilitate Firth's redundant national industry as a living heritage attraction.

This amnesiac neoliberal renaissance of white liberal state-making's poetics—its translations between nature, territory, and capital, between state organs and transnational fantasy, and between antimodernist nostalgia and (neo)imperialist zeal—was accompanied by a renewed intimacy between tourism and politics. The tripartite touristic topography of the Liberal era, for example, was mapped onto contrasts between the rustic Shire, the primeval forests and sublime mountains of kingdoms of Man, and the netherworld of Mordor, with Māori returned to the "spaces of savagery" of the central North Island as a thrilling but threatening elemental phenomenon. In one instance, the arrangement was not only endorsed but also *performed* by New Zealand's head of state. A promotional travelogue titled *New Zealand: The Royal Tour*, sponsored by TNZ and produced by the U.S. Travel Channel to coordinate with the release of *The Fellowship of*

ALTERED STATES

the Ring, featured Helen Clark, Prime Minister and Minister for Culture and Heritage, accompanying anchor Peter Greenberg on a tour. With their journey punctuated by clips from the films, the pair hike, kayak, spelunk, and abseil their way around this "land on the edge of a dream," with nary a hint of the country's bicultural character until the pair briefly visit a marae (community center) in the Rotorua region.[42] It is as if they have stepped into a troll camp: "Whoa, I'm getting outta here!" our American host exclaims as the swirling steam clears to reveal a fearsome warrior grimacing threateningly at him. At the same moment that Māori operatives in TNZ and the Ministry of Tourism struggled to find a semiotic that would make Māori modernity deliverable to tourists, the global cultural technologies of New Zealand's second tourism age crossbred with the colonial racial imagination of its first to return Māori to a primitive and alien past.

Few remarked on this irony at the time. The screen apparatus's renunciation of biculturalism was paired with a public discourse that manufactured consent in the name of the state: "Saying you don't like *LOTR*," one columnist opined, "is tantamount to treason."[43] After the demoralizing years of postreform recession, the country was suddenly flush with promised but long-elusive success on the global stage. Runaway production presented New Zealanders with their ideal neoliberal, if racially undifferentiated, self-image. It made them known to the world as "enterprising, hospitable, casual and down-to-earth" people, "improvisers at need" who, like hobbits, "looked to their mates for help and sustenance," an image notably congruent with the well-established colonial mythos of *settler* character.[44] Publicity literature was at pains to emphasize that "it wasn't the filmmakers who made this film, it was the general public of New Zealand," with, for example, citizens working gratis as extras and the state pitching in with national resources. The Minister of Tourism, dubbed by the press the "Minister of the Rings," pronounced, "Almost everyone in the country has been touched by it, feels part of it. This has become part of our very culture."[45]

PUBLIC CULTURE, CORPORATE PROPERTY, AND THE NATIONAL SYMBOLIC

Public discourse proposed a unified national public of citizens bonded in affect and conduct by this freshly forged "culture," while *Lord of the Rings*

The filmic value of landscape was leveraged by the TNZ campaign. Tourism New Zealand.

took up residence at the heart of the state's symbolic, sovereign mechanisms in *Rings*-themed stamp series and coin issues, for example. In one poetic instance of interpellation into the new national imaginary, incoming passengers to Auckland International Airport faced a row of immigration officers ensconced in cubicles labeled "orcs," "trolls," and "hobbits," under a sign emblazoned "Welcome to Middle-earth." At the very site where the state marks its sovereign power over citizenry and territory, it did so—if only in jest—in the name of a neoglobal, corporate-owned fantasy that both elevated whiteness and parodied ethnic contestation. The sign that "Welcome to Middle-earth" would have obscured was a recent addition in the bicultural renovation of New Zealand's major port of entry: "Haere Mai o Aotearoa," welcome to Aotearoa.

In the extensive appendixes to the DVD set, Peter Jackson remarks that the production team felt at the time that they were making cinematic history.[46] In fact, they were also producing a historical heritage that, although entirely fictional in nature and corporate property of foreign provenance, was nonetheless taken up by the pedagogical technologies of the national symbolic. This process was vividly illustrated when an exhibition on the making of *Lord of the Rings* opened at the new Te Papa Tongarewa National Museum of New Zealand in December 2002, to coincide with the release of *The Two Towers*.[47] The exhibition was a boon to the museum's "commercially positive" mandate from the state, enabling it to reach demographically representative visitorship targets and stimulating the development of its international touring exhibition program (the show toured to science museums in London, Singapore, Boston, and Sydney from 2003 to 2005).[48] The three-year-old bicultural museum had drawn criticism for its chatty populism and its radically deconstructive, leveling, self-critical idiom (especially in its displays of Pākehā art history).[49] In the *Lord of the Rings* galleries, by contrast, all the piety that the museum had refused to bestow on the treasures of its national art was lavished on whimsical clichés that had inspired the *Lord of the Rings's* art directors: the hush of contemplation, auratic lighting, and reverential hanging schema rendered each work valued and autonomous. In the sections introducing the characters and cultures of Middle-earth, costumes of heroic leaders were mounted on dummies, their precious jewels of office displayed on velvet cushions in vitrines. Likewise, wall-mounted narratives told of their character, genealogy, deeds, and the distinct characteristics of "their culture" (singular), while waxwork dioramas thrilled with lifelike recreations of defining historical moments, such as Boromir's funeral. This was realist, objectivist museology of a fantasy tradition ("We're only here to tell the story," one of the exhibition designers announced, "we need to erase our own tracks"). At the same time, the exhibition laid bare the technological devices by which that tradition was invented and replaced the cultural work of imagining community with the filmic work of imaging it.

The *Lord of the Rings* exhibition excelled museologically where Te Papa (at least according to a vocal sector of the Pākehā public) had failed: it performed reverence toward a stabilized and purified tradition, a tradition cosmopolitan in ethos but indisputably white in its attributes, affirming its heroic narrativity, racial destiny, and moral probity. On the one hand, the exhibition reaffirmed *Lord of the Rings*'s success as an inspiration to national self-regard and international recognition. On the other, it invoked the "glimmering object" of tradition, albeit an extravagantly manufactured one, to produce "the feelings necessary for social harmony . . . and a new globally inspirational form of national cohesion."[50] *Lord of the Rings* stepped into the ethnonational vacuum created by biculturalism's assault on the state's sovereign indivisibility and neoliberalism's erosion of its sovereign autonomy: with settler whiteness no longer the "unmarked" default of national identification, and with appropriation of Māori identity a newly problematic move, a global fantasy of whiteness became the surrogate object of attachment and solidarity. International tourists (more than half the museum's patronage) played the role of corroborating witnesses to this state-branded performance of national identification.

Elsewhere in Wellywood, tourism also played a part in solidifying the films' weld of territory, identity, historicity, and runaway fiction. Since the first film's release, tour companies have led tourists on pilgrimages to the now vacated filming locations around a city still peppered with banners that brand it as the home of the new national industry, a city materially transformed by that industry, with whole suburbs (and schools and high-end businesses) flush with the cash of Jackson's studio's cosmopolitan, high-skilled workforce. The sites toured are nondescript nooks in tiny city parks or narrow vistas that CGI postproduction cobbled together with others from many hundreds of miles away, rendering them largely unrecognizable. In the place of cinematic presence's plenitude, the guides' scripts offer the (often disappointed) tourists a wealth of site-specific anecdote, augmented by flip books of film stills, layering manufactured mythos over local history, mixing "making of" tales of Kiwi creativity and collective perseverance with made-up ones of hobbit heroism. Guides incite tourists to share their investment in the fantasy, while they serve up their own with a large helping of civic pride and (as one guide put it to me) "basic Pākehā culture."

This process gives the lie to theorists' claims that as "place is governmentalised and commodified," by Global Hollywood "as an industrial setting of sites and services, its stature as a cultural-historical space is obliterated."[51] Instead, in a tourist state, acts of performative spatial poesis complexly refashion localities, hybridizing them with global fantasy and subtly shaping the future terms of place's intelligibility and value. Such processes bear even on indigenous space: the New Zealand Māori Tourism Board campaign to raise tourist awareness of Māori Aotearoa (discussed in chapter 4) hinged on abandoning the delocalized and racial semiotics of past campaigns in favor of an emphasis on site- and iwi-focused storytelling, unified by a single pan-tribal epic, that of Maui, which echoes the *Heimat* and the heroic narrativity of the *Rings* trilogy.

This global racial fantasy, then, invested in and supported by the state in the name of a culture-driven neoliberal renaissance, has both saturated the national symbolic and insinuated itself into local imaginaries, routed through the apparatus of tourism. In other ways, also, the state's intimacy with Global Hollywood has brought pressures to bear on the rationality of substate agencies and the very conduct of citizens. Film New Zealand, the state–industry partnership founded to attract foreign film ventures, is enjoining regional governments to conform their bylaws and consent procedures to earn "film friendly" status and urging iwi (extended kin group) councils to codify their own protocols and representative authorities for dealing with filmmakers.[52] Governmentally speaking, being "film friendly" demands administrative smoothing of state space through which capital and its mythic signs can move without friction; it also demands of citizens a mode of conduct as conductivity. New Zealanders must attune themselves to the practices and expectations of the visiting companies, a Film Venture Taranaki report advised after the filming of *The Last Samurai*. In turn, they would find themselves transformed into a new kind of cultural citizen, as flows of capital and culture left in their wakes a residue of affect: positive energy, optimism, a new "sophistication" learned from interaction with knowledge-industry elites, and a new scale of entrepreneurial ambition.[53]

IDENTITY CAPITAL AND DOMESTIC FILM

Flexible, expansive, buoyant, and shaped by currents of capital, this imagined citizen–subject of the neoliberal renaissance could, state agents implied, find expression as well as economic benefit in domestic film. Yet the dominance of Global Hollywood seemingly imperiled domestic production. The greater the success of the runaway industry, the more ambitions for domestic film grew: it was newly charged with articulating "our" (emergent) national identity, with capturing socially generated creative capital on behalf of the state, and with trafficking it (through the same global circuits of the culture industry as racial melodrama), inviting reciprocal circulation in the form of tourism and trade. This neoliberal mandate under which the industry operated put pressure on domestic film content, in turn setting the racial conditions of cultural citizenship. Not all culture, it seemed, was equally valuable as capital, and not every citizen could become its legitimate bearer.

New Zealand's film career as "best supporting country," policy makers agreed, had clear limits: Global Hollywood's tight hold on its intellectual property meant restrictions on film's use in cross-marketing and spin-off initiatives (in tourism, for example). To be "sustainable" and of long-term benefit to the nation, the screen production industry needed to create value as well as trade it. Domestic production with distinctively national content was called for. But the challenges faced were those familiar to many smaller producers: with a tiny domestic market, New Zealand feature films had to sell internationally to be profitable, yet they struggled to distinguish themselves internationally from competitors and to fund the level of production value that would make them marketable; furthermore, investment capital was scarce and international marketing costs prohibitive.[54] State subvention of both production and distribution was a clear necessity, but domestic film policy had been rudderless for much of the neoliberal 1990s, with stagnant funding and erratic tax relief provisions. Adding to national cinema's woes, the runaway industry threatened to push up production-service and labor costs, making the country prohibitive for local producers.

For all parties to the ensuing policy debates, global profitability was the unquestioned condition of state investment. Keynesian holdouts and neoliberal industry entrepreneurs differed, not on this fundamental, but on whether the straightest road to profitability lay in an industrial, generic, production-driven model or in a national tradition germinated through public patronage of artistic talent. For some, the existing national idiom, fostered by NZFC decisions, was too art-house, too *bleak*, and too particularist to be appealing to international audiences; others thought that focusing on the three *As* ("attractive story with attractive people in an attractive setting") would establish artistically restrictive norms, making New Zealand product indistinguishable from its competitors and uninspiring to its domestic audience.[55] Prime Minister Clark presented her solution as part of the Cultural Recovery Package. The New Zealand Film Production Fund (NZFPF), established in 2000, was to operate as an autonomous public–private partnership, partially funding one major feature per year (to ten times the average level of NZFC support) provided it (1) drew at least 40 percent of its funding from offshore sources; (2) was commercially viable; and (3) had "significant" New Zealand content.[56]

The NZFPF was a typically "third way" initiative, harmonizing local expression with global consumption, equating the production of value with the value of culture, and operating at arm's length through leaving the selection of national representatives to a combination of market forces and technocratic mechanisms that rested on critically unexamined norms rather than public debate.[57] It was undergirded by a vastly different rationality and a vastly different understanding of the relationship between cultural technologies, economies, identity, prosperity, and population than that which had presided over earlier film policy, animated by the mandate of cultural sovereignty. For the former, Keynesian generation, national solidarity was thought to be strengthened in its autonomy, distinctiveness, and collective resolve by the opportunity to witness (and contest) its own artistic self-articulation, independent of economic pressures. For the Clark-era NZFC chair Ruth Harley, however, "national identity" had an altogether different end:

> It is a key resource both economically and psychologically for New Zealand's future . . . a building block for knowledge based industries. . . . As Pākehā Englishness fades away, we have a new sense of US-NESS coming forward. The trick is to work out how to convert this unique property into sellable stories around the range of goods and services New Zealand can produce for the international market; as well as into stories which promote our own confidence, mutual respect and creative energy. . . . Film is important

not just as a potent advertising medium for New Zealand; not just as a way of creating and personifying our country as a brand in all its diversity; not just as a high growth, high margin knowledge based business. It is all of these, but it is also as a statement to ourselves. It is a central ingredient in constructing our identity for ourselves, as a lever to help New Zealanders get the confidence and boldness to foot it aggressively on the international stages.[58]

In the neoliberal culturescape, then, film is no longer simply mimetic and pedagogic but also performative.[59] It produces a thing beyond itself, a reservoir of the same "identity" it claims to be extracting and "converting," as well the "creative citizen," a buoyant individual who is productive of further intellectual property, properly endowed with liberal toleration ("mutual respect"), and a competent global bearer of the national brand. The national brand, in turn, is understood as "created and personified" by film. Further, for Harley, film has the power to compel belief in the national brand—in the population, where it evolves the "internal conviction that brings truth to the image," and in the global ecumene, where it inflects marketing efforts across the entire spectrum of export goods and services— a twist on what Toby Miller and Marie Claire Leger have called the "Global Effects Model" of screen-cultural citizenship.[60] Hollywood had done it for America, Harley argued, and New Zealand's film industry could do it too. This is rather a lot to ask of any medium, especially one formerly embraced as an artistic site of political contestation and experimentation, and especially when that medium is simultaneously responsible to *non*-national agendas imposed in the process of soliciting and negotiating co-production financing.

MARKET APPEAL, MĀORI STORIES, AND THE (OLD) DIVISION OF CULTURAL LABOR

This debate about *"our"* national film industry proceeded unembarrassed by bicultural claims. Yet it was no coincidence that the fund's first choice of film, *Whale Rider*, featured Māori cultural material (if not Māori cultural producers) as the primary marker of that national brand, identity, and citizen. The film community took this decision as evidence of the selection panel's sound market instincts. New Zealand's "top performing movies had told universal stories," marketers argued, "but with characters and backgrounds that could not have come from anywhere else."[61] Pākehā culture had notoriously failed in past film-marketing efforts to gain recognition as either universal or sufficiently distinctive, reading instead to global audiences as a mawkish, outmoded, and humorless Anglo localism (a perception that Pākehā New Zealand's first major global media success, *The Flight of the Conchords*, managed to turn into its animating joke). Māori difference, on the other hand, had proved eminently saleable, as New Zealand's top-grossing film export at the time, Lee Tamahori's *Once Were Warriors*, attested. Māori difference, then, promised to lend a stickiness to the slick space of the runaway industry, capturing film's elusive capital benefits (intellectual property and recognition) on behalf of the state.

As in the nationalist ventriloquy of a century earlier, the traffic in Māori difference formed the ground of consensus between global profiteers and nationalist pundits. The NZFPF decision to support *Whale Rider* traced a division of labor between indigenous providers (those who have the asset of distinction) and cosmopolitan consumers (those who profit from its circulation and purchase rights to access), while indigenous property formed the symbolic currency with which New Zealand's sovereignty-compromised state could purchase recognition in a global forum.[62] At the same time, this film's status as the flag bearer of such a pivotal knowledge-economy policy initiative introjected indigeneity silently but forcefully into the state's propositions about cultural citizenship. Meanwhile, any lingering reservations about the implications for *Māori* cultural sovereignty (this was a Māori story, after all, although directed, produced, marketed, and distributed by Pākehā) were trumped by the unquestioned appeal to profitability. (At the time of *Whale Rider*'s release, only four of 170 feature films made in New Zealand had been directed by Māori, and no dedicated production company existed for Māori film, a situation for which some held the NZFC largely responsible.)[63]

But what specific form would Māori personhood and property have to take to be legible, valuable, and trafficable in the global culturescape? *Whale Rider*, I will argue, proposed an appealing answer to this question, first driving a wedge between race and indigeneity, and then forwarding and fashioning the indigenous subject as the engine of collective futurity and prosperity. To get at the novelty and distinctively neoliberal cast of *Whale Rider*'s indigenous subject—as well as the place that tourism would occupy in the economy it served—a comparison is useful with that earlier landmark of Māori cinema, the 1994 feature film *Once Were Warriors*. Based on a novel written by Māori author Alan Duff and directed by then-novice Lee Tamahori, *Once Were Warriors* was made on a shoestring budget, employing Māori at all levels of production. Its commercial success in the global art-house circuit was largely unexpected. Set in the urban slums of South Auckland against a background of gang violence, domestic abuse, alcoholism, unemployment, and poverty, and filmed with a grittily realist aesthetic, the film was an unblinking portrait of Māori modernity as high tragedy. Its protagonists are at once heroic and brutally deformed by the twin legacies of colonialism and structural racism; its largely invisible antagonist is a state by turns despotic, oblivious, negligent, and suffocatingly paternalistic. *Once Were Warriors* figured racial consciousness as the mark of social exclusion and impotent dissent (in, for example, its young characters' gangsta bravado) and ethnic consciousness as salvation from urban modernity's ignominy: the film concludes as Beth, the female lead, returns with the remnants of her family to her tribal homeland and, by implication, to a more stable, fulfilling, and authentic life.

Where the film begins, however, is equally telling: an archetypal panoramic still of New Zealand's alp-backed, bucolic paradise, which, as the shot begins to track, is revealed as a billboard adorning an urban motorway, adjoined by sagging barbed wire fences and abandoned factories, burned-out cars, boarded-up shops, and dilapidated council houses. The sequence seems to argue that, in generating their own filmic practices of decolonization, Māori must first reckon with the nationalist triumphalism of the tourism industry, whose fetishized images of nature sublime are the screen of Pākehā fantasy, obscuring Māori dispossession, evacuating Māori history, and eclipsing Māori futurity in a single bloodless gesture. The original setting for Duff's novel, tellingly, was not South Auckland but a thinly disguised Rotorua (fictionalized as "Two Lakes," Rotorua's English translation). At the time of Duff's writing, the tourism center's blighted history of Māori poverty and deep racial and class divisions was painfully accentuated by the depredations of neoliberalization's "structural adjustment," with thousands of (mainly Māori) jobs in state-owned enterprises such as forestry and energy lost to privatization. In *Once Were Warriors's* opening sequence, the billboard advertises an energy corporation and bears the legend "eNZpower: bringing New Zealand a brighter future." With pitiless efficiency, these few shots expose the ironic, and touristic, synchrony of colonialism and neocolonialism, liberal state making and neoliberal post-nationhood, and their racial costs.

"WHALE RIDER" AND THE NEW NATIONAL

The genesis of *Whale Rider* provides a sharp contrast to the polemic urgency of *Once Were Warriors* and its linkages to indigenous activism.[64] *Whale Rider* began production in 2001 after nearly fifteen years' gestation in the hands of John Barnett (the Pākehā executive of New Zealand's most successful TV and film production company, South Pacific Pictures), who had acquired the rights to adapt Witi Ihimaera's 1987 novella of the same name. When Barnett finally appointed Niki Caro (a Pākehā independent) as director, she penned her own screenplay in consultation with Ihimaera (one of New Zealand's foremost authors, a professor and erstwhile ambassador to the United States, who also acted as executive producer of the film). The combination secured NZFPF support, with international cofinancing from a German company. On its release, *Whale Rider* broke all records for a New Zealand film in international takings, running away with awards at the Toronto and Cannes film festivals and securing an Oscar nomination for its young star, Keisha Castle-Hughes.

Marketed to independent filmgoers as a sophisticated family drama with a "magical realist" style, the film narrates the story of Paikea Apirana, born into the chiefly line of a coastal tribe in contemporary New Zealand, the Ngāti Konohi people of Whāngārā.[65] Her mother dies in childbirth, along with her twin brother, and her father departs the country in grief, leaving her to be raised by her adoring Nanny Flowers and her grandfather, Ngāti Konohi leader Koro Apirana, whom she loves devotedly. Tribal lore holds that the tribe will fall on dark times but that a leader will arise from the descendants of the line of Paikea, the founder of the community who, on the journey from the ancestral homeland of Hawaiki, saved his people from extinction by riding to land on the back of a whale after a shipwreck. Young Paikea defies her grandfather's orthodox interpretation of the prophecy, in which only a firstborn son could lead the tribe away from dissolution and despair. She takes up the mantle and, in the movie's symbolic climax, saves a beached shoal of whales by riding their leader back out into the life-giving waters.

The ancestral story, hapū (extended kin community), and location are real, the subject and setting of much of Ihimaera's fiction, but the changes made in the adaptation of the book—written only three years before Duff's novel—are striking, limning concurrent transformations in ethnogovernmental logic. The novella takes place against the broad sweep of global postcolonial activism, making explicit connections between indigenous rights, ecological justice, and antiracist causes. It is narrated by Rawiri, the uncle of Pai (or Kahu, as she is called in the book, where the character takes much less of a central role), who details his time spent in the Māori diaspora in Sydney and his encounters with expatriate racism and neocolonial economics as a plantation hand in Papua New Guinea. Nanny Flowers is not the staunchly suffering helpmeet she is in the film but a feisty, ribald community leader, while Koro is exhausted from his work representing the tribe in Treaty negotiations with the state. In the book, the beaching of the whales prompts a coalition between environmentalists, police, gang members, and locals, both Māori and Pākehā, while the whales themselves (who can speak) voice their own commentary about the environmental devastation of French nuclear testing in the Pacific. The girl's heroic act in this context has truly millennial significance, reanimating the ecology of the ancients (the "partnership between land and sea, whales and humankind") and healing the rifts of modernity between "the natural and the supernatural. The present and the past. The scientific and the fantastic."[66] It is this restoration of the oneness of the world, Ihimaera suggests, on which the future of Māoridom depends.

By contrast, Caro's screenplay narrows the focus to Pai's emotional struggle, winnowing out all contextual material and with it the social, historical, or political ramifications of Ihimaera's tale. As in a number of other New Zealand films (but in contrast to the strident masculinism of the *Lord of the Rings* films), a girl-child is the point of identification for the audience, a "vehicle of hope" who—in her innocence and emotional vulnerability—sees with a wisdom that adults do not.[67] But what malaise afflicts the tribe that the girl must redeem? The film's Whāngārā is a haven of ambient, exclusively Māori gemeinschaft, with a supportive school, loving families, and strong community bonds. True, Rawiri's mates smoke pot, and Pai's friend's dad is in prison, but they all dutifully turn up to the marae when Koro calls.[68] While it is clear that nobody in the community is wealthy, poverty is not a concern either: money is never mentioned, and the camera inhabits the working-class interiors of the homes with respectful affection. Pai's leadership skills find their target only in a campaign among her family to get fit and give up smoking and in her own precocious achievements (her skill in oratory, for example, or her uncanny gifts in ceremonial combat). In comparison with *Once Were Warriors*'s gang and generational violence, alcoholism, juvenile delinquency, unemployment, and poverty, *Whale Rider* seems to contend (neoliberally enough) that any ethnic travails can be solved by a combinational of personal discipline, ambition, and ability.

Instead, in a typically touristic paradox, the film suggests that what is lacking in Whāngārā is precisely what appeals about it: that it stands still, temporally and spatially. Its people see little incentive to change and less to travel: indeed, when Pai tries to leave with her father for Germany, the whales call her back before she has passed the headland. At the core of the film is not so much ethnic renewal as a generalized narrative of collective faith, aspiration, and historical continuity that is also an incitement to motion: "I do know," the child's voice-over concludes the film, "that my people will go on, into the future, together." In the final, triumphant scene of the film, emplacement and motion are mythically reconciled as the tribe puts to sea in the waka (canoe) carved by Pai's father, Porourangi. The one who left has now returned, to show his people how to move toward the future while staying in place.

While, in *Once Were Warriors*, ethnicity was figured unapologetically as a space of exclusion and resistance to the state—in effect, as race—ethnic solidarity in *Whale Rider* was oriented not with respect to the Pākehā state (the teachers, welfare officials, judges, and police so powerfully entangled with the fates of *Once Were Warriors*'s characters) or to the scene of global political activism (the postcolonial coalitions so prominent in the book) but to a broader sphere of white cosmopolitan address. The only non-Māori character in the film is Paikea's father's German girlfriend (Caro's addition to the tale, presumably an offering to the German cofounders), who appears in the closing scene conspicuously, and emblematically, pregnant with the global progeny of a newly traditional Māoridom. The two structural anchors of ethnonationalism, past and place, are the subject of both an intense investment by the cinematography and thoroughgoing evacuation. Whāngārā is a representational space of saturated, nostalgic locality that is simultaneously unlocatable: like its protagonist, the film never leaves the windblown village and the stunning bay. Temporally, the film is marked by the same scrupulous avoidance of historical particulars that might link it to nation-time or politics; its only historical referent is the mythic past. (In Ihimaera's other novels set in the East Cape, the vertical span of human and nonhuman history—from the time of the gods to the present, including the violence and dispossession of the colonial era—is immanent in every feature of the landscape.)[69] Instead, *Whale Rider* is situated partway between a mythic past and an equally mythic future, which it promises to reconcile. Its aspirant time gestures toward a kind of homogenous empty futurity to which the powerless but plucky child is the conduit.[70]

In the figure of the indigene, rerooted and rerouted, purified of racial stigma and referents, the film magically reconciles ethnonationalism's—and tourism's—antimodernist nostalgia (which identifies authenticity with autochthony, stasis, isolation, and place, all under the banner of tradition) with neoliberalism's deterritorializing and dehistoricizing impetus. If liberal modernity's inaugural wave of cultural nationalism rested on "invented tradition" as the foundational essence of present solidarities, neoliberalism rests on tradition's reinvention as the sacrificial object to a future destiny actualized through determined, individual enterprise.[71] It was a return to tradition that ultimately rescued the stranded, dispersed urbanites of *Once Were Warriors*; *Whale Rider*, on the other hand, simultaneously reveres, valorizes, commodifies, and defies tradition. "One young girl dared to confront the past, change the present, and determine the future," the movie's website declared, while the reviews celebrate Pai's "dragging Māori traditionalism into the 21st century."[72] The proposition that "ancient traditions must evolve" for the tribe to survive is as timely as it is claimed to be "timeless." As Bob Berney, U.S. distributor of the film, noted, *Whale Rider* is part of a trend of "female characters bucking tradition and blending their family's traditional cultural values with contemporary freedom"; he cites *Bend It Like Beckham* (2002), *My Big Fat Greek Wedding* (2002), and *Real Women Have Curves* (2002) to support this statement. "People feel in the mood for that right now," he adds.[73] The story conforms to an easily replicable (neo)-liberal formula: indeed, Caro has gone on to direct other "universal studies of female empowerment" (specifically, *North Country* in 2005) that aestheticize locality while picturing exceptional individuals smashing moribund solidarities (in this case, male-dominated unions) in a revivifying fight for justice and opportunity.[74]

The politics of postracialism, however, explains this trope's contemporary currency: disingenuously displaced onto gender, it is a structure of feeling that generalizes ethnic tradition as a conservative force binding the aspirant energies of individuals. At the same time, it *markets* that tradition, converting it into identity capital. *Whale Rider*'s adaptation has been critiqued for distorting Ngāti Porou's complex gender and generational relationships to pander to Euro-American liberal feminist mores.[75] Its girls-can-do-it appeal also works to purify indigenous tradition of its freight of historical grievance, alterity, and antagonism to the normative idiom of the state. In short, it works to purify indigeneity of race to valorize it for circulation through the markets of Global Hollywood.

Whale Rider, then, was not only a product but also an instrument of policy, charting the way for future knowledge-economy initiatives that traded in indigenous materials in the name of the national welfare. As in the new generation of tourism initiatives discussed in chapter 4, *Whale Rider* modeled the bicultural subject's conduct with respect to the traffic in cultural property. Māori pundits celebrated the film's purported "universality," inciting Māori to surrender cultural goods to the market and thus to the national good. For John Tamihere, Associate Minister of Māori Affairs, "the international success of the film *Whale Rider* demonstrates how taking themes and ideas that are undeniably Māori and making them accessible to all has huge potential benefits for not only Māori but New Zealand as a whole."[76] Meanwhile, the well-publicized documentary detailing *Whale Rider*'s making positioned the film as an exemplar of bicultural protocols of artistic collaboration between iwi and filmmakers that would ease the passage of intellectual property from commons to market.[77] "The Paikea legend belongs to the people of Whangara," director Caro stated. "I couldn't have, wouldn't have wanted to take it to the screen without their blessing."[78] In this narrative, Caro won the tribe over through her humility, diplomacy, and sheer talent until they "eventually accepted her as a tangata whenua—a Māori," and she was able to make something about Ngāti Konohi that they would "feel good enough about . . . to claim as their own."[79] *Whale Rider* was a ritual exorcism of the specter of Māori ethnonationalism for the majority state: a sign that the knowledge economy's opportunity to profit from Māori resources would not be curtailed and that the state's capacity to mediate Māori value was undiminished.[80]

OPPORTUNITY, MOBILITY, AND UNIVERSALITY

As Anna Tsing has argued, the "universal" names "knowledge that moves—mobile and mobilizing—across localities and cultures"; its mission is "to form bridges, roads, and channels of circulation," to inspire expansion.[81] In this sense, *Whale Rider's* claim to universality was as promising for Māori forging a pathway in the global knowledge economy as it was for Pākehā pundits. Domestic Māori audiences warmed to the film's depiction of the contemporaneous vitality of "myth" or "magic"; its emphasis on intergenerational relationships; and its intimate portrait of the wairua (spirit) of a rural marae-based community, with the kuia and koroua (elder women and men) who keep the home fires warm for those who migrate in search of work. But commentators also noted the opportunity it presented for branding Māori abroad, foregrounding not only Māori "cultural product" (extraordinary stories and distinctive aesthetics) but also Māori subjects, crystallized in the figure of Paikea, with her natural talent, optimism, and inner determination. In stark contrast to the portrait of dysfunction and misery presented by *Once Were Warriors*, they argued, *Whale Rider* showed the world the "positive face" of Māori modernity. Castle-Hughes became the muse of Māoridom-rising, the darling of the glossy magazines produced by and for a new generation of Māori professionals, representing (like her character, Paikea) a youthful radiance, energy, and aspiration grounded firmly in identity. Meanwhile, the character of Paikea's father, Porourangi (a sculptor), and the actor who played him (Cliff Curtis) proposed global creative entrepreneurialism as the tribe's new life-giving water: Porourangi, like actor Curtis, leaves, succeeds abroad, and returns, his talent and creative leadership vindicated. (Koro, the character's father, dismisses his son's work as "souvenirs": those traditionalists who disdain the market in culture, the film suggests, also risk blinding themselves to creative excellence.)

Once Were Warriors too, it is worth noting, was taken by global audiences as a "universal" tale. The bridges it built, however, might better be described as "analogical structures of feeling" than pathways to future prosperity. Ella Shohat and Robert Stam describe such structures as articulating "filmic identification across social, political, and cultural situations, through strongly perceived or dimly felt affinities of social perception or historical experience."[82] The story that traveled with *Once Were Warriors* was the story of colonial dispossession, cultural loss, and sociopolitical exclusion; what the film realized so poignantly and powerfully was not just the gap between an idealized tradition and contemporary social devastation but also the vitality, fury, passion, and pathos of the culture that had been forged in that gap.[83] If *Once Were Warriors*'s depiction of liberalism's crimes against race had a global resonance—in the hip-hop, reggae, urban gangs, graffiti, and tattoo art that formed its aesthetic canvas—its subjects were immobilized against the background of the state that the film held accountable. Beth's final act, returning to her tūrangawaewae, her ancestral home, was not so much a way forward as a way *back*, posing tradition as a refuge from the present, not a resource for the future. Caro's film, by contrast, with its postnational, postracial morphology, presented structures of feeling that were not so much analogical as fungible; like any good brand, its universalism put projects, products, and people in global motion.

Not surprisingly, then, the potential of the film for tourism marketing was immediately apparent. But while *Whale Rider* was a vehicle to which Māori had access, it was not one over which they had control, and as various initiatives were yoked to the film's momentum, tensions between tribal priorities, state agendas, and market demands emerged. State agents searching for a way to reach beyond the presentational semiotics of Rotorua performance-based tourism to communicate the *feeling* of "the Māori culture tourists don't see" considered that feeling powerfully embodied in the film. The film promised not only to inflect Brand New Zealand with the "Pacific edge" but also to support marketing for small-scale, dispersed Māori tourism start-ups that offered a more intimate introduction to Māori culture. NZFC's Louise Baker bragged abroad of the film's affective power to mobilize tourists: "*Whale Rider* is a movie with the power to move people—all the way from England to New Zealand. . . . As an unofficial advertisement for antipodean holidays, it is proving to be extremely effective."[84] Witi Ihimaera himself pressed the state to take up the banner, but despite his urgings, there would be no Minister for Whale Rider.[85] Nor did the tangata whenua who supported and acted in the film want one: Whāngārā (with around twenty-three residents and long underresourced) had no public facilities and little way of ensuring tourists' respect for residents' privacy or for the strict protocol of the marae featured in the film.[86] Ngāti Konohi made it clear to TNZ and Ministry officials in Wellington that tourism did not feature in the hapū's development plans and that tie-in promotions would not be welcomed. The bay, property of the hapū, remains closed to visitors and can only be viewed from the distant road. Nevertheless, the village faced unbidden traffic: Hone Taumaunu, the kaumātua (elder) who acted as liaison to the film team, finally offered tikanga-focused (custom-centered) tours of the bay as a concession to ensure that visitors did not treat it as an elaborate film set.[87]

However, while disappointed state officials agreed that Ngāti Konohi involvement could not be compelled, commercial operations had no such compunction. One backpacker coach company now offers a package tour of the East Cape, branded "East As," in which a "location tour" features prominently. The brochure evokes a lifestyle inadvertently commodified by the film (the pot-smoking, welfare-funded, dropout life lived in dilapidated sand-swept beach houses, led by uncle Rawiri and his friends) and promises that you will get to "hang with the locals." More than a century of delimited economic opportunity for Māori in the region—hit hard by land alienation, starved of development funds, and depopulated by urbanization first in the 1960s and again in the economic ructions of the 1980s—has left a social and racial legacy that here, ironically, finds itself transmuted into salable identity capital. The residents of Whāngārā may not consent to opening their lives to business now, but in the face of that same legacy, how long will such a resistance seem reasonable? The *Whale Rider* story shows how the political rationality of the knowledge economy and the broad consensus between the market, state, and civil society that undergirds it has not so much expanded the range of choices for Māori regarding their collective and individual futures as it has reorganized the terrain in which such choice is possible—and with it, shifted the grounds of (self-)recognition, representation, and resistance.[88]

ACT 2: POSTRACIAL TRANSLATIONS; OR, ON NOT ACTING MĀORI

Talking at the 2005 Hui Taumata, the Māori summit for economic development, Cliff Curtis (Uncle Bully from *Once Were Warriors* and Porourangi from *Whale Rider*) was among those calling for Māori to "find and promote [their] point of difference," to "take cultural and spiritual depth and turn it into a winning international product."[89] Such pronouncements fused the rationality of the state's "creative innovation" paradigm

with the kaupapa (mission, philosophy) of iwi- and hapū-driven development, resolving the implicit tension between the precepts of competitive
individualism and those of indigenous revitalization. Communities are
strengthened by individual success, and only strengthened communities
able to provide for those within their fold can secure the mana-a-rōpū
(reputation or prestige of the group) from which identity, and in turn creativity, would flow, they argued: "It's about knowing who I am, knowing
my identity, and achieving individually for the collective."[90] This discourse
also equated the right to cultural entrepreneurship with the achievement
of cultural autonomy: Curtis advocated courting overseas investors who
would be free of the prejudices of New Zealand institutions and "consider
applications solely on their ability to deliver a profit."[91] "The hardest place
to be Māori is in Aotearoa," said musician Moana Maniapoto: "Overseas
our culture is embraced, our Māori-ness resonating at a deep spiritual level
with cultures around the planet."[92] For many such commentators, *Whale
Rider* was proof positive that the global market was hungry for Māori cultural product.

     For its Māori advocates, then, the new (cultural) entrepreneurialism of
the self supplants older goals of self-determination; they understand the
capacity to package and globally traffic in their identity as the emancipation
of Māori productivity from the Pākehā state, with its failure to recognize
Māori value.[93] As uncomfortable as such a shift in the trajectory of indigenous dissent makes the academic left, Māori agents of the creative economy counter that academic critiques of cultural commodification work to
curtail Māori economic opportunity and to reprise romantic-colonial constructions of indigeneity as capitalist modernity's unworldly Other.

     In the section that follows, I ask questions of a different nature—ques-
tions about the costs incurred when indigenous identity capital circulates
globally without a critical eye to the supranational economy of race with
which it is entwined. Film makes clear what the terms of that circulation
are, illustrating the fate of indigenous signs when they detach from the
state in relation to which indigeneity comes into political meaning (as a
historical claim to rights, recognition, or redress). As I have already argued,
in a neoliberal moment, indigenous identity becomes globally legible (ana-
logically "resonating") and valorized ("delivering a profit") to the extent
that it divests itself of that political meaning, rendering itself fungible or
"universal." However, the case of Māori actors warrants particular attention

because of the pressure it puts on this novel formulation, identity capital. Literalizing the condition of *Homo economicus*, the actor's capital is insep-arable from its embodiment; however, embodied identity circulates accord-ing to different rhythms and different logic than identity abstracted as cultural property. This rhythm and logic has everything to do with race: the ways in which certain narratives and affects adhere to certain bodies; how those bodies associate with, and are associated with, other bodies; the (symbolic) work they can (be made to) perform; and the mobility they are afforded as a result.

My analysis tracks three actors: Curtis himself, Temuera Morrison (who played the monumentally tragic Jake the Muss in *Once Were Warriors*), and Castle-Hughes. All film actors are at once cinematic commodities and cre-ative agents, but these particular actors, I will argue, also perform a specific kind of racial—racialized and racializing—labor. Contrary to knowledge-economy rhetoric, their value lies not in their identity but rather in their *indeterminacy*. In Hollywood parlance, they can be classified as "ethnic 2": phenotypically nonwhite but not semiotically marked as any specific race, and thus available for racial imprint by the narrative mechanisms of film or the identificatory desire of the consumer. (Ethnic 2 was a moniker de-vised by advertising executives to describe the type that would appeal to the broadest market in an increasingly ethnically diverse United States.) Like the culture workers in chapters 2 and 3 of this volume, who were also launched into global circulation through their participation in state-sponsored cul-tural production, the mobility and marketability of these Māori actors is premised on a finely calibrated performance of racial allusion and elusion. Cast as the threat–promise archetypes of a postracial world, they are simul-taneously called on to renovate and refigure liberalism's racial imaginary for a neoliberal age.

RUNAWAY ACTORS, (POST)RACIAL PERFORMATIVITY

Significantly, many of these archetypes inhabit the future, a space in which the (post)racial imaginary can be elaborated, unrestricted by the limits of realism. Whereas high Fordist, Bretton Woods–era science fiction pic-tured a mosaic of distinct human ethnicities and galactic races (à la *Star Trek*), its neoliberal equivalent proposes a newly normative human subject, phenotypically coded to suggest mixed heritage as a sign of long-harmonized difference and a certain narrative neutrality. These pleasant-looking, coffee-colored individuals speak with middle-class West Coast U.S. accents and bear no other discernible markers of social or geographical origin. They are, in short, entirely assimilable to whiteness.[94] (Even as the principal actors remain, almost invariably, white.) This is the role played by Curtis as Dr. Searle in *Sunshine* (2007), for example. This archetype is shadowed by a sinister double: Jango Fett, played in the *Star Wars* prequels by Morrison. A bounty hunter, stateless mercenary, and genetic template for the vast clone army, Fett manifests the paranoid biopolitical unconscious of the postracial imaginary: his clones are engineered (in deliciously neoliberal terminology) for "diminished independence and accelerated growth."[95] Like the orc army of *Lord of the Rings*, they are figures of expendable, alien labor and threatening anonymity circulating at an economy of scale.

These two Māori actors have also conjured the racial specters and ciphers of a contemporary global condition. Curtis's filmography is prodigious in this respect: Colombian terrorist in *Collateral Damage* (2002), Iraqi in *Three Kings* (1999), African American in *Bringing in the Dead* (1999), Russian in *Traffic* (2004), Indian in *The Majestic* (2001), Arab in *The Insider* (1999), and Mexican in *Blow* (2001). While less substantial, Morrison's filmography includes portraying a Native American in *Renegade* (2004), a South Asian in *Vertical Limit* (2000), and Latinos in *From Dusk till Dawn 3* (1999) and *Speed 2* (1997). These characters are not all villains, but most are suspect, vehicles of the residual racial coding of Hollywood domestic melodrama (bad guy equals swarthy), even as that melodramatic form traces more complex global trajectories.[96] The trajectories of these characters themselves, meanwhile, are what make them such threateningly postracial figures: cosmopolitan, urban, and uninhibited by the laws of borders, they are characters whose prodigious mobility and ability to slip between the cracks of state surveillance depends on a certain skill at passing.

There is nothing particularly new about the phenomenon I name: Hollywood's history is rife with instances of masking, passing, and cross-racial casting (from yellow-face acts to browned-up "Indians," Anthony Quinn, Rita Hayworth, Juanita Hall as Bloody Mary, Naomi Campbell as Pocahontas, and Jennifer Lopez as Selena). Insofar as race is a semiotic construction, it has always both depended on and been unmasked by the capacity of performance technologies (like cinema) to attach histories, properties, and narratives of identity to particular bodies. And institutions such as Hollywood have never been scrupulous about their choice of human material for racial fantasy. Yet I want to suggest that there is something quite present-moment about this specific regime of racial performativity. As Allan Sekula and others have argued, the facticity of race has historically been produced through representational and governmental apparatuses such as photography and the "shadow archive" of bodily taxonomies it made real through its claim to indexicality. Tourist uses of the medium, no less than anthropological or criminological ones, were crucial to this process.[97] Equally, indexicality, as photography's truth claim, has always been shadowed by its theatricality, its capacity to exploit the deceptive human obliquity between being and acting. Scholars of minstrelsy have shown how the popular aesthetics of interracial masquerade have historically tracked the shifting dynamics of interracial appropriation and affiliation, differentiation and derogation, and solidarity and competition, producing hybrids—the Cuban *catedrático*, for example, or the black urban dandy—that crystallize formative national, class, or postcolonial sentiments.[98] Interracial performance, then, might be understood as both a symptom and a mechanism, a symbolic register of racial structures of feeling and a public experiment with the racial properties of an emergent citizenship. What might the contemporary, interracial aesthetics of film reveal about the racial form of neoliberal citizenship? If photography, and by extension film, was a component of liberalism's practical system (in the Foucauldian sense of the term) for racially and biopolitically organizing population, then what is its status in a *neo*liberal age? To answer such questions demands that we engage photography and film not simply at the level of representation (the symbolic, semiotic, and cinematic roles these actors perform) but also at the level of performativity (the subjectivities, capital flows, and opportunity structures that they materialize through their labor).

In one sense, these roles and the choice of Māori actors to fill them are Global Hollywood's high-handed answer to the intransigent materiality of lives, identities, habitus, and bodies structured by racial experience. These actors are valuable because they are detached from the lived and politicized fabric of national ethnic solidarities: they are more likely to be cast as, say, Mexican because they don't "naturally" manifest Mexicanness, in all its regional or class particularity, and can thus *act* Hollywood's imagined Mexican more successfully. This is not minstrelsy (with its constitutive tension between face and cork, racial reality and racial masquerade), nor is this passing, which relies on the occlusion of the racial real as secret. Morrison and Curtis "pass" in a different sense; they move efficiently and inconspicuously through the made-equivalent spaces of global racial topography and the identities of its interchangeable denizens, allowing the narrative material that declares those denizens expendable to pass through them. Their currency is predicated on conductivity, on the absence of both personal celebrity and those markers of identity that might bind them to a state or history. In the flattened social terrain of Global Hollywood's poststate and postracial dominion, they make ideal flexible laborers. They are cheap, mobile, and adaptable: the immaterial laborer of the information economy, in contrast to the productive (factory) laborer, is not molded by and in conformity with the discipline of a specific position in that economy but instead ceaselessly modulates herself or himself, adapting to ceaselessly changing demands. Gilles Deleuze writes (and we might think of this as an analogy for two contrasting modes of racial performativity), "While disciplinary man is a mole, the animal that gets you into spaces of confinement," the immaterial laborer is a snake, "moving among a continuous range of different orbits."[99]

Flexible citizenship and immaterial labor may be the general hallmarks of global neoliberalism, but access to their benefits is unevenly distributed. There is, after all, no shortage of Middle Eastern, Latino, South Asian, or African American actors in Hollywood. Why should roles go to runaway acting talent? Which actors get enlisted as creative labor and which as service providers—who gets a film credit and who gets to work in Hollywood's food halls? What combinations of phenotype and citizenship endow the bearer with mobility, and what combinations immobilize? Which forms of race are construed as inalienable property (and thus cannot be claimed by a person other than their "natural" bearer), and which are treated as fungible?[100] In the 1990s, in an era of late-liberal identity politics, such questions animated fervent debates in the United States and elsewhere as minority actors lobbied for the proprietary rights over race that white actors had always enjoyed (namely the rights to author and have access to roles representing their own peoples).[101] Indeed, such rights remain important to Māori arguments regarding cultural sovereignty: as a rule, directors cast Māori actors in Māori roles—to do otherwise would be highly controversial—while in other contexts, having non-Māori "posing as Māori"

is denounced as "an insult."[102] In this light, the seemingly quixotic casting decisions that put Morrison and Curtis in the roles of African Americans, Native Americans, or Iraqis seem like a deliberate strategy to put
racial style, manners, and history "up for rent," thus allowing the production of racial fantasy to proceed unimpeded by the demands or resistances
of actual racial constituencies.[103]

That such questions no longer rank in public discourse surrounding
Aotearoa New Zealand's Global Hollywood success is indicative of how
much ground racial politics—both the racial politics of the state and of
transnational coalition—has yielded and how invisible the racial asym-
metries of postracial, poststate governmentality have become. In a 2005
episode of *The Tem Show*, a television magazine show hosted by Morrison,
now very much the local celebrity, the actor conversed with his colleague
Curtis about the challenges of playing such a diverse range of ethnic characters.[104] None of these challenges was ethical. Curtis noted the importance
of research, specificity, precise observation, and finely honed technique;
Morrison, meanwhile, repeatedly reminded the audience of Curtis's (and
by implication, his own) remarkable global success. What was most richly
suggestive about this particular conversation, however, was its location: a
hot pool on Mokoia Island, a venerated, storied, and (until recently) highly
trafficked tourist site in the middle of Lake Rotorua. Curtis and Morrison
both hail from Rotorua and are often identified with the Arawa legacy of
entertainment and cultural ambassadorship; both give generously of their
time and profile to iwi culture-driven development initiatives. Like their
tourism-celebrity precursor, Makereti Papakura, their social-geographical
mobility and capacity to capture the benefits of the transnational culture
industry depend on their ability to manipulate racial impressions, capitalizing on their liminal physiognomy to ply the racially striated pathways of (neo)liberalism's global culturescape. Coming after a generation of
race-based, decolonizing activism, however, their profiles point explicitly
to the political costs and betrayals entailed in the transformation of race
into identity capital: to claim postracial mobility is to participate in a global
economy of fantasy still structured by race and to reinscribe the racial distribution of opportunity and value on which that economy still rests.

If Curtis's and Morrison's careers indirectly confer the benediction of success on the state's knowledge-economy project, the figure of Keisha Castle-
Hughes—a third postracial cipher, one who (unlike Curtis or Morrison)

circulates qua Māori—makes starkly visible the state interests to which Māori postraciality is now appropriated.

THE NEW FACE OF INDIGENEITY, THE WHITENESS OF THE WHALE, AND THE MARK OF LOVE

For two brief years of the early millennium, Castle-Hughes was the face of the *new* New Zealand, Aotearoa New Zealand, a cover girl for nearly all the major weeklies. She was a figure who had succeeded in fulfilling Curtis's enjoinder to turn identity into "winning international product," yet one still firmly rooted in both culture and state. She came to exemplify not just Māoriness but also Harley's elusive "US-ness." On the cover of the *New Zealand Listener*'s sixty-fifth anniversary issue, she was pictured frolicking in a field with Sir Colin Meads, also known as Pinetree, a Pākehā farmer and former All Black captain: a figure who bestrode the prosperous 1960s, "a sheep under each arm," representing all the muscular probity of white agricultural nationalism.[105] Next to him, Castle-Hughes, thirteen at the time—radiant, fresh, and playful—presented a figure of national futurity as potent as the half-caste Māori woman at the turn of the previous century: she was a harbinger of the neoliberal state to come, just as the latter had represented the liberal state in the making. For the article's author, film performed crucial steps in this national narrative, which was also a racial narrative: whereas the cultural disconnection and social problems of Māori urbanization were known "all too well from personal experience or *Once Were Warriors*," *Whale Rider* revealed a reconnection and a "merging of the global and the tribal."[106] But it was Castle-Hughes's image, her *face*, that spoke the most eloquently in this article as a stabilizing apotrope for thinking national citizenship biculturally, globally, and positively (at a moment of projected demographic change that would see Pākehā as the largest minority and Māori numbers matched by both Asian and Pacific Island populations within a half-century).

Castle-Hughes recalls another cover girl: the New Face of America, pictured on the cover of *Time* in 1993. "SimEve," as she was called, represented the citizen of America's new racially diverse millennium, a computer-generated media projection animated by white America's fears of accelerated immigration and minority demands. The face figured the alien made human, a sign transmuting apprehension into desire for a prosperous and

Keisha Castle-Hughes and former All Black captain Colin Meads. *New Zealand Listener.*

postracial futurity. As Lauren Berlant has argued, it attempted to stabilize the core image of national society through proposing a new, privatized, political subject: nameless, voiceless, in "pure isolation from lived history" and social (specifically racial) belonging; a monadic incarnation of the economic energies of immigrant corporeality; and a new fantasy norm against which deviancies were to be measured.[107] The Benetton serenity of this face proposed a new political legitimacy for America's ethnic denizens, now available for identification, recognition, and empathy. The paradox, of course, is that the price of inclusion is not merely the renunciation of race—with its attachment to history, grievance, and noneconomic forms of loyalty—but of humanity itself. A digital fabrication is elevated above its flesh-bound referents; a pure dividual replaces the messy unpredictability of individuation. In the same gesture, then, as legitimizing the raced other, *Time* heralded the demise of race as a meaningful category of political community and as a significant component of humanness.

In similar ways, Castle-Hughes became a mythic token of hygienic governmentality, incarnating the aspirant spirit of neoliberalism on behalf of a nation caught between apprehension and anticipation of its ethnic future. But Castle-Hughes's face of Aotearoa New Zealand was generated from the material of a real body, a body not coincidentally young, feminine, and indigenous. It propelled the young actor on her global circulation through other roles, most notably her part as another biblical progenitor, the Virgin Mary, in Catherine Hardwicke's *The Nativity Story* (2006), in which she was cast not only for her "Mediterranean" complexion but because she could "carry a movie with spirituality."[108] The "epic intimacy" Hardwicke sought in her film came, like Caro's, from the conjoining of epochal narrative with a fleshly sign as evocative in its truthing effect as the digitally morphed *Time* cover girl. The stillness and gravity of Castle-Hughes's face—the luminous, flawlessly youthful skin, the eyebrows upturned in an almost permanent expression of vulnerable tenderness, and the soul-deep, faraway brown eyes—was as irresistible a focus for Hardwicke's camera as it was for Caro's. Critics had remarked on the utterly unaffected quality of Castle-Hughes's Paikea not only because the character was coded as "natural" (in the childish vocabulary and simplicity of her first-person voice-over, or in her unkempt gangliness) but also because of the expressive but transparent and pellucid quality of that face, a face that seemed to *conduct* rather than project emotion. As Paikea, Castle-Hughes *non*acted: rather than producing affect through imagining psychological and circumstantial common ground with the character (the "method" technique), she made of herself a space through which affect could flow, in particular a diffuse sense of hurt, yearning, and passive anticipation.[109]

This last quality attracts attention: whereas associations with the natural and spiritual are time-honored clichés attaching to indigeneity, the affective character of Castle-Hughes's face announces itself as a novel structure of feeling. Like the computer-generated New Face of America, this girlchild is a silent and powerless unit of human agency. Driven by the force of messianic fate more than will, absent of struggle except with her own sorrow, Paikea (like Mary and SimEve) does not so much act as yield herself up as the vessel of a communal future. Despite her role as protagonist, she speaks and acts primarily through her suffering, which impels the triumphal self-actualization of the conclusion.

This landscape of affect, touching the audience through the medium of the infantile citizen, was responsible, I submit, both for *Whale Rider*'s national resonance and its global currency. Theorists of liberalism have taken a recent interest in affect, that asignifying dimension of social, political, and aesthetic experience that passes between subjects.[110] The capacity to touch and be touched, to move and be moved, has historically formed the ligaments of moral obligation at the foundation of liberalism's portrait of political collectivity, all the more powerful for its ability to shrink the realm of public responsibility to the individual, writing structural problems into private sorrows and struggles. At its most disingenuous, "the ethical imperative toward social transformation is replaced by a civic-minded but passive ideal of empathy. The political as a place of acts oriented toward publicness becomes replaced by a world of private thoughts, leanings, and gestures."[111] Neoliberalization has inaugurated what Kathleen Woodward calls a "new economy of the emotions," expanding the repertoire of public feeling, not with respect to narratives of psychological interiority, but instead as a terrain of intensity that acts as an alibi for the privatization of the state, sublating rather than stimulating calls to act from feeling.[112]

Paikea's suffering evokes compassion aplenty, but (unlike the suffering of *Once Were Warriors*'s young Grace Heke, whose suicide is the turning point of the film's plot) it makes no demands on an audience's moral obligation to respond or ameliorate. Rather, it situates the audience in a scene of mourning, loss, and sorrow that is overtaken by love and hope. "There was no gladness when I was born," the voice of the young girl opens the film, referring to the death of her twin brother (significantly, Caro's addition to Ihimaera's story) but also evoking the anxious malaise that has overtaken her leaderless people. The "ideology of true feeling," Berlant argues, insists on the universality of pain but jumbles its cases together.[113] In this instance, Paikea, the generic "wounded subject" of the liberal state, is a diffuse, individualized register not of the trauma of colonization (which has no presence in this film) but of something more akin to the "labor of social mourning" occasioned by the brutality of neoliberalization's reforms: the "conditions of relentless and all-pervading social and economic insecurity, where . . . the present becomes so uncertain that it devours the future and prohibits thinking about it except as fantasy."[114] Just as the heroine's passage leads to celebration and joy, the film produced another political intensity in place of mourning—*hope, love, and the elation of success*—which suffused the production and overspilled it, touching audiences who in turn left their mark on the film as a national taonga (treasured possession), as kaumātua Hone Taumaunu declared it. It was both globally salient and nationally timely: New Zealand has been waiting for this film, Kiwi actor Sam Neill said, a film about the beauty and potency of Māori culture, a film that "reminds us of a child's (and our own) capacity to love unconditionally."[115] Love has a price, however: the proscription of other affects, primarily anger, which have historically subtended the judicial, territorial, and historical claims of indigenes against the state. Castle-Hughes is postracial, postfeminist, *postpolitical* nationalism incarnate.[116]

Ultimately, this neoliberal gambit entails the proscription of the raced body itself as a locus of positive political feeling. This is the unsurprising secret of Castle-Hughes's power as a scion and sign of indigeneity: this vessel of a hope-filled future, this face that conducts the affective plenitude of the neoliberal state, is rendered effectively and cinematically white. *Whale Rider* accomplishes this not simply in the purification and revalorization of indigeneity but also through appropriating the codes of whiteness. Film imaged whiteness as radiance, moral purity, and enlightenment, Richard Dyer has argued, through its construction as a translucent medium, allowing the "spirit" of its lighter-skinned subjects to manifest in the material as light.[117] Just as the medium privileged and elevated whiteness, so the light that signified it also came to signify both rectitude and virtue. Light is also the sign of Pai's difference as the chosen one: next to the other lumpen Māori youth of the town and their parents, she quite literally glows. "When Leon Narbey [the cinematographer] and I were discussing how to light the film," Caro claims, "that was the guiding principle—that Pai is (literally) the light. Koro is in the dark and she is not."[118]

Emptied of history but saturated with tradition, anchored in autochthony but as globally fungible as capital itself, Keisha Castle-Hughes's face was an apt emblem for the brand of the neoliberal tourist state. Kevin Roberts, Saatchi & Saatchi's worldwide CEO (and cited as inspiration for key New Zealand tourism marketing initiatives), coined the term "Lovemark" to describe a future "beyond brands" in which corporations would craft intimate and enduring relationships with consumers, relationships that (like the nation of yore) would inspire "loyalty beyond reason."[119] The Lovemark, the powerful metonym of this relationship, makes consumers feel a sense of ownership. It lures with mystery (stories, myths, icons, and

Keisha Castle-Hughes, luminescent and suffering in *Whale Rider*.

dreams), like *Whale Rider*, weaving together the past, present, and future. It enchants with sensuality, like *Whale Rider*'s haptic redolence of sun and sea breeze, its evocation of oceanic memory.[120] It offers intimacy—commitment, empathy, and passion—to mitigate anonymity or remoteness.

Film and tourism have long been paired in New Zealand's branding-work of statehood: as Harley claimed, film is a powerful technology for discovering and communicating the identity of citizens and for forging the pathways by which they (and their products) might foot it abroad, as well as for drawing international traffic. While *Lord of the Rings* branded the nation as human and territorial raw materials for "Hollyworld's" high-technology, racially regressive, and global economy of fantasy, this new generation of policy-driven domestic film perceives the brand as a technology of affective governmentality and subjectivization.[121] The postracial face of Castle-Hughes helped to set the global conditions of legibility for Māori indigeneity, but it also proposed a repertoire of citizenship—norms, proscriptions, trajectories, attachments, and dispositions—coproduced for and by the global market. This repertoire figured the indigene as the form and alibi of a new order of whiteness and as the emblem of the state. It is against such triumphalist elisions between girl and state, state and population, and population and global corporation that the newly disqualified politics of race might have provided a crucial point of resistance.

RACIAL DISSENT IN A POSTRACIAL WORLD

In 2004, Castle-Hughes starred in another locally produced drama: an episode of the Auckland-produced *South Park* and *Simpsons* copycat cartoon comedy *bro'Town*. Devised and voiced by theatrical comedy troupe The Naked Samoans, *bro'Town* is set in Morningside, a down-at-the-heels, anarchic, ethnically diverse suburb in what could only be South Auckland (the home of *Once Were Warriors*'s beleaguered denizens). It follows the adventures of five boys: four Pacific Islanders and one Māori. Titled "A Māori at My Table," the episode is a satiric grab bag of the nation's media history, with musical and visual quotations from Jane Campion (*An Angel at My Table*, 1992), documentary photography of Māori land-rights marches of the 1970s, references to *Once Were Warriors* and *Whale Rider*, and guest spots by Caro, Ihimaera, Castle-Hughes, and Curtis, all playing themselves.[122] In this episode, the kids of Morningside High go on a school trip to their friend Jeff da Māori's marae at Kia Ora Bay. But when they arrive, they discover that Jeff's auntie Queenie has died, and the land on which the marae stands (right next to Morningside's sewage plant) is now up for grabs. Jeff meets up with his "hot" cousin Keisha and cousin Cliff (just back from Hollywood). Cliff tries to persuade him to sell the bay for "serious cash" to Japanese property developers planning to build a mall. Keisha protests, "But Auntie wanted us to safeguard our assets for the future generations." "Shut up, kid," Cliff snaps back, "the future generations can have jobs in the food hall."

A few minutes of business ensues with a magic flute, some whales, a ghostly grandfather, and a lot of scatological humor. The histrionic and bullying Cliff Curtis (who has abandoned kaupapa Māori in favor of unalloyed greed—"Enough with the mumbo jumbo mystical Māori crap!") is on the verge of getting the signatures he needs. Suddenly, Keisha rides into the scene on the back of a whale, summoned by Jeff's mournful guitar playing. "See, Cliff?" she says. "The whales are back. And see, the tourists are already coming! We don't need a stink mall now!" Even more suddenly, *another* (more bro-like) Cliff appears deus ex machina and tears a rubber mask from the face of the histrionic Cliff to reveal . . . a Japanese investor. All is resolved, and soon the boys are back on the bus to Morningside. Cliff has promised to stay and lead the tribe, but only after striking a covert deal with the Japanese investor. ("Maybe we can still work together. Something that uses the whales but makes you a whole lot of money." "Let's hui," Cliff replies.) Cliff's parting shot is, "Hey, Jeff. I got this choice idea, Cuz. Whaddya reckon we build a drama school to teach Māori actors how to play other ethnic minorities in Hollywood movies?"

The episode understands with perfect, brutal clarity the relationship between the new international division of cultural labor, tourist practice, local opportunity, global coercion, and the fantasies of film—and it understands the cunning salience of racial performativity to them all. It is an ethnographic miniature that brings the viewer full circle from the frictionless identifications of *Whale Rider*, with its seductive call of the Lovemark, back to the gritty political economy of race in *Once Were Warriors* with its stories of perilous urban survival and structural injustice, and its critique of state tourism's disingenuous blandishments. And it goes back even further to the land-rights and solidarity politics of the Māori renaissance. Superimposing the three, it punctures neoliberalism's teleology of progress. Even the episode's casual anti-Asiatic sentiment has a sharp point to it: five times the area of land that has been returned to Māori under Treaty settlements has been sold to offshore investors after the neoliberal deregulation of property-ownership laws. Many buyers hail from Asia, leading to a pervasive sense of insecurity about future sovereignty, welfare, and land-based identity among both Pākehā and Māori, and of course to racial resentment. Amid the environmental degradation, poverty, and generational rupture at Kia Ora Bay, cousin Cliff (the real one) promises that accumulation by dispossession can be stayed by a knowledge-economy solution, ushering in an age of tribal prosperity, but at a price: the transformation of identity to orient it to global desires and the foreclosure of alternative, nonentrepreneurial possibilities for a collective future. Against the background of Morningside's anarchic diversity, the episode makes clear that the tourist state's pious hyperinvestment in a sanitized, romanticized, and deracinated Māoritanga—Māori tales and whales and the beauty of a distant bay—is taking place in the face of a national demographic ever more Asian, more Pacific, and more fractiously, noisily global, and ever less consonant with the instrumental fiction of biculturalism itself. Amid such a clamor, how long, one wonders, can a cinematically sanctified, postracial Māoridom stand in for the core values and promises of the neoliberal state?

Already, the conjuncture that turned *Lord of the Rings* and *Whale Rider* into dramas of national transformation has shifted. Since the films' release, runaway fantasy blockbusters such as *The Lion, the Witch, and the Wardrobe* and *Prince Caspian* have been and gone, without garnering recognition for their supporting landscapes or creating tourism tie-ins. Jackson's racial mythology machine has continued apace, first with *King Kong* and later with special effects and design support for ventures such as *Avatar*, which put forward a hyperbolic neoprimitivist version of the New Indigene as an ideal white self for the postindustrial age: wounded, absent of history or race, sustained by superior information networks, affective relationality, and cultural expertise, rescued from collective dispossession by a dose of heroic (white) individualism. The NZFPF has birthed its share of (mostly parochial) flops and profitable (largely generic) workhorses such as Roger Donaldson's *The World's Fastest Indian*, but it has thus far failed to duplicate *Whale Rider*'s success.[123] Meanwhile, Pākehā quirks and self-deprecating parochialism (*Flight of the Conchords*, *Black Sheep*, and *Eagle vs. Shark*) have garnered a young niche audience internationally. Urban immigrant family comedies from the Pacific Islander community, such as *Sione's Wedding*, have been surprise global and domestic hits. An unexpected engine of domestic screen innovation, Māori Television, was set up on a bare-bones budget from the state in (belated) recognition of its Treaty obligation to serve the Māori audience of public broadcasting.[124] Defying all the odds against national public broadcasting in a postquota, post-GATT era, and overcoming early establishment resistance, Māori TV has earned a broad viewership of both Māori and Pākehā and nurtured a generation of documentarists and producers.

The direst prognoses and loftiest ambitions of those few years early in the century have both proven without ground: the domestic industry has not been swallowed up by a Hollywood behemoth, nor has film become a mainstay of the knowledge economy. What it *was*, for those brief few years at the hinge of Aotearoa New Zealand's neoliberal century, was a laboratory of the tourist state: a space for publicly imagining the racial forms and figures of a global state to come, an index of its racial fears and fantasies, and a machine for putting that imagination in motion.

Living in a Tourist State

As the first decade of the new millennium drew to a close, tourism growth slowed in Aotearoa New Zealand. Rising fuel prices took their toll, as did the nation's stronger currency (the neoliberal economy turned victim of its own success). Then global recession set in. State policy has shifted: the new emerging market is now China, the new mantra "sustainability" rather than growth, with ecological outcomes now ranking alongside high-quality experiences, growing investment, and community partnering as strategic priorities.[1] As at the turn of the previous century, the art of government has always demanded reflexivity, a state ready to propose new analytics and techniques (carbon neutrality, for instance, or environmental impact ratings), and new forms of conduct (such as greening tourism provision and protocols of kaitiakitanga, or guardianship) to manage the territory-population assemblage toward the goal of national welfare. Despite the slowdown, tourism is still big and still a growing business for Aotearoa New Zealand: it is the largest export earner (18.3 percent) and a substantive sector of the overall economy (at 8.9 percent of GDP and one-tenth of total employment).[2] The administration that replaced Helen Clark's Labour coalition in 2009 has appointed the Prime Minister, John Key, as Minister of Tourism and custodian of the national brand, signaling that the industry will remain at the epicenter of governmental strategy. But the breathless excitement of state innovation in the Clark years has dissipated, along with much of its optimism: the new order is now the new normal, its terms little questioned, even if some of its terminology ("national identity," "cultural capital") has come to seem dated.

Māori are increasingly addressed as special stakeholders in tourism, which (strategy documents tell them) offers "important opportunities to celebrate, nurture, and present their culture to the world."[3] And Māori tourism operations continue to proliferate, from large-scale iwi investment to small, regional business start-ups modeled to cater to FIT clientele. But as new policy grows old, its cracks begin to show. Many of the business owners and employees I followed in my fieldwork complain that the market has become saturated, and new competition means new pressure to deliver to larger groups in order to raise profit margins. So, while most of these businesses remain focused around ecological themes, are site-specific in character, and are upscale in execution, many have sacrificed the intimacy that lay at the core of their promise. Moreover, the majority of jobs in these businesses are precarious and poorly paid—hardly surprising, given the highly stratified service economies that characterize neoliberal states, producing new, complicated (and usually racialized) topographies of opportunity and advantage. Yet despite the seeming failure of the "identity capital" model to deliver the gains or equality it promised, still iwi and hapū turn to tourism as a development instrument: cultural policy has created the conditions whereby this choice, this exercise of economic agency, seems inevitable. No one is pressing tourism on hapū, state agents argue: "They can go at their own pace."[4] But the direction seems predetermined, and in a climate of tough competition, the fear that someone else will get there first is pressing.

Meanwhile, there has been an apparent resurgence in hāngī-'n'-haka tourism. Tamaki Tours has recently expanded, opening two new facilities in Auckland and Christchurch. Its repackaged product still centers on a feast and a dance, but it has taken more than a leaf from Peter Jackson's book, now promising a fully immersive theatrical and racial spectacle: a melodramatic epic, the "Chronicles of Uitara," told in three episodes across the three sites. It is a story of "grit and glory," told with unapologetic glitz and greasepaint, part heritage reenactment, part historical pageant, and a large part old-fashioned ethnological show business. But there is nothing old-fashioned about their mission statement. Reconciling capital ambition with indigenous emancipation, it epitomizes the neoliberal political rationality that equates community empowerment with cultural

At the 2007
opening of the
Giant Rugby Ball,
Prime Minister
Helen Clark poses
with members of the
Te Arawa kapa haka
troupe. Tourism
New Zealand.

asset management: "The real magic of the Tamaki formula is the way it marries indigenous spirit and storytelling tradition with the necessary and robust business practices that allow communities to enjoy sustainable economic independence."[5]

The 100% Pure campaign flourishes now past its tenth anniversary, with a new generation of images in which Māori are prominent. But the Māori subjects cast as signs of national purity ironically resemble those from a much older generation of state tourism. A recent campaign centered on the Rugby World Cup, to be held in New Zealand in 2011, following the strategy of leveraging major events to maximize limited publicity budgets. At the campaign launch in Paris in 2007, Helen Clark, Prime Minister at the time, is pictured flanked by two burly warriors in make-up tattoos standing in front of a giant rugby ball. Containing dazzling 360 degree multimedia displays dramatizing the "New Zealand journey" and "showcasing everything the country has to offer—from stunning scenery, tourism, trade, culture, lifestyle, food, wine and technology," the ball is emblazoned 100% Pure New Zealand, and behind it rises the unmistakable profile of the Eiffel Tower. In another publicity shot, a kapa haka group works its routine before the same backdrop. The images are resonant and troubling. When the Tower was constructed for the Paris Exposition of 1891, it epitomized the technological triumphs and transcendent ethos of European modernity. A man-made attraction, it also expressed the promise of a newly democratized tourist industry: ocular and epistemological mastery of the city (for a modest price), and the idea that a place and a practice (taking the view) might come together to brand a nation and help shape the expectations, dispositions, conducts, and imperial identities of its subjects. Yet it accomplished this in large part because of its perceived contrast to the ungovernable, exotic riot of ethnological attractions that the exposition was equally famous for—including Egyptian bazaars, Dahomeyan villages, and Turkish dancers—and that underwrote its arguments about the imperial droit of *liberté*.

Is TNZ, one wonders, replicating the exposition's strategy by offering panoramic mastery to cosmopolitan consumers while ornamenting and offsetting its national modernity with primitive spectacle? Is it recapitulating the spectacular diplomacy of a century earlier, the ventriloquist act whereby the New Zealand state put forward Māori performers to distinguish it in a competitive market of nations and to dignify its claims to sovereign and liberal consensus? (Helen Clark was none too popular in Māoridom at the time, after her summary abridgement of Treaty-guaranteed rights with the Foreshore and Seabed Act and her support of a police campaign against Māori sovereignty activists under antiterrorism laws.) After decades of critique of presentational aesthetics, appropriative dynamics, and primitivist racial metonymy in tourism marketing, what are we to make of this revenant? Is it evidence of the continued Pākehā possessive investment in Māori culture? The Pākehā state's cynical bet on the enduring currency of modernist racial aesthetics in a neoliberal age? An admission that the small and vulnerable cannot afford to be too scrupulous in a cutthroat global economy?

TNZ's World Cup campaign may be all of these things. Yet to claim that it outright exploits Māori property and/in performance in the name of a white state is to assume that Māori—and whatever agency they might exercise—stand outside that state. Instead, the achievement of neoliberal cultural policy has been to bring the interests of the state and those of Māori into alignment. Māori have a high stake in tourism traffic to Aotearoa New Zealand, and for Māori entrepreneurs looking to find markets for cultural products, these kinds of promotions are likewise a boon. Māori state and trade development agencies aim eventually to craft a *Māori brand* under which indigenous marketing efforts could be harmonized. (Although it should be anathema to a people who increasingly favor iwi or hapū identifications over the colonialism-derived moniker Māori, the idea of a Māori brand stands as an ironic testament to circulation's power to produce solidarities.) The haka, associated with the mana (prestige) of more than a century of sporting success, and already a recognizable and coveted (indeed, appropriated) international property with considerable affective charge, is ripe to be enlisted into this branding effort as the quintessential Lovemark. The more 100% Pure mobilizes Māori performance property in its campaigns, the more a Māori brand can leverage the recognition, trust, and appeal of 100% Pure (despite its questionable racial semiotics).

The tourist state's art of government works by producing the conditions that make exercising economic self-interest and pursuing indigenous cultural expression synonymous, both directed to the cause of national welfare via their global circulation. From *Homo economicus*, it forges *Homo indigenalis*. (Pākehā, meanwhile, conform their conduct to, and roundly benefit from, this new governmental ecology.)

When the Giant Rugby Ball opened in Sydney in September 2010, a Te Arawa kapa haka troupe exchanged performances with the Aboriginal Doonooch Dance Company, and a "smoking ceremony" was undertaken to welcome these fellow members of their "indigenous family." "Everyone has adopted manaakitanga [hospitality]," said Pita Sharples, Minister of Māori Affairs, invoking what is now a brand value and principle of conduct for TNZ.[6] One of the national social laboratory's most recent inventions and exports, these events make clear, is the conceptualization of indigenous alliance as a global pathway for capital, and of capital as a pathway for global indigenous renaissance. The ceremony was presided over by Māori King Kiingi Tuheitia, Sharples, and Trevor Maxwell, Kaupapa (mission) Director for TNZ: there could be no greater show of support from Māoridom than such an alliance. This kind of traffic, this delicate dance in which the interests of Māori and the state come into and out of alignment, is not only the price of survival in a global economy, it is the field of agency in which all now act. We might even call it the tourist state.

It is a dance that has gone on for more than a century. For many Māori working in the cultural economy, the touristic diplomacy of their Liberal-era forebears is a usable past. In a slew of recent documentaries and popular histories—about touring rugby teams, for instance, or about the life of Makereti Papakura—Māori authors identify the Liberal era as the onset of economic and cultural renaissance and the crucible of bicultural, globally oriented nationhood. "Our people saw the future," they argue: their exploits established the pathways of entrepreneurialism and ambassadorship traversed by Māori today, using performance as an authentically Māori way of engaging with nascent global opportunity and of combating its colonial curtailments.[7] My own research in this book has been enlisted in this project by the descendants of the Hippodrome performers, for whom their ancestors' exploits inspire the ongoing work of reuniting and reinvigorating a whānau (extended family) dispersed first by colonial and then by neoliberal economic duress. New indigenous historiography looks back and sees not only colonial appropriation, exploitation, and racism (although they are ever-present) but also a people empowered, with respect to the state, by virtue of a cultural wealth valorized in the attention of global audiences.

In academe, we want to tell stories about tourism that have clean endings and unequivocal morals. We want to tell of the tragedy of exclusion or exploitation, or of the triumph of "antitouristic" crusades to redeem the authentic integrity of indigenous culture or expose the white imperialist underpinnings of tourism's cultural logics.[8] The picture here only shows us the complexity of liberal life, the myriad agencies, compromises, calculations, investments, desires, and ambivalences that constitute the liberal exercise of freedom, mobility, and opportunity in a world still structured by race.

Tourism is a border art, poising its practitioners between cultures and markets, between the insides and the outsides of communities, nations, and places. At borders, we stand between, but never outside, states: because the very act of crossing, the very conditions of that act, are what give the state its solidity. There, states are *imagined* most forcefully and most consequentially. Borders—we do not need scholars to tell us—are dangerous places. Tourism's border artists live every day with cultural danger, risk, contradiction, and accommodation. Borders are also violently unequal places, but danger and risk are not experienced equally by all. At borders, the gulf between what is normalized and valued and what is abjected is made most starkly visible; the tension between liberal life and its promises (those broken and those still glimmering) is most acutely felt. But borders are also inventive places, where propositions and hybrids have to be made to move forward, where ideas, objects, and identities must be made and remade over and over in a process both irreducibly complex and complexly generative. This is what it means to live in a tourist state.

ACKNOWLEDGMENTS

In the long process of completing this book, I have incurred more debts—personal, professional, and intellectual—than I can name or number. First, I gratefully acknowledge the generous funding of phases of my dissertation research and writing by the American Association of University Women, the Wenner-Gren Anthropological Foundation, and scholarships from Northwestern University's Center for International and Comparative Studies, Department of Performance Studies, and Office of Research and Sponsored Programs. Later work on the manuscript was supported by the Woodrow Wilson National Fellowship Foundation, Pennsylvania State University, and the University of Minnesota, where I have been assisted by the McKnight and Imagine funds, the Institute for Advanced Study, and a College of Liberal Arts grant-in-aid.

During my New Zealand–based research for this book, many individuals took up where the written archive left off. My special thanks to Dorothy "Bubbles" Mihinui, Witarina Harris, and Jim Dennan for generously sharing their experiences and insights with me. Huge mihi to Kingi Biddle, the late and much-respected Robert Biddle, and the mokopuna (descendants) of Kiwi Te Amohau and Kiri Matao. Thank you for welcoming me into your whānau and allowing me to share your stories—it has been an honor and a pleasure. In conducting research for chapters 4 and 5 of this volume, I interviewed approximately thirty individuals working in tourism, government, Māori development, and the arts. Most spoke to me in a professional capacity and were happy to be identified by name when quoted, but to protect the anonymity of those who were not, none of their names appear in the following volume. I am deeply grateful to all of them for giving so fully of their time and expertise.

The archival research for this project spanned four countries and many collections. My particular thanks go to the terrific staff at the Alexander Turnbull Library and to the National Library of New Zealand, the Archive of Te Papa Tongarewa National Museum of New Zealand, National Archives of New Zealand (including the Auckland and Rotorua branches), Rotorua Museum and Archive, Auckland War Memorial Museum Archive, Auckland Public Library, Rotorua Public Library, and New Zealand Film Archive. In the United States, I am grateful to librarians at the New York Public Library, Billy Rose Theatre Collection, American Museum of Natural History, and Library of Congress. In the United Kingdom, Elizabeth Edwards and the archivists at the Pitt Rivers Museum were unfailingly helpful, as were staff at the Museum of London. For the use of images, I thank Tamaki Tours Ltd., Melissa Crockett at Mōhio Tours, and Tourism New Zealand.

The first readers of two of these chapters (in their painful dissertational form) were Tracy Davis, the late Dwight Conquergood, and Micaela di Leonardo. To them and to my other mentors at Northwestern University, Margaret Thompson Drewal and Tom Gunning, I offer humble thanks for the intellectual foundation on which this book rests. Among the other readers who have since offered invaluable insights and sensible advice, I would like to thank Rob Wilson, Christopher Balme, Della Pollock, Helen Gilbert, Paul Rae, Gil Rodman, Phaedra Pezullo, Jean Graham-Jones, Roisin O'Gorman, Shannon Steen, and Guillaume Boccara. In New Zealand, I have been grateful for the curiosity and kindness of Brian Opie, Huhana Smith, Charles Te Ahukaramu Royal, David O'Donnell, and for early monitory advice, Ngahuia Te Awekotuku. Paul Tapsell, Lydia Wevers, and Don Stafford also offered kind assistance during the research process.

The unspoken heroes of academe are those unofficial sponsors who provide roofs, wine, company, and couch space to wandering researchers. My heroes include my dear friends Tom Lawson and Kenrick Davis, Elinore Wellwood, Frances Rowntree, Vlatka Horvat, Megan Huber, and, of course, my forbearing and unflagging champion, my mum, Beverley Werry.

I regard myself as enormously privileged to be part of a broad and deep intellectual community; it has been the wind in my sails throughout the long journey of this book. At numerous conference presentations, the community of theater and performance studies scholars proved a challenging and generous audience. Other interlocutors in cultural studies (especially the folk at Conjunctures), anthropology, and area studies have also pushed this work in productive directions. To my colleagues in Theatre Arts and Dance at the University of Minnesota, especially Sonja Kuftinec, Cindy Garcia, Michal Kobialka, and Megan Lewis, I offer thanks for your unstinting support and intellectual generosity. Thanks also to our smart (and funny and ribald and caring) graduate students and to the veritable army of brilliant and bodacious colleagues who have buoyed my spirits over the past seven years. Space prevents me from naming more than a few of you: Jeani O'Brien, Lisa Disch, Karen Till, Maria Damon, and especially Anne Carter, Anna Clarke, Jani Scandura, and Juliette Cherbuliez, who cheered me on, read my drafts, and still respected me in the morning. I daily count myself honored and lucky to number among you.

This project has followed me through three moves, three jobs, and three states. If at times it seemed like a journey that would never end, it was not one traveled alone. Michael Giblin and Gilbert Rodman have both left their subtle imprint on these chapters, for which I thank them sincerely. Finally, the greatest thanks of all go to Jim Levi and my precious John Solomon, who arrived just in time to help me finish this journey and to embark with me on the best voyage of all.

NOTES

INTRODUCTION

1. Peter Biggs, "Islands of Imagination," www.creativenz.govt.nz/files/resources/biggs_nyc.rtf.

2. Nigel Morgan and Annette Pritchard, "New Zealand, 100% Pure: The Creation of a Powerful Niche Destination Brand," *Journal of Brand Management* 9, nos. 4 & 5 (2002): 335–45.

3. Kevin Roberts, *Lovemarks: The Future beyond Brands* (New York: Powerhouse Books, 2005).

4. "PM Celebrates NZ National Day at Shanghai Expo," July 9, 2010, http://beehive.govt.nz/release/pm-celebrates-nz-national-day-shanghai-expo.

5. See Jane Stafford and Mark Williams, *Maoriland: New Zealand Literature, 1872–1914* (Wellington: Victoria University Press, 2006).

6. On "imperialist nostalgia," see Renato Rosaldo, *Culture and Truth: The Remaking of Social Analysis* (Boston: Beacon Press, 1999).

7. James Cowan, *Official Record of the New Zealand International Exhibition of Arts and Industries* (Wellington: Government Printer, 1910).

8. Margaret Orbell, "Maori Writing about the Exhibition," in *Farewell Colonialism: The New Zealand International Exhibition, Christchurch, 1906–7*, ed. John Mansfield Thomson (Palmerston North, N.Z.: Dunmore Press, 1998), 144, 148.

9. See Simon Anholt, *Brand New Justice: How Branding Places and Products Can Help the Developing World* (Amsterdam: Elsevier, 2005).

10. Haunani-Kay Trask, *From a Native Daughter: Colonialism and Sovereignty in Hawai'i* (Monroe, Maine: Common Courage Press, 1993); Teresia Teaiwa, "Reading Paul Gauguin's *Noa Noa* with Epeli Hau'ofa's *Kisses in the Nederends*: Militourism, Feminism, and the 'Polynesian' Body," in *Inside Out: Literature, Cultural Politics, and Identity in the New Pacific*, ed. Vilsoni Hereniko (Lanham, Md.: Rowman & Littlefield, 1999), 249–63.

11. Noel Kent, "A New Kind of Sugar," in *A New Kind of Sugar: Tourism in the Pacific*, ed. Ben R. Finney and Karen Ann Watson (Honolulu: East-West Center, 1975), 169–98.

12. For a review of this literature, see Bruce Ziff and Pratima Rao, "Introduction to Cultural Appropriation: A Framework for Analysis," *Borrowed Power: Essays on Cultural Appropriation* (New Brunswick, N.J.: Rutgers University Press, 1997), 1–37; and Nicholas Thomas, *Possessions: Indigenous Art, Colonial Culture* (London: Thames & Hudson, 1999). For New Zealand specifically, see Peter Gibbons, "'Going Native': A Case Study of Cultural Appropriation in a Settler Society" (PhD diss., University of Waikato, 1992). The concept of surrogation is elaborated in Joseph Roach, *Cities of the Dead: Circum-Atlantic Performance* (New York: Columbia University Press, 1996) as the process by which survivors attempt through performance to fit satisfactory alternates into the "cavities created by death or other forms of departure" (3). Clearly, the case of ethnic tourism in settler states, where "authentic natives" are called on to represent their own living but departed past, thereby extinguishing that past's claims on the nonnative present, is a fascinating variation on this process.

13. See Nigel Thrift, *Non-Representational Theory: Space, Politics, Affect* (London: Routledge, 2007).

14. Elin Diamond, ed., *Performance and Cultural Politics* (New York: Routledge, 1996), 1.

15. Timothy Mitchell, "Society, Economy, and the State Effect," in *State/Culture: State-Formation after the Cultural Turn*, ed. George Steinmetz (Ithaca, N.Y.: Cornell University Press, 1999), 76–97.

16. I borrow the term "racial formation" from Omi and Winant's well-known formulation: "the process by which social, economic, and political forces determine the content and importance of racial categories, and by which they are in turn shaped by racial meanings." Michael Omi and Howard Winant, *Racial Formation in the United States: From the 1960s to the 1980s* (New York: Routledge, 1986), 41.

17. Benedict Anderson, *Imagined Communities: Reflections on the Origin and Spread of Nationalism* (London: Verso, 1991 [1983]); Anderson, "Nationalism, Identity, and the World in Motion: On the Logics of Seriality," in *Cosmopolitics: Thinking and Feeling beyond the Nation*, ed. Pheng Cheah and Bruce Robbins (Minneapolis: University of Minnesota Press, 1998), 117–33. I am also informed in this discussion not only by the breadth of cosmopolitanism literature (cited in full in chapter 2) but by recent work on "cultures of circulation" by scholars such as Benjamin Lee, Edward LiPuma, and Arjun Appadurai.

18. Raymond Williams, "Structures of Feeling," in *Marxism and Literature* (Oxford: Oxford University Press, 1977), 128–35.

19. Tony Bennett, "Civic Laboratories: Museums, Cultural Objecthood, and the Governance of the Social," *Cultural Studies* 19, no. 5 (2005): 521–47, 524.

20. Periodizations differ, with some histories taking the Liberal era as the period in which the Liberal Party held the parliamentary majority (1891–1912), and others as the period in which the Liberal Party's broader agenda defined the political character of

the nation (1890–1919). Influential historians analyzing this era as the "hinge" of New Zealand history include James Belich, *Making Peoples: A History of the New Zealanders from Polynesian Settlement to the End of the Nineteenth Century* (Auckland: Penguin Books, 1996); David Hamer, *The New Zealand Liberals: The Years of Power, 1891–1912* (Auckland: Auckland University Press, 1998); and Keith Sinclair, *A Destiny Apart: New Zealand's Search for National Identity* (Wellington: Allen & Unwin, 1986).

21. Alys Lowth, *Emerald Hours in New Zealand* (Christchurch, N.Z.: Whitcombe & Tombs, 1906), 6.

22. These estimates come from records of visitors to the Rotorua spa, published from 1901 onward in the Department of Tourist and Health Resorts Annual Report in *Appendices to the Journal of the House of Representatives.*

23. Tom Brooking, "Busting Up the Greatest Estate of All: Liberal Maori Land Policy, 1891–1911," *New Zealand Journal of History* 26, no. 1 (1992): 78–98, 93.

24. Ranginui Walker, *Ka Whawhai Tonu Matou: Struggle without End* (Auckland: Penguin Books, 2004 [1990]); Lindsay Cox, *Kotahitanga: The Search for Maori Political Unity* (Auckland: Oxford University Press, 1993); Alan Ward, *A Show of Justice: Racial 'Amalgamation' in Nineteenth Century New Zealand* (Toronto: University of Toronto Press, 1974); Michael King, *Te Puea: A Life* (Auckland: Penguin, 2008 [1977]). Throughout, I use Liberal with a capital *L* to signify liberalism as it was practiced by the Liberal government in Liberal-era New Zealand.

25. Barbara Kirshenblatt-Gimblett, *Destination Culture: Tourism, Museums, and Heritage* (Berkeley and Los Angeles: University of California Press, 1998).

26. The state was the nation's largest employer, its largest investor, the statutory representative of labor interests, provider of cradle-to-grave welfare and public services, and overseer of numerous nationalized industries (electricity, airlines, health, forestry, and agricultural shipping, to name a few).

27. David Lange, *My Life* (Auckland: Viking, 2005), 193.

28. Unemployment rates in 1983 for Māori were 41.3 percent for men and 27.3 percent for women, compared with 12.5 percent for men and 8.5 percent for women among Pākehā. Maori Economic Development Summit Conference, 1984, cited in Walker, *Ka Whawhai*, 264. The social cost of neoliberal reform is well documented in Jane Kelsey, *Economic Fundamentalism* (London: Pluto Press, 1995), and Andrew Sharp, ed., *Leap into the Dark: The Changing Role of the State in New Zealand since 1984* (Auckland: Auckland University Press, 1994).

29. See Walker, *Ka Whawhai.*

30. On postneoliberalism, see Wendy Larner and Maria Butler, "Governmentalities of Local Partnerships: The Rise of a 'Partnering State' in New Zealand," *Studies in Political Economy* 75 (2005): 79–100; and Wendy Larner and David Craig, "After Neoliberalism? Community Activism and Local Partnerships in Aotearoa New Zealand," *Antipode* 37, no. 3 (2005): 402–24.

31. Nicholas Bain, "Maori Can Show the Way to New Zealand's Knowledge Economy," *Tū Mai* 16 (August 2000): 13. See also Brian Easton, *The Whimpering of the State: Policy after MMP* (Auckland: Auckland University Press, 1999).

32. Elizabeth Povinelli, *Empire of Love* (Durham, N.C.: Duke University Press, 2007), 13, 4.

33. Thomas Blom Hansen and Finn Stepputat, eds., *States of the Imagination: Ethnographic Explorations of the Postcolonial State* (Durham, N.C.: Duke University Press, 2001), 1; Michel Foucault, *Security, Territory, Population: Lectures at the Collège de France, 1977–78*, trans. Graham Burchell, ed. Michel Senellart (New York: Palgrave Macmillan, 2007), 109; Philip Abrams, "Notes on the Difficulty of Studying the State," *Journal of Historical Sociology* 1, no. 1 (1977): 58–89.

34. Michel Foucault, *The Birth of Biopolitics: Lectures at the Collège de France*, trans. Graham Burchell, ed. Michel Senellart (New York: Palgrave Macmillan, 2008), 202.

35. See Tony Bennett, *Culture: A Reformer's Science* (London: Sage, 1998); Bennett, *The Birth of the Museum: History, Theory, Politics* (London: Routledge, 1995); Toby Miller, *Cultural Citizenship: Cosmopolitanism, Consumerism, and Television in a Neoliberal Age* (Philadelphia: Temple University Press, 2007); Toby Miller and George Yúdice, *Cultural Policy* (London: Sage, 2002).

36. I refer here to the argument made by interpreters of biopolitics that governmentality did not succeed and supersede sovereignty, nor do the two coexist as apexes of the "triangle, sovereignty–discipline–government." Rather, sovereignty—in particular, the sovereign's control over the "bare life" of subjects and right to define states of exception to liberal guarantees—*grounds* governmentality, even in its most benign and rationalized forms. Michel Foucault, "Governmentality," in *The Essential Foucault: Selections from the Essential Works of Foucault, 1954–1984*, ed. Paul Rabinow and Nikolas S. Rose (New York: New Press, 2003), 102. Giorgio Agamben, *Homo Sacer: Sovereign Power and Bare Life*, trans. Daniel Heller-Roazen (Stanford, Calif.: Stanford University Press, 1998). See Timothy Brennan's critique in *Wars of Position: The Cultural Politics of Left and Right* (New York: Columbia University Press, 2007).

37. Barry Hindess, "Liberalism—What's in a Name?" in *Global Governmentality: Governing International Spaces*, ed. Wendy Larner and William Walters (London: Routledge, 2004), 23–29, 24.

38. Hansen and Stepputat, *States of the Imagination*, 9.

39. Aiwha Ong, *Neoliberalism as Exception: Mutations in Citizenship and Sovereignty* (Durham, N.C.: Duke University Press, 2006), 6.

40. Elizabeth Rata, *A Political Economy of Neotribal Capitalism* (Lanham, Md.: Lexington Books, 2000); Aiwha Ong, *Flexible Citizenship: The Cultural Logics of Transnationality* (Durham, N.C.: Duke University Press, 1999).

41. See, for example, David Theo Goldberg, *The Racial State* (Malden, Mass.: Blackwell, 2002); John Gray, *Enlightenment's Wake: Politics and Culture at the Close of the Modern Age* (London: Routledge, 1995); and Emmanuel Chukwadi Eze, ed., *Race and the Enlightenment: A Reader* (Malden, Mass.: Blackwell, 1997).

42. Kwame Anthony Appiah, *The Ethics of Identity* (Princeton, N.J.: Princeton University Press, 2005).

43. Nancy Fraser, "From Redistribution to Recognition? Dilemmas of Justice in a 'Post-Socialist' Age," *New Left Review* 212 (1995): 68–93.

44. On Foucault's failure to admit the centrality of colonialism, see Mitchell Dean, "'Demonic Societies': Liberalism, Biopolitics, and Sovereignty," in *States of the Imagination*, ed. Hansen and Stepputat, 42. See also Jonathan Xavier Inda, ed., *Anthropologies of Modernity: Foucault, Governmentality, and Life Politics* (Oxford: Blackwell, 2005); Laura Ann Stoler, *Race and the Education of Desire: Foucault's "History of Sexuality" and the Colonial Order of Things* (Durham, N.C.: Duke University Press, 1995); Thomas Biolsi, "Race Technologies," in *A Companion to the Anthropology of Politics*, ed. David Nugent and Joan Vincent (Oxford: Blackwell, 2004); Guillaume Boccara, *The Making of Indigenous Culture: Neoliberal Multiculturalism and Ethnogovernmentality in Post-Dictatorship Chile* (Minneapolis: University of Minnesota Press, forthcoming); and James Ferguson, *Global Shadows: Africa in the Neoliberal World Order* (Durham, N.C.: Duke University Press, 2006).

45. See J. G. A. Pocock, "Tangata Whenua and Enlightenment Anthropology," *New Zealand Journal of History* 26, no. 1 (1992): 28–53; and Makere Stewart-Harawira, *The New Imperial Order: Indigenous Responses to Globalization* (New York: Zed Books, 2005).

46. Likewise, definitional distinctions between race and ethnicity are difficult to sustain in practice: ethnicity can operate functionally in identical ways to race, merely euphemizing race's associations with social negativity and stigma.

47. Ronald Niezen, *The Origins of Indigenism: Human Rights and the Politics of Identity* (Berkeley and Los Angeles: University of California Press, 2003).

48. On the role of tourism in the building of solidarities and mediating of ethnic relations, see Robert E. Wood, "Tourism and the State: Ethnic Options and Constructions of Otherness," in *Tourism, Ethnicity, and the State in Asian and Pacific Societies*, ed. Robert E. Wood and Michel Picard (Honolulu: University of Hawai'i Press, 1997); and Wood, "Touristic Ethnicity: A Brief Itinerary," *Ethnic and Racial Studies* 21, no. 2 (1998): 218–41.

49. For a historical perspective, see James Ritchie, "The Grass Roots of Maori Politics," in *The Maori and New Zealand Politics*, ed. J. G. A. Pocock (Auckland: Blackwood and Janet Paul, 1962), 80–86.

50. Francesca Merlan, "Indigeneity: Local and Global," *Current Anthropology* 50, no. 3 (2009): 303–33.

51. See notes to chapter 4 for a survey of this literature.

52. Richard Schechner discusses "restored behavior," his famous formulation, most recently in *Performance Studies: An Introduction* (New York: Routledge, 2006), 34.

53. Tourism studies' recent interest in performance supports this project in its focus on the social systematicity inherent in roles and routines, learned and habitual behaviors. This work on the sociology and geography of tourism includes Tim Edensor, "Performing Tourism, Staging Tourism: (Re)producing Tourist Space and Practice," *Tourist Studies* 1 (2001): 59–81; Edensor, "Staging Tourism: Tourists as Performers," *Annals of Tourism Research* 27 (2000): 322–44; Mike Crang and Simon Coleman's introduction to *Tourism: Between Place and Performance* (New York: Berghahn Books, 2002); and Philip Crang, "Performing the Tourist Product," in *Touring Cultures:*

Transformations of Travel and Theory, ed. Chris Rojek and John Urry (New York: Routledge, 1997). By contrast, Ed Bruner's collected work in *Cultures on Tour* (Chicago: University of Chicago Press, 2004), that of Kirshenblatt-Gimblett in *Destination Culture*, and that of Jane Desmond in *Staging Tourism: Bodies on Display from Waikiki to Sea World* (Chicago: University of Chicago Press, 1999) are more closely aligned with anthropological and performance studies perspectives on cultural and social performance.

54. Richard Baumann, *Verbal Art as Performance* (Prospect Heights, Ill.: Waveland Press, 1977), 11.

55. Michel de Certeau, *The Practice of Everyday Life*, trans. Stephen Rendall (Berkeley and Los Angeles: University of California Press, 1984).

56. See Barbara Kirshenblatt-Gimblett, "Performing the State: The Jewish Palestine Pavilion at the New York World's Fair, 1939/1940," in *The Art of Being Jewish in Modern Times*, ed. Jonathan Karp and Barbara Kirshenblatt-Gimblett (Philadelphia: University of Pennsylvania Press, 2008), 98–115.

57. Michel Foucault, "Nietzsche, Genealogy, History," in Foucault, *Language, Counter-Memory, Practice*, ed. Donald F. Bouchard (Ithaca, N.Y.: Cornell University Press, 1977), 139.

58. Akhil Gupta, "Blurred Boundaries: The Discourse of Corruption, the Culture of Politics, and the Imagined State," *American Ethnologist* 22, no. 2 (1995): 393.

59. Fredric Jameson, *The Political Unconscious: Narrative as a Socially Symbolic Act* (London: Routledge, 2002 [1981]), 289; Saba Mahmoud's interview with Talal Asad, "Modern Power and the Reconfiguration of Religious Traditions," http://www.stanford.edu/group/SHR/5-1/text/asad.html.

60. Jon McKenzie makes a similar point in his important study *Perform or Else: From Discipline to Performance* (New York: Routledge, 2001), although this book makes no reference to the broad literature on governmentality. On performance management in policy, see Margaret Werry, "Nintendo Museum: Intercultural Performance, Neoliberal Citizenship, and a Theater without Actors," in *Neoliberalism and Theater: Performance Permutations*, ed. Lara D. Nielsen and Patricia Ybarra (Ann Arbor: University of Michigan Press, forthcoming).

61. Jeffrey T. Nealon, *Foucault beyond Foucault: Power and Its Intensifications since 1984* (Stanford, Calif.: Stanford University Press, 2008), 106.

62. John Law, "Traduction/Trahison: Notes on ANT," *Convergencia* 42 (2006): 47–72.

1. THE STATE OF NATURE

1. Alfred Ginders, *The Thermal-Springs District of New Zealand and the Government Sanatorium at Rotorua* (Wellington: Government Printer, 1890), 5.

2. *New Zealand Parliamentary Debates* 40 (1881): 493; *Appendices to the Journals of the House of Representatives*, H. 2, vol. 3 (1903): vi.

3. "Whereas it would be advantageous to the colony, and beneficial to the Maori owner of the land in which natural mineral springs and thermal waters exist, that such

localities should be opened to colonization and made available for settlement." *The Thermal Springs District Act, 1881, New Zealand Statutes* 20 (1881). For one of its architects, Minister of Lands William Rolleston, the Act was an experiment in government protectionism with respect to Māori lands. Rolleston, *New Zealand Thermal-Springs Districts: Papers Relating to the Sale of the Township of Rotorua* (Wellington: George Didsbury, Government Printer, 1882). See also R. N. Jones, chief judge, "Report Submitted to Native Minister," 1936, reprinted in Don Stafford, *Te Arawa* (Wellington: Reed, 1967), 527–40.

4. According to Guy H. Scholefield, state investment in baths and resorts was virtually the only profitable enterprise in the district. During this era, state expenditure accounted for approximately half of all capital formation. Scholefield, *New Zealand in Evolution: Industrial, Economic, and Political* (New York: Scribner, 1909), 257; Gary Hawke, *The Making of New Zealand: An Economic History* (Cambridge: Cambridge University Press, 1985), 68.

5. Ngāti Whakaue question whether outstanding arrears were satisfactorily resolved or whether the titles established by the Native Land Court accurately represented groups' relative interests in the area. See Peter Waaka, "Whakarewarewa: The Growth of a Maori Village" (master's thesis, Auckland University, 1982); David Armstrong "Te Arawa Land and Politics," a report prepared for the Crown Forestry Rental Trust, Wellington, November 2002.

6. R. C. J. Stone, "The Thames Valley and Rotorua Railway Company Limited, 1882–9: A Study of the Relationship of Business and Government in Nineteenth-Century New Zealand," *New Zealand Journal of History* 8, no. 1 (1974): 22–43.

7. *Appendices to the Journals of the House of Representatives*, C. 1, vol. 1 (1891): 5.

8. The phrase "the Māori at home" was ubiquitous.

9. C. W. McMurran, *From New York to New Zealand; or, the New Century Trip* (Wellington: Government Printer, 1904), 23. The careers of tourism proponents such as S. Percy Smith were bound up with the survey enterprise. See Giselle Byrnes, *Boundary Markers: Land Surveying and the Colonisation of New Zealand* (Wellington: Bridget Williams Books, 2001).

10. *Cook's Excursionist and Tourist Advertiser*, February 1, 1889, 7.

11. James C. Scott, *Seeing like a State: How Certain Schemes to Improve the Human Condition Have Failed* (New Haven, Conn.: Yale University Press, 1998).

12. E. W. Payton, *Round about New Zealand: Being Notes from a Journal of Three Years' Wanderings in the Antipodes* (London: Chapman & Hall, 1888), 99.

13. Yrjö Haila and Chuck Dyke, "Introduction," in *How Nature Speaks: The Dynamics of the Human Ecological Condition* (Durham, N.C.: Duke University Press, 2006), 1–47.

14. Simone Abram and Jacqueline Waldren, "Introduction," in *Tourists and Tourism: Identifying People with Places*, ed. Simone Abram, Jacqueline Waldren, and Donald V. L. McLeod (Oxford: Berg, 1997), 5. To humanistic geographers (such as Yi-Fu Tuan or Edward Relph, often drawing on Gaston Bachelard and Martin Heidegger), for whom place *becomes* through the intimacy of dwelling, the geopiety sensed in certain

tourist sites can only ever be a manufactured, superficial, or transient phenomenon. Tourism produces *lieux* rather than milieus of memory and the sign—not the experience—of emplaced identity. To a subsequent generation of theorists, however, the notion of genuine spatial identities as the exclusive property of dwellers reeks of the kind of exclusionary, primordialist territorialism that has secured ethnonationalism and exemplifies a methodological prejudice toward the place–culture equation in the social sciences. See Doreen Massey's summary critique of this debate in *For Space* (London: Sage, 2005), 183–89.

15. Kirshenblatt-Gimblett, *Destination Culture.*

16. Agamben, *Homo Sacer,* 5.

17. Andrew Barry, Thomas Osborne, and Nikolas Rose, "Introduction," in *Foucault and Political Reason: Liberalism, Neo-liberalism, and Rationalities of Government* (Chicago: University of Chicago Press, 1996), 1–18.

18. Bruno Latour, *We Have Never Been Modern,* trans. Catherine Porter (Hemel Hempstead, England: Harvester Wheatsheaf, 1991), 37; see also Latour, *Politics of Nature: How to Bring the Sciences into Democracy,* trans. Catherine Porter (Cambridge, Mass.: Harvard University Press, 2004).

19. Dean MacCannell, *The Tourist: A New Theory of the Leisure Class* (New York: Schocken Books, 1976); Umberto Eco, *Travels in Hyperreality: Essays,* trans. William Weaver (San Diego: Harcourt Brace Jovanovich, 1986). For the theatrical analogy applied to tourism, see Geoff Park, *Theatre Country: Essays on Landscape and Whenua* (Wellington: Victoria University Press, 2006), 142; or Nicholas Thomas, *Colonialism's Culture: Anthropology, Travel, and Government* (Princeton, N.J.: Princeton University Press, 1994), 21–22. Landmarks in the literature on tourism and landscape include Raymond Williams, *The Country and the City* (New York: Oxford University Press, 1973); John Urry, *The Tourist Gaze: Leisure and Travel in Contemporary Societies* (London: Sage, 1990); Urry, *Consuming Places* (London: Routledge, 1997); and Nicholas Green, *The Spectacle of Nature* (Manchester: Manchester University Press, 1990).

20. Jules Joubert, *Proposed New Zealand Exhibition in London* (Dunedin, N.Z.: Caxton, 1890), 4. For Joubert's biography as transnational entertainment entrepreneur, investor, developer, civic leader, travel writer, and trans-Tasman nationalist booster, see his memoir, *Shavings and Scrapes from Many Parts* (Hobart, N.Z.: Gordon, 1894 [1890]).

21. William Pember Reeves, *The Fortunate Isles: Picturesque New Zealand* (Wellington: Government Printer, 1897), 5. Reeves was Minister of Labor from 1893 to 1895 and Agent General in London from 1896 to 1909; he was a poet, Fabian, and the country's best-remembered nationalist historian of the era. He gave frequent illustrated lectures about the colony, its resources, and investment conditions that melded tourism promotion with these other agendas. Keith Sinclair, *William Pember Reeves: New Zealand Fabian* (London: Oxford University Press, 1965).

22. Massey, *For Space.*

23. Michael Walzer, quoted in Michael Shapiro and Deanne Neaubauer, "Spatiality and Policy Discourse: Reading the Global City," in *Contending Sovereignties:*

Redefining Political Community, ed. R. B. J. Walker and Saul H. Mendlovitz (Boulder, Colo.: Lynne Rienner, 1990), 97–124.

24. Judith Adler, "Travel as Performed Art," *American Journal of Sociology* 94, no. 6 (1989): 1366–91. See also Adler, "Origins of Sightseeing," *Annals of Tourism Research* 16 (1989): 7–29.

25. Civic tourists often followed in the footsteps of state or semistate visitors such as Alice Egerton, Duchess of Buckingham and Chandos, whose travel account (reported in the national papers and published on her return home) became a benchmark and model. Egerton, *Glimpses of Four Continents: Letters Written during a Tour in Australia, New Zealand, & North America in 1893* (London: John Murray, 1894), 160.

26. F. W. Pennefather, *A Handbook for Travellers in New Zealand* (London: John Murray, 1893), 11–12.

27. *Cook's Australasian Travellers' Gazette,* January 1889, 15.

28. T. E. Donne, *New Zealand: A Fairyland,* pamphlet (n.p., 1908), 22; J. G. Greenhough, *Towards the Sunrising; or, A Voyage to the Antipodes* (London: Stockwell, 1902), 106. On arcadianism and the Little Britain trope, see Belich, *Making Peoples,* and Miles Fairburn, *The Ideal Society and Its Enemies: Foundations of Modern New Zealand Society, 1850–1990* (Auckland: Auckland University Press, 1989).

29. Scott, *Seeing Like a State;* Robert Roberts, *Diary of a Voyage to Australia, New Zealand, and Other Lands* (Birmingham, England: Publishing Offices, 1896), 105.

30. Union Steamship Co., *New Zealand: An Earthly Paradise* (Dunedin, N.Z.: Union Steamship Co., 1889), 11.

31. Thomas Bracken, *The New Zealand Tourist* (Dunedin, N.Z.: Union Steamship Co., 1879), v.

32. Lydia Wevers, "The Pleasure of Walking," *New Zealand Journal of History* 38, no. 1 (2004): 39–51; Kirstie Ross, *Going Bush: New Zealanders and Nature in the Twentieth Century* (Auckland: Auckland University Press, 2008).

33. Paul Carter, *The Road to Botany Bay: An Essay in Spatial History* (London: Faber, 1988); Wevers, "Pleasure of Walking"; Ian Wedde, *How to Be Nowhere: Essays and Texts, 1971–1994* (Wellington: Victoria University Press, 1995).

34. Wedde, *How to Be Nowhere,* 46.

35. See, for instance, William Pember Reeves, *The Long White Cloud: Ao Tea Roa* (London: Allen & Unwin, 1950 [1898]).

36. *New Zealand Parliamentary Debates* 126 (1903): 713. The generically liberal nature of this gesture is suggested by its repetition in the context of other national parks movements, including in the United States. See, for example, Freeman Tilden, *The National Parks: What They Mean to You and Me* (New York: Knopf, 1951), x. See also John F. Sears, *Sacred Places: American Tourist Attractions in the Nineteenth Century* (New York: Oxford University Press, 1989).

37. Reeves, *Long White Cloud,* 46.

38. Simon Schama, *Landscape and Memory* (New York: Knopf, 1995), 12.

39. Quoted in Barbara Bender, *Landscape: Politics and Perspective* (Providence, R.I.: Berg, 1993), 23.

40. See Raymond Williams, *Culture and Society* (Harmondsworth, England: Penguin, 1963).

41. David Lloyd and Paul Thomas, *Culture and the State* (New York: Routledge, 1998), 15, 5. See also Ian Hunter, "Aesthetics and Cultural Studies," in *Cultural Studies*, ed. Lawrence Grossberg, Cary Nelson, and Paula Treichler (London: Routledge, 1992), 347–72.

42. Dona Brown, *Inventing New England: Regional Tourism in the Nineteenth Century* (Washington, D.C.: Smithsonian Institution Press, 1995), 33.

43. S. Percy Smith (also, notably, a salvage ethnographer, historian, cofounder of the Polynesian Society, and former head of Lands and Survey) headed the Scenery Preservation Commission from 1904–8, overseen by the DTHR. On the relationship between New Zealand's new urban majority and anxieties about overdevelopment, overcrowding, and racial degeneration, see David Hamer, *New Towns in the New World* (New York: Columbia University Press, 1990). On the "conversion" of New Zealand, see Alfred W. Crosby, *Ecological Imperialism: The Biological Expansion of Europe, 900–1900* (Cambridge: Cambridge University Press, 1986).

44. *Appendices to the Journals of the House of Representatives*, H. 2, vol. 3 (1902): 21.

45. Ralph Waldo Emerson, "Nature," in *The Essential Writings of Ralph Waldo Emerson*, ed. Brooks Atkinson (New York: Modern Library, 2000), 364–77.

46. William Pember Reeves, report to Richard Seddon, TO1 1901/208, 5–6, Archives New Zealand, Te Rua Mahara o te Kāwanatanga (hereafter cited as ANZ).

47. *Scenery Preservation Act, New Zealand Statutes* 54 (1903). The Act allowed land to be purchased as under the Public Works Act (1894), but as Hone Heke (member for Northern Māori) protested, the Native Land Court that assessed the value of Māori lands for these purposes did not guarantee as fair a price as that assigned to Pākehā land, and the process was blind to customary or religious uses. *New Zealand Parliamentary Debates* 126 (1903): 711.

48. "Accumulation by dispossession" is a central concept in David Harvey, *The New Imperialism* (Oxford: Oxford University Press, 2003).

49. Elsdon Best, *Waikare-Moana, the Sea of Rippling Waters: The Lake, the Land, the Legends; With a Tramp through Tuhoe Land* (Wellington: Government Printer, 1897), 3.

50. This was standard copy in advertisements for the DTHR from 1903 through 1910, but derives from John Muir, quoted in Tilden, *National Parks*, 19.

51. James Anthony Froude, *Oceania; or, England and Her Colonies* (London: Longmans, Green, 1886), 239.

52. Martin Bernal, *Black Athena: The Afroasiatic Roots of Classical Civilization* (New Brunswick, N.J.: Rutgers University Press, 1987), 209. Also quoted in Richard Dyer, *White* (London: Routledge, 1997), 21.

53. Dyer, *White*, 21.

54. Roland Barthes, *Mythologies* (London: Grafton, 1973), 74.

55. Barthes, *Mythologies*, 74.

56. Edward J. Smith, *A Yorkshireman Abroad: 35,000 Miles in Six Months* (London: John Long, 1914), 63, 108.

57. Wevers, "Pleasure of Walking."

58. A. S. Wohlmann to T. E. Donne, December 11, 1902, TO1/1901/5/10, ANZ.

59. A. Tramp, "Casual Ramblings," *Auckland Weekly News*, August 18, 1899.

60. Mitchell Dean, *Governmentality: Power and Rule in Modern Society* (London: Sage, 1999), 11.

61. Margaret Bullock, *The World's Sanatorium: A Sketch of Rotorua and Its Environs* (Wellington: John Mackay, Government Printer, 1897), 3; Thos. Cook and Sons, *New Zealand as a Tourist and Health Resort*, 3rd ed. (Auckland: n.p., 1899), 27.

62. C. S. Phillips (née Brayton), "Journal 1896–25," May 1897, manuscript papers 961, Alexander Turnbull Library, Wellington.

63. *Weekly Press*, August 16, 1889, 21; Bullock, *World's Sanatorium*, 3.

64. Frederick Dolman, "An Infernal Region," *English Illustrated Magazine*, May 1900, 122–27, 122.

65. Malcolm Andrews, *The Search for the Picturesque: Landscape, Aesthetics, and Tourism in Britain, 1760–1800* (Aldershot, England: Scolar Press, 1989), 160.

66. *Appendices to the Journals of the House of Representatives*, H. 2, vol. 3 (1902): 12.

67. The Arawa Maori Council presented a claim to Parliament (finally won in 1920) on the basis of customary rights ensured in the Treaty of Waitangi regarding Māori ownership of the lakebed.

68. *Appendices to the Journals of the House of Representatives*, C. 1, vol. 1 (1891): 6.

69. E. Way Elkington, *Adrift in New Zealand* (London: John Murray, 1906), 90. Tellingly, the geysers were given the names of Englishwomen—Victoria, Nelly, and May—and put into action on the queen's birthday. See Camille Malfroy, *On Geyser-Action at Rotorua* (Wellington: George Didsbury, Government Printing Office, 1892).

70. *Appendices to the Journals of the House of Representatives*, H. 2, vol. 3 (1903): vii.

71. See Ian Rockel, *Taking the Waters: Early Spas in New Zealand* (Wellington: Government Print Office Publications, 1986).

72. Spas in New England and Canada also followed this pattern. See Susan E. Cayleff, *Wash and Be Healed: The Water-Cure Movement and Women's Health* (Philadelphia: Temple University Press, 1987); Deborah Wightman and Geoffrey Wall, "The Spa Experience at Radium Hot Springs," *Annals of Tourism Research* 12 (1985): 393–416.

73. Bullock, *World's Sanatorium*. See also Claire Toynbee, "Class and Social Structure in Nineteenth-Century New Zealand," *New Zealand Journal of History* 13 (1979): 65–82.

74. Eric Jennings, *Curing the Colonizers: Hydrotherapy, Climatology, and French Colonial Spas* (Durham, N.C.: Duke University Press, 2006).

75. Alison Bashford, *Imperial Hygiene: A Critical History of Colonialism, Nationalism, and Public Health* (London: Palgrave, 2004), 1.

76. A. S. Wohlmann to Hon. J. G. Ward, Minister, DTHR, February 5, 1903, TO1/1901/5/10, ANZ; A. S. Wohlmann, enclosure with T. E. Donne to Hon. R. J. Seddon, Premier, February 14, 1903, TO1/1901/5/10, ANZ.

77. The statues were by Charles Francis Summers of Melbourne and were purchased from the New Zealand International Exhibition after its close in April 1907.

Roger Blackley, "Beauty and the Beast: Plaster Casts in a Colonial Museum," in *On Display: New Essays in Cultural Studies*, ed. Anna Smith and Lydia Wevers (Wellington: Victoria University Press, 2004), 41–63.

78. A. S. Wohlmann, enclosure with T. E. Donne to Hon. R. J. Seddon, Premier, February 14, 1903, TO1/1901/5/10, ANZ.

79. Constance Frederica Gordon Cumming, *At Home in Fiji* (New York: Armstrong, 1883), 24.

80. *Appendices to the Journals of the House of Representatives*, H. 2, vol. 4 (1908), 2.

81. Bullock, *World's Sanatorium*, 2; engineer in charge to superintendent, September 19, 1908, TO01–0044, ANZ.

82. "Snapshots of Rotorua," unidentified clipping, New Zealand newspaper, 1908, Makereti Papakura Manuscripts, box 8, Pitt Rivers Museum, Oxford.

83. I have traced the emergence of this discourse in detail elsewhere, through a reading of health education, urban reform, census, Young Māori Party literature, and parliamentary debates. Margaret Werry, "Tourism, Ethnicity, and the Performance of New Zealand Nationalism, 1889–1914" (PhD diss., Northwestern University, 2001).

84. Raeburn Lange, *May the People Live: A History of Maori Health Development, 1900–1920* (Auckland: Auckland University Press, 1999).

85. Thomas Osborne, "Security and Vitality: Drains, Liberalism, and Power in the Nineteenth Century," in *Foucault and Political Reason*, ed. Barry, Osborne, and Rose, 116.

86. Jonathan Xavier Inda, "Analytics of the Modern: An Introduction," in *Anthropologies of Modernity*, ed. Inda, 2.

87. Engineer in charge to superintendent, September 19, 1908, TO01–0044, ANZ. Sir Peter Buck (Te Rangi Hīroa) and Frederick Bennett, both Māori reformers, drafted plans for the "ideal whare" (or Māori house), combining Māori architectural aesthetics with European structure and hygiene, and submitted them to the Young Māori Party conference. Te Aute College Student Association, *Report of the Tenth Conference Held at Ohinemutu, Rotorua, December 25, 1905, to January 1, 1906* (Rotorua: Hot Lakes Chronicle, 1906); Young Maori Party, Southern Division, *Report of the Thirteenth Conference, Ohinemutu, Rotorua, April 13–16, 1909* (Gisborne, N.Z.: Office of Gisborne Times, 1909).

88. These distinctions applied until 1921. Ian Pool, *Te Iwi Maori: A New Zealand Population Past, Present, and Projected* (Auckland: Auckland University Press, 1991); Paul Meredith, "A Half-Caste on the Half-Caste in the Cultural Politics of New Zealand," http://lianz.waikato.ac.nz/.

89. Miller and Yúdice, *Cultural Policy*, 17.

90. Tramp, "Casual Ramblings," 4.

91. Jennings, *Curing the Colonizers*, 4. See Sir Hermann and F. Parkes Weber for contemporary definitions of the suite of terms applied to water curatives. Weber and Weber, *Climatotherapy and Balneotherapy: The Climates and Mineral Water Health Resorts (Spas) of Europe and North Africa, Including the General Principles of Climatotherapy and Balneotherapy, and Hints as to the Employment of Various Physical and Dietetic Methods* (London: Smith, Elder, 1907), 299.

92. Cayleff, *Wash and Be Healed.*

93. *Appendices to the Journals of the House of Representatives,* H. 6, vol. 3 (1891): 2.

94. Bashford, *Imperial Hygiene.* The training of Sir Māui Pōmare (Māori Health Officer and member of Parliament) at the evangelical Battle Creek Sanatorium in Michigan is notable, although he never had oversight of the Rotorua facility.

95. Arthur Stanley Wohlmann, *The Mineral Waters and Health Resorts of New Zealand* (Wellington: DTHR, Government Printer, 1907), 5.

96. Alfred Ginders, *The Thermal Springs, Rotorua, New Zealand: Hints on Cases Likely to Benefit by Treatment Thereat* (Wellington: Government Printer, 1885), 5; James Muir, *How to Take the Baths and Drinking Waters at Rotorua and Te Aroha* (Wellington: New Zealand Times, 1900), 15.

97. *Appendices to the Journals of the House of Representatives,* H. 6, vol. 3 (1891): 2.

98. Ginders, *Thermal Springs,* 1.

99. M. P. K. Sorrenson, ed., *Na To Hoa Aroha: From Your Dear Friend; The Correspondence between Sir Apirana Ngata and Sir Peter Buck, 1925–50,* vol. 1 (Auckland: Auckland University Press, 1986), 26.

100. W. B. Hunter, "Hydropathy," in Muir, *How to Take the Baths,* n.p.

101. Weber and Weber, *Climatotherapy and Balneotherapy,* 299.

102. David N. Livingstone, "Climate's Moral Economy: Science, Race, and Place in Post-Darwinian British and American Geography," in *Geography and Empire,* ed. Anne Godlewska and Neil Smith (Oxford: Blackwell, 1994), 137, 141. For climatology's use in tourism and migration promotion, see John Murray Moore, *New Zealand for the Emigrant, Invalid, and Tourist* (London: Sampson Low, Marston, Searle, & Rivington, 1890).

103. Wohlmann, *Mineral Waters,* 4.

104. Jennings, *Curing the Colonizers,* 44; Weber and Weber, *Climatotherapy and Balneotherapy,* 355.

105. Elkington, *Adrift in New Zealand,* 79; *Appendices to the Journals of the House of Representatives,* H. 2, vol. 4 (1906): 14.

106. Arthur Stanley Herbert [Wohlmann], *The Hot Springs of New Zealand* (London: Lewis, 1921), vi.

107. Barry, Osborne, and Rose, "Introduction," 9.

108. Michel Foucault, *The Hermeneutics of the Subject: Lectures at the Collège de France, 1981–82,* ed. Frédéric Gros, François Ewald, Alessandro Fontana, and Arnold I. Davidson, trans. Graham Burchell (New York: Picador, 2005), 407.

109. E.H.M., "'Roughing It' round the Hot Lakes," *Poverty Bay Herald,* Gisborne, N.Z., 1889, 7.

110. Roach, *Cities of the Dead,* 28; Gregory Siegworth and Michael Gardiner, "Rethinking Everyday Life: And Then Nothing Turns Itself Inside Out," *Cultural Studies* 18, no. 2 (2004): 139–59.

111. Kevin Hetherington, *Badlands of Modernity: Heterotopia and Social Ordering* (New York: Routledge, 1997), x.

112. Urry, *The Tourist Gaze.*

113. C. R. Sail, *Farthest East, and South and West: Notes of a Journey Home through Japan, Australasia, and America* (London: Allen, 1892), 211.

114. Tom Gunning, "The Whole Town's Gawking: Early Cinema and the Visual Experience of Modernity," *The Yale Journal of Criticism* 7, no. 2 (1994): 193; Georg Simmel, "The Metropolis and Modern Life," in *On Individuality and Social Forms: Selected Writings*, ed. Donald N. Levine (Chicago: University of Chicago Press, 1971), 410.

115. Dolman, "Infernal Region," 126.

116. Mrs. Edward Melland, "Personal Experiences among Maoris and Mountains in New Zealand," *Journal of the Manchester Geographical Society*, February 17, 1914, 31.

117. Roland Barthes, "The Eiffel Tower," in *The Eiffel Tower and Other Mythologies*, trans. Richard Howard (New York: Hill & Wang, 1979), 9.

118. Bullock, *World's Sanatorium*, 21; guide quoted in full in Don Stafford, *The New Century in Rotorua: A History of Events to 1900* (Rotorua, N.Z.: Rotorua District Council, 1988), 44.

119. Gordon Cumming, *At Home in Fiji*, 24.

120. Melland, "Personal Experiences," 29.

121. Lydia Wevers details this in *Country of Writing: Travel Writing and New Zealand, 1809–1900* (Auckland: Auckland University Press, 2002).

122. Dolman, "Infernal Region," 124; Andrew Garran, *Picturesque Atlas of Australasia* (London: Picturesque Atlas, 1886), 391.

123. Mary Stuart Boyd, *Our Stolen Summer: The Record of a Roundabout Tour* (Edinburgh: Blackwood, 1900), 46.

124. Payton, *Round about New Zealand*, 105.

125. Thomas Cook and Sons, *New Zealand as a Tourist and Health Resort*, 5th ed. (Auckland: n.p., 1905), 37.

126. Pierre Bourdieu, *Outline of a Theory of Practice*, trans. Richard Nice (Cambridge: Cambridge University Press, 1977), 77.

127. Kathleen Stewart, *Ordinary Affects* (Durham, N.C.: Duke University Press, 2007).

128. Lowth, *Emerald Hours*, 11.

129. Steven Feld, "Waterfalls of Song: An Acoustemology of Place Resounding in Bosavi, Papua New Guinea," in *Senses of Place*, ed. Steven Feld and Keith Basso (Santa Fe, N.M.: School of American Research Press, 1996), 91.

130. Elkington, *Adrift in New Zealand*, 91.

131. Mary Douglas, *Purity and Danger: An Analysis of Concepts of Pollution and Taboo* (London: Kegan Paul, 1966), 369.

132. Katherine Mansfield, *The Urewera Notebook*, ed. Ian Alistair Gordon (Oxford: Oxford University Press, 1978 [1907]), 65.

133. Karen Shimakawa, *National Abjection: The Asian American Body Onstage* (Durham, N.C.: Duke University Press, 2002), 160.

134. Dolman, "Infernal Region," 125.

135. Bullock, *World's Sanatorium*, 7.

136. Elkington, *Adrift in New Zealand,* 91; Sigmund Freud, *Civilization and Its Discontents,* trans. James Strachey, standard ed. (New York: Norton, 1961), 17–18.

137. Josiah Martin, "Geysers, Their Cause and Action," in Cook and Sons, *New Zealand,* 3rd ed., 100; Bullock, *World's Sanatorium,* 16, 19; Elkington, *Adrift in New Zealand,* 91.

138. Phillips (née Brayton), "Journal 1896–25."

139. Bullock, *World's Sanatorium,* 14.

140. Michel Foucault, "Questions of Method," in *The Foucault Effect: Studies in Governmentality,* ed. Graham Burchell, Colin Gordon, and Peter Miller (Chicago: University of Chicago Press, 1991), 73–86, 81.

141. Nikolas Rose, *Inventing Ourselves: Psychology, Power, and Personhood* (Cambridge: Cambridge University Press, 1998), 54.

142. Diana Taylor, *The Archive and the Repertoire: Performing Cultural Memory in the Americas* (Durham N.C.: Duke University Press, 2003), xviii.

143. See the arguments of Jane Bennett, *The Enchantment of Modern Life: Attachments, Crossings, and Ethics* (Princeton, N.J.: Princeton University Press, 2001).

144. Descartes, quoted in Genevieve Lloyd, "Reason," in *New Keywords: A Revised Vocabulary of Culture and Society,* ed. Tony Bennett, Lawrence Grossberg, and Megan Morris (Malden, Mass.: Blackwell, 2005), 298.

145. Michel Foucault, "Technologies of the Self," in *Technologies of the Self: A Seminar with Michel Foucault,* ed. Luther H. Martin, Huck Gutman, and Patrick H. Hutton (London: Tavistock, 1988), quoted in Tony Bennett, "Culture and Governmentality," in *Foucault, Cultural Studies, and Governmentality,* ed. Jack Z. Bratich, Jeremy Packer, and Cameron McCarthy (Albany: State University of New York Press, 2003), 59.

146. Toby Miller, *The Well-Tempered Self: Citizenship, Culture, and the Postmodern Subject* (Baltimore: Johns Hopkins University Press, 1993); see also Hunter, "Aesthetics and Cultural Studies."

147. Michel Foucault, *The History of Sexuality,* vol. 1, *An Introduction,* trans. Robert Hurley (New York: Vintage Books, 1978), 139.

148. Rob Shields, *Places on the Margin: Alternative Geographies of Modernity* (London: Routledge, 1991).

149. Barry, Osborne, and Rose, "Introduction," 11.

150. David Scott, "Colonial Governmentality," in *Anthropologies of Modernity,* ed. Inda, 31.

2. THE CLASS ACT OF GUIDE MAGGIE

1. Hugh Reginald Haweis, *Travel and Talk, 1885–93–95: My Hundred Thousand Miles of Travel through America, Canada, Australia, New Zealand, Tasmania, Ceylon, and the Paradises of the Pacific,* vol. 2 (London: Chatto & Windus, 1897), 146.

2. Union Steamship Co., *New Zealand,* 25.

3. Kirshenblatt-Gimblett, *Destination Culture,* 18; Edward Bruner and Barbara Kirshenblatt-Gimblett, "Maasai on the Lawn: Tourist Realism in East Africa," *Cultural Anthropology* 9, no. 2 (1994): 435–70.

4. For the most influential articulation of this argument in the context of Pacific tourism, see Trask, *From a Native Daughter*.

5. Mary Louise Pratt, *Imperial Eyes: Travel Writing and Transculturation* (London: Routledge, 1992).

6. On the guide's liminal role as a "culture broker" or "middleman," see Erik Cohen, "The Tourist Guide," *Annals of Tourism Research* 12 (1985): 9–29; Cynthia Werner, "The New Silk Road: Mediators and Tourism Development in Central Asia," *Ethnology* 42, no. 2 (2003): 141–61; and Hazel Tucker, *Living with Tourism: Negotiating Identities in a Turkish Village* (London: Routledge, 2005).

7. For the locus classicus of this critique, see the essays collected in Craig Calhoun, ed., *Habermas and the Public Sphere* (Cambridge, Mass.: MIT Press, 1992).

8. Seyla Benhabib, "The Pariah and Her Shadow: Hannah Arendt's Biography of Rahel Varnhagen," *Political Theory* 23, no. 1 (1995): 5–24, 14; on liberal self-fashioning, see Appiah, *Ethics of Identity*.

9. Michael Warner, *Publics and Counterpublics* (New York: Zone Books, 2002).

10. Jacques Carré, ed., *The Crisis of Courtesy: Studies in the Conduct-Book in Britain, 1600–1900* (Leiden, N.Y.: Brill, 1994); John F. Kasson, *Rudeness and Civility: Manners in Nineteenth-Century Urban America* (New York: Hill & Wang, 1990); Karen Haltunnen, *Confidence Men and Painted Women: A Study of Middle-Class Culture in America, 1830–1870* (New Haven, Conn.: Yale University Press, 1986); Andrew St. George, *The Descent of Manners: Etiquette, Rules, and the Victorians* (London: Chatto & Windus, 1993).

11. Unidentified clipping, January 31, 1908, in Makereti Papakura Manuscripts, box 8, Pitt Rivers Museum, Oxford (hereafter cited as Papakura MSS).

12. "Rotorua: Some Impressions; By a Lady Visitor," *Evening Post*, January 25, 1908.

13. For a summary of similar arguments, see Nancy Fraser, "Transnationalizing the Public Sphere: On the Legitimacy and Efficacy of Public Opinion in a Post-Westphalian World," *Theory, Culture, and Society* 24, no. 7 (2007): 7–30.

14. An informal "census" of the Whakarewarewa population undertaken by DTHR staff in 1907 showed the majority of the men were working in new state-run industries of the region (predominantly forestry) or in agriculture. Rotorua District Council Archives, TO01–0042. On women's hospitality, see Ngahuia Te Awekotuku, "The Sociocultural Impact of Tourism on the Te Arawa People of Rotorua, New Zealand" (D.Phil. thesis, Waikato University, 1981). The only male guide of the era to achieve any significant reputation among tourists was Alfred Warbrick, who specialized in fishing and hunting expeditions. See his memoir, *Adventures in Geyserland* (Dunedin, N.Z.: Reed, 1934).

15. See Michael King on the de facto segregation of urban Pākehā New Zealand and rural kāinga-based Māori New Zealand until urbanization in the wake of World War II. King, *Penguin History of New Zealand* (Auckland: Penguin, 2003).

16. The major biographical sources on Makereti's life are T. K. Penniman's introduction to Makereti Papakura, *The Old-Time Maori* (London: Victor & Gollancz, 1938) and Ngahuia Te Awekotuku's introduction to the volume's reissue (Auckland:

New Women's Press, 1986); Rangitiaria Dennan with Ross Annabell, *Guide Rangi of Rotorua* (Auckland: Whitcombe & Tombs, 1968); Paul Diamond, *Makereti: Taking Māori to the World* (Auckland: Random House, 2007); and June Northcroft-Grant, "Makereti Papakura, 1873–1930," *Dictionary of New Zealand Biography* (Wellington: Ministry for Culture and Heritage, 1990), http://www.teara.govt.nz/en/biographies/. Other studies include Eilean Hooper-Greenhill, *Museums and the Interpretation of Visual Culture* (London: Routledge, 2000); Elizabeth Cory-Pearce, "In Touch with Things: Tourism, Art Forms and Practices, and the Mediation of Maori/European Relationships" (PhD diss., Goldsmiths, University of London, 2005); and David Andrews, *The Two Worlds of Maggie Papakura* (Great Britain: Greenstone Books, 2005).

17. Judith Simon and Linda Tuhiwai Smith, eds., *A Civilizing Mission? Perceptions and Representations of the New Zealand Native Schools System* (Auckland: Auckland University Press, 2001).

18. Unidentified clipping, December 10, 1907, Papakura MSS, box 8.

19. "Maggie Papakura: The Famous Maori Guide, Whakarewarewa," unidentified newspaper clipping in Papakura MSS, box 8.

20. "Maggie Papakura: Famous Maori Guide."

21. "Maggie Papakura: Famous Maori Guide."

22. *Christmas Globe* (Canada), 1901, Papakura MSS, box 10.

23. "Some Notes for Women" *Manawatu Daily Times*, April 24, 1909. Conditions at Whakarewarewa were competitive among guides, and several complained of Makereti's monopoly on guiding business in the village (see correspondence in TO1, Archives New Zealand).

24. Arawa, despite a number of powerful female community leaders, were known for their unflinching veto on women's speech in the political forum of the marae. See Ngahuia Te Awekotuku, *Mana Wahine Maori: Selected Writings* (Wellington: Huia, 1992). Makereti's papers suggest that she may have acted as an advisor at times to Mita Taupopoki, helping him craft speeches or interpreting for him in the context of his interactions with state representatives.

25. "Maggie Papakura: Famous Maori Guide."

26. Donald Denoon, "Settler Capitalism Unsettled," *New Zealand Journal of History* 29, no. 2 (1995): 129–41, 132.

27. Lowth, *Emerald Hours*, 19.

28. Lowth, *Emerald Hours*, 13.

29. Lowth, *Emerald Hours*, 17.

30. William Baucke, "Where the White Man Treads," *New Zealand Herald*, February 27, 1908.

31. "Snapshots of Rotorua," unidentified newspaper clipping, Papakura MSS, box 8.

32. "Maori Women," unidentified clipping, Australian newspaper, Papakura MSS, box 8; "In Wonderland: Round About Rotorua," unidentified clipping, Papakura MSS, box 8.

33. "Rotorua: Some Impressions."

34. "In Wonderland." Of the sixty or so firsthand accounts I have read of encounters with the guide, I can name only one that claims to have detected a trace of her "uncivilized ancestry," in a "discordant note" to her laugh. Anonymous, *All Red Route* (n.p., n.d.), 37.

35. Gwendolyn Foster, *Troping the Body: Gender, Etiquette, and Performance* (Carbondale: Southern Illinois University Press, 2000).

36. On African American etiquette manuals, see Foster, *Troping the Body*; on the Darwinian theory of emotion, see Kasson, *Rudeness and Civility*.

37. Shannon Jackson, "Civic Play-Housekeeping: Gender, Theatre, and American Reform," *Theatre Journal* 48, no. 3 (1996): 337–61.

38. *New Zealand Herald*, January 17, 1907.

39. *New Zealand Herald*, February 8, 1907.

40. Fatimah Tobing Rony, *The Third Eye: Race, Cinema, and Ethnographic Spectacle* (Durham, N.C.: Duke University Press, 1996); Roberta Pearson, *Eloquent Gestures* (Berkeley and Los Angeles: University of California Press, 1992).

41. Foster, *Troping the Body*, 4.

42. "Notes on a Short Trip through New Zealand: By a Son of 'A Fair Maid of Kent,'" *Kentish Gazette*, undated clipping, ca. 1905, Papakura MSS, box 8.

43. Miscellaneous letters and cards in Makereti's papers attest to this practice. Papakura MSS, box 8.

44. See Julio Aramberri, "The Host Should Get Lost: Paradigms in the Tourism Theory," *Annals of Tourism Research* 28 (2001): 738–61 for this critique of Valene Smith's influential *Hosts and Guests: The Anthropology of Tourism* (Philadelphia: University of Pennsylvania Press, 1989 [1977]).

45. Jacques Derrida, *Of Hospitality: Anne Dufourmantelle Invites Jacques Derrida to Respond* (Stanford, Calif.: Stanford University Press, 2000), 151.

46. Maggie Papakura to T. E. Donne, May 20, 1910, QMS–0621, Thomas Edward Donne Papers, Alexander Turnbull Library, Wellington (hereafter Donne Papers, ATL). Sophia Taiawhio applied for a state pension late in life, claiming that she had performed her "duties" as a state agent, honoring "the confidence the Government [had] reposed" in her. I detail this struggle over guiding control, conduct, and content elsewhere. Margaret Werry, "Tourism, Gender, and Ethnicity in the Performance of New Zealand Nationalism, 1889–1914" (PhD diss., Northwestern University, 2001).

47. Mason Durie, "Marae and Implications for a Modern Māori Psychology," *Journal of the Polynesian Society* 108, no. 4 (1999): 351–66.

48. Jacques Derrida, *Of Cosmopolitanism and Forgiveness* (London: Routledge, 2001), 17.

49. *Graham's Guide to the Hot Lakes* (Auckland: Wilson & Horton, 1884), 12.

50. Michael Myers Shoemaker, *Islands of the Southern Seas: Hawaii, Samoa, New Zealand, Tasmania, Australia, and Java* (New York: Putnam, 1898), 56; undated clipping, Papakura MSS, box 8; James T. Goudie, *Notes and Gleanings: Being Leaves from the Diary of a Voyage to and from Australia and New Zealand, in 1893* (Edinburgh: Clark, 1894), 75.

51. On "networks of voluntary association" as publics, see Geoff Eley, "Nations, Publics, and Political Cultures: Placing Habermas in the Nineteenth Century," in *Habermas and the Public Sphere*, ed. Calhoun, 289–339.

52. *The Theatre* (Australia), March 1, 1910 (emphasis mine).

53. "Rotorua: Some Impressions"; "A Famous Guide: A Talk with Maggie Papakura; Some Interesting Reminiscences," unidentified clipping, Papakura MSS, box 8.

54. Unidentified clipping, Papakura MSS, box 8. Not all were impressed: "Maggie's . . . stock adjectives of admiration now are 'nice' and 'charming,' and she mouths them with the drawl of a Society Dame. She tells us the Duchess of York was 'very, very nice,' the Duke was 'just as nice,' and a line or two further something else was 'nice.'" *Exhibition Sketcher* 7, no. 1, December 8, 1906.

55. "Maori Queen as Critic," *Daily Chronicle*, August 23, 1911, Eva Skerrett (Princess Iwa) Papers, Papakura MSS.

56. Benhabib, "The Pariah," 14, 17.

57. Makereti Papakura to T. E. Donne, May 1, 1924, QMS–1387, Donne Scrapbook, ATL.

58. "Notes on a Short Trip."

59. "Rotorua: Some Impressions."

60. "In Wonderland."

61. *Weekly Graphic and New Zealand Mail*, May 25, 1910.

62. *Hot Lakes Chronicle*, August 12, 1910.

63. Anne Salmond, *Hui: A Study of Maori Ceremonial Gatherings* (Wellington: Reed, 1975).

64. Richard Sennett, *The Conscience of the Eye: The Design and Social Life of Cities* (New York: Knopf, 1990), 20–29.

65. Apirana T. Ngata, "Being Suggestions for a Scheme of Reform Work among the Maori People," in *Papers and Addresses Read before the First Conference of the Te Aute College Students' Association, February 1897* (Gisborne, N.Z.: Herald Office, 1897), 41–43; Maui Pomare's paper presented before the Australian Medical Congress, "The Maori," in *The Maori of New Zealand: Past, Present, and Future*, ed. Hoani Parata (London: Hughes & Sons, 1911), 7–21; James H. Pope, *Health for the Maori: A Manual for Use in Native Schools*, 3rd ed. (Wellington: John Mackay, Government Printer, 1901). See also the reports of the Māori Medical Officers, *Appendices to the Journals of the House of Representatives*, H. 31 (1902–8).

66. The DTHR proposed razing and rebuilding the whares of the village, retaining their "effective and highly picturesque" exteriors while avoiding the "insanitary and unwholesome" aspects of the traditional construction in favor of "convenience and hygiene" in the interior. *Appendices to the Journals of the House of Representatives*, H. 2, vol. 3 (1904): 9.

67. Kasson, *Rudeness and Civility*, 117; Sennett, *Conscience of the Eye*, 82.

68. David Spurr, *The Rhetoric of Empire: Colonial Discourses in Journalism, Travel Writing, and Imperial Administration* (Durham, N.C.: Duke University Press, 1993), 19.

69. MacCannell, *Tourist*; Erving Goffman, *The Presentation of Self in Everyday Life* (New York: Anchor Books, 1959).

70. Miriam Hansen, *Babel and Babylon: Spectatorship in American Silent Film* (Cambridge, Mass.: Harvard University Press, 1991), 82.

71. Martha W. S. Myers, "Modern Maori Snapshots," undated newspaper clipping, Papakura MSS, box 8.

72. Kasson, *Rudeness and Civility*, 174.

73. Makereti Papakura to T. E. Donne, May 1, 1924, QMS–1387, Donne Scrapbook, ATL.

74. "Notes on a Short Trip."

75. Makereti anticipated contemporary museological practice, which honors the living mana of the taonga in its relationship to kaitiaki (guardian) communities. See, for example, Sidney Moko Mead, "The Nature of Taonga," in *Landmarks, Bridges, and Visions: Aspects of Maori Culture* (Wellington: Victoria University Press, 1997), 179–89.

76. Kirshenblatt-Gimblett, *Destination Culture*.

77. "Maori Women," unidentified clipping, Australian newspaper, Papakura MSS, box 8.

78. "Famous Guide."

79. Undated, untitled newspaper clipping, Papakura MSS, box 8.

80. "Famous Guide."

81. See, for example, Myers Shoemaker, *Islands of the Southern Seas*, 8. Donne also understood himself as an authority on Māori ethnology and published a frothy and derivative popular volume on the subject, *The Maori Past and Present* (London: Seeley Service, 1927). Makereti's access to this male-dominated milieu did not translate into support for her own ethnological efforts later in life. See Diamond, *Makereti*, 152.

82. Haweis, *Travel and Talk*, 131; Edgar Watson Howe, *Travel Letters from New Zealand, Australia, and Africa*, 2nd ed. (Topeka, Kans.: Crane, 1913), 58–59. For Sophia at work, see E. I. Massy, *Memories of Maoriland* (London: William Clowes & Sons, 1911), 30–47.

83. Haweis, *Travel and Talk*, 128.

84. Maggie Papakura, *Maggie's Guide to the Hot Lakes and Some Maori Legends* (Auckland: Brett, 1905), 18.

85. St. George, *Descent of Manners*, 33; "Maori Queen as Critic."

86. Foucault, "Governmentality," 237. The law of tapu (respecting sacred objects and values), Makereti argued in another context, maintains "universal order" among Māori, like an invisible hand adjudicating social and property relations through a system of prohibitions and obligations. "Notes on the Maori," Papakura MSS, box 3.

87. Myers, "Modern Maori Snapshots."

88. "Maori Queen as Critic."

89. Unidentified clipping, Papakura MSS, box 9.

90. *The Theatre* (Australia), March 1, 1910.

91. Papakura, "A Talk on the Maori (of New Zealand)," Papakura MSS, box 6.

92. James Belich, "Myth, Race, and Identity in New Zealand," *New Zealand Journal of History* 31, no. 1 (1997): 9–22; Kerry Howe, "The Fate of the 'Savage' in Pacific Historiography," *New Zealand Journal of History* 11, no. 2 (1977): 137–54; M. P. K. Sorrenson, *Maori Origins and Migrations: The Genesis of Some Pakeha Myths and Legends* (Auckland: Auckland University Press, 1979); D. R. Simmons, *The Great New Zealand Myth* (Cambridge: Cambridge University Press, 1976); Edward Tregear, *The Aryan Maori* (Wellington: Whitcombe & Tombs, 1886).

93. Reeves, *Fortunate Isles*, 15. For Makereti on Aboriginals, see Diamond, *Makereti*. The "whitening" of Māori is examined in detail in Belich, "Myth, Race, and Identity," and Bernard Smith, *European Vision in the South Pacific* (New Haven, Conn.: Yale University Press, 1960).

94. *Madame*, September 1911, 412.

95. Makereti's claim would have recalled Irish resistance to forcible annexation, very much in the mind of her British patrons during this era. Statesman Apirana Ngata had in fact used home rule as an analogy for the Kotahitanga parliament's agenda of Māori separatist self-government. Ngata, "Maori Politics and Our Relation Thereto," in *Papers and Addresses Read before the First Conference*, 34.

96. The guide's birth name was Margaret Pattison Thom, her name by marriage Margaret Dennan. Makereti is a Māori transliteration of Margaret. Māori locals also referred to her as Makereta Tame, and (to friends) she signed herself Herete, Ereti, Reti, Rereti, or Reta, all shortenings of Makereti. In her professional capacity, she was known to Pākehā as Guide Maggie or Maggie Papakura. Makereti herself regarded the Papakura moniker and the name Maggie (with its assumption of familiarity and class inferiority) as stage names of sorts. After her second marriage in 1912 and her relocation to England, she took on her new husband's double-barreled pedigree, and all her public interaction was undertaken under its auspices (see, for example, "The Traditions and Customs of the Maori" for the BBC *Radio Times*, September 27, 1926, 18). She declared herself *"quite* retired into private life," insisting that *"My old name must not be used in either shape or form whatever."* Margaret Staples-Brown to T. E. Donne, March 30, 1924, Maggie Papakura annotated scrapbook, Donne Papers, QMS–0621, ATL (emphases in the original).

97. Arthur H. Adams, *Tussock Land* (London: Fisher Unwin, 1904), 26. See also Elspeth Probyn, "Bloody Metaphors and Other Allegories of the Ordinary," in *Between Women and Nation: Nationalisms, Transnational Feminisms, and the State*, ed. Caren Kaplan, Norma Alarcón, and Minoo Moallem (Durham, N.C.: Duke University Press, 1999), 47–62.

98. See, especially for their discussion of Alfred Domett's revision of the Rotorua tale of Hinemoa and Tutanekai as an interracial romance, Stafford and Williams, *Maoriland.*

99. Donne, "Romance of Two Worlds," *British Australasian*, May 8, 1930; Apirana Ngata, "A Plea for the Unity of the Maori People," *Papers and Addresses Read before the Second Conference of the Te Aute College Students' Association, December 1897* (Napier, N.Z.: Daily Telegraph Office, 1898), 24–25.

100. Pomare, "The Maori."

101. Donne, "Romance of Two Worlds"; Judith Binney, "'In-Between' Lives: Studies from within Colonial Society," in *Disputed Histories: Imagining New Zealand's Pasts*, ed. Tony Ballantyne and Brian Moloughney (Dunedin, N.Z.: Otago University Press, 2006).

102. Tracy Davis, *Actresses as Working Women: Their Social Identity in Victorian Culture* (London: Routledge, 1991), 100.

103. "Notes on a Short Trip."

104. Cynthia Enloe, *Bananas, Beaches, and Bases: Making Feminist Sense of International Politics* (Berkeley and Los Angeles: University of California Press, 1990). See Jennifer Craik, "The Culture of Tourism," in *Touring Cultures*, ed. Rojek and Urry, 113–36, 131. On Hawai'i, see Trask, *From a Native Daughter*; on Tahiti, see Miriam Kahn, "Tahiti Intertwined: Ancestral Land, Tourist Postcard, and Nuclear Test Site," *American Anthropologist* 102, no. 1 (2000): 5–26. See also Ross Gibson, "I Could Not See as Much as I Desired," in *Pirating the Pacific: Images of Travel, Trade, and Tourism*, ed. Ann Stephen (Adelaide: Powerhouse Publishing, 1993), 22–42.

105. Florence Harsant, for example, claimed the "relaxed standards" of Maggie's concert party "led to the spoiling of some of the pretty young girls who took part." Harsant, *They Called Me Te Maari* (Christchurch, N.Z.: Whitcoulls, 1979), 71.

106. "Notes on a Short Trip."

107. Margaret Staples-Brown to T. E. Donne, December 14, 1911, QMS–0621, Maggie Papakura annotated scrapbook, Donne Papers, ATL.

108. Undated clipping, ca. 1907, Papakura MSS, box 8.

109. On the "folkloric" as a performance mode, cultural commodity, and structure of racial feeling, see Robert Cantwell, *Ethnomimesis: Folklife and the Representation of Culture* (Chapel Hill: University of North Carolina Press, 1993). For the distinction between ethnological show business and folklorist performance, see Annie E. Coombes, *Reinventing Africa: Museums, Material Culture, and Popular Imagination* (New Haven, Conn.: Yale University Press, 1994), 187–213.

110. QMS–0621, Maggie Papakura annotated scrapbook, Donne Papers, ATL.

111. Craig Owens, "The Medusa Effect," in Owens, *Beyond Recognition: Representation, Power, and Culture*, ed. Scott Bryson et al. (Berkeley and Los Angeles: University of California Press, 1992), 198. See also Owens's essay "Posing" from the same volume, 201–7.

112. Letter to the editor, *New Zealand Herald*, ca. 1908, Papakura MSS, box 8.

113. Craig Calhoun, "The Class Consciousness of Frequent Travelers: Toward a Critique of Actually Existing Cosmopolitanism," *South Atlantic Quarterly* 101, no. 4 (2002): 869–97.

114. "Discrepant mobility" is the focus of Rebecca Stein's *Itineraries in Conflict: Israelis, Palestinians, and the Political Lives of Tourism* (Durham, N.C.: Duke University Press, 2008). It is a term adapted from the literature on "discrepant cosmopolitanisms," coined by James Clifford in *Routes: Travel and Translation in the Late Twentieth Century* (Cambridge, Mass.: Harvard University Press, 1997), 36.

115. The works that have influenced my thinking about cosmopolitanism include Arjun Appadurai, *Modernity at Large: Cultural Dimensions of Globalization* (Minneapolis: University of Minnesota Press, 1996); Carol A. Breckenridge et al., eds., *Cosmopolitanism* (Durham, N.C.: Duke University Press, 2002); Cheah and Robbins, *Cosmopolitics*; David Rodowick, "Mobile Citizens, Media States," *PMLA* 117, no. 1 (2002): 13–23; James F. Ferguson, "Of Mimicry and Membership: Africans and the 'New World Society,'" *Cultural Anthropology* 17, no. 4 (2002): 551–56; Caren Kaplan, *Questions of Travel: Postmodern Discourses of Displacement* (Durham, N.C.: Duke University Press, 1997); Clifford, *Routes*; Timothy Brennan, *At Home in the World: Cosmopolitanism Now* (Cambridge, Mass.: Harvard University Press, 1997); Kwame Anthony Appiah, *Cosmopolitanism: Ethics in a World of Strangers* (London: Norton, 2006); Stephen Vertovec and Robin Cohen, eds., *Cosmopolitanism: Theory, Context, and Practice* (New York: Oxford University Press, 2003); David Held, "Cosmopolitanism: Taming Globalization," in *The Global Transformations Reader: An Introduction to the Globalization Debate*, ed. David Held and Anthony McGrew (Cambridge, England: Polity Press, 2003), 514–29; Aiwha Ong, *Flexible Citizenship: The Cultural Logics of Transnationality* (Durham, N.C.: Duke University Press, 1999).

116. Walter Mignolo, "The Many Faces of Cosmo-polis: Border Thinking and Critical Cosmopolitanism," *Public Culture* 12, no. 3 (2000): 721–48, 723. On discrepant cosmopolitanism, see Clifford, *Routes*; for postcolonial cosmopolitanism, see Benita Parry, "Overlapping Territories and Intertwined Histories: Edward Said's Postcolonial Cosmopolitanism," in *Edward Said: A Critical Reader*, ed. Michael Sprinker (Oxford: Blackwell, 1992), 18–47; and on vernacular cosmopolitanism, see Pnina Werbner, "Vernacular Cosmopolitanism," *Theory, Culture, and Society* 23 (2006): 496–98.

117. Derrida, *Of Cosmopolitanism*; Charles Taylor, "The Politics of Recognition," in *Multiculturalism: Examining the Politics of Recognition*, ed. Amy Gutman (Princeton, N.J.: Princeton University Press, 1994).

118. Elizabeth Povinelli, *The Cunning of Recognition: Indigenous Alterities and the Making of Australian Multiculturalism* (Durham, N.C.: Duke University Press, 2002).

119. Henry James, *Portraits of Places* (New York: Lear, 1948 [1883]), 83.

120. Anderson, "Nationalism, Identity," 117–33.

121. "Famous Guide."

122. Maggie Papakura, *Maggie in Australia: Places Visited & Friends Met*, reprinted from *Hot Lakes Chronicle and Advertiser*, Rotorua, 1903.

123. Pope, *Health for the Maori*; see also *Notes of Meetings between His Excellency the Governor (Lord Ranfurly), the Rt. Hon. R. J. Seddon, . . . and the Native Chiefs and People . . . in Respect of the Proposed Native Land Legislation and Native Affairs Generally, during 1898 and 1899* (Wellington: John Mackay, Government Printer, 1899).

124. "The Travelled Maori: A Widened Horizon; What Maggie Papakura Thinks," *New Zealand Herald*, November 12, 1910.

125. See Michael King on the vituperative Pākehā press coverage of the Kīngitanga diplomatic missions to England in 1884 and 1914. King, *Te Puea*. For deft theorization

of the native "out of place in the metropolis," see Saloni Mathur, "Living Ethnological Exhibits: The Case of 1886," *Cultural Anthropology* 15, no. 4 (2000): 492–524.

126. "Travelled Maori."

127. The correspondence can be found in the Public Record Office files for the Colonial Office; see also correspondence in the Imre Kiralfy Papers, Museum of London Archive.

128. See Coombes, *Reinventing Africa.*

129. "Maories in Battle: Lively Time in New Zealand; The Return from London; Maggie Papakura's Eyes Blackened," Newspaper clipping, QMS–0621, Maggie Papakura annotated scrapbook, Donne Papers, ATL.

130. Frederick G. Hall-Jones, *Sir William Hall-Jones: Last of the Old Liberals* (Invercargill, N.Z.: Hall-Jones Family, 1969); Diamond, *Makereti.*

131. Te Awekotuku, "Sociocultural Impact," 148. Here is but one example of Makereti's praise for the British: "I think there will come a time . . . when the Maori will be lost. . . . All their individuality as a race will disappear. The Government is very good to the Maoris." "Famous Guide."

132. De Certeau, *Practice of Everyday Life.*

133. Dorothy Mihinui, personal communication, 1998.

134. Paul Ricoeur, "Reflections on a New Ethos for Europe," *Philosophy and Social Criticism* 21, nos. 5 & 6 (1995): 9.

135. Warner, *Publics and Counterpublics;* Jill Dolan, *Utopia in Performance: Finding Hope at the Theater* (Ann Arbor: University of Michigan Press, 2005).

3. TRANSLATION, TRANSNATION

1. Thomas Babington Macaulay, "Von Ranke," in *Critical and Historical Essays Contributed to the Edinburgh Review,* vol. 3, 12th ed. (London: Longman, 1965), 99–146, 101.

2. Belich, *Making Peoples,* 297–98.

3. Union Steamship Co., *New Zealand,* 1.

4. *Christchurch Press,* October 30, 1906. Reprinted from the London *Times.*

5. *New Zealand Herald,* December 3, 1888.

6. Michael Bassett reviews some of this literature, including works by Frank Parsons, André Siegfried, Andre Metin, Henry Demarest Lloyd, and the English Fabian Party. Bassett, *The State in New Zealand, 1840–1984: Socialism without Doctrines?* (Auckland: Auckland University Press, 1998), 93.

7. The distinction between expression and representation that I employ here is a Deleuzian formulation, adroitly summarized in Brian Massumi, "Introduction: Like a Thought," in *A Shock to Thought: Expression after Deleuze and Guattari* (London: Routledge, 2002).

8. Anderson, *Imagined Communities;* Anderson, "Nationalism, Identity," 117–33.

9. Dipesh Chakrabarty, *Provincializing Europe: Postcolonial Thought and Historical Difference* (Princeton, N.J.: Princeton University Press, 2000); Charles Taylor, "Modern Social Imaginaries," *Public Culture* 14, no. 1 (2002): 91–124; Appadurai, *Modernity at Large.*

10. Benjamin Lee and Edward LiPuma, "Cultures of Circulation: The Imaginations of Modernity," *Public Culture* 14, no. 1 (2002): 191–213.

11. Cornelius Castoriadis, *The Imaginary Institution of Society*, trans. Kathleen Blamey (Cambridge, Mass.: MIT Press, 1998 [1987]), 3.

12. Gayatri Spivak, "The Politics of Translation," in *Outside in the Teaching Machine* (London: Routledge, 1993), 398.

13. Naoki Sakai, *Translation and Subjectivity: On Japan and Cultural Nationalism* (Minneapolis: University of Minnesota Press, 1993).

14. Raymond Williams, *Drama in Performance* (Harmondsworth, England: Penguin, 1968), 185. I discuss theories of spectacle in more depth elsewhere. Margaret Werry, "The Greatest Show on Earth: Spectacular Politics, Political Spectacle, and the American Pacific," *Theatre Journal* 58, no. 3 (2005): 4–35.

15. Michael Warner, "Publics and Counterpublics," *Public Culture* 14, no. 1 (2002): 49–90, 82.

16. As Gordon Selfridge, department store magnate, said in lauding the work of the Hippodrome, "Imagination urges us on. . . . No great thing was ever accomplished by the world's greatest merchants without imagination. . . . It pictures the desirable." Woody Register, *The Kid of Coney Island: Fred Thompson and the Rise of American Amusements* (New York: Oxford University Press, 2001), 43.

17. Michael Hardt and Antonio Negri, *Empire* (Cambridge, Mass: Harvard University Press, 2000), xii. While I do not believe that Hardt and Negri's thesis is supportable analytic ground for contemporary political strategy, I find it historiographically useful in characterizing the distinction between the form of colonial, extractive, or territorial imperialism associated with British or European rule, and Roosevelt's imperial ambitions during this era. Roosevelt disseminated a mode of decentered, deterritorialized sovereignty hospitable to the free movement of capital and encouraged the establishment of "peaceful" global equilibrium secured by the "policing" function of U.S. military power. Throughout, I capitalize Empire (and Imperial) to distinguish their specific theoretical formulation from more general uses of the term.

18. Hardt and Negri, *Empire*, 10. Theodore Roosevelt characterized the 1908 tour of the Fleet as the perfect expression of his presidency's achievement: seven and a half years of "absolute peace," which he called "the peace of righteousness." Theodore Roosevelt, *The Rough Riders: An Autobiography* (New York: Library of America, 2004 [1913]), 800–804.

19. *Rotorua Times*, August 13, 1909; see also Franklin Matthews, *Back to Hampton Roads: Cruise of the U.S. Atlantic Fleet from San Francisco to Hampton Roads, July 7, 1908–February 22, 1909* (New York: Huebsch, 1909), 47.

20. Diary of surgeon Eugene P. Stone, quoted in James Reckner, "A Maori Welcome for the Fleet," *Historical Review: Bay of Plenty Journal of History* 37 (1989): 63–70, 63.

21. *New Zealand Herald*, August 14, 1908.

22. Walter Benjamin, "The Task of the Translator," in *Illuminations: Essays and Reflections*, ed. Hannah Arendt, trans. Harry Zohn (New York: Schocken Books, 1968), 72.

23. Emily Rosenberg, *Spreading the American Dream: American Economic and Cultural Expansion, 1890–1945* (New York: Hill & Wang, 1982).

24. On the fallacy of "the Chinese market," Washington's reticence about the concerted development of the Philippines, and the weak transportation and communication linkages between the United States and Australasia, see Jerry Israel, *Progressivism and the Open Door: America and China, 1905–1921* (Pittsburgh: University of Pittsburgh Press, 1971); Donald D. Johnston, *The United States in the Pacific* (Westport, Conn.: Praeger, 1995); Arthur Power Dudden, *The American Pacific: From the Old China Trade to the Present* (New York: Oxford University Press, 1992); Ronald Takaki, *Strangers from a Different Shore: A History of Asian Americans* (New York: Penguin Books, 1989); William F. Nimmo, *Stars and Stripes across the Pacific: The United States, Japan, and the Asia/Pacific Region, 1895–1945* (Westport, Conn.: Praeger, 2001); John Eperjesi, *The Imperialist Imaginary: Visions of Asia and the Pacific in American Culture* (Lebanon, N.H.: University of New England Press, 2001).

25. *Times* (London), September 1, 1908.

26. Adrian Franklin, "Performing Live: An Interview with Barbara Kirshenblatt-Gimblett," *Tourist Studies* 1, no. 3 (2001): 211–32.

27. Letter from Sperry to Roosevelt, September 12, 1908, box 2, Admiral Charles Sperry papers, Library of Congress (hereafter cited as Sperry Papers).

28. Letter from Sperry to Roosevelt, September 12, 1908, box 2, Sperry Papers.

29. Address by U.S. ambassador Thomas J. O'Brien at the Imperial Hotel, Tokyo, October 19, 1908, Sperry Papers, box 13; letter from Emperor of Japan to Roosevelt, October 20, 1908, Sperry Papers, box 13.

30. For accounts of the tour as a whole, see Robert A. Hart, *The Great White Fleet: Its Voyage around the World, 1907–1909* (Boston: Little, Brown, 1965); Kenneth Wimmel, *Theodore Roosevelt and the Great White Fleet: American Sea Power Comes of Age* (Washington, D.C.: Brassey's, 1998); and James R. Reckner, *Teddy Roosevelt's Great White Fleet* (Annapolis: Maryland Press, 1988).

31. Sperry privately asserted that the tour would "establish a curious sort of protectorate—a new Monroe Doctrine." Charles Sperry to Edith Sperry, September 9, 1908, Sperry Papers, box 5.

32. "In Greeting to the Fleet," introduction to the descriptive account of New Zealand, Department of Tourist and Health Resorts subject files, TO10/2, National Archives of New Zealand (hereafter cited as DTHR subject files).

33. The words were Sperry's in a speech to the Australian Premier. *Daily Telegraph,* August 22, 1908.

34. Franklin Matthews, *With the Battle Fleet: Cruise of the Sixteen Battleships of the United States Atlantic Fleet from Hampton Roads to the Golden Gate, December 1907–May 1908* (New York: Huebsch, 1908); Matthews, *Back to Hampton Roads.* Sailor's point of view accounts include Roman J. Miller, *Around the World with the Battleships* (Chicago: McClurg, 1909) and the fictionalized account by Margaret J. Codd, *With Evans to the Pacific: A Story of the Battle Fleet* (Chicago: Flanagan, 1909).

35. Christopher Endy, *Cold War Holidays: American Tourism in France* (Durham: University of North Carolina Press, 2004).

36. That accounts of the tour also culled liberally from travel and tourism literature is an indication that for the American public to "follow [the sailors] around the globe" and take "a share in the welcome" they were accorded meant not only witnessing their own recognition as a world power but also enjoying the cosmopolitan prerogatives of vicarious tourism. Miller, *Around the World*, 368.

37. Letter from Sperry to Mr. and Mrs. Denison, June 19, 1908, Sperry Papers, box 2.

38. Letter from Charles Sperry to Edith Sperry, September 16, 1908, Sperry Papers, box 5.

39. The Chinese Immigration Amendment Act (1907) is but one example of this anti-Asiatic sentiment. Its restrictive conditions included a poll tax and, revealingly, an English-language literacy test. Without the capacity to translate, Chinese were denied the option to migrate. See Peter O'Connor, "Keeping New Zealand White," *New Zealand Journal of History* 2 (1968): 41–65.

40. *Weekly Graphic and New Zealand Mail*, August 19, 1908; "In Greeting to the Fleet."

41. *New Zealand Parliamentary Debates*, vol. 143 (1908): 728.

42. "American Fleet: Visit to Australia; Complete Story in Pictures," pamphlet reprinted from *Sydney Morning Herald*, August–September 1908.

43. *Auckland Weekly News*, August 11, 1908; address from the government of New Zealand to Roosevelt, DTHR subject files, TO10/2.

44. Sperry's speech is quoted in Matthews, *Back to Hampton Roads*, 28.

45. See Joseph Ward's comments in Parliament. *New Zealand Parliamentary Debates*, vol. 143 (1908): 864.

46. *Weekly Graphic and New Zealand Mail*, August 19, 1908; "In Greeting to the Fleet"; *New Zealand Parliamentary Debates*, vol. 143 (1908): 555.

47. *The Mosquito* (published onboard USS New Jersey), October 2, 1908, Mitchell Library Archives, Sydney.

48. Couze Venn, "Translation: Politics and Ethics," *Theory, Culture, and Society* 23 (2006): 82–84, 83.

49. Roach, *Cities of the Dead*, 2.

50. Akarana is significantly a transliteration of the Scottish "Auckland," not the Māori name for the region, Tāmaki Makaurau.

51. With a classically liberal eye to racial norms of citizen conduct, objections centered around the risk of disorderly behavior and unhygienic camp sites if visitors were to be hosted by Ngāti Whātua tangata whenua (local indigenous peoples).

52. Address to Rear Admiral Charles S. Sperry from representatives of the New Zealand parliament, DTHR subject files, TO10/2.

53. *Auckland Weekly News*, August 20, 1908.

54. John Bell Condliffe, *Te Rangi Hiroa: The Life of Sir Peter Buck* (Christchurch, N.Z.: Whitcombe & Tombs, 1971), 78.

55. *Auckland Weekly News*, August 20, 1908.

56. "In Greeting to the Fleet."

57. In fact, it was Buck (Te Rangi Hīroa) who persuaded the Rotorua hapū to participate. T. E. Donne to Augustus Hamilton, July 6, 1908, MU152, box 6, folder 9, Te Papa Tongarewa National Museum of New Zealand Archives.

58. Buck quoted in *New Zealand Herald*, August 7, 1908.

59. *New Zealand Parliamentary Debates*, vol. 144 (1908): 203.

60. *New Zealand Herald*, August 7, 1908.

61. *Auckland Weekly News*, August 20, 1908 (emphasis mine).

62. *New Zealand Herald*, August 7, 1908.

63. *Auckland Weekly News*, August 20, 1908.

64. Benjamin, "Task of the Translator."

65. Samuel Carter III, *The Incredible Great White Fleet* (New York: MacMillan, 1971), 94.

66. *Auckland Weekly News*, August 13, 1908.

67. Hart, *Great White Fleet*; Reckner, *Teddy Roosevelt's Great White Fleet*.

68. The use of the term "American Pacific" to describe the regional or geographical imaginary that brought the Pacific and Asia into coherent visibility for American capital and culture appears in a number of critical and historical works, but the nuance of the definition put forward here is my own. See Paul Lyons, *American Pacificism: Oceania in the U.S. Imagination* (New York: Routledge, 2006); and Eperjesi, *Imperialist Imaginary*. On "Asia-Pacific" as a regional imaginary, see Arif Dirlik, "The Asia-Pacific Idea: Reality and Representation in the Invention of a Regional Structure," *Journal of World History* 3 (1992): 55–80. This chapter is also indebted to Rob Wilson, *Reimagining the American Pacific: From "South Pacific" to Bamboo Ridge and Beyond* (Durham, N.C.: Duke University Press, 2000).

69. Wilson, *Reimagining the American Pacific*, 29.

70. Rob Wilson, "Imagining 'Asia-Pacific' Today: Forgetting Colonialism in the Magical Free Markets of the American Pacific," in *Learning Places: The Afterlives of Area Studies*, ed. Masao Miyoshi and Harry D. Harootunian (Durham, N.C.: Duke University Press, 2002), 239. On early "exploratory" performances in and of the Pacific, see Greg Dening, *Performances* (Chicago: University of Chicago Press, 1996). The locus classicus on Edenic imaginings of the South Seas is Smith, *European Vision in the South Pacific*. On Broadway's Pacific, see Andrea Most, *Making Americans: Jews and the Broadway Musical* (Cambridge, Mass.: Harvard University Press, 2004); Christina Klein, *Cold War Orientalism: Asia in the Middlebrow Imagination, 1945–1961* (Berkeley and Los Angeles: University of California Press, 2003); Adria Imada, "Hawaiians on Tour: Hula Circuits through the American Empire," *American Quarterly* 56, no. 1 (2004): 111–49; and Wilson, *Reimagining the American Pacific*. On the mystical marketing of APEC, see Rob Wilson and Arif Dirlik, eds., *Asia/Pacific as a Space of Cultural Production* (Durham, N.C.: Duke University Press, 1995).

71. Wilson, "Imagining 'Asia-Pacific,'" 234.

72. Edward Said, *Orientalism* (New York: Vintage Books, 1979).

73. The following discussion draws on R. H. Burnside, "Secrets of the Hippodrome," 1932, Robert H. Burnside Collection, New York Public Library Theatre

Collection (hereafter cited as RHB Collection); Norman Clarke, *The Mighty Hippodrome* (New York: Barnes, 1968); Milton Epstein, *The New York Hippodrome: A Complete Chronology of Performances from 1905 to 1939* (New York: Theatre Library Association, 1993); and Register, *Kid of Coney Island*.

74. Register, *Kid of Coney Island*, 57.

75. Gretchen Finletter, "Deadheads and the Hippodrome" in *The Passionate Playgoer*, ed. George Oppenheimer (New York: Viking Press, 1958), 359–67. The Hippodrome also offered motion picture shows, titled "New York Hippodrome Travel Festivals," in collaboration with the famous travelogue lecturer Lyman H. Howe.

76. The season before *A Trip to Japan* featured a melodrama called *Battle in the Skies*, a science fiction potboiler that also involved a plot about the secret traffic in weapons of mass destruction and a U.S. fleet (albeit an air fleet).

77. Janet M. Davis, *The Circus Age: Culture and Society under the American Big Top* (Chapel Hill: University of North Carolina Press, 2002).

78. Davis, *Circus Age*, 10.

79. Hardt and Negri, *Empire*, 33.

80. *A Trip to Japan* and *Inside the Earth*, 1909, RHB Collection.

81. The atmosphere of conspiracy and suspicion pervading the stage Tokyo resembled that of the real Tokyo the year before, as the diplomatic situation on the Fleet's arrival at Japanese ports was so volatile that the admiral feared the misbehavior of sailors on shore leave might precipitate war. They kept the coal supplies under armed guard, lest Japanese, Korean, or Chinese subversives attempt to plant explosives.

82. *Trip to Japan*, 23.

83. MacCannell, *Tourist*, 47–51.

84. Finletter, "Deadheads," 360.

85. *Trip to Japan*, 19, 23.

86. *Trip to Japan*, 31.

87. *The Sun*, undated clipping in Burnside production scrapbook 1909–11, RHB Collection.

88. The programs of the Mission Choir and other performances can be found in Misc: B ConcertsNZ, 1901–10, Alexander Turnbull Library, Wellington.

89. The Hudson–Fulton Celebration was a paean to Progressive-era techno-economic imperialism. A "magic three centuries of change" in the "virgin" expanses of the Hudson River saw the hollow log canoes of the native Indians give way to "the treasure-laden argosies of the world" and the urban wonders of New York, soon to be the "first city . . . a civilization which rivals that of any other part of the world." Promoters argued that the celebration would enable the foreign-born population of New York to claim the pioneer history as their own, celebrate the cosmopolitan origins of American Empire, and rejoice together in the technological transcendence of global space that had "narrowed the ocean in point of time to one-sixth its former dreary breadth, increased the productive power of mankind and multiplied the world's commerce . . . given to all the navigable waters of the earth a value which they did not previously possess, and by increasing the neighborliness of nations promoted . . . the

brotherhood of mankind." "Introduction," *The Hudson–Fulton Celebration: The Fourth Annual Report on the Hudson–Fulton Celebration Commission to the Legislature of the State of New York, May 20, 1910* (Albany, N.Y.: Lyon, 1910).

90. *Standard Union,* September 29, 1909. The show became the scene of the circulatory diplomacy it mimed when Prince Kuni of Japan, on a state visit for the Hudson–Fulton celebrations and accompanied by Lord Charles Beresford (the British ambassador to Japan during the Fleet tour), visited the Hippodrome.

91. The Hippodrome initially approached T. E. Donne, the head of the DTHR, who had referred them to Makereti Papakura. She had already committed her troupe to a tour of Australia and the United Kingdom, so she referred the Hippodrome to Frederick Bennett, the future archbishop of New Zealand and a member of the Ngāti Whakaue group. Correspondence in Donne Papers, Maggie Papakura Scrapbook, Alexander Turnbull Library. For more on Bennett's selection, see correspondence between Augustus Hamilton at the Colonial Museum in Wellington and Lawrence Birks, engineer in charge at Rotorua, MU152, box 4, folder 8, Te Papa Tongarewa National Museum of New Zealand Archives.

92. I thank Robert and Kingi Biddle and their whānau (family) for sharing kōrero (stories) about their tipuna (ancestors), Kiwi Te Amohau and Tuoro Akapita Pango (his son-in-law and Robert Biddle's grandfather). It was an honor to bring the kōrero home to you.

93. "Te Haere ki Amerika," letter to *Te Pipiwharauroa,* August 1909, trans. Kingi Biddle.

94. The words belong to Kiri Matao, named after her illustrious great-grandmother. W. B. Baucke, quoted at length in chapter 2, argued that the true wonders of Wonderland were the members of Rev. Bennett's Māori Mission Choir, paragons of domestic discipline, manly industry, wholesome leisure, hygiene, and learning. He predicted that these performers would, by their example, "beshame [Pākehā] with their clamours in the Councils of the Nations" for the slights to citizenship at the hands of the state. *New Zealand Herald,* January 17, 1907.

95. She also went by the names of Piata Pahiriko or Te Taotahi/Te Tautahi.

96. Correspondence between the engineer in charge at Rotorua (Lawrence Birks) and Augustus Hamilton at the Colonial Museum suggests that a skeptical Bennett drove a hard bargain with the Hippodrome promoters. MU152, box 4, folder 8, Te Papa Tongarewa, National Museum of New Zealand Archives.

97. *New York Daily Tribune,* August 28, 1909.

98. *New York Press,* September 12, 1909.

99. *New York Press,* September 5, 1909; *New York American,* September 5, 1909.

100. *The Evening Sun,* undated clipping in Burnside production scrapbook, 1909–11, RHB Collection.

101. Production notes found in Burnside production scrapbook, 1911–19, RHB Collection.

102. Edward LiPuma and Thomas Koelble, "Cultures of Circulation and the Urban Imaginary: Miami as Example and Exemplar," *Public Culture* 17, no. 1 (2005): 153–79.

103. The cause was a suspected outbreak of trachoma, an eye infection.

104. *New York Daily Tribune*, August 28, 1909.

105. *New York Press*, August 28, 1909 (emphasis mine).

106. *Morning Telegraph*, August 28, 1909.

107. *Daily Citizen*, August 28, 1909. Speculations were rife, and they issued from several quarters, one paper even suggesting that the Schuberts would set the group up in an amusement park in Manhattan. There is, however, no evidence to suggest that any of their number stayed on after the conclusion of the Hippodrome season.

108. *The World*, November 28, 1909.

109. "Maori Terrors as Football Players," *The World*, November 28, 1909. The connection between the turn-of-the-century world of ethnological show business and the Hippodrome's venture was a deep one, even leading the Hippodrome publicists to stage a visit of the troupe to the Museum of Natural History, where Professor Lowie took casts of Te Kiwi's and Kiri Matao's faces for display with the Māori collections, and the group entered into negotiations over the sale of their costumes and weapons to augment the Māori collection at the museum. See Bethany Edmunds, "The Mighty Maoris," Anthropology and Photography at the American Museum of Natural History, http://blogs.nyu.edu/blogs/hg26/amnhphotographs/2009/04/the_mighty_maoris.html.

110. *New York Daily Tribune*, October 24, 1909; unidentified clipping in Burnside production scrapbook, 1909–11, RHB Collection.

111. Barbara Fuchs, "Conquering Islands: Contextualizing *The Tempest*," *Shakespeare Quarterly* 48, no. 1 (1997): 45–62.

112. *The Sun*, November 7, 1909.

113. *New York Herald*, January 12, 1910. It is instructive to compare the Māori case to the system of symbolic containment represented by Chinatown, the other Oriental spectacle in New York during this era, which might also be read as an attempt to manage touristically the human consequences of global modernity. A stigmatized but sensationally patronized enclave of putatively "unassimilable" immigrant life, it rhetorically and spatially contained and immobilized its subjects on the margins of urban and national life. Chinatown during this era was theatrically retrofitted as a destination for thrill-seeking urban tourists, a virtual environment with staged opium dens and tong headquarters that could be seen from the safety of a guided tour on a gape wagon that traced a route from Chinatown to Coney Island (the Hippodrome's sister site). The American Pacific mobilization of performance clearly differed from performance's nationalist instrumentation. Jan Lin, *Reconstructing Chinatown: Ethnic Enclave, Global Change* (Minneapolis: University of Minnesota Press, 1998); Michel Laguerre, *The Global Ethnopolis: Chinatown, Japantown, and Manilatown in American Society* (New York: St. Martin's Press, 2000).

114. *New York Press*, October 26, 1909.

115. *The World*, September 12, 1909.

116. Zygmunt Bauman, *Liquid Modernity* (Oxford: Blackwell, 2000).

117. Homi Bhabha, *The Location of Culture* (London: Routledge, 1994), 228.

118. Roman Jakobson, "On Linguistic Aspects of Translation," in *The Translation Studies Reader*, ed. Lawrence Venuti (London: Routledge, 2000), 115. Much like the political theory of nationhood, this theory of translation conceals the global hegemony of English as the universal form of value, while it conducts its ongoing war of "translational violence" against all that cannot be uttered in the commensurating metalanguage of capital modernity. Saranindranath Tagore, "Multiculturalism and the Ethics of Translation," in *Translation, Text, and Theory: The Paradigm of India*, ed. Rukmini Bhaya Nair (New Delhi: Sage, 2002), 289–302; Morinaka Takaaki, "Translation as Dissemination: Multilinguality and De-Cathexis," trans. Lewis Harrington, in *Translation, Biopolitics, Colonial Difference*, ed. Naoki Sakai and Jon Solomon (Hong Kong: Hong Kong University Press, 2006), 39–54.

119. Quoted in Bhabha, *Location*, 228.

120. Sakai, *Translation and Subjectivity*, 11.

121. Oskar Negt and Alexander Kluge, *Public Sphere and Experience: Toward an Analysis of the Bourgeois and Proletarian Public Sphere*, trans. Peter Labanyi, Jamie Owen Daniel, and Assenka Oksiloff (Minneapolis: University of Minnesota Press, 1993).

4. TRAFFICKING RACE

1. Cheryl Harris, "Whiteness as Property," *Harvard Law Review* 106, no. 8 (1993): 1709–91. See also Eve Cherniavsky, *Race, Nation, and the Body Politics of Capital* (Minneapolis: University of Minnesota Press, 2006); C. B. McPherson, *The Political Theory of Possessive Individualism: From Hobbes to Locke* (London: Oxford University Press, 1964 [1962]); and Goldberg, *Racial State*.

2. Marlon B. Ross, "The New Negro Displayed: Self-Ownership, Proprietary Sites/Sights, and the Bonds/Bounds of Race," in *Claiming the Stones/Naming the Bones: Cultural Property and the Negotiation of National and Ethnic Identity*, ed. Elazar Barkan and Ronald Bush (Los Angeles: Getty Research Institute, 2002), 259–301, 260.

3. Pierre Bourdieu, "The Essence of Neoliberalism," *Le monde diplomatique*, December 1998, http://mondediplo.com/1998/12/08bourdieu.

4. David Harvey, *A Brief History of Neoliberalism* (Oxford: Oxford University Press, 2005), 178–79; Povinelli, *Cunning of Recognition*.

5. For comparable cases in other former settler colonies, see Penny Bassett and Bernadette van Gramberg, "Neoliberalism and the Third Sector in Australia" (working paper, School of Management, Victoria University, 2005), http://eprints.vu.edu.au/120/; and B. Mitchell Evans and John Shields, "Neoliberal Restructuring and the Third Sector: Reshaping Governance, Civil Society, and Local Relations" (working paper, Centre for Voluntary Sector Studies, Faculty of Business, Ryerson University, 2006), http://www.ryerson.ca/~cvss/WP13.pdf.

6. For a review of the Māori critique of incursions on tribal ethos and values through the Treaty process, see Maria Bargh, "Māori Development and Neoliberalism," in *Resistance: An Indigenous Response to Neoliberalism*, ed. Bargh (Wellington: Huia, 2007), 25–44.

7. Boccara, *Making of Indigenous Culture*.

8. These interviews began in 2003 and took place in three subsequent research visits, concluding in 2010. In each case, I discussed with the interviewee the nature of my interest in ethnic tourism in Aotearoa New Zealand and my publication plans for the project. Most met with me in the context of their work environments, understanding the interview as part of their professional duties. When the interviewee was a tourism service provider, the interview often took place in the context of a tour on which I was a paying customer, with the understanding that I was on the tour for the purpose of research and might (with further permission) write about my experience. Although most of these individuals were happy to be named in this book, to protect the identity of those who were not, and to maintain consistency, I have identified individuals only by their professional roles.

9. Hansen and Stepputat, *States of the Imagination*, 5.

10. See Massimo de Angelis, *The Beginning of History: Value Struggles and Global Capital* (London: Pluto Press, 2007).

11. Growth averaged 17.5 percent per annum over the decade from 1965 to 1975. Margaret McClure, *The Wonder Country: Making New Zealand Tourism* (Auckland: Auckland University Press, 2004), 212.

12. McClure, *Wonder Country*, 253; see also David Simmons and Neil Leiper, "Tourism Systems in New Zealand and Australia," in *Time Out: Recreation and Tourism in New Zealand and Australia*, ed. Harvey Perkins and Grant Cushman (Auckland: Longman, 1998), 86–105, 92.

13. The "Tourism 2000: Grow for It" conference resulted in *Report of the Taskforce 2000: A Report to the Minister* (Wellington, 1989) and ultimately, from the Tourism Strategy Marketing Group, *Destination New Zealand: A Growth Strategy for New Zealand Tourism* (Wellington: New Zealand Tourism Department, 1990).

14. Helen Clark, "Implementing a Progressive Agenda after Fifteen Years of Neo-liberalism: The New Zealand Experience" (address to London School of Economics, February 21, 2002), http://www2.lse.ac.uk/publicEvents/events/2002/20020221t1512z001.aspx.

15. Clark, "Implementing a Progressive Agenda," http://www2.lse.ac.UK/public events/events/2002/20020221t1648Z001.aspx. For an analysis of these "neo-social techniques" that target "civility, levels of trust, intensity of community feeling, and extent of voluntary endeavors," see Wendy Larner and Maria Butler, "The Places, People, and Politics of Partnership: After Neoliberalism in Aotearoa New Zealand," in *Contesting Neoliberalism: Urban Frontiers*, ed. Helga Leitner, Jamie Peck, and Eric S. Sheppard (New York: Guilford Press, 2007), 85.

16. William Flores and Rina Benmayor, "Constructing Cultural Citizenship," in *Latino Cultural Citizenship: Claiming Identity, Space, and Rights*, ed. Flores and Benmayor (Boston: Beacon Press, 1998), 12; Taylor, "Politics of Recognition."

17. Evan Davies, quoted in *Towards 2010: Implementing the New Zealand Tourism Strategy* (Wellington: Ministry of Tourism, 2003).

18. Emily Martin, "Mind-Body Problems," *American Ethnology* 27, no. 3 (2000): 569–90.

19. Miller and Yúdice, *Cultural Policy*, 2.

20. Miller, *Cultural Citizenship*, 11; see also Ian Hunter, "Aesthetics and Cultural Studies," in *Cultural Studies*, ed. Grossberg, Nelson, and Treichler, 347–72.

21. Miller and Yúdice, *Cultural Policy*, 76.

22. Justin Lewis and Toby Miller, eds., *Critical Cultural Policy Studies: A Reader* (Malden, Mass.: Blackwell, 2003), 4; George Yúdice, *The Expediency of Culture: Uses of Culture in the Global Era* (Durham, N.C.: Duke University Press, 1994), 4.

23. Yúdice, *Expediency of Culture*.

24. George Barker, commissioned by the New Zealand Film Commission in 1997, theorized cultural capital as a shared form of human capital (the capabilities embodied in individuals, which affect their economic, social, and political competencies) and social capital (relationships between individuals that create trust and norms of behavior that facilitate exchange). Barker, *Cultural Capital and Policy* (Wellington: Australian National University, 2000), 11–13.

25. To the end of the Clark administration, the Department of the Prime Minister and Cabinet named national identity as one of the Prime Minister's three strategic priorities: "to be able to take pride in who and what we are, through our arts, culture, film, sports and music, our appreciation of our natural environment, our understanding of our history and our stance on international issues . . . who we are; what we do; where we live; how we are seen by the world." "Statement of Intent, 2008–2013," http://www.dpmc.govt.nz/dpmc/publications/index.html.

26. Yúdice, *Expediency of Culture*, 6, 25.

27. Heart of the Nation Strategic Working Group, *Heart of the Nation: A Cultural Strategy for Aotearoa New Zealand* (Wellington: McDermott Miller, 2000), x, xv.

28. Ruth Harley, "Gluing New Zealand Together," in *Vision Aotearoa: Kaupapa New Zealand*, ed. Roslie Capper, Amy Brown, and Witi Ihimaera (Auckland: Bridget Williams Books, 1996), 76. See also Michael Goldsmith, "Culture, For and Against: Patterns of 'Culturespeak' in New Zealand," *Journal of the Polynesian Society* 112, no. 3 (2000): 280–93.

29. *Heart of the Nation*, vii. Critiques from within the academic and policy establishment are few and recent, including contributions to "Concepts of Nationhood: A Symposium to Mark the Centenary of the Proclamation of Dominion Status," 2007, http://www.nzhistory.net.nz/culture/dominion-status/symposium. See especially Giselle Byrnes's and James Belich's contributions.

30. *Heart of the Nation*, ix. See also Helen Clark, "Growing an Innovative New Zealand" (speech, February 12, 2002), http://www.executive.govt.nz/minister/clark/innovate/speech.htm.

31. On culture as compensatory stabilization, see Jennifer Lawn, "Globalizing the Cultural Imaginary in New Zealand," in *Global Fissures: Postcolonial Fusions*, ed. Clara A. B. Joseph and Janet Wilson (Amsterdam: Rodopi, 2006), 227–45. See also Lydia Wevers and Mark Williams, "Going Mad without Noticing: Cultural Policy in a Small Country," *Landfall* 204 (2002): 16; Tim Corballis, "Against Creativity," *Landfall* 205 (2003): 53–65.

32. Hui Taumata Māori Economic Development Conference, *Māori in Tourism* (Wellington, 1986).

33. Te Puni Kōkiri and the Office of Tourism and Sport, *He Mātai Tāpoi Māori: A Study of Barriers, Impediments, and Opportunities for Māori in Tourism* (Wellington, 2001), from a report by The Stafford Group.

34. Māori Tourism Advisory Group, appendix to *Strategy 2010* (Wellington: Tourism New Zealand and Ministry of Tourism, 2003), 24. The authors cite the terms of the United Nations Draft Declaration on Indigenous Rights as they note that the Ministry's data-gathering practices frame Pākehā as normal and Māori as the exception.

35. During this era, adventure tourists constituted 20 percent of visitorship. Activities included jet boating, bungee jumping, and ecotourism, including some Māori-owned ventures such as Whale Watch Kaikōura.

36. The Tourism Board had drawn censure from a parliamentary select committee for focusing on growth over yield: high numbers of Asian wholesale package operators were cutting profit margins with New Zealand providers, taxing infrastructure, and giving low-quality experiences.

37. Colmar Brunton Group, *Demand for Māori Cultural Tourism* (Wellington: TNZ and Ministry of Tourism, 2004).

38. The New Zealand Way, *Brand New Zealand* (Wellington, 1993), 1; Ulrich Beck, *World Risk Society* (Cambridge: Polity Press, 1999).

39. Mike Moore was, significantly, also Minister for Overseas Trade and Marketing and future leader of the World Trade Organization. Quoted in P. Cloke and Harvey C. Perkins, "'Pushing the Limits': Place Promotion and Adventure Tourism in the South Island of New Zealand," in *Time Out*, ed. Perkins and Cushman (Auckland: Longman, 1998), 271–87, 271.

40. Nikolas Rose, *Powers of Freedom: Reframing Political Thought* (Cambridge: Cambridge University Press, 1999). According to McClure's informants, Kevin Roberts's first iteration of the campaign focused on New Zealand as "the last undiscovered Paradise" and troped the New Zealand spirit as modeled by Lucy Lawless as Xena the Warrior Princess. McClure, *Wonder Country*, 283.

41. Morgan and Pritchard, "New Zealand, 100% Pure."

42. TNZ and Ministry of Tourism, *Strategy 2010*, 20.

43. See the discussion of the relationship between distinction, authenticity, affective charge, loyalty, and the Lovemark in chapter 5.

44. New Zealand Māori Tourism Council (NZMTC), *Living Landscapes* (Wellington, 2009).

45. Celia Lury, *Brands: The Logos of the Global Economy* (London: Routledge, 2004).

46. This language was used by numerous interviewees.

47. Kaumatua (elder) Wiremu Williams, Ngāpuhi, in an interactive essay on the hongi, www.tourismnz.govt.nz (accessed October 5, 2008).

48. "Māori in Tourism Portfolio," www.nzgs.co.nz/download/Manaakitanga.pdf (accessed May 10, 2008). Rotorua RTO introduced "Manaakitanga" as the first Māori brand in 1997.

49. NZMTC, *Statement of Intent* (Wellington, 2008–9).

50. NZMTC, *Living Landscapes*.

51. Zygmunt Bauman, "Culture and Management," *Parallax* 10, no. 2 (2004): 63–72.

52. See, for example, Robert Jahnke and Huia Tomlins Jahnke, "The Politics of Māori Image and Design," *He Pukenga Kōrero* 7, no. 1 (2003): 5–31; Aroha Te Pareake Mead, "Legal Pluralism & the Politics of Māori Image and Design," *He Pukenga Kōrero* 7, no. 1 (2003): 34–37. Managerial remedies (such as Toi Iho, a Māori "mark of authenticity") attempted to assuage such fears in the context of tourism but raised yet more concerns about the adjudication of the value and authenticity of Māori creative property resting in the hands of authorities whose power is delegated by the state.

53. Christopher Balme, *Pacific Performances: Cross-Cultural Encounter in the South Seas* (Basingstoke, England: Palgrave Macmillan, 2007); Desmond, *Staging Tourism*; Kirshenblatt-Gimblett, *Destination Culture*.

54. See Kirshenblatt-Gimblett, *Destination Culture*; and Edward Bruner, *Culture on Tour: Ethnographies of Travel* (Chicago: University of Chicago Press, 2004).

55. Johannes Fabian, *Time and the Other: How Anthropology Makes Its Object* (New York: Columbia University Press, 1983).

56. Timoti Karetu, *Haka! The Dance of a Noble People* (Auckland: Penguin, 1993); Teurikore Biddle, "Māori Performing Arts: A Forum for Passive Resistance" (unpublished paper, 2009); Mervyn McLean, *Maori Music* (Auckland: Auckland University Press, 1996); Apirana Ngata, "Maori Past and Present," in Robert Andrew Loughnan, *Royalty in New Zealand: The Visit of Their Royal Highnesses the Duke and Duchess of Cornwall and York, June 1901; A Descriptive Narrative.* (Wellington: Mackay, Government Printing Office, 1902).

57. Charles Te Ahukaramū Royal, "Te Whare Tapere: Towards a New Model for Māori Performing Arts" (PhD diss., Victoria University of Wellington, 1998).

58. See, for example Ngata, "Maori Past and Present." Siegfried Kracauer, "The Mass Ornament," *New German Critique* 5 (Spring 1975): 59–66.

59. For "new traditionalism," see James Clifford, "Indigenous Articulations," *The Contemporary Pacific* 13 (2001): 468–90.

60. See McClure, *Wonder Country*, and Ngahuia Te Awekotuku, "The Sociocultural Impact of Tourism on the Te Arawa People of Rotorua, New Zealand" (D.Phil. thesis, Waikato University, 1981).

61. My fieldwork was conducted before a recent (2009–10) rebrand, which I address briefly in the conclusion, that pushed the company even further toward immersive theatrical idioms.

62. Tamaki does not share its market research, so I cannot confirm what the ratio is between package and independent travelers.

63. See Paul Tapsell's discussion of this principle in relation to Te Papa Tongarewa National Museum of New Zealand in "Taonga: A Tribal Response to Museums" (D.Phil. thesis, School of Museum Ethnology, Oxford University, 2001). When the state attempted to produce a national tourism attraction at Whakarewarewa reserve

in the early 1900s, they constructed—controversially and tellingly—a simulacral pā (fortified village) on the historical site of an actual one, Rotowhio.

64. Te Awekotuku's interlocuters in *Mana Wahine Maori* talk of gender selectivity in the hotel shows in the 1970s and 1980s. For the case of Hawai'i, see Desmond, *Staging Tourism.*

65. Barbara Kirshenblatt-Gimblett, "The Ethnographic Burlesque," *TDR: The Drama Review* 42, no. 2 (1998): 175–80.

66. See MacCannell's influential structural analysis of tourism in *Tourist.*

67. I have explored this link between higher education and tourism elsewhere. Margaret Werry, "Shameful Lessons: Pedagogy of/and/as Tourism," *The Review of Education, Pedagogy, and Cultural Studies* 30, no. 1 (2008): 14–42.

68. This flag has been the subject of considerable debate over whether it should be taken to represent Māori or is too (negatively) identified with a specific activist movement.

69. Niezen, *Origins of Indigenism.*

70. Maurizio Lazzarato, "General Intellect: Towards an Inquiry into Immaterial Labour," in *Immaterial Labour: Mass Intellectuality, New Constitution, Post Fordism, and All That* (London: Red Notes, 1994), 1–14.

71. Yúdice, *Expediency of Culture,* 20.

72. Even Te Puia, the nation's largest attraction, struggles to reach the 10 percent of its visitorship that is domestic. The FIT proprietors I spoke with could remember only a handful of Pākehā clients; by contrast, every Tamaki performance I have attended has included at least one Pākehā family.

73. Rosemary Coombe, "Legal Claims to Culture in and against the Market: Neoliberalism and the Global Proliferation of Meaningful Difference," *Law, Culture, and the Humanities* 1 (2005): 35–52, 40.

74. Michael Hardt, "Affective Labor," *boundary 2* 26, no. 2 (1999): 96; B. Joseph Pine and James H. Gilmore, *The Experience Economy* (Boston: Harvard Business School Press, 1999).

75. Michael Volkerling, "The End of Economic Man: Cultural Holism as State Policy," in *The Second International Conference on Cultural Policy Research, 2002: Proceedings* (Wellington: n.p., 2002), 530–42, 530.

76. Lazzarato, "General Intellect"; Paolo Virno, *A Grammar of the Multitude: For an Analysis of Contemporary Forms of Life,* trans. Isabella Bertoletti, James Cascaito, and Andrea Casson (Los Angeles: Semiotext(e), 2004); Michel Callon, Cécile Méadel, and Vololona Rabiharisoa, "The Economy of Qualities," *Economy and Society* 31, no. 2 (2002): 194–217.

77. Michel Callon, "Introduction: The Embeddedness of Economic Markets in Economics," in *The Laws of the Markets* (Oxford: Blackwell, 1998), 1–58, 51.

78. Povinelli, *Cunning of Recognition.*

79. For "rooted cosmopolitanism," see Anthony Appiah, *Cosmopolitanism: Ethics in a World of Strangers* (London: Norton, 2006).

80. Micaela di Leonardo, *Exotics at Home: Anthropologies, Others, American Modernity* (Chicago: University of Chicago Press, 1998).

5. ALTERED STATES

1. David Crouch, Rhona Jackson, and Felix Thompson, "Introduction," in *The Media and the Tourist Imagination: Converging Cultures*, ed. Crouch, Jackson, and Thompson (London: Routledge, 2005), 1–13.

2. Walter Benjamin, "The Work of Art in the Age of Mechanical Reproduction," in *Illuminations*, 223.

3. Toby Miller, *Technologies of Truth: Cultural Citizenship and the Popular Media* (Minneapolis: University of Minnesota Press, 1998).

4. Toby Miller et al., *Global Hollywood* (London: BFI, 2001), 15.

5. Paul Gilroy, *Against Race: Imagining Political Culture beyond the Color Line* (Cambridge, Mass.: Harvard University Press, 2002), 30; Howard Winant, *The New Politics of Race: Globalism, Difference, Justice* (Minneapolis: University of Minnesota Press, 2004), 69.

6. Deborah Solomon, "Questions for Henry Louis Gates Jr.: After the Beer Summit," *New York Times Magazine*, February 11, 2010, 13.

7. Appadurai, *Modernity at Large*, 19; Gilroy, *Against Race*.

8. See Martin Blythe, *Naming the Other: Images of the Maori in New Zealand Film and Television* (Metuchen, N.J.: Scarecrow Press, 1994); and Jonathan Dennis and Jan Bieringa, eds., *Film in Aotearoa New Zealand* (Wellington: Victoria University Press, 2000 [1992]).

9. John Grierson, quoted in Sarah Davy, "Images of New Zealand in Government Film-Making, 1923–1940" (unpublished paper, New Zealand Film Archive); state official quoted in Dennis and Bieringa, *Film in Aotearoa*, 197.

10. Merata Mita, "The Soul and the Image," in *Film in Aotearoa*, ed. Dennis and Bieringa, 36–54.

11. *The Piano* was technically not a New Zealand film, either by official nationality or by funding, but it was widely identified as such because of the subject matter, cast, location, and nationality of the director. See Lindsay Shelton on the finance and distribution channels opened by new "independent" subsidiaries of media multinationals, such as Miramax and New Line. Shelton, *The Selling of New Zealand Movies* (Auckland: Awa, 2005).

12. Miller et al., *Global Hollywood*.

13. New Zealand Institute of Economic Research (NZIER), *Scoping the Lasting Effects of "The Lord of the Rings"* (Wellington: New Zealand Film Commission, 2002), v. For the game-changing innovation of *Lord of the Rings* in Hollywood, see Kristin Thompson, *The Frodo Franchise: "The Lord of the Rings" and Modern Hollywood* (Berkeley and Los Angeles: University of California Press, 2007).

14. NZIER, *Scoping the Lasting Effects*, vi.

15. For a skeptical assessment of the "Rings effect," see Jennifer Lawn, "Arts, Culture, and Heritage," *Social and Cultural Studies* 5 (2005): 16–34.

16. NZIER, *Scoping the Lasting Effects*, v.

17. Morgan and Pritchard, "New Zealand, 100% Pure."

18. *Tourism News*, July 2004, 6–7.

19. Quoted in Louise Baker, presentation at Cineposium (2003), http://www .filmnz.com/news/archive/cineposium-2003.html.

20. Ruth Harley, "Cultural Capital and the Knowledge Economy" (presentation at Public Service Senior Management Conference, 1999), http://pssm.ssc.govt.nz/1999/ papers/rharley.asp.

21. *Sydney Morning Herald,* January 17, 2002.

22. Gordon Campbell, "Lord of the Tax Deals," *New Zealand Listener,* October 21, 2000, 18–24; Russell Baillie, "Rules Could Stifle Next Blockbuster," *New Zealand Herald,* January 22, 2002. Thompson, *Frodo Franchise,* estimates the savings at 50 percent.

23. Gordon Campbell, "Planet Middle Earth," *New Zealand Listener,* December 15, 2001, 16–24.

24. Film Venture Taranaki, Investment New Zealand, and New Zealand Trade and Enterprise, *Economic Impact Assessment for the Filming of "The Last Samurai" in Taranaki* (New Plymouth, 2004), 52.

25. Miller et al., *Global Hollywood,* 42.

26. I have seen this statement cited without clear attribution by commentators in other first-world runaway production sites (including Australia and Canada). If it is indeed an urban myth, it is one that speaks volumes about the level of racial anxiety the loss of cultural and economic sovereignty engenders in erstwhile settler colonies.

27. See Sue Kim, "Beyond Black and White: Race and Postmodernism in *The Lord of the Rings* Films," *Modern Fiction Studies* 50, no. 4 (2004): 875–907.

28. See Jane Chance, "Introduction," in *Tolkien and the Invention of Myth,* ed. Chance (Lexington: University Press of Kentucky, 2004).

29. Patrick Curry, *Defending Middle-earth: Tolkien, Myth, and Modernity* (New York: St. Martin's, 1997), 24.

30. For example, see James Pinkerton, "The Once & Future Christendom," *The American Conservative,* September 10, 2007, accessed online. See also Ken Gelder, "Epic Fantasy and Global Terrorism," in *From Hobbits to Hollywood: Essays on Peter Jackson's "Lord of the Rings,"* ed. Ernest Mathijs and Murray Pomerance (Amsterdam: Rodopi, 2006).

31. "And just as in our world everybody's culture—European, American, South American, African, Australian—represents the evolution of those people through history, so it is in Middle-earth." Brian Sibley, *"The Lord of the Rings": Official Movie Guide* (Boston: Houghton Mifflin, 2001), 19. Sandra Balliff Straubhauer argues that Jackson's approach actually effaced the history of intermixing that Tolkien explored in the books. Balliff Straubhauer, "Myth, Late Roman History, and Multiculturalism in Tolkien's Middle-earth," in *Tolkien and the Invention,* ed. Chance, 101–18.

32. See Kim, "Beyond Black and White."

33. Lisa Hopkins, "Gollum and Caliban: Evolution and Design," in *Tolkien and Shakespeare: Essays on Shared Themes and Language,* ed. Janet Brennan Croft (Jefferson, N.C.: McFarland, 2007), 281–93.

34. Film Venture Taranaki et al., *Economic Impact;* Screen Actors Guild, *U.S. Runaway Film and Television Production Study Report* (Los Angeles, 1999).

35. McKellen, quoted on TNZ website, www.newzealand.com (accessed September 23, 2003).

36. Claudia Bell and John Lyall, *The Accelerated Sublime: Landscape, Tourism, and Identity* (Westport, Conn.: Praeger, 2001).

37. Mark Sinker, "Talking Tolkien: The Elvish Craft of CGI," *Children's Literature in Education* 36, no. 1 (2005): 41–54.

38. The designers describe the landscape in colonial terms, as "a different world, a different land, a primitive land and a primitive time in history," and "a slightly surreal version of a European landscape," "uncluttered with the impedimenta of civilization." Sibley, *"Lord of the Rings,"* 21.

39. Josiah Clifton Firth, *Nation Making, a Story of New Zealand: Savagism v. Civilization* (London: Longmans, Green, 1890).

40. "Immersive simulation" is the *Lord of the Rings's* designers' phrase, quoted in Erik Davis, "The Fellowship of the Ring," *Wired,* October 2001.

41. Crosby, *Ecological Imperialism.*

42. Travel Channel, *New Zealand: The Royal Tour,* directed by Kate Hall, 2002.

43. Michele Hewitson, "Random Play: I Hate Hobbits," *New Zealand Herald,* December 15, 2001.

44. Mary Boyd, quoted (uncritically) by Thompson, *Frodo Franchise,* 68.

45. Mark Burton, quoted in video clip on www.purenz.com (accessed April 3, 2002).

46. *The Lord of the Rings: The Motion Picture Trilogy,* DVD, directed by Peter Jackson (Los Angeles: New Line Home Video, 2004).

47. The following remarks are based on my observation of the exhibition in 2006 when it was remounted at Te Papa after its global tour.

48. *Museum of New Zealand Te Papa Tongarewa Act 1992,* Public Act no. 19, 1992; Museum of New Zealand Te Papa Tongarewa, *Annual Report 2003/4* (Wellington, 2004).

49. For a critique of the early missteps of the museum, see Paul Williams, "Te Papa: New Zealand's Identity Complex," *Journal of New Zealand Art History* 24 (2003): 11–24; Goldsmith, "Culture, For and Against."

50. Elisabeth A. Povinelli, "Settler Modernity and the Quest for an Indigenous Tradition," *Public Culture* 11, no. 1 (1999): 19–48, 22.

51. Miller et al., *Global Hollywood,* 58.

52. See for example, Te Runanga o Ngai Tahu, "A Guideline for Filming within the Rohe of Ngai Tahu," http://www.filmnz.com.

53. Film Venture Taranaki et al., *Economic Impact.*

54. With a domestic market of four million people, even on average budgets of US$1–1.5 million, these productions stand little chance of recouping costs on domestic sales.

55. Timothy Ord, managing director, United International Pictures, quoted in Frances Walsh, "'Lord' . . . What Next?," *New Zealand Listener,* March 9, 2001, 50–53.

56. The NZFC's mission statement indicates that the agency aims "to contribute to the creation of cultural capital in New Zealand through audience-targeted feature

films within a sustainable screen industry." This and all following references to NZFC policy are drawn from the website www.nzfilm.co.nz.

57. The charter defines "significant" New Zealand content in terms of subject matter, locations, or personnel, defaulting to the phrasing of 1978 legislation.

58. Harley, "Cultural Capital."

59. On the performative quality of policy, see Miller and Yúdice, *Cultural Policy*; and Yúdice, *Expediency of Culture*. On the difference between pedagogic and performative articulations of nationhood, see Bhabha, *Location of Culture*.

60. Rod Oram, "Brand New Zealand," *Unlimited* 34 (December 2001); Toby Miller and Marie Claire Leger, "Runaway Production, Runaway Consumption, Runaway Citizenship: The New International Division of Cultural Labor," *Emergences* 11, no. 1 (2001): 89–115.

61. Shelton, *Selling of New Zealand Movies*, 175.

62. Barbara Kirshenblatt-Gimblett, "World Heritage and Cultural Economics," in *Museum Frictions: Public Cultures/Global Transformations*, ed. Ivan Karp et al. (Durham, N.C.: Duke University Press, 2007).

63. See "An Open Letter to John Barnett from Barry Barclay," *Onfilm*, February 2003, 11; Merata Mita's comments in Tapu Misa, "Stories Worth Telling," *Mana*, December 2002– January 2003, 30–35; or Ian Mune's comments in Lana Simmons-Donaldson, "Where Is the Maori Voice in Storytelling?," *Tū Mai*, August 2000, 20.

64. It is worth noting that Duff himself was at odds with culturally based, iwi-driven revitalization efforts and erred to the right in his diagnosis of postcolonial Māoridom's woes. The redemptive return at the conclusion of the film was the screenwriter's addition.

65. Witi Ihimaera, *The Whale Rider* (New York: Harcourt, 2003 [1987]). The name Apirana evokes Apirana Ngata, the early twentieth-century Ngāti Porou politician whose profound influence on the course of Māori politics forms the background to the earlier chapters of this book.

66. Ihimaera, *Whale Rider*, 147, 116.

67. Sabra Thorner, "Changing the Rules of Engagement: How *Rabbit Proof Fence* and *Whale Rider* Forge a New Dimension of Ethnographic Media," *Visual Anthropology Review* 23, no. 2 (2007): 137–50, 138; Kylie Message, "*Whale Rider* and the Politics of Location," *Metro* 136 (2003): 86–90.

68. For a more nuanced discussion of the 1990s ethnic pedagogy of the film, see Chris Prentice, "Riding the Whale? Postcolonialism and Globalization in *Whale Rider*," in *Global Fissures*, ed. Joseph and Wilson, 247–67.

69. See, for example, Witi Ihimaera, *Whanau II* (Auckland: Reed, 2004).

70. Anderson, *Imagined Communities*, 24.

71. Eric Hobsbawm and Terence Ranger, eds., *The Invention of Tradition* (Cambridge: Cambridge University Press, 1983).

72. Sandra Hall, "Whale Rider," *Sydney Morning Herald*, May 10, 2003, C5.

73. Lorenza Munoz, "Summer Sneak: And a Girl Shall Lead Them," *Los Angeles Times*, May 6, 2003, E31.

74. Ryan Mottesheard, "Girl Power: New Zealand Writer/Director Niki Caro Talks about 'Whale Rider,'" http://www.indiewire.com/article/girl_power_new_zealand_ writerdirector_niki_caro_talks_about_whale_rider/.

75. Tania Ka'ai, "Te Kauae Mārō o Muri-rangi-whenua (The Jawbone of Muri-rangi-whenua): Globalizing Local Indigenous Culture—Maori Leadership, Gender, and Cultural Knowledge Transmission as Represented in the Film *Whale Rider*," *Portal Journal of Multidisciplinary International Studies* 2, no. 2 (2005), http://epress.lib.uts .edu.au/ojs/index.php/portal/article/view/92.

76. *New Zealand Parliamentary Debates*, vol. 609 (June 12, 2003), accessed online at www.parliament.nz.

77. Thorner, "Changing the Rules"; *The Making of "Whale Rider,"* directed by Jonathan Brough (2003).

78. "Whale Writer: An Interview with Niki Caro," *Write Up*, magazine of the New Zealand Writers Guild, Summer 2003, 4–7, 5.

79. *Los Angeles Times*, May 6, 2003.

80. Barry Barclay, a Māori independent filmmaker of stature, was one of the few naysayers. Insofar as *Whale Rider* is "an absolutely international" story, he argued, it is "a story which, because of that internationality, that universality, anybody, including South Pacific Pictures, may freely make use of," trumping any recourse to indigenous intellectual property rights. Barclay, "An Open Letter," 11. Significantly, the Screen Production Industry Taskforce report argued for NZFC-funded producers' rights to retain and exploit the intellectual property generated by their films (which currently rests with the state agency). *Taking on the World: The Report of the Screen Production Industry Taskforce* (Wellington, 2003).

81. Anna Tsing, *Friction: An Ethnography of Global Connection* (Durham, N.C.: Duke University Press, 2005), 7, 9.

82. Ella Shohat and Robert Stam, "From the Imperial Family to the Transnational Imaginary: Media Spectatorship in the Age of Globalization," in *Global/Local: Cultural Production and the Transnational Imaginary*, ed. Rob Wilson and Wimal Dissanayake (Durham, N.C.: Duke University Press, 1996), 161.

83. Nicholas Thomas, "Gender and the Politics of Tradition: Alan Duff's *Once Were Warriors*," *Kunapipi* 15, no. 2 (1993): 57–67.

84. Louise Baker, presentation at Cineposium 2003, www.filmnz.com. Baker is quoting an article by Jo Joiner, "A Whale of a Time," *The Guardian*, July 5, 2003.

85. Philip Matthews, "Mythmaking," *New Zealand Listener*, February 1, 2003, 18–24.

86. Louisa Cleave, "Whale Rider Fans Overwhelm Whangara," *New Zealand Herald*, August 3, 2003.

87. Edward Wilkinson Latham, "Feeling Alive on the 35," *Outpost Magazine* 46, July/August 2005, http://www.wilkinsonlatham.com/highway35.php.

88. Scott, "Colonial Governmentality," 23–49.

89. "Developing Enterprise/Creative Sector" (summary of discussion, Hui Taumata Māori development conference, Wellington, 2005), http://www.huitaumata.maori.nz/

2005/. See also Nathan Hoturoa Gray, "What's Good for Maori is Good for NZ," *Tū Mai*, April 2005, 8–12, 10.

90. Kirikōwhai Mikaere, "The Best of Both Worlds," *Kōkiri Paetae*, March/April 2005, 6.

91. "We Have to Invest in Ourselves," *Kōkiri Paetae*, March/April 2005, 6.

92. Gray, "What's Good for Maori," 8.

93. Michel Foucault, "Entrepreneur of the Self," in Foucault, *Birth of Biopolitics.*

94. See two articles from Mary Beltrán and Camilla Fojas, eds., *Mixed Race Hollywood* (New York: New York University Press, 2008): Mary Beltrán, "Mixed Race in Latinowood: Latino Stardom and Ethnic Ambiguity in the Era of *Dark Angels*," 248–68; and LeiLani Nishime, "*The Matrix* Trilogy, Keanu Reeves, and Multiraciality at the End of Time," 290–312.

95. "Clone Troopers," http://www.starwars.com/databank/organization/clone troopers/; Lianne McLarty, "Masculinity, Whiteness, and Social Class," in *From Hobbits to Hollywood*, ed. Mathijs and Pomerance, 173–88.

96. Significantly, these specters of racial pollution and desire are channeled through male figures. Castle-Hughes and Rena Owen (Beth Heke in *Once Were Warriors*), have both been cast in future-normative postracial roles in the *Star Wars* films, but (leaving aside Castle-Hughes's foray as an Arab girl in Prince's ill-conceived video for "Cinnamon Girl") Owen's roles have tended more toward the mystical or exotic, in independent films: playing a Tibetan nun, a Rotuman Warrior Woman, and a Roma witch.

97. Allan Sekula, "The Body and the Archive," *October* 39 (1986): 3–60; Nicholas Mirzoeff, "The Shadow and the Substance: Race, Photography, and the Index," in *Only Skin Deep: Changing Visions of the American Self*, ed. Coco Fusco (New York: Abrams, 2003), 111–26. See also Elizabeth Edwards, ed. *Anthropology and Photography, 1860–1920* (New Haven, Conn.: Yale University Press, 1992).

98. See, for example, Eric Lott, *Love and Theft: Blackface Minstrelsy and the American Working Class* (Oxford: Oxford University Press, 1993); Catherine Cole, *Ghana's Concert Party Theatre* (Bloomington: Indiana University Press, 2001); Jill Lane, *Blackface Cuba, 1840–1895* (Philadelphia: University of Pennsylvania Press, 2005).

99. Gilles Deleuze, *Essays Critical and Clinical*, trans. Daniel W. Smith and Michael Greco (Minneapolis: University of Minnesota Press, 1997), 180.

100. Harris, "Whiteness as Property." See also Eva Cherniavsky, *Incorporations: Race, Nation, and the Body Politics of Capital* (Minneapolis: University of Minnesota Press, 2006).

101. The ongoing debates over "colorblind" casting and affirmative action on the U.S. stage have coalesced around public controversies, such as protest over casting in *Miss Saigon* or the acrimonious public debate between August Wilson and Robert Brustein. See David A. Schlossman, *Actors and Activists: Politics, Performance, and Exchange among Social Worlds* (New York: Routledge, 2004); and Brandi Wilkins Catanese, *The Problem of the Color[blind]: Racial Transgression and the Politics of Black Performance* (Ann Arbor: University of Michigan Press, 2010).

102. Iria Whiu, quoted in Anna Rushworth, "Maori Greeters: 100% Pure Fake," *New Zealand Herald,* January 24, 2010, http://www.nzherald.co.nz/nz/news/article .cfm?c_id=1&objectid=10621953.

103. "Our manners, our style, our gestures, and our bodies are not for rent. The history of our bodies—the lashings, the lynchings, the body that is capable of inspiring profound rage and pungent cruelty—is not for rent." August Wilson, *The Ground on Which I Stand* (New York: Theatre Communications Group, 2001 [1996]), 24.

104. *The Tem Show,* season 1, episode 1, 2005.

105. Greg McGee, *Foreskin's Lament* (Wellington: Price Milburn, 1981), 52.

106. Tim Watkin, "Nation Far Walking," *New Zealand Listener,* July 10, 2004, 10–11. Watkin's title is an appropriation of the title of a play by Witi Ihimaera, *Woman Far Walking* (Wellington: Huia, 2000).

107. Lauren Berlant, "The Face of America and the State of Emergency," *Disciplinarity and Dissent in Cultural Studies,* ed. Cary Nelson and Dilip Parameshwar Goankar (New York: Routledge, 1996), 398. See also Gilroy, *Against Race,* for a reading of such liminal racial figures as Castle-Hughes as signs of "timeliness, vitality, inclusivity, and global reach" (21).

108. Interview with Hardwicke on www.popsyndicate.com/site/story/nativity_ director.

109. Rawiri Paratene, for example, claimed that there "were no performances" in *Whale Rider.* Paratene, "Something to Be Proud Of," *Mana,* December 2002, 41.

110. I refer to the work of Lauren Berlant, Elizabeth Povinelli, Wendy Brown, Sara Ahmed, Brian Massumi, Erin Manning, Eve Sedgwick, Patricia Tincineto Clough, and Elspeth Probyn, among others.

111. Lauren Berlant, "Poor Eliza," *American Literature* 70, no. 3 (1998): 635–68, 641.

112. Kathleen Woodward, "Calculating Compassion," in *Compassion: The Culture and Politics of an Emotion,* ed. Lauren Berlant (New York: Routledge, 2004).

113. Berlant, "Poor Eliza," 641.

114. Lois Wacquant, quoted in Berlant, "Introduction," in *Compassion,* 8.

115. "FW: Whale Rider Thunders into Toronto," *Onfilm,* October 2002, 5.

116. For an explicit endorsement of these politics, see Philip Matthews, "The Chosen One," *New Zealand Listener,* January 25, 2003, http://www.whaleriderthemovie.co .nz/articles/article20.html.

117. Dyer, *White.*

118. "Whale Writer," 7.

119. Roberts, *Lovemarks.*

120. See Laura U. Marks, *The Skin of the Film: Intercultural Cinema, Embodiment, and the Senses* (Durham, N.C.: Duke University Press, 2000).

121. Aida A. Hozic, *Hollyworld: Space, Power, and Fantasy in the American Economy* (Ithaca, N.Y.: Cornell University Press, 2001).

122. "A Maori at My Table," *bro'Town,* season 1, episode 4, DVD (Auckland: Firehorse Films, 2004).

123. Flops include Vincent Ward's messy national epic, *River Queen*, and Gaylene Preston's insular psychodrama, *Perfect Strangers*. NZFPF attempted to duplicate *Whale Rider*'s success with *Boy*, Taika Waititi's coming-of-age drama, also set in an East Coast Māori community and featuring a cast of child actors.

124. There is yet to be a comprehensive history written of Māori TV, but the early steps of its astounding story are told in Ranginui Walker, *Ka Whawhai Tonu Matou: Struggle Without End*, rev. ed. (Auckland: Penguin Books 2004). Nga Aho Whakaari, a body advocating for Māori presence and growth in the screen industry, has only recently (2007) announced a NZ$600,000 fund, the first of its kind, devoted to fostering Māori film talent.

CONCLUSION

1. Ministry of Tourism, Tourism Industry Association of New Zealand, and Tourism New Zealand, *New Zealand Tourism Strategy 2015* (Wellington, 2007), http://www.nztourismstrategy.com/.

2. Ministries of Economic Development and Tourism, *Vote Tourism: Briefing to the Incoming Minister, 2008* (Wellington, 2008).

3. Ministry of Tourism et al., *Tourism Strategy 2015*.

4. This was a phrase I heard several times in interviews with Māori development appointees in the Ministry of Tourism and Tourism New Zealand, and with representatives of Maori Regional Tourism Organizations. All those interviewed in a professional capacity in this volume retain anonymity.

5. Tamaki Heritage Experiences, "Global Storytellers," http://www.christchurch info.co.nz/PicsHotel/TamakiChch/CustomPages/GlobalStorytellersPres.aspx?ID= 17481.

6. "Giant Rugby Ball Opens in Sydney," September 2, 2010, http://www.tourism newzealand.com/news-and-features.

7. Kiri Matao, speaking of her eponymous tupuna's travels in New York, described in chapter 3 of this volume.

8. Paul Lyons, *American Pacificism: Oceania in the U.S. Imagination* (New York: Routledge, 2006).

GLOSSARY

The following glossary provides brief translations of key Māori terms, as they are used in this volume. As the author is not a scholar of the Māori language, and many of these terms have tremendously complicated, subtle, and evolving definitions that defy translation, readers are referred to the source list at the conclusion. Most of these Māori terms are in common usage in New Zealand English.

Aotearoa. The Māori term now used to designate New Zealand as a political and geographical entity. Concatenated with New Zealand, it is commonly used strategically—as in this volume—to mark the bicultural character of the nation or the bicultural sympathies of the speaker. In fact, Aotearoa originally named only the North Island, as the Māori system of iwi and hapū had no use for a term that unified the islands into a single geographical entity. Those writing in Māori during the Liberal era used a transliteration of New Zealand (Niu Tireni) when referring to the *nation-state* and used Aotearoa (North Island) and Te Wai Pounamu (South Island) to refer to the territory. However, Liberal-era Pākehā nationalists, such as William Pember Reeves, naturalized the use of Aotearoa to refer to the nation as a whole.

haka. A rhythmic posture-dance and chant.

hāngī. A meal cooked by burying wrapped food in a pit filled with heated stones.

hapū. A term referring to a unit of Māori society in which members claim common ancestral bonds and share territorial identification. Because of the significance of membership units in the process of adjudicating claims by the Treaty of Waitangi Tribunal, and because of the ways in which forms of membership transformed under the pressures of colonialism, the definition and history of hapū and iwi have been much debated by scholars. See, for example, Angela Ballara, *Iwi: The Dynamics of Māori Tribal Organisation from c. 1769 to c. 1945* (Wellington: Victoria University Press, 1998). When referring to Māori political collectivities in general, most commentators will use the terminology "iwi and hapū" or "iwi, hapū, and whānau" in order to avoid controversy and to include all the ways in which these collectives define themselves. (While New Zealanders will frequently use the adjective "tribal," this is falling out of usage, and the noun "tribe" is no longer considered appropriate.)

hongi. A gesture of greeting, in which the two parties press their noses together, usually accompanied by a handshake.

hui. A meeting or gathering.

iwi. A unit of Māori society. As with hapū, the state-recognized definition states that iwi members claim genealogical affinity and share territorial identification; it also suggests that they retain a degree of functional political unity. An iwi is usually understood as a broader unit of membership than a hapū, often comprising a confederation of different hapū. However, iwi membership and definition is a great deal more complex and contested, and many scholars argue that the state approach to iwi is a strategy of control and manipulation of more fluid and evolving processes of Māori representation. In practice, the distinction between hapū and iwi is impossible to make categorically; there are examples of iwi invented without ancestral or territorial grounds, and many Māori claim multiple iwi memberships. See **hapū.**

kāinga. A village or settlement. Often used simply to mean "home."

kaitiakitanga. Guardianship, custodianship, or care. Denotes the ancestral responsibility to care for resources for future generations.

kapa haka. Used to describe Māori performance arts that take the form of an ensemble performance, a sequence of routines that might include haka, waiata-ā-ringa, poi, and mōteatea.

karakia. A prayer, blessing, or dedication.

karanga. A chant, call, or invocation, such as that performed by women at the beginning of a pōwhiri, to invoke the ancestors of the two parties meeting.

kaumātua. An elder in a Māori community. A kaumātua commands both respect and authority.

kaupapa. Mission, philosophy, or purpose.

kia ora. Literally meaning "be well," it is a common and informal term of greeting. Also used colloquially as "thank you."

kōrero. Story, saying, news, or speech.

kowhaiwhai. The patterns painted on the internal rafters of Māori houses, usually interconnected, curved, lineal forms.

kuia. An elderly woman, a grandmother. As with kaumātua, the term usually connotes both respect and authority.

kūpapa. Describes those hapū and iwi who allied with the Crown during the wars of the mid-nineteenth century.

mana. An enormously complicated, and contested, term denoting prestige, standing, authority, charisma, and qualities of leadership or accomplishment, whether god-given, endowed by ancestry, or earned through deeds.

manaakitanga. Loosely, hospitality. The responsibility of iwi, hapū, and whānau to care for, and the prestige derived from, caring for guests.

Māori. The indigenous peoples of Aotearoa New Zealand. The term Māori is an artifact of the postcontact era: precontact iwi and hapū had no need or desire to designate themselves as an ethnic or racial group. In a retribalizing nation, most now prefer to identify themselves by iwi or hapū affiliation; similarly, scholars of the Liberal era have argued that few Māori of the era would have found the term a useful identity descriptor. My use of the word in this book is attuned to the ways in which the term has manifested in state or public discourse in both periods, to make arguments for understanding Aotearoa's indigenous peoples as an ethnic or racial collectivity.

Māoritanga. A neologism used to refer broadly to Māori culture, custom, or lifeways.

marae *and* **marae ātea.** The symbolic, spatial, and political center or gathering point of a Māori community. The marae ātea is the forecourt area in front of the wharenui (the meetinghouse); in precontact times, it was the area in front of the predominant rangatira's dwelling. It is the highly charged site for speech making and reciprocal performance, where hosts and guests meet. Today, the marae usually refers to an entire community center complex, usually including a wharenui and marae ātea, as well as a kitchen, dining hall, and other amenities for hospitality.

mauri. Life force.

pā. A fortified Māori settlement. In the nineteenth century, the term was also used to refer to substantive or long-standing settlements, regardless of whether they were fortified.

Pākehā. A contested term used now to describe all New Zealanders of non-Māori descent (although Pacific Islanders or New Zealanders of non-European ethnicity are unlikely to self-designate using the term). I use it here to describe non-Māori New Zealanders generally, recognizing that despite the increasing racial and ethnic diversity of the nation (Pacific Islanders now make up 12 percent of the population and those of Asian descent 11 percent), the combination of contemporary bicultural logic and the historical hegemony of European-descended populations means that in the dyad Māori–Pākehā, the latter is presumptively white.

piupiu. An ornamental skirt, often worn by kapa haka performers, made of dried tubes of flax hanging from a waistband; the tubes move with a lightly percussive effect.

poi. A performance form in which female performers dance while twirling and slapping balls of flax attached to either short or long strings, in unison, producing stunning visual and percussive effects. Poi is usually performed to the accompaniment of waiata.

pōwhiri, *also* **pōhiri.** The ceremony of encounter and welcome between two parties, between hosts and guests.

rangatira. A paramount leader and figure of mana.

rangatiratanga. Usually translated as chieftainship, autonomy, self-determination, or sovereignty. The definition is the anchor of the Waitangi Tribunal process, because the fundamental promise of the Treaty (in its Māori, not English, version) was that Māori would retain tino rangatiratanga (where tino means absolute or highest).

tamariki. Children.

tangata whenua. People of the land. Used to refer either to the community with ancestral rights to inhabitance in a specific territory or to Māori generally.

taniwha. A water-dwelling supernatural creature, the guardian of a specific place, who may be either benign or malign.

taonga. A treasure, a possession of great value, either tangible (objects of art, an heirloom, a useful plant, or a person of great gifts or standing) or intangible (the language, a technique, or a song).

tapu. Often loosely translated as "sacred," tapu describes objects, people, places, or things, tangible and intangible, that have a special spiritual status, demanding careful treatment and strict adherence to certain protocols in order to guarantee safety. It is also used to refer to this system of categorization as a whole.

tikanga. Customary law, the rules prevailing over correct or appropriate behavior.

tiki. An ornamental carving representing a human figure, usually in greenstone, worn as a pendant.

tupuna, *also* **tipuna.** Ancestors or forebears.

tūrangawaewae. Ancestral homeland, the territory to which one belongs and to which one owes loyalty. Literally, "a place to stand."

utu. Active redress of past wrongs. Retributive justice.

waharoa. Ceremonial gateway, usually a carved edifice representing a founding ancestor.

waiata. A song.

wairua. Spirit.

whaikōrero. A speech, or the art of oratory generally (understood as both a rhetorical and an embodied skill).

whānau. Family, usually meaning an extended family or kin group.

whanaungatanga. Kinship, the principle and experience of interrelationship, and the responsibilities toward kin.

whare. House or dwelling.

whare whakairo *and* **wharenui.** Literally "carved house" and "big house." Since the late nineteenth century, wharenui have been built as the embodiment of the mana of specific hapū, iwi, and whānau and have been used as the main locus of political and ceremonial gatherings. A wharenui or whare whakairo is the centerpiece of a marae.

whenua. Land. The term also means birth, afterbirth, or place.

FURTHER SOURCES

Clive Barlow, *Tikanga Whakaaro: Key Concepts in Māori Culture* (Auckland: Oxford University Press, 1991).

Hirini Moko Mead, *Tikanga Māori: Living by Māori Values* (Wellington: Huia, 2003).

John C. Moorfield, *Te Aka Māori–English, English–Māori Dictionary and Index* (Aukland: Pearson Education New Zealand, 2005), http://www.maoridictionary.co.nz/.

James Ritchie, *Becoming Bicultural* (Wellington: Huia, Daphne Brasell Associates, 1992).

Te Ara: The Encyclopedia of New Zealand (Wellington: Ministry for Culture and Heritage, n.d.), http://www.teara.govt.nz/.

INDEX

Aboriginal Doonooch Dance Company, 243

Actor Network Theory, xviii, xxxvi

adventure tourism, 147, 148, 149. *See also* FIT tourism

agency: economic, 239; human, xvi, xxxiv, 230; indigenous, xxxiv, 186–87; liberal, xxxvii, 50; as passage, xxxvi; performative, xxxii, 79, 169; political, xiii, 87, 151, 185, 186; and state interests, xxxv, 243

American Museum of Natural History, 127–28

American Pacific: and diplomacy, xvi; formation of, xvi, 99, 100; imaginary of, 115, 129; and performance, 116, 117–22, 127, 131–32; and spectacle, 118–20, 126–27, 132–33; and tourism, 102; use of term, 276n68; and U.S. Fleet, 101

Anderson, Benedict, 93

Angel at My Table, An (film), 195

Aotearoa New Zealand: and agency, xxxv; biculturalism in, xxvii; biopolitics in, xxxi; branding of, ix–x, xiii, xxxvii, 4, 148–49, 152–55; demographics, xviii–xix, xx; governmentality of,

143–44; as Little Britain, 203; neoliberalism/postneoliberalism in, xxiii, 140, 186, 192, 237; as social experiment, xvii–xxiii; as tourist state, xi, xiv–xv, xxxviii, 136, 237; use of term, 151. *See also* Maoriland; New Zealand; tourist state

APEC. *See* Asia-Pacific Economic Cooperation

Appiah, Kwame Anthony, 79

Arawa people: and ethnic tourism, xx–xxi, 57, 124; guiding tradition, 48, 50; performers, 53, 82–84, 124, 126–30, 161–62, 165–66, 240; poverty of, 55, 57

Asia-Pacific Economic Cooperation (APEC), 115

autonomy: and film industry, 210; and liberalism/neoliberalism, xxiii–xxiv, xxxiv, 138, 207; of Māori, 146, 184, 222; and performance, 161. *See also* rangatiratanga

Avatar (film), 236

Baker, Louise, 220

balneology, 28–33, 41

Barnett, John, 214

Barthes, Roland, 16

303

36–38; tour guides tradition, 44, 50; tourist responses to, 40

Whale Rider (film), xxxviii, 191; development of, 214–17; Māori cultural material in, 211–12, 222; postracialism in, 218; success of, 214; tradition in, 217; universality of, 219–21

whānau (extended kin group): development of, 150; and leisure travel, 81; and modernization, 24; touristic performance by, 154, 243

Whāngārā (village), 214, 215, 216, 218, 220, 221

whare, 64–68

whiteness: and assimilation, 224; attributes of, 30, 137, 201; and conduct, xxviii, 11, 17, 28, 187; criteria for, 193; and definition of race, xxix, 111; and ethnic tourism, xxxvii, 8, 11; and mobility, 162; as normative, xxxi, 41;

origins of, 16, 202; and personhood, 137; and social advantage, xxviii; and spa, 28, 31, 40; symbols of, 232, 234; and tourism, 8. *See also* race

Wohlmann, Dr., 29–30, 33

women's suffrage, 128

Wonderland (spa resort). *See* Rotorua Wonderland

Wordsworth, William, 13

World's Fastest Indian, The (film), 236

World Trade Organization (WTO), xxi, xxvii

Xena: Warrior Princess (series), 195

Yates, Waapi Tungi, 128, 129, 130

Young Māori Party, 27, 108, 109, 123

Yúdice, George, 28, 145

Zander, Dr., 30

MARGARET WERRY is associate professor in the Department of Theatre Arts and Dance at the University of Minnesota.

www.ingramcontent.com/pod-product-compliance
Lightning Source LLC
Chambersburg PA
CBHW020821270326
41928CB00006B/403

* 9 7 8 0 8 1 6 6 6 6 0 6 5 *